A Theme for Reason

BOOKS BY ELISABETH OGILVIE

A Theme for Reason

The Face of Innocence

Bellwood

Waters on a Starry Night

The Seasons Hereafter

There May Be Heaven

Call Home the Heart

The Witch Door

High Tide at Noon

Storm Tide

The Ebbing Tide

Rowan Head

My World Is an Island

The Dawning of the Day

No Evil Angel

BOOKS FOR YOUNG PEOPLE

The Pigeon Pair

Masquerade at Sea House

Ceiling of Amber

Turn Around Twice

Becky's Island

The Young Islanders

How Wide the Heart

Blueberry Summer

Whistle for a Wind

The Fabulous Year

A THEME FOR REASON

ELISABETH OGILVIE

Amereon House
MATTITUCK

Reprinted by Special Arrangement
with Elisabeth Ogilvie

International Standard Book Number 0-89190-394-1

To order contact
AMEREON HOUSE, the publishing division of
Amereon LTD.
Post Box 1200
Mattituck, New York 11952-9500

Printed in the United States of America

Dear love, for nothing less than thee
Would I have broke this happy dream,
        It was a theme
For reason, much too strong for fantasy,
Therefore thou wak'd'st me wisely; yet
My dream thou brok'st not, but continued'st it.

JOHN DONNE

CHAPTER 1

"WHATEVER WILL YOU DO when something happens to that cat?"

Dodie prided herself on being an absolutely unique thinker, but her tone was exactly the same in which the question was so often asked by other people. Alix tried to analyze it, gazing meanwhile at William, who boldly stared back at her dark glasses while he used a forbidden chair for a scratching post.

"That cat is going to tear this place to pieces," said Dodie. "Did you hear what I asked you?"

"Yes," said Alix. "I was thinking how I'd describe the way people ask it. It's a kind of rich curdly mess of self-satisfaction, and gratitude for there being no possible chance of getting peculiar like me."

Dodie opened her mouth and then snapped it shut. If Alix had been feeling anything positive these days she'd have experienced some pleasure at having struck Dodie temporarily mute. She threatened William with a magazine, more because he expected it than because upholstery could have any possible meaning for her now, and William snarled, took a swipe at the magazine with a huge double paw, and bounded off across the room with his thick tail bent sidewise.

[1]

"How about some tea?" Alix asked, slowly getting up and stretching her long arms and legs in what had lately become a nervous reflex. "Or a drink? How would you like to get drunk this afternoon, Dodie? We could sit here and slide gracefully into tipsy melancholia like the decayed gentlewomen we are."

Dodie's eyes were bulging and swimmy, sad pug eyes in her little pug face. Alix felt a dim shame. After all, Dodie had come here to be kind to her.

"It's not just you," she explained. "But somebody's always asking me that, as if there's something wrong with me for taking William into account. If I had five children and was fond of my cat besides loving my children, I'd be normal. As it is, I'm not supposed to have anything but maybe a nice row of African violets on the window sill."

"It's not that with *me*," said Dodie angrily. "*I* don't think you're neurotic for loving William. But now that you're—" She blushed, and her eyes watered even more. "Well, where you're all alone and he's so—well, he's likely to become so over-important to you that you'll have nothing to draw you out of yourself and out of this place."

Alix leaned an elbow on the mantel and watched her. Under the blind stare of the dark glasses Dodie fumbled, but she had a pug's tenacity to match her face. "You always wanted to go to Greece for a year, Alix. Way back in school you talked about it. You mentioned it again just last year. Now's the time to go, right *now!* William's not a child, for heaven's sake. If you can't bear to board him in a kennel, you could have him painlessly put away, and be off tomorrow for anywhere you want to go. It's not as if he was a *young* cat. He can't have too much longer, though I don't know how long cats live. . . ."

Her voice had grown faint, not in itself but in Alix's ears. She gazed out the windows through the perpetual twilight of the dark glasses. Go to Greece alone? she silently questioned Dodie, or someone unseen but omniscient who was always opposing her or accusing her or demanding explanations.

[2]

". . . no use," Dodie's voice, raspy with impatience, scraped at her. "The instant I try to talk sense to you, you go away."

"Did you say you wanted tea or a drink?"

"Neither," snapped Dodie. She stood up, reaching only to Alix's shoulder. "I told you when I came in that I'm on the way to the dentist. But Alix, now is the time to do something drastic. If you don't do it now, you never will. Already you're withdrawing. How long since you've been outside this apartment? Look at those feet! Talk about your *hippies!* And when did you brush your hair last, to say nothing of washing it?" She tapped Alix on the chest. "You've got to rouse yourself. It's like getting right back on a horse after you're thrown. I know whereof I speak," she said, squinting and nodding sagely.

"Incontestably," said Alix, "and I'm not being sarcastic. You did it, but I don't know how you did it."

"And don't tell me I couldn't have loved Ed as much as you loved Shane. Think about what I've said, Alix. And listen, I didn't mean you should do away with William this minute. But don't let an animal stand in the way of your making a change."

"I shan't," Alix promised so obligingly that Dodie gave her a suspicious glance.

"You eat every bit of that casserole. It's *loaded* with protein."

"I'll eat glass and all," said Alix. "Delicious crunchy-munchy Pyrex. Yum yum." She walked Dodie to the elevator and wished her good luck at the dentist's office. When she came back into the living room William thudded to meet her. He was a big gray tiger cat, solidly muscular, with a broad face of childish innocence and eyes like green tourmalines. He leaned against Alix's leg, his purr loud and uneven like the sound of eggs boiling, and heavily impeded her progress across the room.

"I know," she said. "You want supper . . . they probably think I rock you to sleep at night, and secretly dress you in baby clothes. No, little sailor suits. And read to you about

[3]

Winnie the Pooh." Her voice, husky these days as if with a perpetual cold, seemed to die of its own weight; the effort ex-
pended on Dodie had exhausted it.

She left William eating noisily, and went into the studio, not
for any particular reason, and found herself standing there
looking at work she hadn't touched since Easter. She took off
the dark glasses and saw more clearly the three children gazing
back at her from their separate canvases. She could not even
remember the last time the children had come.

At the far end of the studio, where the shadows always gathered first like the incoming tide filling a pool among the Tiree
ledges, there was a full-length mirror, and she saw herself there,
a vague figure hovering tentatively like a trespasser who isn't
sure he's trespassing or how he got here in the first place.

"Which I don't know," she said wonderingly. "I really don't
know." The mystery was how Alexia Horne, a sixteen-year-old
hoyden with sharp elbows and narrow waist, the fall of fox-red
hair, the ability to yell like Tarzan, to shoot straight up from
the gym floor like a red-tipped arrow as she led her basketball
team to victory, to weep over a poem and, ultimately, to paint,
had suddenly become this distraught and mourning woman.
Twenty years had been condensed to overnight. She was like
the girl in Gertrude Atherton's short story who lost consciousness in the boating accident that killed her lover, and when she
woke up, thinking it was the next day, it was to find herself an
old woman about to die.

Alix took off the dark glasses and went closer to the mirror
as if to make sure this was she. The thin straight height in
slacks and turtle-neck jersey made the same silhouette as always. But a closer look showed her the dullness of the hair
pinned carelessly up off her nape, the new sharpness of cheekbones with the freckles dark on a pallor from three weeks indoors. The skin around her eyes was bluish-lavender.

She stood there in her bare feet, lost in time and place, un-
thinking as it so often happened these days, forgetting even the
faint curiosity that had brought her to the long mirror.

This wasn't depression. It was an enormous indifference. A nothingness, as if all her apparatus for feeling, smelling, tasting, and hearing had died when Shane did. For nine years they had spent every summer together in their own home on Tiree. The rest of the year they lived apart, she in New York and he on the campus of the small liberal arts college in Vermont where he taught government. During those months they met when they could, but they had never openly displayed their affair in the world away from Tiree.

Alix had had two destructive love affairs and a flurry of doomed attempts to force life to act like the poems young Alexia had wept over. She met Shane when they were both skiing, and at the end of their first hour together she knew that he was what Alexia Horne had been born for. They had become friends long before they became lovers, and he was all the friend she had ever dreamed of.

His wife was a Catholic and would not divorce him, though they had separated before he and Alix met. This spring he had given away his older daughter at her wedding a few days after Easter, had suffered a heart attack at the breakfast, and died almost instantly.

A colleague of his who had once come unexpectedly to visit Shane in Maine, and had thus found out that Alix existed, had had the kindness to tell her about Shane's death. Otherwise she might not have known until a letter came back stamped "Deceased," so meticulously had they kept their two worlds from brushing.

That had been three weeks ago, and it was still so incredible to her that she hadn't yet cried about it. She had gone to her doctor and got some sleeping capsules, which he thought he was giving her for being a thirty-six-year-old spinster with secret frustrations that kept her awake. Because she wasn't used to sedatives she had slept very heavily at first. Waking up in the dark, confused and thick-tongued, she would orient herself by thinking, *Shane is dead. He died suddenly and I wasn't there.*

It meant nothing. It was just words. She would try again. *I wasn't there, but she was. He loved me, but she was the one who was there. If he said anything, she heard it. If he said my name, I'll never know. I don't even know where his grave is.*

She had some idea that if she could hammer the facts into her consciousness like nails into the flesh, she would suffer great agony, and that would be better than this vacuum. But no matter what she said to herself, nothing happened. She was merely oppressed by her own dullness and apathy.

At first she'd kept having the feeling that when she went to the island everything would be as usual, that he had died only in their separate lives. In fact, her first impulse when she heard the news was to go straight to Tiree, where she would find him.

Now, sitting on a tall stool in the studio, watching William wash up after dinner in the smoky orange light of a city sunset, her grimy bare feet braced on a rung and her strong bony hands hanging useless between her knees, she thought how strange it all was. How strange *she* was. She knew Shane wasn't on the island, that there'd been no gorgeously complicated, lunatic, and successful ploy to fool Cathleen. But as long as she didn't go there, she didn't have to admit it. She would never go there again.

In any case, without Shane the place had ceased to exist except as words on a deed and in her will. They had bought the place together nine years ago, a small island as far down East as they could find one, well away from popular yachting waters and resorts. She went there every May, and he came in June when the college year ended, and stayed until it began again in the fall. Sometimes he had to go away to conferences and seminars, but for those three months it was their home, and they had learned how to live their time there with a careful leisure and a miserly savoring of every instant. They never mentioned autumns and parting, but were always making plans for next year. The essence of those summer months was undiluted by the presence of other people, except for the Goodwins, from whom they'd bought the place and who had reserved one distant section for themselves.

When Shane and Alix had gone to look at the island, they'd had supper and spent the night with the Goodwins in the old house which would be theirs if they were lucky enough to suit. Alix had been falling more deeply in love with the place all that summer afternoon. At supper, facing the sea-filled windows, she could not wait any longer to end the suspense. When Ozzie called her Mrs. Mannering, she had burst out like the young Alexia, with neither tact nor forethought, "I have to tell you something. We're not married, Shane and I, and we don't know when we can be."

She felt herself going white with shame and despair as she said it, thinking *Now we don't get the island, and what a scene to spring on Shane!* She couldn't look at him.

Ozzie went on stirring his coffee and said gently, as if she'd been an overwrought ten-year-old, "Well, now, that's no concern of ours."

"Goodness, no!" Madge exclaimed, bringing in the pie. She was scarlet with the effort to convince them that she wasn't shocked. "After all," she cried, "you love the place, and that's what matters to us. And we know artists and people like that, well, they *think* different—I mean—"

"Don't beat it to death, woman," said Ozzie. "Set, and cut the pie."

Alix sat looking at her plate, trying to fight down the ache in back of her nose, silently cursing her sentimentality, saying to herself no wonder they didn't care; they were going to get fifteen thousand, weren't they? For that money anyone could set up a free-love colony or a bordello right under their noses.

When she couldn't stand it any longer she rolled her eyes sidewise at Shane, and found him giving her a long flinty blue look that terrified her by its pure objectivity.

Then he winked.

[7]

For nine years the Goodwins and the island had been insepa-
rable in her and Shane's minds. Now everything else had gone
at one stroke, with Shane.

"Now that's something to conjecture about," she said to William in the loud, cheery, games-mistressy tone she'd adopted as
if to fool somebody who might be listening, the one she was always explaining to or arguing with. It was certainly not William, who looked peculiarly at her. "Which is the real existence of a place or a thing or of a person? The corporeal, or
somebody's idea of it? I mean, how do we know something exists when we're not actually touching it? It's like the old theory
of the big tree falling in the forest—" Her throat seemed to
shut itself off for a moment; she had to struggle to get going
again.

"It makes no sound if there's no one to hear," she went on.
"So who knows, William, if the tree actually existed? All that
makes it a real, genuine, honest-to-goodness tree with bark and
bugs and nests of robins in its hair and so forth is the fact that
somebody's seen it, touched it, climbed it—I think I've lost
sight of my original premise."

William yawned. She said, "Thank you for that well-
thought-out comment. Anyway, that place doesn't exist any
more, if it ever did; if the whole thing hasn't been one long
wish-fulfillment dream of sixteen-year-old Alexia Horne, all
taking place in one night before exams or after too much
Christmas. ... So you and I'll camp out for the summer up
here, William, and I'll sneak out every night for provisions,
and we'll open no doors to Dodie Anson or anybody else.
Their worst fears will be realized, and it will make their own
lives all the sweeter."

Only Dodie knew about Shane; the rest believed that she
had been inexplicably odd for the past few weeks, and thought
like her doctor that her spinsterhood was catching up with her.
The younger ones were fond of believing that anyone from
Boston had to be rigidly inhibited, and you know what *that* led
to.

She looked at her watch, pure habit because time meant nothing when you had so much of it and no way to spend it. If she went to bed now, one capsule wouldn't get her through till morning, and a kind of animal caution had kept her from using more than one a night. Should she go out for an hour or two? Walk up one street and down another? She hadn't been out for three weeks, except to go to the doctor's that time.

For a few minutes she seriously considered it. She could always drop in somewhere and be welcomed to the everlasting shop talk over beer or the cheap wine the kids bought by the gallon. They liked her. Their common involvement with painting dissolved the difference in ages. Besides, she was generous, both with her listening and her interest.

"You're a good painter, though you're limited, of course," she had been told kindly by a boy of twenty-two. "You know it —you're no fool. You're narrow and noncreative, but you can't help it. Probably the way you grew up inhibited your creativity. But you're damn good in your field, and we have to have portrait painters, I suppose."

"So you can live another day, Alix," someone broke in, laughing. He ignored that and went on earnestly. "You've really got a feel for kids. Must be your suppressed maternal instincts."

"Why, Tony, how perceptive you are," she told him, and he exclaimed radiantly, "What I like about you is that you're a painter before you're a woman!" Then he explained confusingly the symbolism of his own work, and invited himself home to dinner with her. He was missing his mother back in Illinois, though torture wouldn't have made him admit it.

Alix had written out the whole thing in a long letter to Shane two nights before his daughter's wedding. She wondered now if he'd ever got the letter, and if Cathleen had exercised her conjugal rights after his death by going to his rooms in Vermont and reading his mail.

Alix got up abruptly. Her feet and ankles were cramped because she had been sitting so long with them braced on the rung, and she almost fell down. But she welcomed the pain and went wincing to her room, moaning with enthusiasm at every step. She took a capsule and got into bed in her clothes, and pulled the covers over her head.

✦ CHAPTER 2 ✦

WILLIAM AWOKE HER, starting on one of her knees and walking up her body. Each of his large feet seemed to support in turn his full fifteen pounds. Crouching on her chest he thrust a damp nose into her face, and stared into the eye that struggled open. Satisfied that she was awake, he jumped over onto the window sill, looking out into the dusty sunlight and chattering his teeth at the insolent pigeons.

To her blurred vision he was insubstantial against the light, a phantom cat flickering in and out of focus as her consciousness did. The shadows of the pigeons' wings flashing on window and ceiling made her feel dizzy and sick. When she could fix one eye on her watch, she saw that it was almost ten.

All her professional life she had been an early riser, to catch the morning light. Now habit gave a start of consternation, at least it made an effort to break through as she realized she must have taken a second capsule in the night but couldn't remember it.

Then with an almost voluptuous surrender she sank back, thinking, What does it matter? There is nothing to get up for any more.

[11]

William began a loud, keening wail that was pure gem-cut misery. Instantly she was ashamed of herself. William, who bore his winter captivity with remarkable good nature, was crying because it was spring, and somewhere outside the glass lay the things of which he had become a part every May for all his life; it *was* his life that awaited him out there. The island hadn't ended for him.

"You shall go there, William," she told him thickly. She got cautiously out of bed and felt her way into the bathroom, and kept splashing cold water on her face until she was more awake, though she still felt as if she were tilting sidewise, and wouldn't be able to get her head up again from the basin. She did, and William followed her to the kitchen, complaining and blandishing. She gave him some milk, and made coffee, drinking two cups as fast as the heat would allow.

This was the first morning since it happened that she had got up with any sense of purpose. The extra capsule bothered her, both in its lingering physical effects and in the fact that she had taken it and couldn't remember. Angrily she walked around the apartment and through the studio, breathing deeply, flailing her arms, trying to get her blood to circulating faster.

"You damn fool," she said aloud. "You'd better lock them up tonight if you can't trust yourself. And don't say *Who cares?* If you don't look out you'll turn into an object other people can take charge of. Imagine being taken over by Dodie. Grrr!" She growled and shuddered, thought the vibrations were doing her good, and repeated the growl for William, who looked astounded. Then she touched her toes ten times, and after the roller-coaster plunge of the first few attempts her head cleared rapidly.

When her hands had stopped feeling puffy and unhinged, and didn't tremble when she held them up, she went to her desk to write to the Goodwins. They would have had no way of finding out about Shane.

She typed as fast as she could and still be legible. "I won't be able to come to stay this summer, but if I bring William down and pay his board, will you look out for him? It doesn't seem fair to make him lose his summer when it's the only time he can really be a cat." Then, her fingers rigidly crooked, she wrote, "Shane died suddenly three days after Easter."

There was something like a hammer blow inside her head. Her brain seemed to crash in on itself; at least that was the picture forming before her eyes. Physical and mental chaos became one, so that the pain slashing across her belly was the scarifying attack of grief, and the sensation inside her head was the struggle of a maniacal rage to express itself. Through it all she heard herself howling like William at the window.

The vacuum had smashed, and she was spared nothing. She knew now, and her body knew, that Shane was dead.

It all took place within a half-hour. At the end she was still sitting at the desk; she had been snatched up by a cyclone, like Judy Garland being Dorothy, and then neatly set back in her chair. She felt exhausted from the trip, but calm. It would have been impossible to be anything else.

She ripped the letter out of the typewriter and threw it in the wastebasket. Then she took a long soaking bath and washed her hair. Still damp, she called the mother of the children in the paintings and said she had at last gotten rid of the troublesome virus, and if she could have the children a couple of times this week she'd have the portraits finished by Saturday afternoon.

"You sound awfully husky," the woman said.

"It's nothing catching," Alix said. "It's from coughing so much."

"You poor thing, you've really had a siege. Well, I'm simply delighted to think I'll have the pictures to show off on Mother's Day. Can't you come to dinner one night soon? I'd like to have you see how we've had them framed and hung."

"I'd love to," said Alix, playing it so graciously that she actually smiled at the telephone. "But I'm due in Maine next week."

"Oh, dear! Well, perhaps in the fall then. My husband and I would love to have you, and I know the children would. They talk about Miss Horne so much. They've quite missed the sittings."

"They're great youngsters," said Alix. "Yes, I'll enjoy that. I'll call you when I come back, shall I?" Her smile deepened into what Shane called her Cheshire-cat grin, because it was three-cornered between her narrow chin and high cheekbones. She agreed briskly that the children should come after school tomorrow, said yes, the weather *was* marvelous, and good-bye.

Then she called her doctor and made an appointment for this afternoon, and followed this by writing a note to the Goodwins to let them know when she would be arriving. This time no chaos exploded from the message about Shane. The end of the world had already occurred. She picked her way among the smoking ruins and wrote, "Please don't mention it when I come."

Now that she knew that she would not and could not live without Shane, she had at last a sense of direction. It was as if the long period of anesthesia had come about simply because she couldn't think of the right thing to do.

The wonder was that it had taken her so long to recognize the truth, when it was something she had always known; or rather, she had known it since that period when their life had voyaged in the night, as it were, from one sea to another. Now, half-dreaming of the Mediterranean cruise they had planned to take when Shane retired, she saw their life as a ship gliding past distant blue headlands and mysterious islands like lilac clouds on the horizon, through uncounted dawns and sunsets, occasionally experiencing storms but never anything catastrophic, and always with no sense of urgency or even time passing, until suddenly, one day, the ship is on the other side of the world.

So they had crossed the unseen line, the equator between the temporary and the permanent. There was no more thinking *When this breaks up,* or even *If this breaks up.* It was then that she had become aware of the third passenger.

Whatever Browning had meant by "the shadowy third," for Alix it was the knowledge that Shane had become her reason for existence and not merely an agreeable adjunct to it. And as he went into his forties and she into her thirties, there was no reason not to believe that this unity would last for the rest of their lives.

And so it has, she thought ironically. For him, anyway. If I were a true Christian, I would believe him to be waiting for me on some other shore. One step, and I'd be in his arms. But doubtless Cathleen believes the same thing . . . anyway, I know I'm not going to him. I wouldn't believe it even if there were no Cathleen. I'm just going because he's no longer here, so I've got no further use for here, either.

"Ah, well," she said aloud. "I can't ask for heaven even if I believed in it. I've already had it. But one keeps on hoping for a little more. It's only human, I suppose . . . or it's only avid little Alexia." She chanted, derisive and nasal, "Green eyes, greedy gut, eat all the world up!"

William stopped washing to stare at her. "I didn't mean *your* green eyes, my boy," she said, then thought all at once, And I don't even know if he got that last letter.

The doctor told her candidly that she looked terrible. She answered with her Cheshire-cat grin that she'd had a rotten cold and probably needed vitamins. "Or iron, I should think. I'm rather white."

"If you know so much, why did you bother to come to me?" he asked, a little too casual.

"Because I want to renew my Seconal prescription," she said. "They won't refill it the third time, and I'd like to take some to Maine."

"You'll sleep up there without help," he said enviously. "All that silence and pure air."

"You're probably right," she agreed, "but I've got this nutty little phobia about not sleeping, because if I run short of sleep my painting falls off, my eyes are bothered, my hands no good . . . I'm just not *keen*, don't you see?" She cocked her head, but winsomeness was not her thing; under his benignly skeptical gaze she realized how unconvincing she sounded. They were like two fencers in the preliminary stages of a match. She gave up and said bluntly, "If I have something in the house I won't need it, that's all."

"What are you worried about, that keeps a healthy, hard-working young woman awake?"

"Nothing."

"Can you look me straight in the eye and say that?"

She did, willing her hands to be absolutely quiet on her handbag. He stared back at her, absently twiddling his pen, then said, "How about a checkup before you leave for Maine?"

"I had one last fall."

"Oh yes," he murmured.

"Look," she said with asperity, "if you think this not-sleeping is simply female jitters, you're mistaken. Maybe it's professional jitters, who knows? Maybe I'm tired of doing portraits and want to do something wild and adventurous. Maybe I wish I'd *been* wild and adventurous, raised a little hell here and there instead of sowing my wild oats in flowerpots."

He laughed hard at that, and she laughed too, in relief and triumph at a small victory. "Seriously, though," he said when he stopped laughing, "how about that checkup? Six months isn't overdoing it."

"After I come back from Maine," she promised. "But I feel fine really, everything's in good working order, I just have this—"

"Nutty little phobia about not sleeping," he finished.

"I don't know why you're being so difficult. Surely I can be allowed a few eccentricities? Only one, really. Most of the women I know brag about all kinds of things, their little fibroids and polyps, and they have migraine if anyone disagrees with them, and I know at least one who claims her stomach's so delicate she has to live on champagne and oysters. And then there's—"

"All right, all right!" He was already writing a new prescription. "Don't overdo it. One more argument, and you'll really be in trouble." He pushed the slip toward her. "Remember what I told you about drinking with these things. Oh, I forgot, you aren't going to take any. They're just a kind of charm, like garlic to keep away vampires."

"I wonder how your wife puts up with that smile," said Alix, putting the slip away before he could change his mind.

"That's why she married me. To find what it meant."

"It's obviously meant to be superior and maddening. And it succeeds, too."

He laughed, a gray-headed man sounding suddenly youthful and mischievous. At the door they shook hands, and he wished her a good summer.

"I envy you that island," he said.

She smiled. "It solves everything, always."

❧ CHAPTER 3 ❧

Now she could be very busy making arrangements. She was greedily delighted to hurl herself into activity, and her mind rushed from one detail to another, so exceptionally clear and efficient after the weeks of stupidity that she could hardly believe it. Without effort she remembered minutiae that would have ordinarily been cast off as nuisances. In fact she remembered all sorts of unnecessary items, so that while she was deciding who was to have what of her belongings, and who would get the most out of using up the rest of her studio lease, she was plagued by a constant kaleidoscopic shifting of time and events. It was as if her mind, having no future, were driven back to the past, far back to young Alexia observing the illogical (to her) behavior of bereaved aunts, neighborhood women, her mother.

"Good heavens," she said to William, "some of them weren't much older than I am now. And I know at least one was younger. And I thought that if they weren't dripping with tears and black veiling they weren't suffering." She lifted him for the fifth time out of a carton containing her Impressionist prints. They were to go to Tony. "Let him swash around in all that color for a while," she told William, "and then see who's limited and inhibited, him with his beige and brown squares."

She wrote lists covering everything and tucked them away with her will. The island was all attended to; it had been in her name from the first, going to Shane if anything happened to her, and back to the Goodwins if she survived Shane. Ozzie and Madge had been friends beyond the name of neighbor all those years. If they had a chance to sell the island a second time, no one deserved it more.

She should mention the doctor to them as a possible buyer. *Dear Dr. Smollet: A close friend of ours who recently killed herself with Seconal (prescribed by you) and hard liquor has suggested*—no, not *has*, that sounded as if she'd gotten a message to the Goodwins via Ouija board or table-tapping—*wrote in her farewell letter that you might be interested in buying her island property.*

"And I guess *that* would smack a wet sock into Old Smiley's twinkle," she said. But when she sat down to compose the letter for the Goodwins to find, she decided not to give in to her sense of humor and mention the doctor. "Bad taste is a cardinal sin, Alexia," she said crustily. "Die if you must, but with dignity, please. No crude jokes. It's not necessary to leave them laughing."

She drew money from the bank and sealed the cash in the letter. It should be enough to pay for cremation, and to take care of William for the rest of his life. They had given him as a kitten to her and Shane, and had always had a proprietary affection for him.

She had two good sessions with the children. While she worked with one child, the other two amused themselves with books and drawing materials, and with William. The smaller boy would patiently drag a catnip mouse on a string for as long as William cared to pursue it, which sometimes appeared to be forever. The girl did a large and dashing watercolor of Alix painting the older brother.

"When I grow up I'm going to be just like you, Miss Horne," she said. "I'm going to be a famous artist and everything. I think I've got a good early start, don't you? Did you paint this good when you were eight?"

"Not nearly as well," said Alix, and the child looked smug. I must remember this conversation, Alix thought, and then remembered there was no one to tell it to. Her hand shook slightly. The boy sitting in the captain's chair on the model stand, his sailboat on his knees, watched her with bottomless dark eyes.

"What are you thinking about, Clark?" she asked.

"I think you don't feel very good," he said in a gruff young voice.

"Whatever gives you that idea?" She put a red pennant on the sailboat.

"I don't know. I just know. Like you've been worrying, or having bad dreams, maybe." He added so low that she could hardly hear him, "Crying."

She moved the brush just in time before her jumping hand could make a smear. The girl said in a bored tone, "He's always saying things like that. He thinks he's so smart. ... It makes Daddy and Mummy nervous."

Her complacency was a relief. "Does it make you nervous?" Alix asked.

"Nope." She sozzled her brush luxuriously in a puddle of Prussian blue. "Miss Horne, if a person's a genius they can go to art school when they're still a child, can't they? I don't mean art classes for children. I mean real art school, like where you went."

"If a person's a genius, I suppose anything's possible. Not being a genius, I can't be certain. ... There you are, Clark. I'll try the Moving Target for fifteen minutes now."

"You'll be lucky if he sits still for five," said Clark. He moved the captain's chair and substituted a smaller chair and table, and got out the wooden train of cars. "Come on, Raisinhead."

Roger squatted to hug and kiss an accommodating William, then climbed into position. He was an uncomplicated three-year-old who beamed every time he caught her eye, and was neither psychic nor smug. He played quietly with the train for all of ten minutes, and she worked with a feeling of accomplishment. Unexpectedly she reached the point where the painting needed nothing more.

"Roger, you're a gentleman and a scholar," she said.

He thought that was extremely witty. When he had finished laughing he said, "When do we have our cookies?"

"Right now." She washed her hands, and they followed her into the kitchen, where she mixed up a jugful of the revoltingly magenta-colored fruit drink they loved, and set out a plate of their favorite cookies. She made coffee for herself, and they all sat at the table. It came to Alix that once she had enjoyed these children far more than most, and that ordinarily she would have been sorry to see the sessions end. Ordinarily, too, there would have been no cause for the boy to display his disturbing empathy. Now she was glad this was the finish.

Right now he was soberly applying himself to his eating and drinking. His sister could do both and talk at the same time, no doubt another proof of genius. "I think when I'm a famous artist I'll have a bigger apartment than this," she said. "I saw this movie once where a woman was an artist, and her place was just beautiful. Even the kitchen. She had a cook. She was beautiful, too."

"The cook?" asked Alix.

"No, the artist. And ooh, her *studio!* It went way up high—" she raised her arms and her eyes to cathedral heights—"and it had big windows and this *huge* fireplace with big logs in it. And she had all these lovers—"

"To bring in those big logs, I suppose," said Alix. Clark snorted into his drink. Roger looked enchanted, and began blowing bubbles in his. The older two spoke severely to him. Then the doorbell rang. It was their mother, and the session was over.

Dodie was always dropping in unexpectedly, bringing little delicacies; she could not believe, knowing Alix of old, that any disaster whatever could affect her appetite. It was simply a question of finding the right thing to start the machinery going again.

This time she said in astonishment, "You look better!"

"Don't sound so outraged."

"I'm not. I'm just indignant. I've been worried sick about you, and here you are wearing something decent, your face is scrubbed, your hair's been washed, and you've got *shoes* on."

"They wouldn't let me into the bank barefoot."

Dodie blew out smoke from her nostrils like a small dragon, and squinted around the living room. "What have you been doing to the place? There's a lot of stuff missing. You aren't planning. to move, are you?" She sounded alarmed.

"I'm just moving to Tiree, as usual. I've put some things away for the summer," said Alix, thinking of the labeled cartons in her bedroom closet. There was one marked *Dodie,* and dispassionately she imagined Dodie weeping over the old Spode plates she'd always coveted.

"I must say," said Dodie, "that when I said you should brace up, I didn't expect to see you actually grinning. You're a little too braced up to be true." She came close, trying to look at Alix's eyes. "Are you sure you're not taking some kind of pep pills?"

"I am not taking anything," said Alix blandly. "I'm getting ready for Maine, that's all. It gives me something to do. I make lists. In fact, I make lists of lists."

Dodie was determined to worry. "*Should* you go to Maine? Why not take a nice Scandinavian cruise? It would be lovely, and a lot cooler than Greece. Besides, there's something about this new government—and that poor young king in exile—no, Scandinavia it *is*," she said decisively. "You must go."

I could jump overboard in a fjord, Alix thought. She said, "But what about poor William? You see, I'm getting abnormally attached to him, just as you said. Now let's have coffee, and that cheesecake you brought. William loves cheesecake, don't you, William?"

Dodie looked not so much annoyed as deeply hurt, and Alix was disgusted with her own malice. She and Dodie had been friends since high school. With two marriages and a family, and a circle of organizations for which she worked very hard, Dodie was still faithful to the tight juvenile partnership of tall skinny Alexia and short stocky Dodie. And she had been the one person to whom Alix, in the first incredulous reaction, had communicated the news about Shane.

"I'm just teasing you, Dodie love," she said. "I don't know what I'd do without you to worry about me. Some day I'll be really able to tell you how much you mean to me." Dodie would know when she saw what was in the box.

Dodie's little eyes filled with tears that bounced out over the dark liner and ran among the creases. She said crossly, "You can show me by taking care of yourself, that's all."

"On my honor as a Wildwood Camper," said Alix, holding up her right hand and staring glassily at the ceiling. Dodie giggled.

"Remember the Iron Maiden? I think she was trying to model us on the Coldstream Guards."

"Hitler Youth was more like it," said Alix. They burst into relieved laughter, assured that another difficult moment had been superbly dealt with, and went out to the kitchen on a wave of vigorous reminiscence.

✤ CHAPTER 4 ✤

SHE SPENT a night at a motel near Damariscotta, not the one in which she'd always stayed, where the owners welcomed her each year as an old friend. Her stop there and her dinner in the restaurant had become ritual of the sort that had always been precious to her, like the special routines of childhood. (Always clam chowder for supper on the boat between Boston and Bangor.)

It occurred to her now that not only Shane had died but so had a good many reflexes and associations, both conscious and unconscious; they had composed so much of her that without them she was almost as unfleshed as a skeleton.

Going to bed in a strange place where only William, indelicately devouring his supper, was familiar, she felt like a skeleton, that wandering and rattling one in the poem by Frost, trying to get back to its own place.

The surrounding countryside was bleak in a raw dusk. She took a Seconal to help her forget its hostility. She'd been struggling along without them, hoarding the drug for the important time ahead, and so tonight it worked fast. William sprawled against her feet, the security of a live teddy bear, lulling her into sleep with his egg-boiling purr. He knew where he was going.

In the morning the sun was shining undefiled across a windy world full of red-winged blackbirds, and gulls flying in to find newly ploughed fields. She drove northeast through transparent young greens overlaid with gold and silver, and firs dark and tossing in the wind that ruffled every scrap of water to cobalt.

William rode tensely beside her, sitting on his haunches with his front paws braced on the door handle. He rose up lashing his tail whenever he saw a dog, a cat, or crows.

Another part of the ritual had been the stocking-up at Emery's, the village store. This time she stopped in a town ten miles west of the Harbor, and went into a large chain store. She didn't need much food for the little while left, but slow starvation wasn't the end she had in mind, and she needed physical strength to do the final tidying-up chores. Besides, she was so thin now that if she got any leaner Madge would fuss at her—in soft tearful bleatings, as compared to Dodie's terse nagging—and the whole idea was to accomplish this business without drawing too much attention to herself beforehand.

After she put the groceries in the car, she left William nosing excitedly over the boxes while she went to the state liquor store and bought two bottles of Scotch and a bottle of the best brandy the place offered. She wasn't sure how fast the liquor and barbiturate combination worked; whether you took your drink and your dose every night until it built up to the lethal point, in a form of Russian roulette, or if it took only a couple of tries. She decided that to be on the safe side she'd have everything done before she began to experiment.

This was going to be complicated, she thought in some exasperation. She'd had a rather poetic picture of herself setting out the letter to Madge and Ozzie, perhaps on her pillow, then swallowing half-a-dozen capsules, drinking a toast to Shane, and going to sleep with the sound of the sea in her ears.

It would be simple and beautiful all around. The Lady of Shalott drifting down to Camelot.

This way she was going to have to get things ready every night, just in case, and what an anti-climax to wake up the next morning. Feeling absolutely foul, she'd have to stagger around putting that envelope out of sight and pulling herself together in case one of the Goodwins should come in early, though it probably wouldn't be early but midday, and if they should find her passed out in a drugged stupor—

It didn't bear thinking about, Roger Goodwin bringing a doctor out and the rest of the whole revolting fiasco. If you had any guts, she thought, you'd do something quick and violent like drowning or hanging. There'd be nothing poetic about it, but it would be efficient, if that's what you want. But no, either it's the Lady of Shalott syndrome or you don't want it to hurt.

"Oh, Lord, William," she said irritably, "you've found the chops." She climbed into the back of the car and removed fifteen pounds of determined cat from the box, and piled her raincoat and parka on top of the food, then her paintbox. "I may be a lost cause," she told him as she got behind the wheel, "but I'll be damned if I'll eat a chop you've been gnawing on."

William turned his back on her. It seemed to become very broad when he was displeased.

In midafternoon she drove down the narrow winding road between spruces and blueberry fields to the Harbor. On such a day the scene always burst upon one with the gaudy glory of a calendar picture: the bright water blue as turquoise, the gulls sailing on the wind, homecoming boats with bones in their teeth, a broad-beamed seiner going out with a string of orange dories astern; the uncorrupted light outlining the men with gold, gilding the fishhouses, flashing off the wet rocks, dazzling on the white cubes of houses among the dark spruces.

Now, though she saw it all, and her nostrils were filled with the cold oceany scent that always came with this wind, she felt nothing. It was as if certain nerve ends had been totally destroyed.

William's head was up, he was sniffing hard, and when she

stopped the car he started across her toward the open window. She seized him and stuffed him expertly into his case, and took it down to the end of Roger Goodwin's wharf. Here she set him high on a row of lobster traps. He could see the harbor and growl at gulls that swung too close, and still be above the notice of local dogs.

Ozzie's boat was at his brother's float, with no one aboard. Over at the lobster wharf three boats were tied up around the car, and she saw Ozzie among the men there. He was a bean-pole of a man with brown skin and an imposing nose which he claimed came direct from an Indian ancestor. He was helping another man to swing a heavy crate of lobsters from a boat to the scales. He didn't see Alix, and she didn't linger to enjoy the scene as she would have once done. She went back to her car and began unloading it.

She hadn't much this time, and it was all out of the car and on the brassy slope when Ozzie arrived. "Hi," he said, with a very slight grin, as if anything wider would be offensive under the circumstances. "I'll start lugging while you get the rest of your gear out."

"There isn't any more," she said. One of his eyebrows went up, but otherwise he showed no astonishment. "It's good to see you, Ozzie," she said, putting her hand out. He gripped it hard, then dropped it abruptly and said, "Well, I'll take the stuff down anyway. You go park. Madge is in the house."

"All right, and thanks." She was proud of her businesslike tone. She drove the car up into Roger's driveway and across a flat face of ledge, then under a row of thick-trunked tall old spruces where Ozzie's car and pickup were parked. As she stood by the car, pulling on her parka, the wind blew through the boughs overhead, stirring them to massively gentle motion. They made a sound she had always wished she could paint. But it's just there now, she thought tiredly. Everything's just there, so many sounds and smells and sights. A primrose by the river's brim, and so forth.

Robins flew up sputtering from the lawn as Madge came

running from the kitchen door. She was overweight, but light and fast, and as she ran Alix knew that her request not to mention Shane was going to be ignored. She knew gloomily that she was going to be embraced, and she would have to accept it or hurt Madge's feelings. She knew that Madge was going to burst into tears, which she did. Furiously embarrassed, Alix found herself hugging Madge back. Madge was softly plump, fragrant with some new scent Roger's wife was selling. She kept saying thickly somewhere under Alix's ear, "It's a crime, it's just a *crime!*"

Worse than the embarrassment was the fear that in another moment she'd begin to cry too. "Stop that, Madge," she said crossly. "Or you'll have me doing it." They backed off to look at each other, holding each other's arms, Alix forcing her aching face into the Cheshire-cat grin and Madge trying to wink back the freshet. Incongruously, Alix realized that she had never been this close to Madge, and that when you saw someone in enlarged sections a few inches away from you, their total geography was forever changed.

Madge gave a final convulsive squeeze and went digging for a handkerchief, whispering little laments to herself, and then blew her nose. Alix turned and frowned into the car as if looking for what she'd forgotten. She saw nothing; she was trying not to tremble. She wished she hadn't come, William or not.

"*Now,*" said Madge loudly. "What about a cup of coffee in the house before we start out? Daisy's got the kettle on."

"Can I take a raincheck on that?" asked Alix. "I'm just thinking of getting home. Besides," she lied, "I stopped for a big lunch in Edwardstown." She kept her head in the car, fiddling aimlessly with objects in the glove compartment. "Tell Daisy, will you? Tell her I'll be in one of these days as soon as I've rested up." She backed out and finished locking the car. "Here are the keys." They were always left with the Roger Goodwins.

"She'll understand, dear," Madge said tenderly, and hurried back to the house. Alix wondered how long it would take Madge to stop treating her like a hospital case. Freezing her face into blankness, she stalked down to the wharf as if ignoring everyone would make her invisible. Thank God there'd soon be an end to the whole business.

Thank God? she repeated to herself. Excuse, please. Figure of speech. Rank cliché, in fact. If there is a God, I couldn't possibly share Him with Shane's wife, and she's got the priority. She's got all the credentials of a God-loving, God-fearing woman; she's got a direct line to His ear, even if the battered babies and the starving ones don't. Sparrows may fall in clouds, but not Cathleen Mannering. So what does her God have to do with me? He wouldn't give me the time of day.

"Alix—"

"What?" she snapped.

Ozzie's voice was mild. "I thought you were going to walk off the end of the wharf, the way you came down all winged out."

She laughed. "I might have at that, Ozzie. Thanks." She went down the ramp onto the float. William's case was on the engine box. He protested to Alix, and clawed at his wire-mesh window.

"He's been talking a blue streak," said Ozzie. "Give me quite a yarn. Says this year he's going to catch him a sea gull, see if he don't."

"He was ever a dreamer," said Alix. Where in hell was Madge? Giving Daisy a full description, no doubt, and weeping again. *Oh the poor thing ... skin and bones, and black as ink around the eyes. ... Wait till you see her.*

There was an explosive flapping of sails as a little yawl came about close by them. A young couple waved, and she forced herself to say, "Who's that? It's early for summer people."

"Oh, they ain't summer complaints. They moved into the old Dunton place this winter. He's an artist." Ozzie gave the word no special inflection. Knowing Alix had educated him about artists, and so many had come and gone in the mainland community in the last few years that the whole village was now sophisticated about the species. In fact, there were quite a few amateur painters among the natives.

"Seem like nice kids," Ozzie said. "That old yawl was in the barn up there. They've fixed her up, and made her a new suit of sails. Got Roger to tell 'em how. He has all Grampa's tools . . . that was our mother's father," he went on, and she knew he was talking to fill up space, because it wasn't like Ozzie to repeat himself as he was doing now. "He was a sailmaker by trade. Last ship he made sails for, she was a five-master, the *Gladys B. Hart,* and she was launched upriver in Edwardstown, in—let me see—"

Nineteen hundred and one, she almost told him, but she only stood there listening bleakly to what she had heard before. This nervousness in Ozzie upset her more than Madge's tears, which always came easily anyway. She was relieved to see Madge hurrying down the wharf.

"Here they come," said Ozzie, also relieved. "Seems like Madge and Daisy never run out of talk. Being married to Goodwins must give them plenty of material. My ears have been burning for the last ten minutes."

Madge came down the ramp tying her kerchief under her chin. Halfway she stopped and cried, "Ozzie, you never thought to get Jonas's tobacco and outboard oil!"

"I did, and I also thought to get his traphead twine *and* his gloves *and* his sparkplugs. Get aboard, old woman, and stop treating me like your backward son."

"No need to be sarcastic," said Madge, resuming motion. It was then that Alix saw the child close behind her; it had been hidden by Madge's blowing coat.

"She was hoping I'd forget," Ozzie said to Alex. "You see her face? I disappointed her something awful."

"Twarn't disappointment, 'twas shock," said Madge. "Because you remembered, for once." She climbed nimbly aboard. "And here's William! How's my old Sweet William today?" She leaned over the case cooing baby talk to the purring and arching cat.

The child stood on the washboard a moment, then jumped down into the cockpit. She was about ten, wearing red stretch slacks and a quilted and hooded red jacket that turned her skin milk-white. White-blond bangs fluttered on her forehead. She wore thick glasses with pink rims. Alix half-expected to see pink eyes too, but the enlarged and unwinking stare was bachelor-button blue.

"And who's this?" Alix asked, trying to sound jovial. Ozzie had started the engine and they were backing away from the float; above the churning of water and the vibration Madge cried in astonishment, "Why, this is Thelma's Karen! You remember her being here when she was a baby, and just last year you and—" She swallowed something back, blushed, but pushed on. "You sent her that lovely doll you won on chances at the church fair."

"Oh yes," said Alix, regarding Karen with what she hoped was a winning expression. But she had a feeling that Thelma's Karen was not deceived. Her chilly gaze didn't change as she stood without moving under her grandmother's patting hand. "What did you name the doll, Karen? I never heard."

Karen's lower lip moved out a little. She shrugged, and said nothing. It seemed safer not to inquire into the fate of the doll; not even to think of it. "Has Thelma moved back to Maine, then?" Alix asked Madge.

"Lands, no," said Madge. "You'd never get Einar to move away from that good job in Connecticut. Karen's visiting. She was real sick this spring, and they sent her down to Gramp and Gram to get some roses in her cheeks."

"Well, this is the place to find them," Alix replied brightly. Madge winked and grimaced over the child's head to let Alix know there was more to the story. Then she went into the cuddy to see if everything was there.

The boat was out of the harbor now, and meeting the deep swell of open water. The bow waves rushed past the low sides of the cockpit and joined the splendidly foaming wake astern. Alix sat on the washboard watching the way ahead for a few minutes; ordinarily at this point the joy of homecoming would be almost too intense to be borne.

She turned her back to the bow, propping her shoulder

against a canopy post, and felt aimlessly in all her pockets. She and Shane had given up smoking a few years ago—anything to prolong life—and now she thought how handy it would be to do all that fussing with cigarettes and lighters. She had to settle for her dark glasses as a form of refuge, and had them in her hand when her attention was drawn to Karen.

Motionless, her new red sneakers set close together, her hands folded on her stomach, she stood contemplating Alix.

A child on the island in May. Alix had never anticipated such a thing. They sometimes came in midsummer, but never this early. How could she carry out her plans when there was a child around who would be upset by the goings-on? Though this one looked as if the death of one adult more or less couldn't possibly dent her.

I wish I'd never left New York, she thought, turning away from the magnified blue scrutiny to look ahead again. The island was about two miles away now, sharp in outline as a colored cutout in this preternaturally clear light. The spruces on the height were blue as plums above fields that descended toward the shore in rich green terraces. The occasional single trees or small groups, the thickets of wild rose, alder, and bay, seemed to have been placed in certain spots for landscaping purposes. The rocky footing shimmered between greens and blues in a band of subtle grays, tawnies, and a pale pinkish apricot she'd always enjoyed. Since the contours of the island hid Beauty Cove, where the Goodwin house was, the island looked uninhabited. It should have the ruins of a temple somewhere up there on the highest part facing the east and the rising sun; it floated on the sea in a sort of ancient Aegean dream of its own.

Alix felt the need to do something exaggerated and vehement before she burst, but she could only put on her dark glasses and shove her hands deep into her pockets where they could clench away with no one seeing.

Madge was contentedly mulling over things in the cuddy, like a plump bird treading round and round in her nest. Ozzie stood watching ahead, his pipe between his teeth. Suddenly William cried out forlornly, as if the journey had gone on entirely too long. Until then Karen had apparently not noticed him, for now she approached the case like one hypnotized. She peered in at William. Without speaking to him or even smiling, she stabbed her forefinger in through the mesh.

Instantly her face contorted with surprise and pain. She pulled her finger out and put it to her mouth, but Alix had already seen the bright beaded line of blood.

"He does that if you move too fast," she said. Am I *pleased?* she thought, shocked.

Ozzie looked down on them, unmoved. "Ayuh, William's real quick on the trigger. You want to respect him, Karen. Don't go taking liberties."

Alix reached for Karen's hand, but she kept it up to her mouth and turned away. Alix was confronted by a rigid shoulder and a tight elbow. The child walked to the stern of the cockpit and stood back to the others, immobile.

"I'm sorry," Alix said to Ozzie.

"No harm done."

"But she thinks we're against her, we're on William's side."

"She poked him," said Ozzie reasonably. "Now she knows better. When she came we told her what Sidney doesn't like. Don't pull his ears or his whiskers, we said, and be careful around his tail, it's real tender since he got run over on the mainland that time. So first thing she did was give his tail a yank and he bit her. Not enough to draw blood, but she was hard put not to cry about it." He shrugged. "She's an awful lot politer to old Sidney now. . . . You poke in where you hadn't ought, you get clipped. That's simple, ain't it?"

"What's simple?" Madge came out of the cuddy. "Ozzie, you know *what?* Jonas got a letter today from some law firm in Rockland."

Ozzie lifted a hand in salute as a lobster boat passed them on her way home. "It's probably about the divorce," Madge went on.

"Who's Jonas?" Alix asked. "Somebody else trying to get roses in his cheeks?"

Madge started to laugh, then remembered and drew her mouth down; her eyes took on a humid pathos. "Now, he won't bother you no more than Karen will. You'll likely only see him at a distance when he's hauling. Oh, we have him to eat once in a while, a man alone, you know. . . . We've rented him the Home Camp for a while."

She went on talking and Alix tried to look as if she were listening. The words "Home Camp" registered as a picture; it was the much-repaired, patched, and renewed dwelling that Gibraltar Goodwin had built originally as a one-room cabin for himself and his bride when he first bought the island of Tiree from a Scottish settler, who had bought it from an Indian. The Scot had named it for an island he knew at home. He had come to the United States as a quarry worker, and it was the granite dust in his lungs that sickened him before he'd had time to enjoy his island. So he'd sold it and gone back to Scotland to die.

Alix's mind reviewed the story, returned briefly to the Home Camp, set a faceless man in the camp, and forgot him. She was much more conscious of the inimical little figure in the stern. *Perhaps she's only here for a week or so,* she calmed herself. *I'll need a week anyway for going through things.*

Things. Shane's clothes, books, tools. His guitar. His notebooks. No one else was ever to touch them. Even the thought of such sacrilege suffused her body with heat, and a pounding began in her head. Hiding behind the dark glasses she battled for poise and came gradually back to Madge's voice purling on like a brook. She'd lost the thread of the narrative and forgotten the subject, but when Madge stopped and looked at her expectantly, she said with feeling, "Imagine it!"

Madge nodded fervently. "That's what *I* say." Then she went aft, calling to Karen, "What do you see, chickabiddy?"

☙ CHAPTER 5 ☙

THEY WERE THERE, or almost. The Head, the high northeast prow of the island, reared up over them like the crest of a monstrous wave frozen into stone. The thirty-five-foot boat danced like a chip in the backwash from the base. Ozzie concentrated on threading among the reefs and ledges, some marked by a constant play of surf, some unseen at this tide. Madge bubbled on to the child about the eiders that rode the swells. She pointed, gesticulated, grew ecstatic about the ducklings to come. Her gift of perpetual wonder and astonishment at the world around her was perhaps more ingenuous than Alix's had been, but it was as strong as ever. Knowing how her own had gone so swiftly, Alix looked from Madge to Ozzie and saw them for the first time as aging and mortal, terribly frail against the forces that could attack without warning. In a night Madge could lose that innocent amazement, or the peace could be shattered out of Ozzie's eyes for good.

While Madge explained and exclaimed, the child stared impassively at the long line of black-and-white drakes and brown ducks. It occurred to Alix that Karen might be either retarded or disturbed, and that was the reason for Madge's winks and nods. Still, Madge had always talked freely of her children and grandchildren. If there were anything wrong with Karen, and she knew it, she couldn't have kept it a secret.

Perhaps Karen was simply a stolid and noncommittal child. Her mother was a pretty and lively dark-eyed girl, but her husband was so quiet that their marriage had been the source of many mild family jokes. Karen took after him, apparently, and the unnerving stare turned on Alix meant no more than curiosity about the stranger of whom she must have heard much. Alix remembered her own merciless scrutiny of adults, and now secretly apologized to those whom she must have disconcerted.

Now she recognized the black buffalo humps of ledge they were passing. If she looked up she would see her house, or at least its steep pitched roof and chimneys above the high bank. She went down into the cuddy and began setting her things out in the cockpit. With a plunging sensation in her stomach she felt the boat make a turn into smooth waters, which meant they were in Gib's Cove and gliding toward the wharf.

The engine was shut off, gulls called stridently as they took off from the wharf and circled over the intruders, and William began to howl again. Alix found herself reading avidly over and over again the lettering on the side of a carton of groceries. *Barbara Brewster's Angelfood Mix.* Whispering them like an incantation she went out to the cockpit. They helped. She was able to say cheerfully, "William's in distress. All he can think of is that beach out there. God's great sandbox."

Ozzie and Madge laughed, and Karen turned her glasses slowly from one to the other. Alix went up the ladder, keeping her own laughter-fixed on her face, and Ozzie handed William's case up. She undid the clasps and lifted the lid. They all watched while the big cat arched his back, then stepped out with great deliberation, stretching first one hind leg and then the other. He looked up at the gulls, sniffed the air, went over to examine the detritus of bleached crab shells on the gulls' favorite corner of the wharf. Two tree swallows came sailing down on him like miniature hawks. All at once William's tail crooked sidewise, he galloped across the wharf and took a speedy and familiar route to the sand and began to dig. The adults burst out laughing again, to Karen's apparent mystification. As they began unloading Alix's things, she kept watching the cat with the same attention she gave to everything.

"I don't need help getting this stuff to the house," Alix said. "The wheelbarrow's right here, and I need the exercise."

"It don't seem right for you to have so little gear to lug," Madge fretted. "Now you be sure to come to supper, dear."

Alix had to promise; if she didn't go Madge would bring the food over to her.

"I mowed the back lawn, Alix," Ozzie said, "but the front isn't high enough yet, where there's all that ledge underneath. Takes it longer to get going. Besides, I know how you like the dandelions."

"Oh, I do. All that gold spattered around free, and then the goldfinches coming." Her voice rattled vivaciously in her empty head, like dried peas in a salt shaker. "Thanks, Ozzie."

After the lower point of Gib's Cove had cut off the sound of *Marjorie C.*'s engine, she stood on the wharf in silence almost unblemished except for the rote from the windward side, and the slight chatter of the swallows as they headed back to their houses up on the hill.

The gulls had settled again on the ledges and shallows. William had disappeared, already an island cat. Well, she had brought him here as she'd promised, and she wished that now she could go up to the house, put out the envelope for Madge and Ozzie, and lie down on her bed and die. What if she didn't go through her things and Shane's? What sort of neurotic placed so much importance on objects? Maybe it was just procrastination. If she took all her Seconals at once tonight and washed them down with whiskey—

"It's that infernal kid," she said aloud. "You never know about them. She looks like a lump but she may not be. I don't want to send her up the wall." Angrily she began loading the wheelbarrow.

Usually she brought enough working materials to do her

into October: rolls of canvas, bundles of stretchers, watercolor blocks, her typewriter, boxes of books. No wonder Ozzie's eyebrow had gone up at the sight of two bags and her old paintbox. The paintbox was to be burned along with Shane's guitar and the other things that were too intimate a part of their life to be left behind them.

The squeak began in the wheelbarrow as she pushed it across the planks. The squeak that could never quite be greased out of existence was as much a part of the life as the gulls' crying. Maybe I ought to chuck the wheelbarrow onto the pyre too, she thought. If there's an afterlife it might come in handy.

From the woods toward the west came a constant chipping and fussing. William was disturbing the birds. He had never killed one, to Alix's knowledge, but the birds still knew him as The Enemy. They knew well the shape of terror, they were born knowing it.

Up there at the top of the hill, in the house facing the east, her Enemy waited, and she too had been born knowing its shape, but it seemed to her now that all her life had been a frivolous, irresponsible avoidance of the knowledge. If the truth was so terrible now it was because she had ignored it for so long.

And ignorance was bliss—oh, pure bliss that she looked back upon with burning eyes and finally wept for, letting go the wheelbarrow because she couldn't see where she was going. Without shame she let herself go in noisy blubbering sobs while the tears rushed down her contorted face.

But, being Alix (once Alexia had bawled in the same wholehearted way), she couldn't ever give in completely, either because someone appeared or her nose got so stuffed up she couldn't breathe. Now she groped in all her pockets for a handkerchief and found only hard little wads of tissue. "Of course you wouldn't have one, you slut," she wept around hiccups. "A clean handkerchief is the mark of a lady, so you know where that puts *you*." Finally she found a scarf jammed in the pocket of her raincoat. After she'd blown her nose on one end and wiped her tears with the other, she realized it belonged to Shane.

"Oh, Shane, why did you have to go to that goddamn wedding?" she asked plaintively. "Why the devoted father bit all of a sudden? You gave them away years before, you know. You damn well did when you moved out and gave their mother free rein to tell them what a lustful scoundrel you were. What happened, did you go all squishy-squashy about another man taking your daughter, you old fox? Or did Cathleen ni Houlihan or whoever put the pressure on you about shaming your child by letting her uncle take her down the aisle? And how did she get the priest to let you inside the church, you adulterer? Or is adultery forgivable but not divorce?"

She grabbed up the handles of the wheelbarrow and ran it off the wharf and onto the path. "I suppose," she went on in the brittle, crackling voice he'd always hated when they argued, "that they gave you the last rites in spite of yourself, and now she's happy that she was the death of you, because that makes her a blessed widow whose husband came back to her and the church. *He's* in paradise, and everybody knows where *I'm* going."

She jolted the wheelbarrow hard over the hump of ledge in the path instead of going around it. The paintbox bounced off. "Her and her private God that says I'm an evil woman for loving you and she's a virtuous one for keeping the hooks in you all these years. She got you back in the end, didn't she, Shane? Or she thinks she did, and that's the same thing. Oh, Shane, I'm so *furious*, don't you see I can't do anything else but what I'm going to do?"

The wheelbarrow jounced down into the hollow she knew was there, another spot usually avoided. The shock went up from her wrists to her shoulders.

"If I try not to think about you," she explained, "there's this rotten apathy, as if I'm some sort of cretin. If I give in, there's all this rage and pain, and this hatred eating away at my guts like cancer. I can't live with it, that's all there is to it."

She was halfway to the house and she had to stop, gasping for breath while her heart seemed to slam around unmoored behind her ribs. She pulled off her parka in panic at its constriction, stripped off the sweater under it, and yanked her shirt out of her slacks to let the air reach her wet back and midriff. She forced herself to breathe evenly, to look around and fix her attention on externals. A warm vernal fragrance came up from the earth. Strawberry blossoms and violets edged the path, the bay twigs showed tiny coral buds, the hardhack and wild roses were in tight new leaf. Song sparrows were unquenchably energetic from alder sprays and wild apple trees; the whitethroats' whistle was so limpidly melodious it was impossible to consider it a war cry.

Now, some pressure temporarily relieved, she looked openly up at the house. Sunlight warmed its weathered gray shingles, turned its white trim to cream, stippled with dull gold the lichened and faded brick of the chimneys. The windows flashed reflections of the day. Madge would have washed them while Ozzie was lighting the gas refrigerator and the stove pilots, or mowing the grass.

What was Karen doing all the while this was going on, she wondered. There was probably nothing in the house that she had missed. Alix felt a prickle of belligerence like hackles rising on her nape, but it was a vestigial remnant from her past and quickly subsided.

The original story-and-a-half house that Gibraltar Goodwin had built was small and low-posted with a steep roof. Ells, dormers, and "warts" had been added to it according to the whims of successive Goodwins. Its freakish irregularities, its slanting floors and odd steps, were a constant delight to Shane.

"There's not a line in this house that's plumb!" he had exclaimed as if announcing that he'd found a trunkful of gold doubloons in the cellar.

The front stairs were steep enough to be formidable if you

felt unsteady at all. The back stairs curved from behind a door in one corner of the kitchen up into the space and light of the ell chamber, whose gable end faced north. They'd filled this wall with glass to give Alix a good painting light.

Downstairs they had made three rooms into one to make a large living room, but they had done nothing more in the way of structural changes. Only the colors were their own, dull and soft so as not to war with the perpetual change outside the windows. They cherished the kitchen the way it was, with the cupboards Gib's son had made, the wide pine boards of the floor, the mantel shelf behind the stove for lamps. Alix kept the black sink like black satin, and never forgot to coat it with mineral oil when she left in the fall.

Bottled gas for cooking and refrigeration was an enjoyable convenience, but it was a matter of pride with them that when they first came they had cooked on the wood range and kept food cold in the cellar or in the well.

The well curb had been replaced many times over the well that Gibraltar had dug and rocked up. Shane had built the last one and had been naïvely proud of it. Madge couldn't believe that he really enjoyed drawing water and carrying the pails to the house. She and Ozzie had done it for years, and she left with paeans of joy for the new little house over on Beauty Cove, electrified by a power plant. They had running water in the house, and television.

"All right," she said crossly, "you don't need television because you're out stramming around like young ones half the night. And you think oil lamps are real picturesque. But you could have a bathroom, for heaven's sake! And you could have water running right in the kitchen sink! I can't for the life of me see what's so thrilling and romantic about hauling a pail of water out of an old well and lugging it into the house."

"But Madge, lugging water like that makes us realize what a precious thing pure water is," Alix told her. "You take it for granted because you've always had it. We don't. This water deserves to be worked for. When you bring up a pailful and think how many years this same well has been in use, it's almost a religious thing."

"Give me a good religious reason for hanging onto an outdoor toilet when you don't need to."

"I admit that could rapidly lose its charm in winter," said Shane. "So could going to the well. But on a good summer day with the door open and the birds talking all around, and the whole Atlantic spread out before you—oh, I've had some very sublime thoughts out there, Madge love. You'd be amazed."

"Yes, I would be." She gave him a half-irritated, half-flirtatious eye. "And you a professor. I don't get it. Seems as if the more brains a man has, the more peculiar his notions."

The memory of that conversation had carried Alix to the house. She even found herself smiling, entirely absorbed in the past. As a startled robin exploded into flight before her, she was knocked back into the present. Each time one forgot for a moment, the return of memory was worse.

Her room was upstairs, but she put her bags in a small downstairs room at the back of the house, which they had used as a study. Its one window looked up across the gently sloping field toward the woods along the western height. There was a couch here, where she had never slept before; now she would feel like a stranger in someone else's house, and that was what she wanted.

But the first thing she saw in the room was Shane's guitar case lying on the desk. He loved classical guitar music but he was self-conscious about his attempts to play it, and worked on it only in the summers. In his rooms at the college he couldn't be sure of privacy. Alix gathered that Cathleen had always been exasperated and a little ashamed by such a peculiar hobby for a grown man, and her criticism had made its mark on him; in some ways he was absurdly sensitive.

Alix stood looking at the case now, then abruptly turned her back on it and went out to the kitchen. She put the food away in cupboards and refrigerator. There was a fresh pail of cold well water on the counter by the sink, and outside the white-painted rain barrels had been put in place under the downspouts, and were half full. She brought in some of the soft water and heated it enough to take off the chill, then undressed and washed. She put on jeans and a checked shirt, then made a mug of instant coffee and walked barefoot through the house carrying the mug, not looking at anything around her as she passed.

Crossing the living room she felt herself caught by eyes like a crossfire, and her neck ached as she tried not to look at Shane's portrait. The two paintings faced each other across the room, Shane's over the fireplace; he had white-capped ocean behind him and sun on the side of his dark-burnt face. Alix's portrait was above an old chest he'd refinished. She'd done it from a mirror, up in the studio. "You've caricatured yourself," he had accused her. "False modesty. You want people to say, 'My God, woman, beside *that* you're a raving beauty.'"

She opened the front door and the wind came in, briny and cold. The eastern sea was dark blue, streaked and spangled with curling crests to the horizon, which had been done with a ruler along a glazed yellowish-blue sky. The lush grass powdered with the first dandelions was like a child's joyous experiment with vivid greens and incandescent yellows; the scene jumped and vibrated in Alix's tired vision. The lawn sloped to the high bank, where there were dense thickets of the rugosa roses that grew and prospered out here on the eastern side the way the tough bay and juniper did. Perhaps it was because they were no longer tame. No one knew in what garden or how long ago the parent stock had lived. These once-Japanese roses had been sown by the birds and had grown up wild and tough.

Now they were wiry tangles, but later the air would be voluptuously scented with red and white roses for weeks. The fragrance would flow into the house on the sea wind, and hover like a cloud when there was no wind.

The roses and the wild flowers had been enough garden for Shane and Alix. Shane kept the grass mowed all around the house, and the old paths cleared through the woods, occasionally making a new one to some special spot they had discovered; they were always discovering them.

"But we can get around here by the shore," Alix objected once last year when he wanted to cut a short way through the woods to a group of massive old spruces at the southwest tip. "That's how we found the place."

"Now we can," he answered seriously, "but when we're old we'll want an easy way to come. We'll have two chairs out here under the trees, and we'll sit and gaze at the ocean and hold hands all afternoon."

She said something rude, and he grinned. "Age isn't the bubonic plague, love. Don't you like the Darby and Joan touch?"

"*No!*" She spat the word at him, then jumped for a maple branch and swung from it, glaring at him, reassured that she could still do it, comforted by the easy stretch of muscles and the strength in her hands.

Shane laughed at her and shook his head. There were spills and twigs in his thick, rough, graying-black hair and beard. He'd burned off the winter's extra weight, and his normally dark skin had tanned even darker. Stripped to the waist, the machete in his hand, he had an air both tropical and piratical, like a man slashing his way through the jungle to find a lost temple and take the giant ruby from the Buddha's forehead.

"Of course old age won't begin for us until we're about a hundred," he said. She looked down at him, narrow-eyed and defiant, wondering how much longer she could hold on, and suddenly he dropped the machete, grabbed her around the hips, and gave her a quick boost upwards. She lost her grip and collapsed with a shriek on his head.

"You idiot! I could have broken your neck!"

"I had to grab aholt just to prove to myself I wasn't living licentiously with Huck Finn. Pederasty never was my thing, but you can't ever tell about a man when he gets by forty." He let her slide down him, then slapped her bottom hard. "Yep, it's my woman all right. I'd know that flat fanny anywhere. Who says we aren't just a couple of kids? What are you worried about? We're barely adolescents yet."

She tried to think of something witty and insolent, but she could not. Something was with them that had the shapeless menace of black shadows massed in a corner, or a closet door that was never opened. Shane took her by the upper arms, squeezing them gently, and said, " 'To me, fair friend, you never can be old, for as you were when first your eye I eye'd, such seems your beauty still.' I think I did that rather well, don't you?"

"Olivier and Gielgud would be sick with envy," she said.

She turned away from the door and shut out the wind. She had never been afraid of age until he spoke of it. Now she wondered if it was because she'd known all the time that they'd never make it.

Never make old bones. She heard the dry, wispy voice of one particular collection of old bones, a great-great aunt, when Alexia had been a peeled twig of a child.

She'll never make old bones, that one. You can see through her now.

And her mother had answered merrily that her child was tough and wiry, and she'd be the lucky kind who could eat everything and never get fat, and she would end up as a terrifying old lady with hundreds of descendants.

And here I stand now, Mother, she said now, with not even one descendant. All I own is misery. You'd be sorry for me if you knew, not because Shane is dead but because you'd believe that I'd either sold my life or destroyed it when I began living with a married man.

She went back through the house to the little study, took the guitar out of the case, and hung it on the wall in the living room where it always hung in the summer. For some reason she felt, not better, but satisfied.

✿ CHAPTER 6 ✿

WILLIAM WASN'T AROUND when she left to walk to the Goodwins' for supper. She went out around the woods, over the high windswept field of the Head, then down into the sun-flooded basin of Beauty Cove. It was not named for its beauty, which was considerable, but for one Goodwin's favorite ox. Ozzie and Madge had built their house here with part of the money they got for selling the rest of the island. Madge, though born at the Harbor, had no quarrel with island living; this was Ozzie's place. But she wanted to face the mainland and see the far lights twinkling in the dark, and she wanted a modern house.

The old house was full of ghosts, she said, and Old Gib was the head hooter. When the others laughed at her, her fair skin went red to the roots of her hair, even her ears glowed, but she insisted that she *sensed* things. "I was born with a caul. That makes me different. ... I was never happy in that house with all those old Goodwins disapproving of me and anything I did. Like painting the cupboards blue that time. Gib acted up something fierce. Ozzie said the old-timers thought blue was unlucky, and I said, 'That's all right, whatever he *thinks,* if he'd only stay in his grave and not be moving things around in my kitchen all night.' "

"Did you know," Shane asked her solemnly, "that if you bring a red-headed woman into a house, and she knows the right things to say, you can make a ghost go away?"

"Or at least shut up," said Alix. "I don't want anyone to be driven away from the place they loved. I don't care how many of them live with us as long as they don't keep me awake. I have to have my sleep."

"Oh, you two!" Madge decided to laugh about it. "One'll lie and the other swear to it."

There couldn't possibly be any ghosts around the new house unless the spirits of long-past cows were looking in the windows, or the velvet-eyed Beauty and his partner Babe. Alix doubted that even a supernatural beast could see very much through windows that were beruffled, bedraped, and garnished with colored glass trinkets and potted plants. The house itself, of the generic type known as "three-bedroom ranch," could have been in any new development anywhere in the United States. Ozzie's oilclothes hanging in the back hall and his rubber boots arranged neatly on the plastic boot tray looked absolutely exotic.

Ozzie had drawn the line at Venetian blinds, on the grounds that they made him think of Cy Merrick's funeral home in Edwardstown. This had always seemed funny until now, when Alix shied away from the word "funeral" as if from an obscenity, which it was if you thought of it in connection with Shane.

She shut her eyes against the hot dazzle of the western water and stood on the path a little while, pretending to be looking around and listening to the plovers in case anyone should be watching from the house. She wished that Shane had been drowned from the catboat and never recovered; she wished that she had been drowned with him.

She heard excited snorts and the scamper of paws on the short turf, and opened her eyes just as the dog threw himself at her. She leaned down and he leaped up trying passionately to lick her face. "On my ear," she said, turning it toward him. "There. That's enough. How are you, Sidney?"

Sidney pranced and barked. He was a woolly gray-black mongrel of great charm and like William he was a help in awkward moments. Talking to him, she went more confidently down to the house. Gulls on the ridgepole marred the suburban demeanor of the three-bedroom ranch, and no Levittown ever had the lichened faces of granite ledge surfacing on a front lawn that went all the way to the shore. Ozzie had beached his boat after getting home, and coppered the bottom; the scent of the fresh paint had a sharp pungence that blended agreeably with that of new-mown grass and low tide. Shane's catboat, *Golden-Eye*, was hauled up into the field beyond Ozzie's fishhouse, where he always kept her in the winters. Alix ignored her now, as she had tried to ignore everything in the house except what she must positively touch.

She was hungry at supper. She couldn't help it. Her body seemed to be operating quite independently of her, and she had hard work not to bolt her food. She was glad to be able to show a good appetite for the traditional supper of her arrival; baked stuffed lobster, baked potatoes, young dandelion greens, hot yeast rolls, a tart lemon-flavored custard.

She didn't have to talk. Madge gave her a detailed and rambling recital of all the news of the family—except the reason for Karen's presence—and of the Harbor and the road halfway to Edwardstown. It was accented with dramatic pauses and eloquent eye-widenings when something was considered not fit for juvenile ears. She seemed determined to have no embarrassing silences when, presumably, either she or Alix would burst into tears. Now and then Ozzie gave her a quizzical look, his fork suspended, then shook his head slightly and went on eating. Karen worked stolidly through a large plateful of food and managed at the same time to watch everybody.

"I asked Jonas to come over," Madge said. "But he wouldn't. That letter today must have upset him."

Alix thought it was more likely that he hadn't wanted to face a strange woman as well as Karen. Anyway, she was glad he hadn't come.

She left at sunset, saying she was going home through the Tangle and wanted plenty of light.

"You *aren't!*" Madge objected. "Not through *that* place at *this* hour! Ozzie, you'll just have to go with her."

Ozzie started to get up but Alix waved him back. "I'd refuse your company even if you wanted the walk, which I know you don't. What's going to eat me in the Tangle, Madge?" She caught Karen's gelid stare and winked at her, getting no response. "There's no four-footer on the island besides William and Sidney. Of course the peepers could suddenly band together and attack humanity, but I doubt it."

"It's all those cellar holes," said Madge. She rubbed her arms where genuine gooseflesh showed. "And all those nasty stories Ozzie's father used to tell about the folks who lived there in French and Indian War times." She rolled her eyes at Karen, who went on impassively wiping the silver. "*You* know," Madge said portentously to Alix, with more of those manic noddings. "You've heard Ozzie tell them, and Shane took some down—" She stopped herself with a gasp and a hand to her mouth. Tears came into her eyes.

Ozzie cleared his throat. "I'm thinking I may have to lug her to the main and set her up in one of those apartment houses. When she's got folks on either side and underfoot and overhead, she'll be fussing about flesh-and-blood pests, not those poor critters been long gone."

"Oh, Madge isn't really scared," said Alix. "This is all for fun, the way we've kept the Old Gib business going for years." Madge wiped wet bright eyes which immediately flooded again, and bit down on her lower lip. Alix said with loud breeziness, "Well, I'll be off, then! It was a gorgeous meal, Madge. The first food I've really tasted in weeks."

Silently, her handkerchief at her nostrils, Madge handed Alix a paper bag of rolls. "Oh, these will be wonderful for breakfast!" Alix cried, as if she were the sturdy friend whose duty was to brace up the bereaved. Madge said nothing because she couldn't. Ordinarily she would have walked up to the edge of the woods with Alix. This time it was Ozzie who went out into the yard with her and wished her good night, and she heard Madge's sobs burst out before she'd gotten off the doorstep.

The glow from the western sky washed the hillside in deep saffron, as if it were all seen through a tawny glass. Sidney overtook her and charged on ahead, sending birds up in every direction. She was surprised to hear the faint scuff of other footsteps on the worn turf behind her, and looked around and saw Karen silently trudging up the path.

"Oh, hello, Karen," she said. She turned forward again, not shortening her long stride for the child. "Are you going to take a look at the Tangle? Or have you been there already? I imagine you've just about covered every inch of the island by now."

There was silence behind her, then a small flat voice. "Gram won't let me."

"She probably worries about you when you're out of sight. We all worry about something. Don't you?"

No answer. Karen wasn't giving anything away, even small talk. They reached the first spruces, and from far within their gloomy corridors Sidney's bark echoed weirdly. It had to be for something no more frightening than a woodpecker or a crow; Sidney made the most of what Tiree offered in the way of excitement.

Alix stopped and looked back out over the bay toward the flowing dark waves of the mainland hills. "The water looks like gold foil, doesn't it?" she said. "You know, the kind that comes around candy sometimes."

Karen ignored the view. "Are those ghost stories Gram was talking about?" she asked.

"Some of them were," Alix admitted. "But people just tell them for fun. Even your Gram's just pretending to be scared. It's like Sidney making believe a yellowhammer's an eagle."

Karen hunched her shoulders toward her ears, her mouth

went tight and turned down at the corners. Impossible to guess what it meant. The rich light through her short silvery hair made a genuine aureole around her head, but the thick spectacles and dour little face took away any angelic effect.

"Do *you* believe in ghosts?" she asked.

"No," said Alix, "and I don't believe your Gram does either, when it comes right down to the truth."

"But once I heard her talking to Gramp about that man in your house."

Alix went perfectly cold and still, as if her heart had stopped beating and her brain had blacked out. Then, with an exertion that almost nauseated her she said, "Oh, you must mean Old Gib. Gibraltar Goodwin. He'd be your grandfather with six or seven 'greats' tacked on, maybe not that much . . . well, he's a kind of joke we've all had over the years. If we can't find anything we say Old Gib took it. If something falls down we say he did it, but it's usually the cat. How's your finger?"

Karen held it up, ornamented with a Band-Aid. "Gramp says I'll live till morning."

"Fine!" She despised her artificial heartiness, but she couldn't seem to quench it. "Here comes Sidney. He's probably scared all the birds clear to Europe. You two had better go home while the light's still good."

Karen appeared to plant herself more solidly. "I'm not afraid of the dark."

"But your Gram won't know where you are. You can see the Tangle another time." Slyly she asked, "How much longer will you be here? Is your mother coming for you soon?"

She got the shrug and the turned-down mouth again. Sidney arrived with all the élan of a cavalry charge. Alix leaned down to him and let him swab her ear lobe with his tongue. She straightened up and said, "Good night, Karen. Good night, Sidney. Go home now."

She didn't wait to see them go, but went abruptly into the woods. A ruby glow shone among the tree trunks, and sent her elongated shadow ranging and flickering ahead of her like a

mysterious entity on a quest of its own. The little plants pushing up through the floor of spills looked as artificial as green
plastic. Unseen above the interwoven boughs something took
off with a heavy flapping of wings but no cry. The tree frogs
were chiming from the swampy spot where the early settlers
had had their well.

In a few minutes she had left the fiery light behind a wall of
spruces and had come into the Tangle. The peepers stopped at
the sound of her feet on last year's leaves, no matter how
stealthy she tried to be.

The Tangle was illuminated by the last of the day's light,
coming from overhead where there remained an area of blue
sky flecked with pink-edged feathers of cloud. A diffused and
gentle light lay among the white birches, the still-bare shad-
bushes, and the Japanese attitudes of wild cherry trees. The
leafless alders were hung ornamentally with perfumed tassels
that spilt their gilt dust at a touch. Over the years old trees had
died and fallen, or had remained upright as multiple housing
for flickers, woodpeckers, chickadees. Young trees rushed to fill
the gaps. The cellar holes of the first settlers were almost obliterated now, though one could still find faint hollows here and
there with the feet if not with the eye. An ancient stone wall
went through the Tangle, marking one boundary of a pasture
that had long since been stolen back by the woods.

The Tangle was where Alix's ashes were to be scattered. She
sat down on the thick springy cushion of dry bracken. Now
that she was quiet the hylas began again.

Maple boughs flowered red against the paling sky, and the
tightly furled new leaves of the moosewood were like hundreds
of green and rosy candle flames burning along the gray
branches. Above them the swallows sped through space like
free-form skaters, crossing and recrossing the circle of sky. At a
higher level gulls flew home in quiet groups. Chickadees were
busy with old alder cones, while down in the warm dry leaves
the sparrows went on energetically scratching as if Alix weren't
there.

I'm really not, she thought, and they know it already. It was a soothing idea. In another year, in another few months, in another few weeks if that child would only go home, who would be able to tell where Alix was? The bracken would grow waist-high, the Tangle would be roofed with green leaves; it would fill with blossoms and the flashing jewels that were warblers. The long-stemmed violets would flood the swamp with blue, and the peepers give way to the thrushes and whitethroats. But Alix would be gone. Home safe. *All ye, all ye in free!* the children's voices sang out in the summer dusk, calling the last ones in from the hiding places behind the garage and under the syringa.

Safe. Free. Alexia had dreamed in the nights after the long twilight games, but ashes couldn't dream when they were lost in the grass and the old leaves, with the sparrows scratching among them. . . . No one had ever told Alexia that there wasn't an endless supply of tomorrows and that one day she would be glad of the fact.

She lay back on the bracken, her arms under her head. It was a deep cushion for her tired bones. Once when the Goodwins had been away for a week she and Shane had made love up here in the Tangle. Black flies and a noisily persistent mosquito had made the experience something less than idyllic. There had been a good deal of swearing, lunging, and swatting, and Alix hadn't been able to keep from laughing wildly at the whole picture. Shane had furiously grabbed up his clothes and gone home without speaking to her.

A fierce quarrel had then blown up. Cathleen had been dragged in somehow, as she always was in spite of their vow to live on Tiree as if they'd never known anyone else. Alix couldn't remember now who had mentioned her first, but it was fatal. It always was. Later they would swear with all the religious ardor of adolescent lovers that they would never mention her again. And they'd agree that the fight had been worthwhile because the making-up had been so unspeakably marvelous.

All gone now. Her body was of no further use to her. Facts is facts, Alexia, she said. Instead of a woman with a lover you are now exactly what Old Smiley thinks you are, a frustrated, unloved thirty-six, obsessed with the futility of existence. Of hers, anyway.

She got up. The swallows had ceased, the scratchings stopped; here and there one small chickadee voice called out the last message of the day. Only the peepers chimed on. She was just able to see the path, but she could have walked it blind. It crossed a break in the stone wall, passed under some lightning-scarred old maples, then again into a belt of spruces which held shadow as brown and cold as brook water.

She came out from that to the amethyst pallor of the eastern sky. In its strange light the slope unrolled before her like smoke-colored velvet all the way to the small dark huddle of her house.

She was used to coming back alone to it on May evenings, because Shane had never been here with her then. But because now he would never come to it at any time, there was a difference about it tonight, as if it had clutched itself together against loneliness and the dark. When William greeted her from the back doorstep, she dropped the bag of rolls and swept him up, hugging him harder than he liked, rubbing her face in his neck.

"You smell so *good,*" she said. She held one of his big double forepaws to her nose. "Sweet fern and seaweed and sand. A soupçon of bay. Absolutely delicious. You smell like a poem, my William."

He wriggled peevishly.

"Oh, all right," she said. "All you think of is your stomach."

He was bubbling eagerly around her legs as she opened the door, but when he went in he stopped short just over the threshold and nearly tripped her up. "What's the matter with you?" she asked him. "Struck with Spanish mildew?"

He wasn't purring, and her voice emphasized the peculiar quality of the silence within the house; it was different from the great primitive stillness outside. Why should walls change its essence? She felt the hair tightening on her nape, and a desire to make no sudden move. She turned her head slowly, looking around the dim room. The windows held the last glimmering of the sky, and she could just make out the shapes of the furniture; a spectral gleam represented the teakettle Madge had so lovingly polished, as if this would help Alix to feel better.

Nobody had wound the mantel clock. Perhaps the absence of that loud ticking made all the difference. But William, welcoming her home and thinking about his supper, should have been noisy. Instead he remained just inside the door, unpurring. Then it struck her that this hush was not the silence of emptiness but of listening.

By someone else besides her and William.

Consciously she rejected the idea at once, but her conviction of its impossibility didn't last. Someone could have beached a boat below the lawn, climbed the bank, and walked up to the unlocked house. Just because it had never happened, and she'd never feared it, didn't mean it *couldn't* happen.

Thievery, even violence, could reach three miles out; not only "good" people had access to boats with powerful outboards. A house facing the sea, out of sight of other buildings —why not? Everyone along the immediate coast knew the place, though only those at the Harbor would know that she was already here. A couple of youngsters or grown men in a fast boat could carry off anything they thought was valuable, and no one would ever know who they were, they could have come and gone so quickly.

She went noiselessly across the kitchen to the doorway that opened into the living room. "Hello!" she called in a strong, challenging voice. "You can go out the front door. I won't put a light on you, I'll never know who you are. Just *go!*"

She listened. The silence flowed away from her shout in widening rings. She could almost see it lapping like ripples of water against furniture and walls. A board creaked, very faintly. She stiffened and held her breath, but reminded herself that the old house had its own noises. Then she heard, tiny but piercingly clear, the twang of a guitar string.

She walked forward into the room. *"Shane?"* she whispered. "Is it *you?* Are you here?" Down around her legs William began suddenly to purr. All her resources collapsed in either laughing or crying, she couldn't tell which. "Oh, my love," she whispered. *"Be* here! Let it be you!"

She held out her arms and called as loud as she could, "Shane, Shane!"

There was nothing but the ringing echo of her voice. She could feel the portraits watching her but nothing else. Exhaustion fell upon her all at once, bone-dissolving, stupefying. Her hands felt hot, swollen, and heavy enough to drag her arms from her shoulders. If she tilted her head sidewise she would fall that way.

Touching things lightly for balance, she got to the study and fell onto the couch. With her thick-feeling weakened hands she pulled a blanket over her and curled up in it. It was a going-down into darkness, sinking like a stone into black water that would close unmarked over her head.

From far off she heard William complaining, padding rapidly back and forth with occasional polishings of chair legs. Finally he got up on the couch and settled heavily behind her knees. In the next instant she was out.

❦ CHAPTER 7 ❦

DAYLIGHT BROUGHT her awake with the immediacy of a wet towel snapped into her face. For a moment her greatest trouble was remembering just where she was, and then wondering why she'd chosen to sleep in the study instead of her own room, with its dormers opening out over the sea.

Then she knew, and shut her eyelids down tightly to seal herself back into unknowing. But it was no good. There was a yellowhammer on the lawn near the window, his voice as piercing as his bill. The Sabre Dance, they used to call that machine-gun delivery. She felt every jab. Then something was knocked over in the kitchen, not by Old Gib but by William prowling where he shouldn't be.

She rolled out of the blankets, aching with having lain so long in one tight position, and went stiffly out to the kitchen. William greeted her with a loud chirrup from the table, where he'd been rolling the salt and pepper around, and had knocked the sugar spoon out of the bowl. He tracked sugar to the edge of the table and jumped down and went to the refrigerator. She fed him and let him out, standing on the back doorstep while she waited for the teakettle to boil. The air was cold, and the

[5 7]

thick grass soaking with dew. William walked gingerly across it, shaking each paw in succession, trying not to get his belly wet.

The chill was salutary. Alix found herself coming alive, however unwillingly. Efficiency took over; she knew what had to be done today. She washed up and had a breakfast of coffee and Madge's rolls. The sun was beginning to come in now, and she didn't build a fire for warmth, but sat in the patch of light like a cat.

When she went into the living room on the way upstairs the front windows were filled with the pallid glitter of eastern sea and sky, but her attention was drawn as if by a shout to the lustrous dark auburn curves of the guitar hanging on the off-white wall. Her coffee seemed to come up horridly into her throat. She recollected last night half with repugnance, half with a cautious reaction that was hard to define. Fascination? A degrading, hysterical eagerness to believe anything? No, not that bad, but not outright joy, certainly; her capacity for that had gone forever. ... *Gone, alas, like our youth, too soon,* the words crooned idiotically in her head. Shane used to sing those songs when he felt excessively Celtic.

Irish treacle, she'd called it when she wanted to needle him. She strode forward and boldly plucked each string. Out of tune. That was it, a peg had slipped last night. Changes of atmosphere or something. Contractions. *Oh, for one of those hours of gladness, gone, alas, like our youth, too soon. Oh, to think of it, Oh, to dream of it—*

Shane, be here! she had cried. And it had seemed possible in the twilight-filled room that Shane had fled straight to her from whatever safe heaven Cathleen thought she had tucked him away in.

Yet in daylight she could not even imagine how the room had been in the dusk, or the certainty that had pervaded it. But what if she denied him? What if, for fear of losing her own good opinion of her sanity—to hell with what other people thought of it—she shut herself away from him?

He watched her from the painting with blue sparks in his
eyes, bearded like Frobisher, an ironical buccaneer amused by
his captive's struggles. Or—worse—as if he knew something
she didn't and were laughing at her from some point so far
away her mind couldn't even begin to reach it. It was like the
times when as a child she tried to imagine limitless space and
would come upright in bed, cowering and shaking, appalled by
the whole idea.

Here it was again, the breathless, brain-rocked reaction to
the unimaginable.

She tried to run away from it, upstairs, but it was inescapa-
bly present while she handled his clothes. She kept seeing an
aunt of hers whose one child had been drowned. She had
begun going to a medium, whose hold over her the husband
couldn't break. As the woman prospered, so did the mother's
misery grow fat and vigorous. No matter how many messages
she received, there were never enough. She wanted more and
more. To hear him but never to hold him again, to know that
this bit of something laughing and dancing through the darkened room like light from a prism, and as untouchable, was
her baby, finally became more than she could endure.

She recovered from her collapse. She was apologetic for the
trouble she had caused. She never spoke of her experiences and
never went to another medium. She was quiet and kind, and
apparently the soul of common sense.

But in the glare of now Alix wondered what torments had
continued behind the quiet eyes. What if she had still believed,
and thought that her breakdown had betrayed Davy and driven
him away from her forever?

Alix dropped a sweater of Shane's and ran downstairs and
out the front door, across the lawn and down over the bank
past the rosebushes. She took the hardest part of the shore, the
glacial rubble around the base of the Head. It meant fingers as
well as toes in some places, a cautious sliding down on one's
seat in others. She kept going, seeing nothing but the way
ahead, until her mouth and throat were dry and she was out of

breath. Then she sat down in a niche of rocks directly under the highest thrust of the Head.

The sea was azure to the horizon except in the sun's path, rippled by currents and catspaws into sinuous bands of light and dark, like Alexia's best watered-silk hair ribbons and sash. They made her uncomfortable *on*, but oh, just to look at them when she first opened her eyes in the morning—

Oh, to think of it, Oh, to dream of it fills my heart with tears.

They'd never be the same, once they were worn. Nothing ever was.

Gulls stood on the tawny shelves below her, breasts to the light wind. The eider ducks rode the swells offshore, proud in their size and strength, preening and gabbling constantly; not for them any looking-ahead to the time when the big blackback gulls would be watching hungrily for ducklings.

Men were setting traps in the crystal morning, boats scattered over the sea but none close to the island, which had been Goodwin territory ever since lobstering had become a paying business. Ozzie's red and yellow buoys bobbed beyond the ducks like another exotic variety of sea bird. Ozzie himself was working just beyond the taurine shape of Old Bull Ledge; she could see his mast and the red and yellow buoy mounted on the canopy roof as legal identification.

Suddenly a gray dory shot into sight from around the northern side of the Head. A man in yellow oilpants and black-and-white wool shirt slowed down the heavy outboard motor and gaffed an orange buoy that she hadn't noticed before; now she saw them everywhere among Ozzie's. The man began to haul the trap by hand, braced back in the rolling dory. The visor of his cap shadowed his face and she couldn't tell if he were looking toward her or not. She knew a person could be almost invisible among these rocks, but she shrank back instinctively into the cleft between the granite slabs.

This had to be the man Jonas, of course. She didn't know his last name, and she wished she didn't know his first. He was an acutely painful intrusion, he and Karen both, like cinders blown into an already infected eye. She found herself holding her breath as if she were actually in hiding. Then he headed off toward a surfy reef to the southeast, engine wide open, and she got up to return home.

She went back even faster than she'd come and climbed the bank to the lawn, resolved not to stop even for a cup of coffee until she had finished her job.

Karen was sitting on the front doorstep.

The sight of her stopped Alix short. She almost turned and went back to the beach, but she forced herself to go on. She had a picture of the child at her leisure in the house, going through every room, her hands busy, her eyes gobbling every-thing as the blackbacks gobbled the new-hatched ducklings if they got the chance.

Karen sat immobile, her glasses blind circles of sunlight, red sneakers together, knees drawn up in green jeans with the plaid lining folded back in cuffs. Her stubby hands were cupped over her knees. She wore a green sweatshirt with a peaked hood, and she looked like the sort of brownie who would just as soon sour the milk as do the cobbler's work for him. Would rather.

"Hello, Karen," Alix said nicely, to atone for her evil thoughts. "Which way did you come?"

"That way," said Karen, with a wooden gesture of her hand back toward the house.

"That figures," said Alix. "Straight through from back to front. Though probably not straight. A lot of detours. Or do you mean you came through the Tangle?"

Karen nodded. "Gram told me not to." It was not a confi-dence, but a report of authority defied.

"See any ghosts?"

"Nope. Not even where the man was scalped by the Indi-ans."

"I don't know that place," Alix lied. It was one of Ozzie's fa-vorite stories. "Where is it?"

"Right where you come over the stone wall. They caught him on his way home from plowing. There was a field there once."

"Did Gramp tell you that story?"

For the first time Karen showed a flicker of something. Impatience? Contempt for stupidity? "No. *He* wouldn't tell me. He thinks I'm scared of things with blood in them."

"Most little girls are."

"Well, I'm not," said Karen. "My mother told me, anyway."

"Oh," said Alix. "Well, I have to go in and go to work now. Good-bye, Karen." She crossed the doorstep with the intention of shutting the door behind her and pushing the bolt across. But Karen was suddenly standing between her and the door, and a folded envelope had appeared as if by sleight-of-hand.

"I've got this note," she said, thrusting it at Alix.

Madge had a round, careful hand so ornate in places it was hard to read. She'd never forgotten that for five grades her penmanship had been the best in the Harbor school.

She wrote, "We meant to ask you last night if you wanted the skiff and outboard brought around. Ozzie's got the engine all tuned up if you want it. Ozzie can tow it around after he gets in from hauling. Hope you were all right last night. Love, Madge."

Alix looked away from the note to the blue moire sea. On such a morning one might strike out for the horizon as if there were no need to think of returning.

"Yes, I'd like that," she said aloud. Not to drown; she couldn't bear to drown herself, she knew she couldn't throttle her reflexes by pure will power. But just knowing the two strangers were on the island made it too crowded, and the boat offered temporary escape. "Will you tell Gram I would like the boat? And thank you very much."

Karen didn't say, You're welcome. Maybe she expected a nickel, or candy, or to get into the house again.

"Come," Alix said, "and I'll see if I can find you something to eat while you're going back." Not quite touching the child she managed to sweep her along toward the kitchen at a good pace. Karen was obviously reluctant, she was trying to see everywhere at once, and suddenly Alix felt intolerably petty. I *am* turning odd, she thought, just as everybody thinks, only worse. Malicious. Cruel. It's time I was leaving. I could become a horror.

She gave Karen a packet of cheese crackers, thanked her again for bringing the message, and saw her out the back door. Passing Shane's workshop Karen hesitated, gave it a long look, glanced back at Alix, then went on, insolently casting away the cellophane wrapper.

When she was well up the slope toward the woods, William came out from beneath the workshop and approached Alix with his eyes blandly opening and shutting.

"Yes, she's gone," said Alix. "And you're right to stay out of her way. She hasn't forgiven you yet for scratching her. We're lucky she doesn't know how to shoot Gramp's rifle."

William fell over on his head. "Knock on wood," said Alix, doing so. "Maybe she *can* shoot. Maybe that's why she's here. They had to get her out of town because she gunned down a little playmate in cold blood."

William had more to eat, and Alix had more coffee and a package of the cheese crackers. Then she went back to work.

By midafternoon she had filled a sizable number of cartons. They held clothing which had special significance, like the lucky jeans she always wore when they went trolling for mackerel, a tatty old raincoat she'd worn on their long walks through the rain or on nights of dripping cottonwool fog. Shane's aged Donegal tweed jacket, a dark orangey red with elbows leather-patched by her; to handle it and smell its indefinable, unique aroma was to see again the Northern Lights streaming and wavering up half the sky, or to re-experience, here in the chilly and austere bedroom, the small fire crackling among the rocks that they sometimes kept going on a still night until suddenly the black creep of the tide was there, licking and hissing at the outer edge, and sparks went showering to their death in the water as the translucent red-hearted sticks collapsed.

Her old jodhpurs, protection against the thorny entwining clutch of blackberry vines; her thick turtle-neck sailing sweater, and Shane's foul-weather gear, which placed him at the tiller of *Golden-Eye* while they raced home heeled over with one side under water and her terror turning to rage, a silent screaming to herself of all the things she would tell him and call him when they got ashore. *If* they got ashore, in which case, after flaying him for an arrogant sadist, she would never step one foot aboard the damn thing *ever again*.

His paratrooper boots. His flannel robe, which evoked moonlight swims and trying to get warm afterward in the kitchen with thick mugs of cocoa, or mulled wine, which sounded better than it was.

She couldn't resist a weary, battle-scarred pride at having gotten through the job. She carried the cartons down to the study where they wouldn't show with the door open if Madge happened to come in. She collected her and Shane's favorite books and put them in other cartons, then began turning out the drawers of the desk. She was wise enough not to open any of Shane's notebooks, but dropped them rapidly into a box as if they were so much trash mail, thinking all the time of what to do next. Tools would go to Ozzie; Shane would be tolerant of her burning the clothes and books, but not the tools. The books would take a long time burning, so she wouldn't attempt them and the notebooks tonight. At the very end, when everything else had been reduced to white ash and wispy black flakes, she would burn the portraits, her paintbox, and the guitar. She would put the guitar back in its case so she couldn't hear the strings snap.

With the drawers emptied on one side, all at once she felt her efficient vigor turning a little frantic, and she got up and walked fast out through the living room and opened the front door. Dandelions apparently took flight and went away singing: goldfinches. She dragged air down into her cramped lungs.

The southwesterly wind struck her, as cold and boisterous as the choppy seas tumbling shoreward without end. It was good. It blew in her ear and scalded her eyes, went through jersey and slacks to scour her flesh. The Old Bull and Tiree Ledge were explosions now, not rocks.

Over the points that made Gib's Cove, spray jetted into the air with lovely, lazy deliberation. Inside the cove there was an aquamarine rush and sparkle of catspaws.

Marjorie C. was also inside the cove, slipping toward the wharf with the twelve-foot dory skiff in tow, the three-horse outboard tilted up on the stern. Madge and Karen were aboard with Ozzie, and Sidney stood up on the bow, ready to jump onto the wharf at the first graze. Madge saw Alix and waved; Alix waved both arms vehemently, getting into her part like a Method actor, fixing her smile in a glaze of happy welcoming, and ran down the hill to the wharf.

Sidney was already ashore, running to meet her. She took his head in her hands, and playfully roughed him up, let him go, and went to the edge of the wharf with her hands in her pockets and her smile intact, even broader.

"Well!" Madge exclaimed. "Somebody looks a lot better than somebody did yesterday."

"It's sleep that does it," Alix called back. "What about the mooring, Ozzie?"

"She's all down, right where that buoy is, and I've got the crosspiece aboard here, all coppered, and some new line. The old one was starting to chafe."

"Oh, what a lovely color!" said Alix at sight of the canary yellow coil on his arm. "And look at my *Sea Pigeon!* She's always so beautiful when she's just painted, and so proud." That was a little too precious, it all but gagged her, and she thought her tone wouldn't fool anyone, but Ozzie was busy making the boat fast and then hauling the skiff up alongside, and Madge kept nodding and smiling up at Alix as if everything had come out all right.

With such a good and gullible audience it wasn't too hard to

maintain the air of eager involvement, like Sidney waiting to
jump ashore. Ozzie left the coil of line on the wharf for Alix to
pay out, took one end, and rowed out to the pot buoy that
marked the anchor. He took off the buoy and tied on the crosspiece, ran his end of the yellow float rope through the block,
then rowed back ashore. When the two ends of the line were
knotted securely together, the skiff's painter was tied into a
loop in the line, and she was hauled out to the crosspiece,
where she looked innocently proud of herself, dancing on the
skimming ripples as if she couldn't wait to be gone.

"Well!" cried Alix heartily. "How about everybody coming
up for a cup of coffee?"

"I brought a cake, just in case," said Madge, coming up the
ladder one-handed, balancing the cake tin on the other palm.
This particular talent had nothing to do with age or weight;
when you learned about ladders you not only learned how to
go up and down one-handed, you also learned how to pass children, animals, or cakes up and down them with equal ease.
"Come along, Karen," Madge called back, while maintaining
the cake's perfect balance. "You don't want to stay behind all
by yourself in the boat, do you?"

"Maybe she's planning a trip to Europe while your back's
turned," Alix suggested.

Ozzie said, "Wouldn't put it past her. Trying it, anyway."

"Don't look so grumpy," Madge urged her granddaughter.
"Here, Alix, take this ... Karen had a nap. That's why she's
acting so addled. She's only half-awake."

"You got plenty of outboard oil on hand?" Ozzie called up to
Alix.

"I think we—yes, I got some extra last year." She was dema-
terialized in a blast of near-obliterating pain, then blown back
through time and made incarnate in last year, leaning on the
candy counter in Bert's store drinking root beer and studying
Bert's collection of Linen Thread calendars and assorted art
while Shane bought six bottles of outboard oil during the
course of a long and (to her) incomprehensible conversation
about the technique of sailing. And she had been bored; dear

God, bored! Yawning till she had tears in her eyes while Shane had been still alive, in that sweatshirt she couldn't get off him until it was too stiff with sweat and dirt and salt water for even him to stand.

Like ghostly figures in the negative of a double exposure, she, the Goodwins, and Karen moved noiselessly in black daylight against the bright stage of Bert's store and the three there, who talked, drank pop, and yawned. The future was before their eyes but they couldn't see it. Shane was duped and vulnerable as he stood there in his salt-stiff clothes, telling Bert something with his grand large gestures, so confident, merry, so *sure* of everything, like the little girl who was going to grow up to be a genius. And all the time his death had been there in the room with them, and this moment was there too, in embryo; this instant when she listened with her mind to a voice she was terrified of forgetting, and with her hands took the five-gallon can of oil Ozzie handed up to her.

But the voice was fading, the scene dimming out like an artful television dissolve. Madge's voice replaced it, coming in warm buoyant puffs like a changing wind. Karen was up the ladder now, and nothing could be retained under her stare. Far off Sidney was barking. Ozzie was saying, "You want the catboat around here?"

He said it twice before she, staring back at him, realized he was speaking to her.

"No," she said, putting her hands in her pockets and taking an expert kick at a dried crab shell on the planks. "I'll sell her, I think. Maybe I'll put an ad in Bert's store, and another one up at Emery's."

"She'll go quick." Ozzie was blessedly matter-of-fact. "Be sure to put down that Saul Goodwin built her. That fact alone is likely to sell her to anyone that knows cats."

"I'll remember. Come on up and have coffee now. *Real* coffee in your honor, Ozzie. Perked in the pot."

"If that don't toll me up the hill, nothing will," said Ozzie. Madge pounced on her cake tin.

"This is a new recipe I got from Daisy, I'm dying to taste it," she said, happily setting off in the lead. Alix followed her. Ozzie slogged along in his rubber boots, hands in his pockets, gazing out to sea as if he never got enough of it. Karen was at the end, her head down as if she were watching her stubborn feet.

Sidney's hysterical barking was heard faintly through the noise of surf as he pursued sea gulls on the beach below the house.

"Hear that fool dog," said Madge. "He'll be some hoarse to-night."

"How long is Karen staying?" Alix asked without premeditation.

"Oh, that poor little thing!" Madge turned a distressed face to her. "Einar wants her back now, but Thelma—Alix, I *don't understand* that girl. I *don't know* what gets into her! My own daughter, and she's like a stranger to me!"

"What's the matter?" asked Alix, wondering if Thelma had begun to drink, or wanted to go to work.

"I don't know!" Madge wailed. "But she acts just like she wants to be shed of her own young one, and it gets me so worked up sometimes I can't sleep. Ozzie says it's all my imagination, Thelma just wants Karen to have an island summer, but I can't help the way I—" Her wide, distraught eyes shifted from Alix's face to beyond her shoulder, and she whispered loudly, "Here she comes. They always *know* when you want to talk about them. . . . I'll have a chance to tell you, I *hope*. But she can be quiet as a cat, and a darn sight quieter than that William with his big feet. You think she's in one place, you just *saw* her there, and the next minute she pops up so far from it it's like magic."

"Maybe she's a juvenile witch," said Alix, "like the girl and her mother on that program you like to watch."

Madge laughed, an instant, youthful smoothing-out of all dismay and anxiety. "You've got something there."

Inwardly Alix was shaken by some potent force, rage, frustration, or a pure explosion of nerves, she couldn't tell what; and there was the fear that it might show, and she would see the recognition of it suddenly aflame in Madge's face.

But Madge, radiantly smiling, was calling to the child, holding out her free hand. "Come on, punkin! Come walk with Gram!"

Alix stepped off the path to let Karen go by. Without a glance at Alix she went and took her grandmother's hand. The red sneakers were firmly placed in the tender strawberry blossoms and ground down on them, leaving them in torn fragments or obliterated.

⚜ CHAPTER 8 ⚜

THEY HAD COFFEE and cake around the kitchen table, and the hour was far more of a success than Alix had expected. Both Ozzie and Madge had old-fashioned ideas about children, which meant Karen had to stay in one place. Alix prepared a mug of *café-au-lait,* for which she received an almost inaudible thank-you only after Madge insisted. Karen gazed at the mug with suspicion and contempt, tasted the contents with a teaspoon, and the only sign that she liked it was the fact that sometime during the session she drank it all. Otherwise she gloomily entertained herself at the far end of the kitchen table with the large sheets of rough paper and felt-tipped markers Alix brought from the studio.

There was no further chance to discuss the child, and it didn't look as if there would be; Karen herself was probably determined the opportunity would never arise.

I know all the tricks, my girl, Alix thought. How well I remember.

The only thing to do was to go ahead as if Karen weren't there. It had been rather ridiculous to consider her in the first place. After all, she wasn't likely to be the one to discover the

—Alix jibbed at referring to herself as "the body," and yet "me" was a false pronoun for what would be left to discover.

Ozzie was telling about a whale he'd seen while he was hauling that morning, and Madge was faithfully enthralled. "What if he'd ever come right up *under* you, Ozzie?" she asked. "Couldn't he wreck you with just the tiniest flip of his tail?"

"Oh, he didn't mean any harm," said Ozzie. "He was just playing around. I was real good company for him, and him for me . . . awful breath he had, though." He nodded at Karen. "Guess he doesn't brush his teeth reg'lar."

Karen was not amused. She went back to her drawing. She attacked her paper with strong wide sweeps of the black marker, then put that one down and took a red one with no fumbling, no time to make up her mind. From her end of the table Alix couldn't see what the drawing was, but she felt a stirring of curiosity faint as a breath and as short-lived. Sidney scratched at the door and when Ozzie opened it William was also ready to come in. Sidney had a loud splashy drink while William sat and watched him.

"And folks say a cat and dog can't be friends," Madge marveled, as she did every time she saw the two together. Ozzie cocked his head indulgently at her, and said, "Good coffee, Alix. No, no more, I'm all awash now. And I got a halibut trawl to bait up before dark. Come on, girls."

"And we've got a washing to take in, haven't we, chicka-biddy?" Madge said comfortably to Karen, who, as if she'd divined Alix's ephemeral interest, folded up her sheaf of papers and crammed them into her jacket pocket.

Alix walked to the wharf with them, and the instant *Marjorie C.* left the cove she could think only of getting back to the house and lying down before she could lose this beautiful heaviness of the eyelids and the near-blissful ache of exhaustion. The wind caught and pushed at her as she went up the hill, and it seemed to permeate her bones as it did her clothes. She was drugged with it in spite of two cups of strong coffee. When she reached the house she went to the study, her eyes

open only enough so she could find her way but not so that she
could see anything that would remind or divert her. She was
successful in sleeping through the last part of the afternoon, a
deep sleep with no dreams that she could remember when William woke her.

He was sitting on the outside window sill, clawing at the
screen. By the time she'd given him his supper, the sun was
well down behind the woods on the hill, and the wind was
dropping with it. She felt a shaky eagerness to begin. Once the
match was touched to the kerosene-soaked newspapers, she
would be on her way. *C'est le premier pas qui coûte,* trilled the
voice of her high school French teacher, who prided herself on
her pure Parisian accent and mourned Gallicly every day over
the impossibility of passing it on to a class of recalcitrant New
England tongues.

Alix said it aloud now, again and again, with flourishes and
fillips that would have delighted Miss Fairbarn. She loaded the
wheelbarrow and took it down the front lawn to the edge of
the bank, declaiming all the proverbs she could remember
from the Chardenal Grammar. William followed through the
wet grass, listening tolerantly.

"*Tel père, tel fils,*" said Alix, steering recklessly among the
dandelions. "*Petit à petit, l'oiseau fait son nid. Dis-moi qui tu
sais, et je te dirai qui tu es.*" It was like shouting your lungs
out on the rides at Paragon Park; it kept your mind off what
you were feeling.

William stayed with the first load of boxes, trying to figure a
way to get into one. Going back for another load she ran out of
proverbs and declined verbs. *Aimer* had always been the favorite, done with as much expression as could be got by Miss Fairbarn, while the rest of the class were deliciously convulsed with
strangled mirth. She chose *dormir* as safer. *I sleep, I shall sleep.*

Then Shane's voice roaring. Light from a dead star. "*Auprès
de ma blonde, qu'il fait bon dormir, dormir, Auprès de ma
blonde—*"

It drove her into a run across the lawn with the last load. It was twilight now, and the dandelions had lost their gold and were merely pale. The peepers accentuated the silence that followed the end of the wind. There was only a slight swash on the shore, and a grayed-lilac sea stretched away without visible motion until it disappeared in the oncoming dusk.

She slung her boxes down the steep path to the rocks, then farther down the beach where later the tide could swallow the remains. The grass back on the bank and lawn was so wet there was no need to worry about flying sparks.

She had brought with the last load the little kerosene can from which they filled lamps, and a handful of wooden kitchen matches. She collected dried rockweed, dead brush, old laths and chips that had floated ashore, and laid them over and around the pyre. Then she poured kerosene lavishly on everything, made a long spill of a twisted newspaper, lighted it, and tossed it onto the heap.

As the first flame leaped up her throat clamped shut and her breathing stopped as if someone had seized her. She forced air down, and as the flames raced voraciously over the pile the suffocation was replaced by a hopeless dismay, as if she had just set fire to herself and wished she hadn't, but it was too late.

Sick enough to vomit but unable to, she moved back from the heat and sat down on a ledge. William came and sat with her. As the dry rockweed and brush caught there was a tremendous crackling and roaring, and the fire shot straight up high into a roseate shower of sparks. She gripped her knees till her fingers ached. She wished she had the courage to burn the house too and herself with it—dead first, because she had no desire to go screaming out of the world. Screaming "Shane, Shane, help me!" Like Longfellow's wife coming to him wreathed in flame and even he, alive, couldn't save her.

The silhouette of a man appeared between her and the fire. She heard a hoarse half-strangled sound that came from her. William ran. The man was bending over her almost at once, half-laughing, half-embarrassed, smelling of tobacco. Certainly not Shane. "Hey, I didn't mean to scare you! But you scared

[7 3]

me. I saw the glow over the trees and I thought the island was afire, your house anyway. So I came around to see."

She unclenched her hands and tried to loosen her jaw so she could speak, but at once her teeth began to chatter and she locked them shut again. "Look here," he said, sounding angry, or else it was his tense, choppy way of talking. "Are you all right?" He sat down on the log beside her and she felt him staring intently at her profile.

"Yes, I'm all right," she snapped back. "I thought I was alone, that's all. I'm not used to anyone else being on the island, and I knew—" She was out of breath, got it and began again. "I knew Ozzie and Madge would be watching television, and there's nobody out *there*—" She gestured at the ocean, now unseen in a night made blue-black by the firelight.

"Well, I'm sorry I came barging in," he said, a little more aloof. "But when those sparks shot up, it looked pretty deadly."

"I'm sorry I scared you." What an inane conversation. Damn his eyes. "I didn't mean to screech like a night heron. I'm not usually so jittery."

"You didn't really screech. It was more like a loud gasp." She thought he was laughing but it was soundless and she wouldn't look at him to see; she wanted him to go away before he could intrude too deeply into her mood. The fire had settled down now to an unspectacular but steadily devouring flame. It was all going, all those things, and she couldn't think about them as they went because of this character making himself at home by lighting his pipe. She wanted to say to him, in what Shane called her hoity-toity or Louisburg Square manner, Well, now that you've seen the island isn't on fire, why don't you go away?

·She jumped up and her legs almost gave way beneath her. At once he was up too and caught her by the elbow and steadied her. She almost did cry out at him then, Why the hell don't you get out of here and mind your own business?

Instead she said grimly, "Thanks." She picked up a long driftwood pole saved for the purpose and began poking at the fire, separating papers and sending up new flames in places, turning over smouldering clumps of cloth that were the tweed jacket and all the rest. It should have been a sacredly private time. Instead she was as conscious of him as of an attack of poison ivy; he stood behind her complacently smoking his pipe and probably thinking her a hysterical spinster who suspected any strange male of incipient rape, unless Madge had told him about Shane, in which case she was defenseless against something which was almost rape: a destruction of her privacy and an exposure to pitying curiosity.

She turned on him and said brusquely, "It's almost out now. I'll douse it and call it a day. I'm sorry if I shook you up. If you see any more glows in the sky, you'll know I'm doing some burning."

But he didn't move to go, just stood with his hands in his pockets, meditating on the fire. She grabbed up the pail she'd brought and strode down to the water. The sand gave way to slippery stones and clumps of rockweed, which spoiled her stride, and it was difficult in the shallows to scrape up even a half-bucketful of water. But Old Johnny-Jump-Up was there, nimble as a grasshopper without the charm. He took the pail from her in a humorous masculine silence and waded out into the dark with clouds of phosphorus bubbling weirdly about his boots.

Her endurance wore out and gave way to a calm dissociation in which the greenish-silver luminosity of his steps and around the dipped pail became the surrealist elements of a dream. A little way beyond him the dim shape of his dory floated, too quiet to make a rim of cold fire around her hull.

He came back toward her, again illuminating the water, but his face was indistinct. He went by her without speaking, up the beach toward the embers. The water splashed and hissed. He kicked at the last clots of sparks and tramped them out with his boots.

She wanted to cry out at the sacrilege, but in this new calm she could not. "Thank you," she said, more polite than ironic.

It was all gone, and she hadn't had a chance to see the thing properly through. But never let it be said that Alexia Horne forgot her manners, whatever the provocation. "And good n—"

"I'll walk you to your door," he said, "just to be sure you make it."

Miss Horne's good manners could wear thin, after all. "I've been walking this island in the dark for nine years."

"And I've been here only a month. I know it. But you're shaky tonight, only you won't admit it." He had a soft quick voice, the pure coastal accent and intonations coming out more strongly when he spoke faster. "Mebbe you don't feel good, or you're almost out on your feet. You just scared hell out of me with that blaze, so now you can humor me, can't ye?"

She walked by him and went up over the bank and across the lawn. She heard the hollow thump and brush of rubber boots on the grass behind her. William came among the glimmer of dandelions, interrogative, but she ignored him and went on toward the house. The chimneys were sharp black against a prickle of stars, the Dipper poised to pour over the front gable, and the dark panes on the face of the house reflected other stars with a phantom watery gleam.

Within the house Shane could be waiting. She walked faster, expertly avoiding William's erratic turns across the path as he tried to force her to pick him up. The boots came on behind, and she wondered if ever the sound of rubber boots—just the sound, no boots, no legs in them—had figured in a ghost story. The Midnight Walker. Shane could have made a good hair-raiser out of this and she'd have done the painting to illustrate it.

Fumbling at the doorknob with William poised boiling on the sill, she sagged with the weight of Shane five weeks dead. It was a guitar peg that had slipped last night, and made the string sound. Nobody was in the house. Nothing.

She said to the man unseen behind her, "I suppose the least I can do is offer you a drink, to settle your nerves."

Moving expertly in the dark kitchen she got a lamp from the

mantel shelf and set it on the table. "I've got some Scotch and probably some ice." She was feeling in her pocket for matches but suddenly a match flared in his fingers, and he tilted back the chimney, lighted the wick, replaced the chimney, and adjusted the flame to a broad symmetrical leaf of fire. Lamps always smoked when Shane first lit them; she resented the show-off competency of the intruder.

He said, "No thanks to the Scotch. Coffee?"

"It'll be instant, and you probably hate it," she said hopefully.

"I do hate it," he agreed, "but I drink it. You allow rubber boots in your kitchen?"

"If I don't, it's too late now."

"Yep, and I've tracked in sand and rockweed and cinders," he said cheerfully. They faced each other across the lighted lamp, she almost insolently looking him over, hoping he wouldn't like it and go. But he smiled a little as if he were challenging her, hands in his pockets, rocking a little. He was only slightly taller than she, ruddily tanned and with thick brown hair cut very short, evidently to discourage curliness. His short nose was almost delicately shaped, and he had the merriest eyes she had ever seen, under oddly thick brows. They reminded her of someone. The impression was baffling and maddening, because it was a pleasant association, whereas she had disliked him from the first moment of his interference.

"Hello, Miss Alexia Horne," he said. "I'm Jonas Hallowell. When did you eat last?" As he said it he pulled out a chair from the table, and with humiliation she was glad to sit down in it.

"I don't remember," she said.

"I'll make the coffee. I'm very good in a kitchen." He ladled water into the teakettle.

"I'm sure you're very good at everything," said Alix. She put her elbow on the table and rested her head on her hand, shading her eyes from the light. William jumped up into her lap and began bunting his head against her chin.

"That's a great cat," the man said. "He's been over at the Home Cove and made a call on me. Where do you keep your mugs? Oh, here they are." He was taking them out of the cupboard. "How about some soul and body lashins? For you, not for me. What have you got on hand? Not much," he answered himself, looking in the refrigerator. "You couldn't have planned on eating, or do you live off the land? Mussels and dandelion greens make damn good fodder for some folks. . . . Here's a couple of lamb chops."

He was outrageous. Tomorrow she'd tell the Goodwins they could keep him on their land and not let him step foot on hers. But her mouth was watering, and she was so hungry her stomach hurt.

"Fix them both," she said. "A growing boy like you can always put down an extra meal."

"What about this growing boy here? Come on, Whisker Bill, haul your head out of there before you lose it."

"Oh, he can chew on the bones," said Alix giddily.

Jonas sang, "And the little ones chewed on the bones-o, the bones-o, the bo-ones-o." He turned the gas on under the frying pan. "They never had such a supper in their life and the little ones chewed on the bones-o."

"Along with everything else, a singer too," said Alix.

"Not really," he said modestly. "My real talent is minding other people's business."

"So I've noticed," said Alix. The smell as the chops went into the pan caused William to howl and Alix to swallow.

"Let's see," said Jonas. "We ought to have bread and butter with this." She asserted her rights over her own kitchen then by getting bread from the breadbox, and putting a fresh stick of butter on a plate. He measured coffee into the cups and poured on the boiling water. She placated William with more food in his dish.

The bread and butter was so good that she was ashamed of herself for being excited about food when she was planning to die. One's body betrayed one in all sorts of unexpected ways. If she wasn't careful she'd have six slices eaten before Jonas finished one, and he wasn't a dainty eater. When the chops were cooked her desire for them gave her an actual pain. She tried to banter about it so he wouldn't know.

"I couldn't have done better myself," she said. "They look elegant. Were you a cook in a previous incarnation? When you weren't minding other people's business, I mean."

"I don't know about you." he said, "but when I eat, I eat."

"Good," she said. "That relieves me of having to make conversation."

William had the bones afterwards, and they finished off with more coffee and the rest of the cake Madge had left behind.

"Madge is a better cake-maker than I am," he said thoughtfully.

"It's perfectly fine of you to admit it, old man," said Alix.

"Something's just dawned on me," he said, grinning. "You don't like me."

She wanted to say, How sensitive of you to pick up all the subtle nuances. But except in a kind of fiery intimacy she could never be that sarcastic. She said, looking away from the amused light-brown eyes, "It's not that. But I never did have much small talk, and I'm hardly civilized right now, anyway. I mean —" She found herself flapping her hand vaguely in a way she disliked. "I'm not sleeping very well, and I'm rather uprooted at the moment, and I—" She couldn't stop that futile flipper-waving, and she could make no more excuses.

"Look," he said, pushing the lamp aside and leaning across the table. "I barged in tonight, right? Down on the beach and up here. Took over. You didn't even get a chance to ask me in if you'd wanted to, which you probably didn't. So who am I to act insulted if you don't fall for the famous Hallowell charm?"

"Is it as famous as your cooking?"

"At least *as*. Only not so useful. It only works till I get someplace where they wish I'd get the hell out." No self-pity; he seemed proud of his capacity to irk.

"Well, it certainly wasn't your charm that got you in here to-

night," said Alix, "but you do cook a marvelous chop and I
thank you very much. I mean that," she added honestly. "I was
feeling rotten, and I guess hunger was a part of it. I just hadn't
remembered to eat."

"You want to watch that," he said seriously. "You could get
anemic." He got up. "What about these dishes?"

"At this hour?" It was after ten. "Never. I'll do them in the
morning."

"All right. Thanks for the mug-up. Good night." He was
gone that quickly, apparently not one to stand upon the order
of his going. It was all of a piece with the rest of him. Probably
he thought such abrupt disappearances were as intriguing as
his frankness and that irritating perpetual amusement. She
hadn't even come close to liking him in the past hour, and the
irritation lasted as she brushed her teeth and went to bed in
the study.

She was so tired and still so preoccupied with him that she
slid quickly into sleep without remembering that she had
planned to concentrate tonight on Shane.

She woke in the dark sitting up, trying to hear over her
heartbeat what had waked her. She was certain that someone
had called her; she could almost remember the voice—no, not
the voice, but the word, her name, made more than audible; all
but tactile, like a Montessori alphabet. Yet William slept on
beside her feet. Last night he had been on the alert from the
moment they had come into the house. But couldn't his peaceful sleep mean that now he recognized and accepted Shane's
presence?

Oh Shane, she appealed in a luxury of penitence, I didn't
mean to fall asleep so fast tonight, it was that bumptious little
man's fault.

Nothing came of the impression that something had waked
her, and she began to sweat from the anguished effort to concentrate. The silence sang in her ears like surf on a far shore.
Her sweat ran icily down her forehead and back. If he were
trying to reach her and she couldn't hear or feel, Oh God, this

was a disaster she hadn't dreamed of, and how could there be anything worse? She'd thought his death was the ultimate, but she'd been wrong. She was always wrong.

Upstairs, upstairs. She didn't ponder that, but got up like a sleepwalker. The cold turned her damp pajamas clammy and her teeth began to chatter. She went through the house by starlight, past the portraits and the silent guitar, up the stairs that creaked as they always did at night and at no other time; her bare soles registered the familiar cracks between the wide boards in the upstairs hall and then the straw matting on the floor of her room.

Stars filled her windows. In the blurry grayness of the room the gap left by Shane's partly open door was a dark slash. Shivering but only carelessly aware of that, she crawled in between the fresh cold sheets and pulled herself up into as small and tight a bundle as she could, and lay watching the black gap.

Come to me, she said inside her head. *Come and warm me, Shane. Wrap me in your arms and legs and watch the stars with me. Shane, come to me.* She could feel herself already beginning to loosen, her limbs falling open as simply and soundlessly as the big petals fell from the rugosas.

Shane, come to me.

But nobody came, and she didn't know when she fell asleep.

❦ CHAPTER 9 ❦

An angry William woke her; it was after ten. Except for the fact that her head felt perfectly clear and her body reasonably agile she'd have suspected herself of having taken Seconal without knowing it.

It was a chilly gray morning, with showers blowing on easterly winds under a Jacob Van Ruisdael sky. She dressed rapidly, staring out the windows the whole time so she wouldn't look at Shane's door. Between rushing clouds and the fast hard showers the sea shifted from glaucous green to gun-metal, dove-gray to dull silver, and when the sun almost came out it turned a tinselly viridian.

It was choppy but not too much for work. *Marjorie C.*, wearing a red jigger sail to keep her up into the wind when Ozzie hauled a trap, moved along to the leeward of Tiree Ledge. Two boats from the Harbor worked around the Timmy Shoal, to the south. Something bright much closer to shore caught her eye, Jonas's wet-shining yellow oilclothes as his dory danced confidently a little way off Alix's eastern shore. He was standing up, braced back against the motion and hauling a trap.

She moved quickly away from her windows. "I wouldn't put

it past you to drop in for a cheery cup of coffee," she said. "I never saw a man so taken with himself, and so obvious about it." Oh, Shane thought he was great, she continued as she went downstairs, but then he *was* great. Tony and the others think what they're doing is the twentieth century's answer to Rembrandt, but they *have* to think it or they couldn't survive. But this one—he's like Beauty in the poem—he's his own excuse for being.

Too bad she had nobody to share this with except William, who was interested only in his breakfast and going out. She attended to him, then built a fire, and an old reflex took over; she could never bear to waste all that good birch heat on just coffee, and besides, she was hungry. She couldn't remember when she last felt hungry in the morning. Well, yes, she could, but she refused to.

She scrambled eggs, and made toast on the stove covers. Once she stepped on one of the chop bones, thoroughly cleaned. But already, with the prospect of another day to get through, she saw the incident by lamplight in the kitchen as long ago and growing dimmer by the moment.

In a sudden shower the rain beat hard on the easterly windows, obscuring vision like a sea breaking over a boat's windshield. Karen wasn't likely to be allowed out in this, which was one small blessing.

William came in again and went under the stove to dry off. She went up the back stairs to the studio. There was a Franklin stove here and she built a fire in it, feeding it with anything small and light enough to easily burn up. Otherwise, everything cleaned out of cupboards and drawers was dumped into cartons.

Here she had done other things besides portraits: landscapes, seascapes, still lifes, nonobjective motifs; worked in watercolor, pastels, charcoal, pencil, dry brush; experimented with tempera, with mixing her own colors; groaned in frustration or experienced hard-won triumphs, like Shane with his poetry and his guitar.

The only portraits she had ever painted on Tiree besides Shane's and her own were those of Ozzie and Madge, Ozzie working in his fishhouse, and Madge in her apron and a rosy new sunburn, with a tin dipper of raspberries. She had given them the paintings, and all their company praised the likenesses so much that Madge had gotten over being flustered at having a housedress and apron on instead of one of her good dresses and her cultured pearls.

The little fire was crackling company, and so was William, who came upstairs and lay before it like a lion. Outside the glass wall the Van Ruisdael sky was all flying lights and darks, slate-blue clouds edged with silver, blue-black masses from which the rain came hard. It beat on the roof close to Alix's head and streamed down the glass while the wind roared past the chimney. The wheeling gulls shone pure white against the storm clouds, as if with a light of their own. In the lulls, frayed-out foggy wisps dissolved in small lakes of clear turquoise, and the great bald brow of the Head showed up as bright as the men's oilskins.

It was enough to madden a painter, and one of the sketchbooks Alix intended to burn was full of reminders of all the times when the weather outside the north window had driven her into fresh torments of creation. Even now, with all that behind her, she found herself standing and staring, enamored of a cerulean patch that disappeared while she looked at it; bemused with the way the high slope of the Head field changed color under the changing skies as the sea did.

She wondered if another painter would ever stand thus in her studio; she imagined the surprise and pleasure at the good light and all the storage space. The Franklin stove, too. She wondered if William would try to move in with them. But maybe they wouldn't like cats. For the first time she felt doubtful about leaving William. He'd never understand being kept out of his own house, and she felt quite upset and almost tearfully sentimental. Which was silly, because William would settle down quite happily wherever he was fed, and the Goodwins were good feeders to anything that could eat.

She went downstairs for more coffee, uttering sardonic blessings on the next tenant. I hate you but I won't haunt you, though Madge will probably make me into a romantic legend. *She left the web, she left the loom, she made three paces through the room ... Out flew the web and floated wide; the mirror cracked from side to side. The curse is come upon me, cried the Lady of Shalott.*

We snickered. The Curse meant one thing to us then. And besides, we didn't want to be emotionally moved. Not in public, anyway. But I wonder how many girls besides Dodie and me saw themselves floating down a flowery English river with their hands crossed on their breasts.

She has a lovely face, God in His mercy lend her grace. Sir Lancelot, looking like Robert Taylor, very stern and sad. At least he was Robert Taylor for Dodie, but for me it was Laurence Olivier. It had to be Olivier. Was there ever such a mouth? And those hooded eyes. I'd settle for no less. Or rather, Alexia wouldn't.

Alix settled for Shane and all that went with him. Of which this, today, is a part.

She put down her coffee cup and returned to the studio as she had done so many times, preoccupied by a problem in her work. She had four cartons to bring down and put in the study. Perhaps tonight, if the rain let up, she could burn these with no dry boughs and rockweed to send up a warning geyser of sparks and bring Peter Pan winging in.

She straightened the blankets on the couch, smoothed and folded them, plumped the pillows in automatic housewifely motions. Then she turned to the desk with the impression that she'd left something undone there, though she knew she had been thorough yesterday. All that was left in the drawers or on the top were ordinary impersonal items that could be found on anyone's desk.

Anyone's. Of the hours that Shane had worked at the desk there was no trace, no lingering in the atmosphere. Curious how nothing of him survived here. In a few days it would be, at least for a stranger walking in, as if Shane had never existed.

She stood staring at the desk with the hair tightening on the back of her head so that, dreamlike, she put a slow hand up there and gripped a fistful of hair. In the middle of the dark green blotter there stood facing her a tiny white toy figure of a Viking, bearded chin thrust up and out, one hand resting on the handle of a broadaxe braced against his foot, the other on the hilt of a sword. He was three inches tall, from his feet to his winged helmet, arms and legs brawny with muscles, the minuscule face perfect in its heavy-browed ferocity.

She knew the toy, they'd picked it up once in a heap of wet rockweed after a storm. What shook her now was the fact that yesterday the Viking had been lying among some pens and pencils, paper clips and rubber bands, in an old knife box in a top drawer. She had opened the drawer, glanced in, and shut it again; she hadn't taken the Viking out and set him on the blotter.

She sat down on the couch without taking her eyes off the figure. If he had suddenly come alive with his chain mail, drinking horn, and cross-gartered legs, and was now threatening her, she could not have been more astounded.

"I *know* I didn't touch it," she said aloud, as if to be sure she still had her voice. When she'd waked up here in the night she hadn't even had a light, she'd just gone bumbling and fumbling out of the room in the dark and upstairs to fall into bed.

"*William?*" she asked. Appearing just then in the study doorway he answered her, and she shook her head at him. "No, you couldn't have." He came to rub around her legs, making his egg-boiling sound.

There remained one other answer. She didn't say this one aloud. Were you here, Shane? Are you here now? Shane, if you could do that, why didn't you wake me?

She felt pathetic, lost, young. She wanted to cry, but couldn't. She sat staring at the toy and it stared back from blind, white, hostile eyes.

They had been walking the shore after a bad southeaster,

finding pot buoys and shattered traps, some good lumber. That day there'd been a grape box with a South African name on it and a crayoned destination, Port of Spain. Lost toy boats were always tragic for some reason. Tennis balls evoked the rich over on Mt. Desert and velvety grass courts one good stroke away from the surf. Fancy liquor bottles went to Ozzie for toggles; they'd picked up an elegant brandy bottle that day and she wanted to use it first with a few of the other finds in a still life she'd call "Beachcomber's Loot."

Then Shane saw the Viking in the rockweed and pounced on it with a whoop of triumph.

"A statue of my ancestor!"

"I thought your ancestors were all wild Irish kings," said Alix.

"Well, no, you haven't heard all my genealogy," said Shane with the almost-brogue and the long face that meant he was creating. He balanced the Viking on the palm of his hand. "I never told you this part because we haven't had time to get to it, you see, my forebears being so numerous and so illustrious. According to their own lights, that is. Well, you see, there was an Irish princess. Deirdre of the White Shoulders, and she was given to a Viking raider to get him into the family, so to speak, so he'd leave off burning the place down every spring. He was Thorvald Yellowmane—or Brawnycalf," he added, squinting at the solid legs.

"You're making this up as you go along," she said. "I'd be ashamed to be such a liar. Is that the Irish or the Norse in you?"

"It's my pious English father," said Shane. "A descendant of an old Cromwellian major general, God forgive him." He pushed his palm and the Viking toward Alix. "Isn't he magnificent? The sea washed him to our feet and we'll take it as a sign."

"A sign of what?"

He frowned at her. "You're being intransigent, Alexia. Anyone would think I was the artist and you the expert on government. Can't you see the poetry of this? And the possibilities? Thorvald may have sailed these shores with Deirdre. He might even have been outlawed and come here, the way Eric the Red took off for Greenland. And now in some marvelous way we've all come together, at least in spirit."

"Well, just so long as you don't revert and go into a berserker rage some night with the carving knife," said Alix. But he seemed almost serious; this was one of the things that she adored in him, like the way he threw himself into his poetry or his guitar playing.

"All right, where do I come in?" she demanded.

"Deirdre had red hair," he said solemnly, and at that they both burst out laughing. He embraced and kissed her roughly, the wind cuffed them and spray licked their ears and cheeks, and for a moment as they held each other tightly so close to the crash and suck of the waves they could have been Deirdre and Thorvald.

For a few days Thorvald stood on the kitchen table. Then she took him up to the studio to include him in her beachcomber group, but he was no good; tiny as he was beside the brandy bottle, a net cork, and a cluster of huge blue mussel shells torn loose from bottom, his arrogance and ferocity dominated the group and turned it into something else. He insisted on becoming a portrait, not an object in a still life.

She returned him to the kitchen, and Shane had taken him to the study, saying straight-faced that he wanted to see if now his work could come any easier. He was trying to buckle down to a commissioned article on some of the lesser-known signers of the Declaration of Independence. But Thorvald invoked too bloody and violent an atmosphere in which to discuss the fortunes of sober and God-fearing Anglo-Saxon types. Then William carried him off a few times, so Shane retired him to the safety of the knife box in the drawer, from which he glared and thrust out his bearded chin whenever anyone came looking for a paper clip.

She had planned to do a portrait of Thorvald this spring,

making him very yellow of hair and blue of eye, and have it hanging on the living room wall when Shane came. She'd say, "Here's your great-great-grandpop." And how he would laugh. She could hear him now. But of course she'd forgotten the painting, she'd forgotten the Viking, he hadn't even registered on her yesterday when she'd glanced into the drawer.

But here he was.

Recollecting the first discovery of him after the storm had steadied her, and she could think more clearly now. Shane had kept saying the toy was a sign. Wouldn't he now expect her to remember that?

It reminded her of something and she jumped up in a fever of irritation and frustration, as if the thing she couldn't remember were somehow a key. Madge was mixed up in it . . . Then she remembered Madge's bringing them a magazine, one of the popular ones, dropping it on the kitchen table and brushing her hands afterward.

"I can't keep it in the house. Just to know it's there gives me gooseflesh."

It turned out not to be one of the outspoken articles on sex that always shocked her, but the shortened account of a reputable clergyman's communication with his dead son.

Shane had kidded her about believing everything she read. "But he's a *bishop!*" she exclaimed. "Now you know he has to be real smart and real *good* to get that high. So it stands to reason he wouldn't rig all this up just to get it printed. I mean using his poor boy like that, and all. So I say that *proves* there's something to it, and it makes me some *nervous!*" She was as wild-eyed as a cow pestered by flies. "I only *half*-believed it about Old Gib all this time, but when a *minister* says it's so— and I don't mean one of them spiritualist ministers at Seal Bay," she added. "*They'd* swear to anything."

After she'd gone home, adjuring Sidney to stay close by her when they went through the Tangle, Shane read the article. "Maybe she's right," he said. "He's a man of integrity, as far as we know."

"But he wanted this communication so badly, he could have rigged things without knowing it."

"He's too intelligent to fool himself. He's applied all kinds of checks and had other people do it too."

"I still think it's possible to fool yourself," said Alix. "Or maybe one of the people close to him knew this would mean a lot to him, so they arranged the little signs and symbols."

They were off on one of those long enjoyable wrangles that often sprang up from even a lesser point than this one, neither wanting to give in to the other or be the first to propose a compromise. Finally Shane said, "What are you so afraid of? Was one of your ancestors hanged as a witch, by any chance? Do you feel weird atavistic stirrings in your psyche when you brush against the occult?"

"I feel a weird atavistic longing to punch you right in the nose," said Alix. "Why are *you* so strong for this hocus-pocus, innocent as it may be?"

"I'm strong for an open mind, that's all. Hey, why don't you get the book and read the whole story, all the details?"

"From a public library. With what you'd pay for that book you could rescue some kid from starvation."

"You're a cynic, but compassionate."

"You're a romantic, but—"

He bunched his shoulders and stalked menacingly toward her. "But what?"

She shut her eyes, swallowed, and then rubbed her throat because swallowing didn't stop it from hurting. . . . They hadn't thought of the book again.

She blinked her eyes hard to clear them, and went to the desk, ignoring Thorvald Yellowmane or Brawnycalf. There was an address book in another drawer, and she turned the pages until she found the shop in Bangor from which they had sometimes ordered books and paper. She wrote the telephone number on a note pad and took it out into the living room, wondering absently what day it was and how long she'd been here;

it felt like forever, a messy blend of light and dark hours like cookies in a tin that had been dropped until there wasn't a whole one of any variety left. By fixing her attention she made it two days, four since she'd left New York. That meant Ozzie wouldn't be going over to the mainland again for at least four more days. He carred his lobsters and took them over once a week, when she and Madge drove to Emery's for groceries, and collected the mail.

She felt distracted, jumpy, full of an unpleasantly seething energy. Four days more might as well be four years, but she would not ask him to make a special trip. She looked back in at the small figure solitary on the broad green field of the desk blotter.

"And how came you there?" she demanded. "For God's sake, answer me that! Or *somebody* answer!"

The harsh clang of her voice shocked her, and aroused William. For the first time she realized that a clear lemon-yellow sunlight was replacing the earlier elusive silvery glints. She hadn't known when the wind let go, but beyond the windows the sea was almost calm, a gentle pastel blue. The voices of birds penetrated the glass.

The skiff would need a little bailing. Otherwise she was ready to go; she would take the remaining chop like the sea pigeon for which she was named.

❧ CHAPTER 10 ❧

SHE TIDIED HERSELF quickly; a fast scrub and brushing, her hair pinned up on her head, a change into respectable tweed slacks and turtle-neck jersey. Billfold jammed into a hip pocket, windproof parka bundled under her arm, William out. Remembering Karen, she locked the doors; times had changed in more ways than one.

William followed her to the wharf and sat watching while she pulled *Sea Pigeon* in and bailed out rainwater with a cut-down plastic bleach jug. The tank was full and the auxiliary can was full also. She pushed off from the wharf with an oar and turned to start the engine, but it didn't catch on at once and she felt the gouging physical pain of disappointment that Alexia had always suffered when she was in a state of high tension and couldn't put her plans in operation at once.

She sat down on the stern seat and forced herself to be still as the boat floated free, counted to ten, and tried again. This time the motor started.

"So long, William!" she called triumphantly. Only the tip of his tail flicked. Then a swallow buzzed him and he lost his dignity and ran under the fishhouse.

Alix headed out of the cove and up across the remaining easterly swells. Keeping the boat over at Beauty Cove would have eliminated the trip around the Head now, but it would also have eliminated her privacy. This way she could go to the Harbor and back without anyone's knowing she'd left the island, unless someone walked around and saw that the skiff was gone. But that didn't matter, she'd have accomplished her errand.

Though she'd been often frightened in the catboat, and accused a hilarious Shane of being a madman under canvas, *Sea Pigeon* was her own trustworthy little boat in which she could putter along at three-horse speed or slower, and row if she had to. She often made trips to the mainland or around to Beauty Cove in fine weather, and this was rapidly becoming fine; the wind was a mere ghost of itself now, the swells flattening fast, and it would turn into one of those tranquil afternoons when she would return with her own reflection for company.

She stayed well off the Head, where the surge never really died down. The eiders were there, as usual, and medricks skimming and squealing. *Sea Pigeon* bounced and rolled a little, but in a few minutes they were away from the wash and heading across a larkspur-colored bay. A warm spruce-scented land breeze blew lightly against her face. The ripples gurgled around the dory bow, the engine ticked on dependably, almost musically, a tribute to Ozzie's loving-kindness. There were other boats in sight but all at a distance. Alix felt small and alone out here, a being not much bigger than Thorvald sailing in a mussel shell, but there was a curious safety in this solitude as if she were free not only of people but of herself.

She was almost sorry to reach the Harbor. With the sight of houses, washings hurried out with the sun, cars, utility poles, she regained all that she had repudiated while she had been out on the bay, and the weight was worse than before.

It was the early afternoon lull. The lobstermen hadn't yet started to come home, and the children hadn't left school yet. The place drowsed and steamed in the fresh sunlight, gulls stood undisturbed on ridgepoles. She tied up at Roger Goodwin's float, and went up the ramp warily. They'd always used Roger's telephone, but this was one call she didn't want overheard. She had just decided to get the keys and drive to the village store, Emery's, where there was a public booth, when she saw that the lobster buyer's car was gone. He left his place unlocked when he was gone on a short errand, in case anyone needed something from there in a hurry; and at this time of day it had to be a short errand, because the men would be coming in soon.

Now if only Daisy didn't call to her about that cup of coffee. But this was her day, all right; Daisy's car was gone.

Bert had a private line. Another plus. There was no waiting in anguished impatience for a pair of defiant marathon talkers to get off the line. She propped her rear against the mammoth old safe in the corner beyond Bert's desk, dialed the operator, and asked to be given the charges after the call. While she waited she looked out the window, watching the gulls picking around on a strip of ledge and shingle left bare by the tide just below the office. She'd never yet been satisfied by any gull she'd sketched, and as one lifted wings and savage beak to warn off a newcomer, she felt just for an instant the familiar nag in her fingers, the unscratchable itch—

The bookstore answered. Alix identified herself, but the clerk was a new one who didn't recognize an old, if seasonal, customer. However, she was ardently helpful when Alix mentioned the clergyman's book.

"Oh, yes, we have that! It's *very* interesting, and quite inspirational and helpful *too*." She dropped her voice. "For people who have lost someone, you know. It gives hope."

"Yes," said Alix. "Well, I'm more interested in the ESP angle than the inspirational part. Do you have any more books on that?"

"On what?"

"Extrasensory perception." It was becoming ludicrous. She was deathly tired of the whole thing and wished she had never started it.

"Oh," said the clerk in a flat tone. "I don't know. I'll have to ask Mr. Chapman and he's out right now." Enthusiasm returned. "But we have a *lot* of spiritualism right now, though, on account of the big camp meeting at Seal Bay this summer."

"I'm not a spiritualist," said Alix. "I'd like only the book I mentioned, and anything Mr. Chapman has on ESP. And will you mail them to me as soon as possible?"

"Certainly," said the woman, perceptibly cool. "Would you repeat the address and zip code, please?"

Alix did, wondering guiltily if she'd been rude; *You sounded so damned clipped and imperious,* Shane said once. *The missing Grand Duchess Anastasia, I presume.* Consciously gentle, she thanked the clerk for taking the order, but it was too late, the woman still sounded aloof, if not hurt.

At once hangdog and defiant—anyone that thin-skinned shouldn't be clerking, besides I wasn't rude, just firm—she waited for the operator to give her the charges. Then she wrote a note to Bert on the pad on his desk. As she was counting the change to leave beside it, the sliding door was pushed slightly open and a young man with a ginger beard slid sidewise through the opening, saying, "Hey, Bert, you got any—" He saw her with transparent surprise. "Why, Bert, how you've changed," he said.

"Well, see, I've got these crazy glands," said Alix, "so every year I switch, like oysters."

"And nobody ever guessed! Well, gosh, Bert, you're a lot prettier this way, got more hair and everything."

He and Alix smiled at each other, then she nodded, murmured "Hello," and started to go past him to the door. He moved quickly into her path, his round face reddening. It was the sort of snub-nosed face with big front teeth and ingenuous eyes, now blinking slightly in self-consciousness, that showed exactly what he had looked like as a small boy, in spite of the ginger beard, mustache, and D. H. Lawrence forelock.

"You're Alexia Horne," he told her rapidly, "and I've always wanted to meet you. I'm Pete Ruskin. You've probably never heard of me, in fact I know you haven't, but some day—"

"But some day the whole world will know," said Alix, putting out her hand. "How do you do? Now can I say I met him when he'd just made a beautiful new suit of sails for his yawl?"

He shook her hand hard, grinning. "I guess I *am* about as proud of that job as anything I've done. Hey, isn't the yawl a little beauty? The reason we swung in so close, we wanted to get a look at you. You're a kind of legend around here, you know."

"I'm leaving," said Alix.

But he held onto her hand. "Well, you are a legend. Everybody told me I'd never get near enough to speak to you."

"*Everybody* meaning who?"

"Oh, not the real people around here," he assured her. "But the arty-farty crowd. Excuse me," he said quickly and turned a little redder.

"I've used the term myself more than once." It was actually Shane who had, but no matter. And had they told him about Shane? *She lives with a man out there on Tiree. Not married. They don't mix.* "Well, Mr. Ruskin, it's been very nice meeting you."

He said with a kind of last-ditch desperation, "Look, Miss Horne, you've never exhibited in the Harbor Day show, have you? That's what they tell me. We just moved here last winter."

"No, I never have," she said. "I've always concentrated on my work in the summertime and never come to the mainland unless it's absolutely necessary." She tried to edge not too flagrantly toward the door, but he managed to get in her way again, blinking harder.

"I don't blame you. If I had Tiree I'd probably be a sociopath. But . . . would you consider the show this year? We'd be honored, and I mean it."

"Honored, when you have Eva Landry and Todd Polanski, people like that?"

"We don't have Alexia Horne, and she belongs to the Harbor more than almost all the rest."

"Well, thank you, you're very nice to say that." He didn't look about to let her go; he was determined to go back to the arty-farty crowd with her scalp. They weren't the working artists, but the fringe, too dull even to be called lunatic. "When is the show?" she asked. "Early in July, as usual?"

"Yes. Will you?"

With any luck she'd be out of the whole thing by then, so she could say yes now and forget it. "All right," she said. "I'll see what I have."

"Hey, thanks! My God, I got you, as easy as that! Don't tell me they never even *asked* you."

"Oh, they asked me," she said. He was so innocently jubilant she felt a twinge at letting him think she'd be around for the show. Oh well, she could always make an addition to her farewell note, which was going to be quite a document when she got through with all the P.S.'s. *Would either of you loan your portrait to the Harbor Day show?*

She took hold of the door and he said wildly, "Can't I treat you to something? Candy bar? Vintage Coke? Orange soda that was laid down the year Victoria became queen and was sent around the Horn?"

"You mean Victoria was sent around the Horn?"

He burst into loud adolescent laughter. The extra hair looked all the more like something stuck onto an overgrown twelve-year-old for Hallowe'en. "No, but seriously," he said, "would you come up to the house and have a drink with us now? My wife would flip. She thinks you look like Katharine Hepburn."

"I won't get close enough to disillusion her, then," said Alix. "Thank you anyway, but I must get back before it breezes up."

"Another time then." Eagerly he shouldered open the door for her. "This is just great, Miss Horne. I came down here looking for Bert and find you. That's the purest essence of serendipity, isn't it?"

"It's something," she admitted. She smiled at him and went out. But he came with her around to Roger's wharf and down to the float, talking all the while; she couldn't have told afterwards what he'd said. She remembered that a long time ago she had been like Pete Ruskin. Now at thirty-six she felt she had been alive for a century and it was much too long.

He held the skiff while she got in, watched while she pushed off and started the engine, waved vigorously and yelled, "So long, see you later!" The first lobster boats were coming in and she had to keep her eye on the way ahead, but she felt that he was still watching her, and then he would rush home to tell his wife and call up someone to gloat. She realized that she hadn't asked him what sort of work he did, that it hadn't even occurred to her to ask it. Such indifference was foreign to her. Or at least it was to the earlier Alix. This one felt a great boredom at the thought of catering maternally to the natural vanity of artists. How the hell had she ever put up for five minutes with that wretched infant Tony?

She'd used the fear of more wind as an excuse, not really expecting it. But the northwest breeze had freshened. Cold-sculptured masses of cloud towered up beyond the spruces and moved with deliberate speed across the sky. All colors had taken on a hard, burnished light.

Alix was in the lee of the land while she went through the harbor, and for a little while outside. Then the puffs of wind came down after her like miniature squalls, sometimes slapping a little water into the boat around the cut-out stern where the engine was placed. She slowed the engine down to trolling speed. She disliked following seas, and though these were small yet, and spasmodic, she took them seriously. The squalls began to come closer together, be stronger, last longer.

She seemed to have no saliva to moisten her mouth. She tried not to look around, which could always jelly her bones. Better to keep staring ahead, never mind the massive lift picking up the boat and driving her forward, then dropping her. The sea was in control, one could only steer, keep her from getting around sideways to the deep chop whose crests went hissing by the boat.

She remembered now that she hadn't checked the tank before she left Roger's float. Damn that idiot boy prattling on. Damn him for holding her up in the first place. Damn *her!* Talk about vanity. *Thank you, you're very nice to say that.* Wasn't it gratifying, after all, to be flattered by one of the kids whose gods were Picasso or Munch?

So you had to stay and hear some more, and you called it manners, and you laughed like a gratified fool, and here you are, fool all right; fool woman all alone out here, and drowning isn't the way I want to die.

In her excitement she'd let the boat get off course a bit. *Sea Pigeon* lurched and shook and water splashed over the side. Alix's feet were wet, but their coldness had nothing to do with water. She was sweating under her parka, and had gone beyond nausea. Tiree came no closer. What about those maniacs who started for England in a dory?

What makes you think you're going to drown? . . . Well, how many people *don't* think they're going to, and then turn up as bodies the Coast Guard's looking for? . . . Well, look, you've got along this far, you must be halfway, just keep on doing the same thing. You can always row, provided you can get the oars out from under the seat, and the oarlock strings unwound from them, and the oarlocks in place and then the oars arranged, all this while you're still steering, so the instant you shut off the engine you can grab the oars before she swings around.

Makes you think, doesn't it?

She leaned forward and took hold of the blade of one oar and pulled it toward her. It came only so far, held by the oarlock string. The boat went off course again for that instant and tried to swing. Alix thought of William as she'd last seen him, dodging the swallows. He'd be all right, Ozzie and Madge would take good care of him. But there was all that stuff in the study that she hadn't got to burn yet, and Thorvald alone and valiant on the desk blotter. Thorvald Yellowmane shouting defiance in the middle of a green Irish meadow.

He'd sent her on this errand. Was it intended to end like

this? "No!" she shouted aloud. She wouldn't accept it; Shane knew how terrified she could get on the water sometimes. Nobody had anything to do with this but herself, good old blockhead one-track Alexia.

How much water would slop aboard in the next two miles, with wind and seas increasing? Could she bail fast enough and still steer straight? If she got there, what then? A direct course would take her right into the surf that leaped along an up-and-down wall of red rock. She would have to swing right to go down toward Beauty Cove or left to go up around the Head. Neither way looked very enticing, each meant turning *Sea Pigeon* broadside to the seas, but the Head way was longer. Beauty Cove it was, then, and maybe she'd be washed to Ozzie's doorstep like "My son's wife Elizabeth" in the poem.

She bailed with the cut-out plastic jug, she kept the other hand on the tiller, and tried to keep her gaze straight ahead. Her eyes kept blurring, either with the sweat running into them or a hysterical myopia brought on by fear, so she didn't see the big boat coming up from the south until she heard a heavy engine and thought it was a low-flying plane; she turned a strained face skyward, thought she heard someone shout, and saw the boat a few hundred yards away and coming fast, dipping her bow into the seas and sending showers of spray back over decks and house.

The windshield was streaming and she had the nightmare notion that the man behind it didn't see her, that she was invisible in the glittering, dancing, rushing water. She waved the white dipper in a wild arc but the boat came plunging smoothly on. Then she slowed down abruptly and began a lazy rolling movement as she came toward *Sea Pigeon*.

She was *Marjorie C*. With a shaky hand Alix steered to meet her, and the two knocked gently together, the smaller one nuzzling along the bigger boat's side like a calf seeking its mother's milk.

Jonas looked around the side of the canopy with a grin. "I was going to yell 'Get a horse,' and keep on going, but I thought better of it. Want a tow?" He took hold of the *Sea Pigeon* with a short gaff.

"Tow nothing, I want to get aboard." She tilted up the engine and holding onto the big boat's guardrail she leaned far forward and got the painter. She stood up cautiously; her legs had been braced in one cramped position since the first squalls had hit. "I'm not disloyal to the *Pigeon*, but she feels like a clamshell right now."

"Oh, you could go to Matinicus in that boat and be safe," Jonas said.

"You can try it sometime," said Alix. "Feel free." As the skiff rose on a sea she swung herself onto the washboard and over into the cockpit. Jonas took the painter and went astern to make it fast to the ring bolt beyond the mast with its furled red jigger sail. He wore, and came back wearing, the male expression of quiet amusement that always made her want to explain at great length and with gestures that she wasn't completely a fool to have gotten into this mess, that she could prove it was somebody else's fault from the start. Masterfully she stifled the impulse and looked around the gently rolling boat as if she'd never been aboard any such craft before.

Karen stood in the companionway watching her. Alix almost jumped. For a moment they considered each other. Then Alix said, "Hello, Karen," and received no answer. Jonas turned up the idling engine and swung the bow around toward the east. "Want to go straight home?"

"Yes, if you don't mind." She was still so bemused with relief that antagonism hadn't yet revived.

He gave her a bright terrierlike glance. "You never know when Karen's going to pop up. I'm beginning to think she's my conscience."

"It must be convenient to have a myopic one."

"It would be. In this case the word is 'amblyopic.' In other words, Karen ambles. Don't you, peanut?" He looked around at Karen and winked, but she was as inscrutable as William. "She ambles all around. She told me you were gone. It kept breezing up, and Ozzie was baiting a halibut trawl, so I took the boat. I thought I'd catch you still at the Harbor. Madge swore you wouldn't start back in this."

"Well, thank you both," said Alix, including Karen in her nod.

"Spoken with a definite coolness."

"No, definite embarrassment. After nine years I should have known better. My pride's suffering."

"It's possible not to know better after twenty years," he said. "If the worst thing you do is misjudge the weather, you're either lucky or a genius. Here, take the wheel while I get my pipe going."

She moved into his place. "What did you do before you came here?" she asked. "Were you always a lobsterman? If it's none of my business, say so."

"Oh, I owe you a little nosiness after last night. It's no secret anyway. I'm not hiding out from the Mafia or the FBI. I started out as a lobsterman, I was in a peapod when I was thirteen. But when I came here this spring I'd been a boat-builder. My yard's down to the west'ard, Williston."

"The sea captain's town," she said. "Where the tall ships went down the river with the tide and out to sea." Something was familiar. "Ozzie had this boat built in Williston."

He nodded. "I built her." Somewhere the last few traces of amusement had been erased completely. He got his pipe going and stood with folded arms, watching the way ahead with eyes narrowed against the brilliant glare outside. He looked older and tougher than she remembered from last night.

"You said you'd been a boat-builder. Isn't that something you always are, even when you're not actually building? It's an art, isn't it?"

He shrugged without looking around at her. She said, "Well, is this a vacation, or a defection? Or an abdication?"

"I won't answer that," he said, "for the simple reason that I don't know yet what it is."

"You'd better take the wheel," she said. "I'm not sure of all the ledges around here." She wished she hadn't asked him anything; it was simpler to keep him a one-dimensional busybody.

Karen had gone aft and now stood staring astern. She had done this before, and Alix wondered if some sorrow or homesickness moved the child behind her impassivity. As they went past the Head and came into the lee waters she thought, Three of us aboard this boat and each one of us obsessed; we know each other's names and that's all.

❧ CHAPTER 11 ❧

WHEN SHE LET herself into her own house again, with William garlanding himself around her ankles and almost tripping her up, she went at once to the study as if drawn by an invisible leash. Thorvald still stood on the blotter, defying what? The mysterious Skraelings? A pack of wild Celts? Calmed now after the excesses of the day so far, she said aloud to herself, "What did you expect, that he'd have moved somewhere else while you were gone?"

Then it came to her that she must have half-expected it, and the vibrato of nerves began in her again. She left the room quickly. She fed William, and then they went out again and she walked the shore beyond the southern arm of Gib's Cove.

Here, between stretches of creased, folded, multistriped rock, there were beaches worn by the sea into steep hollows; barrier beaches with rounded stones rolling underfoot and tossed by winter storms into the edge of the woods or the swamps behind them. There was always a tide-row of flotsam high at the top of the beaches so that beach peas and bindweed and selfheal grew through old lobster traps and around rotting lumber.

The little shore birds flew up from each beach as Alix and William came to it. Plovers, sandpipers, sanderlings; their small musical cries and their swift wings made her hands clench into fists in her pockets. After her first encounter with them she had to force herself to go on. Like everything else at this time of year they meant the rush of new life, and as she walked between their excited busyness at the edge of the tide and the flashing wings in the swamps and woods, her eyes taking refuge from the vivid day behind dark glasses, she felt already like an invader here. She saw herself stalking long and black through spring with her shadow killing everything it touched . . . only that wasn't so. Everything went hurrying and thrusting on, and she was no more to it than to the sandpipers who were not even afraid of William but simply moved back to the part of the beach the cat had just left.

She walked on, automatically registering only familiar things and landmarks, refusing to let herself see, smell, or touch everything for which she had once searched so hungrily. She walked because she did not want to go back to the house.

She came up over a rise where water trickled down over a sculptured flow of rocks. Above here she had always picked cranberries in October before leaving the island, miniature pale green apples with rosy cheeks. She'd done a very good thing in tempera once of the lacy vines straggling onto the bare rock, and a few berries gleaming in their damp nest near a battered old pot buoy that had hardly any paint left on it. She felt a dry satisfaction at how good the thing had been. She'd given it to Shane and he had it in his rooms on the campus. She wondered, not very much, where it was now.

There was a great brouhaha among the birds in the woods nearby, and William appeared from under the low branches of thick spruces above the boggy spot and began picking his way fastidiously toward her. She looked ahead, shading her eyes against the sun, and down into the Home Cove. She saw the big gray dory rocking gently on the haul-off, the traps piled at the edge of the turf just above the beach, and the small gray-shingled cabin back against the spruces.

William said something and started eagerly down over the

creviced stone slope. She caught him by his thick tail and heaved him up into her arms and turned back, everything else forgotten now. The important thing was not to be seen, saluted, possibly summoned. Jonas could still be at Ozzie's after returning the boat, but you couldn't tell; he was almost as ubiquitous as Karen. William growled and squirmed and she said, "Never *mind*. Oh sure, he probably gave you something to eat when you showed up. I thought cats were supposed to be proud and independent, but let anyone feed you and you're ready to move in."

She put him down finally, and he stood growling and lashing his tail. She went on, and when she looked back he was coming behind her but ignored her when she spoke to him.

By not walking too fast on the way back, she was able to stay out till after sunset. The woods darkened steadily against a nectarine sky in the west. The voices of the peepers were blown on gusts of wind that sometimes swept over the trees and down to the house, setting up rattlings and clickings in it. It was a drying wind, even after sundown there was no dew, and she wouldn't be able to burn anything at dusk for fear of one of those errant baffles swooping down on her fire and blowing part of it back to the grassy bank.

She put Thorvald back in the desk drawer and went to bed at dark in the study. She set a lamp on the desk and tried to read one of the leisurely mysteries saved for summer nights. William stretched out about a yard long beside her legs. It was agony to stay awake after the day she'd had in the wind, and the walk on the shore, and she fought the narcotic sensation which once she would have welcomed, because unconsciousness could mean missing Shane.

At least it would mean that if I believed it, she corrected herself conscientiously. It was a little frightening to realize how close she was to taking it seriously. But death threw everything out of focus. What was more frightening was the suggestion that she could have moved Thorvald in the first place without remembering it.

This roused her as efficiently as a shout in the ear and she sat up ready to run, to escape, but where? The Seconal and the brandy bottle? She was half out of bed on her way to them before the soundless words were coldly spoken in her brain: *I did not move the Viking. I know I didn't.*

William dreamed with twitching paws and quivering whiskers. Alix went out to the kitchen, letting the night chill strike through her pajamas, made coffee and took it back to bed with her, sat up with the book on her knees and read. But the combination of warm bed and hot drink worked against her.

She came awake with a jump and a muffled shout, not knowing what she had dreamed to startle her. An offended William leaped to the floor and left the room. Her mouth tasted bad and the small room felt airless because of the lighted lamp; the wind had dropped and the night was silent. She looked with blurred eyes at her watch. It was after one. She got unsteadily onto her knees, turned down the lamp and blew it out, then dropped two of her pillows on the floor and fell back on the remaining one.

I'm waiting, Shane, she said inside her head.

The old mantel clock in the kitchen clanged unmelodiously for the half-hour. After that all she could hear was the soft spiraling rush in her ears which, when she'd first noticed it as a child, had convinced her that silence was really noisier than sound.

Lying flat and straight she breathed evenly, willing herself to receive. A radio telescope getting signals from an unseen planet. A huge dish on a hilltop, turned toward space. She saw SPACE, all in capital letters. Lost civilizations and moonwalks. The Flight of Apollo. *Who drives the horses of the sun shall lord it but a day.* Who said that and who was it lost the vhole damn outfit: Phoebus? No, Phaeton. Anyway, he found out, and so did Icarus. Icarus flew too near the sun. Down down down the plunge into the sea. Seven days and seven nights he fell. Lucifer. Light-bearer. *Brightness falls from the air.* A plane crashing in flames.

The vision of the flaming plane plummeting toward the jungle burned so vividly across her sight that she lunged upward in bed and leaned toward the window, as if the crash had just occurred and she would see and hear the whole monstrous conflagration in the back field.

There was nothing of course but the silent tide of the grass, and up on the hill the black woods against the stars.

She was fully awake, and fully alone. There had been no sense whatever of another presence, and there wasn't going to be. She had been left dangling awake at two in the morning, with the whole round of horror to go over again, beginning with the call from Shane's friend.

"Well, I won't," she defied the silence. "I *can't*. I'm fed up to here with the whole rotten business." She put on her robe and slippers and carried the lamp out to the kitchen, relit it, and built a fire. William appeared and she fed him, remembered she hadn't had supper and made herself a fried egg sandwich. After that she dressed and went out. The dew had come at last and the thick grass soaked her sneakers. It was cold out, and bright from the stars. She went back into the house and began bringing out the cartons that were left in the study. William, who had gone into her blankets after she'd fed him, watched her activities but didn't offer to join.

She wheeled two loads down the lawn. The squeak of the wheelbarrow and the peepers in the swamp were the only sounds, now that the wind had gone. On the shore the water was scarcely louder than breathing. Sometimes there was a little gurgling noise around a rock, or a tiny splash.

She sat hunched up in her hooded jacket among the rocks and this time watched her fire burn undisturbed to the end. When the last sparks had died away she took the wheelbarrow back to the house. William went out as she came in. She took off her wet sneakers and socks and put them under the still-warm stove. She filled a hot water bottle and carried it into the study, wrapped up in the blankets with the bottle at her feet, and went straight to sleep.

Again she had the sensation of being wakened, but this time it didn't fool her. The sound, or alarm, was in her own brain. "Or the kitchen clock," she said aloud. "If nine clanks of that don't get through to you, nothing could."

Nine. The swallows in furious pursuit of a pigeon hawk. The sun high up, a perfect May day full of birds and blossoms, miraculous lights and new gradations of color with each shift of the breeze and every passing cloud; up in the Tangle shadows would become more significant than their origins. You would walk all in a dapple.

If you walked, that is. But to walk in a windy May world where Shane was not—"If it be not fair to me, what care I how fair it be?" she misquoted, and heaved herself out of bed with a groan.

William was crying outside the kitchen door as she washed. She let him in and he entered suspiciously, lowering at corners, his whiskers pointing forward. He prowled around the entire lower floor with head and tail down before he settled down to his dish.

She went up the back stairs and through the studio to her room for clean underwear. She was not going to look out the north window but she couldn't resist it, and there was an osprey pair floating in wide circles above the Head.

She felt the nagging again in her hands or in her head, she could never tell which. Anyway, it was a tiresome desire, worse than hunger, and she wished it would go away. She put her hands in her pockets and turned her back on the window, but her eyes betrayed her, going to the litter on her long table where the charcoal sticks were, and the oil crayons. I'd better burn all that stuff tonight, she thought, and went on into her room.

She encountered herself in the mirror over the chest, not the ghost in the New York studio but a hard thin woman very much alive and fighting it: sunburned, new freckles, loose strands of dark red hair curling around her forehead and ears, and the rest skewered untidily on the top of her head. The old

green jersey turned her eyes the color of William's; they stared
from over the sharpened cheekbones, and she thought, Good
God, maybe I scare Karen into silence when I look at her.
Maybe she thinks I'm Old Lady Witch.

She smiled experimentally, but it wasn't much help, the
smile was too obviously arranged.

She went on past the chest without thinking and into Shane's
room. It was as simply furnished as hers with straw matting on
the floor, a braided rug by the spool bed; a patchwork quilt,
made by some Goodwin wife in the Log Cabin pattern, was the
spread. Shane had refinished this chest of drawers and hers,
finding the soft rich face of the pine under a half-dozen coats of
paint. He'd also refinished the stand beside his bed, turning an
old commode into something of distinction. He'd taken a fancy
to the paper in the room, a small fine design that had faded
well, and had kept it. There was a sturdy chair he'd reclaimed
from the fishhouse, and a bookcase he had made. There were
only two things hanging on the wall, where he could see them
when he lay in bed: a painting of William asleep on the granite doorstep in the sun, and a pencil drawing of Alix by one of
the young group in New York.

She went across to his mirror, ridiculing herself as she did so,
Do you think you'll find another Alix in this one? Shane's
Alix?

She wouldn't look. Her reflection was becoming tiresome,
like everything else. Instead she stared down at the objects on
the chest of drawers. When she had been in here a few days
ago, going over his clothes, everything that he had left on the
chest last September had been neatly squared on the bright
strip of Guatemalan weaving after Madge's dusting and tidying,
and Alix had not touched a thing. As far as she *knew,* she qualified, with a tendency to gulp like a dog about to be sick. It
was the Viking business all over again.

The two paperback adventure novels by Hammond Innes
now lay side by side instead of one on the other. A slab of stone
imprinted several million years ago with the shapes of tiny scal-

loplike shells lay on one of the books. He had found it the day before he left last September, and had intended to take it home with him to give to the young son of a colleague. He had forgotten it, and so had she, later.

There was a small box covered with leather and possessing a lock which was never locked. That had been moved to a back corner of the chest, close to the wall. She picked it up almost gingerly. Her heart was beating unevenly as she lifted the lid. Nothing was changed, no mysterious message for her lay inside among the handful of foreign coins, some odd keys, his Boy Scout knife, a cigarette lighter long unused, a fountain pen. Nothing had been taken away that she could tell, and nothing added. The box still held its secretive, cedary scent. But as she set it down she saw what had been hidden under it: the little fat tiki from New Zealand, carved from some smooth soft stone.

She stood there wondering how long she could stand this. If only she could accept or repudiate. If she could remember, or at least convince herself, that she had absently moved things around here while thinking about something else. But she could not remember; she was as positive as she had been in the middle of the night that she had not set the Viking out on the blotter. But she'd read of people writing anonymous letters to themselves and not knowing it. What if she were going to pieces like this, literally, her personality splitting off into independent fragments?

She was really going to be sick now, the salt water was running in her mouth. Then with a great overwhelming billow of relief she remembered the books she had sent for. She didn't have to make up her mind to anything until the books came.

She went back into her own room and got her clean clothes out and changed into them. Suddenly William came noisily up the back stairs and bounded across the studio into her room, then on into Shane's, and after him she heard feet on the stairs. She went out into the studio fastening her shirt. It wasn't Madge coming, Madge never entered the house without a knock first, then a blithe, "Hoo-hoo! Nobody to home?"

The steps were too light for a man's feet, but not at all tentative. It had to be, and it was, Karen.

Alix waited, her hands in her pockets. As the white-blond head appeared around the curve, the eyes were on a level with the floor and they began at once to swallow the room. The mouth was puckered tight with concentration. The glasses at last came to Alix's feet, and with deliberation they traveled up Alix's legs and finally reached her face.

"Good morning," said Alix. "Looking for someone?"

Karen came up a few more steps. Trying to see around Alix she said, "Gram says come to supper tonight. Gramp maybe'll get a halibut on his trawl."

"I'd love to come," Alix said. "Will you tell your Gram that, and thank you very much for bringing the message." She should have known that Karen would ignore the dismissal. She didn't move. She seemed to miss nothing, from the angles of the roof where wooden pegs held the old beams together to the most distant corners.

"This is my studio," Alix said. "It's not a very interesting place, as you can see." This was false, and she knew it; any new place is as fascinating to a child as to a cat. She was bored by her dreary insincerities as she was by everything else. "I'm just going out," she said. She rummaged around on the long table and found a flat tin box of oil crayons and charcoal, pushed it into a hip pocket and picked up a large sketch pad.

"You'd better get back home, Karen, or your Gram will be wondering what's happened to you." She started toward the stairs and Karen had no choice but to turn around and start down. Looking down on the silky head and the innocent nape Alix felt that she'd been inexplicably cruel. But when in the kitchen Karen turned and faced her again, she had that sensation of facing an adversary without humor or imagination but of an unremitting and therefore unsinkable self-centeredness.

She said, "I haven't any more cheese crackers, Karen, but how about this?" It was a small packet of raisins left from last year. They felt soft enough when she squeezed the box. "Here you are."

Karen took the box reluctantly. Perhaps she couldn't read. "Raisins," said Alix.

"I know it," said Karen.

"Do you like raisins?"

"Sometimes."

"Well, is this one of the times?"

"I don't know," said Karen hoarsely, and Alix burst out laughing. Karen stared at her without emotion and Alix said, "Life gets more foolish by the minute. Come on now, I'm going out."

As she locked the door Karen said, "Why did you do that?"

"Somebody might land on the shore," said Alix, "and come up into the house. I don't like anyone poking around my house when I'm not there. Which way did you come?"

Karen pointed up the hill.

"Through the Tangle? It must be full of birds this morning. Did you see any violets?" Karen shrugged. If she'd seen any, she'd doubtless walked on them. Alix went on with what she considered a gruesome smarminess, "I'm going up there this morning, so I'll walk along with you."

Karen didn't move from the doorstep, so Alix set off briskly. "Come along," she called, and after a moment the child came behind her.

The Tangle was alive with warblers and chickadees, nervous juncoes, downy woodpeckers working unconcerned on the old wild apple trees. The candle flames on the moosewood boughs hadn't changed much, but the new shoots were a sharp translucent red, like Bohemian glass, against the light. More ferns and green plants had broken through the dead bracken, and the star flowers were already in blossom. The old stone wall wound past aged trunks and tender new growth, a benign gray snake in sunlight.

Moving around trying to decide what to use, Alix was at once absorbed; the whole place was almost too rich, with the sort of ephemeral beauty that is best not recorded except in memory. Photography or a painting was like damping a butterfly's wings. Yet, knowing the futility of it, she always began, and when she became involved there was always the hope and then the certainty that this time she would accomplish a breakthrough. Or, at the very least, something that would start up a whole chain of associations for the viewer, like Proust's little cake and limeflower tea.

She walked around squinting through a frame of hands, squatted on her heels and looked again, knelt to consider the slender half-furled fronds of a spray of ferns; beside it there was part of the shell of a robin's egg, so pure a blue that it caused her a pang, half of painful pleasure, half of discovery. Was this it, then? If she could do it as well as the cranberries ... *And the meaning of May was clear.* She'd call it that.

Suddenly a shadow fell across her and the shell, as cold and solid as the child herself. "What are you doing here?" she asked sharply. Then she collected herself, sank back on her heels, and said more gently, "I thought you'd gone along ages ago, Karen. You startled me."

"I don't have to go yet," said Karen, stolidly munching raisins.

"Well, I'd rather you did go home. I'm busy now. I have my work to do."

Without a change of expression, Karen conveyed skepticism. "Up *here?*"

"Yes," said Alix. "You see, I make my living from my paintings the way your grandfather—"

"I should think you'd clean your sink," said Karen. "It's some dirty, all gucky and rusty. My mother never goes out and leaves a dirty sink. Gram doesn't either."

"Oh, go home!" said Alix. "At *once.*" Karen opened her mouth once more, and Alix snapped, "This minute. *Now.*"

Karen turned and tramped back to the path. Seen from the back, she had a certain touching dignity, but whenever she looked one in the eye any illusion of defenseless childhood disappeared. She seemed to be one of those born to move through life flat-footed, ponderous, and intimidating, tolerating no frivolities or weaknesses, making the most harmless little lies curl up and die miserably the moment they were uttered. And at this moment she had just succeeded in making Alix see her profession as pure nonsense for any able-bodied woman.

Alix stood with her hands on her hips watching Karen's red jacket disappear beyond the translucent screen of new leaves. "You are the kind of child," she said softly, "that when I was your age I wanted to hit every time I looked at her, but I couldn't because she wore glasses."

Instantly she and the chief enemy of her fourth-grade year, named Dorothy Gallagher, confronted each other outside the schoolyard gates, Dorothy ineffably smug in pink-checked gingham and glasses, Alexia with doubled fists and pigtails bouncing as she danced back and forth yelling, "Take off your glasses, you coward, you sneak!"

And she never did take them off, at least not to fight me, thought Alix. I wonder what kind of woman she grew up to be. She laughed aloud, surprising herself.

She sat down in the bracken, the sun warm on her head and shoulders, and went to work. Sketches of the newborn fern and the eggshell first, then she went on to other details. She forgot everything but what surrounded her. When the momentum finally died, the sun had traveled past the zenith and was throwing her shadow toward the other side. She was yawning and depleted, and started toward home with an animal instinct for food and drink, and for someone waiting.

When she remembered, she was stopped in her path, rocking a little as if from some great blow across the shoulders. How could I forget, how could I? She marveled. For at least three hours she'd been back in the world which had closed to her on the day he died, and now she paid for it in remorse and guilt that was far worse than the stupid indifference of those first weeks.

She walked slowly, almost without strength, out through the cool sun-shot darkness under the spruces to the top of the long green slope. Against the dazzling sea the house was an indeterminate dark shape whose outlines seemed to flicker and change constantly, as if it were a living entity crouched there in fear of so much sky.

❧ CHAPTER 12 ❧

WILLIAM CAME THUMPING down the steep front stairs express-
ing his displeasure at having been shut in all morning, and
went to the front door. When she opened it for him, the salty
sunlight came in, and voices. For her sins, the lie that she had
told Karen was coming true. People were coming up from the
shore, and she could see the tip of a mast in the cove. She had a
glimpse of a white sweater just coming around the rosebushes,
and from the corner of her eye she saw William dive for the
corner of the house, running low. She shut the door and ran
too, up the front stairs.

People had come like this a few times in the early summers,
and if she and Shane had a chance to avoid them, they did.
Caught, they were civil enough—even charming, on Shane's
part—but they never issued invitations or accepted any. Their
time was too precious to be frittered away on other people.
When the sailing historian appeared, it was because Shane had
told him one night over drinks about Tiree. The man had
been easy and kindly after the first embarrassment of discovering that Shane didn't live alone, and she had worked to keep
him from realizing how scaldingly enraged she was with Shane.

There'd been three days of storm, and in all decency she couldn't think of the man sleeping in a damp and tossing bunk when there was a warm dry bed ashore. So she'd put him in her room, and she had slept in the small downstairs bedroom so she wouldn't be up on the same floor with Shane and have the man wondering, or even taking it for granted that they were in the same bed.

"Puritan!" Shane jeered at her afterward. "You're living openly with me, before Madge and Ozzie. The whole Harbor knows we aren't married. So where's the courage of your convictions?"

"There's such a thing as violation of privacy. Madge and Ozzie aren't in the same house with us. And they can suspect things at the Harbor, but they don't *know*. And I'd rather be a puritan than a big-mouth Irishman! One drink too many and you're spilling out your life history to the nearest ear!"

"Now what did I say to him?" Shane demanded. "Were you there? Did you hear me? Did you count the drinks? Go on, tell me." He was there on the stairs with her the way he had been that day; too vigorous for a ghost, legs braced and thumbs in his belt, his grin savage in his beard, goading her.

"I didn't have to be there! I know about the Irish, I was born in Boston."

He threw back his head at that. "You don't have to be born in Boston to know about the Bostonians, and I don't mean the good healthy ones from Ireland that brought the old place back to life."

"That killed it, you mean. My mother's probably turning over in her grave."

"So's mine," said Shane with ferocious triumph. "Me sleeping with the get of English Protestants."

Alix hooted raucously. "I thought your mother married the descendant of a Cromwell man. Talk about Puritans! She went to bed with one and got you!"

He howled at that, hugging her till she yelped for mercy. "You've cracked a rib, dammit, I know you have!"

"Oh, my blessed Pinky!"

"Oh, my Paddy the bog-trotter!"

"We'd got beyond that, you know. We had lace curtains, and the monsignor to tea. He and my father used to argue about original sin and the wickedness of popes . . . you know, I liked old Martin, but I'm happy as hell that he's gone. Come on to bed before I throw you over my shoulder and lug you off like a Sabine woman."

Hanging to the banister now, she closed her eyes and clenched her teeth. The knock at the door came dimly through to her, then more loudly, and she let go the banister, leaving damp prints. To speak to someone else for just a moment would be a relief; that is, someone who didn't know about Shane. Anyway, they might just be wanting water. That had happened before. She ran down the stairs and opened the door.

Peter Ruskin stood there, smiling expectantly through his ginger whiskers. His expression changed to uncertainty if not actual consternation, and he said rapidly, "Are we interrupting your work? Yes, we are. We'll go away." He whirled around and bumped into the girl behind him, and she cried out, "Ouch! You be careful, Peter Ruskin! You could give anybody cancer of the breast that way!"

"Oh, wait a minute, Peter," Alix said. "I'm sorry if I looked fierce. It's nothing to do with you. Is this your wife?"

"Yes, what's left of me." The girl ducked under his elbow and stood in front of him. She was short and chubby in a large pink sweatshirt and tight jeans, her brown hair in bangs and braids. "I'm Myra." She put out her hand and gripped Alix's. Her eyes were large and pale blue like aquamarines, with short lashes thick as fur. At this moment her eyes were worshipfully shining. "I saw your show at the Harcourt a year ago. I thought it was out of this world. Then we moved into town and I found out *you* lived here *too*—"

"Shut up, Myra," said Peter. "You talk too much. The only improvement over radio is no commercials. Seriously now, Miss Horne, if you think we've got a hell of a nerve just say so, and we'll go."

"Raving all the way home," said Alix. "I can hear you now. 'Who does she think she is?'"

"And he would too," said Myra with enthusiasm. "He gets very uptight about snubs, fancied or otherwise."

Peter said tensely, "Myra, do you want me to pull out yet another fingernail?"

"Come on in," said Alix. "I was just going to have a cup of coffee. I'm afraid I haven't any beer on hand, or anything."

"Coffee with Alexia Horne," said Myra, "is my idea of feeding on honeydew with Kubla Khan." Then she looked puzzled and said, "That sounded funny."

"I take it as a compliment," said Alix. "However undeserved." Peter looked exasperated and embarrassed.

"Don't be upset, Peter," his wife said kindly. "The great ones are always nice. Look, we've got two more with us. They're wandering around on the beach."

"Well, call them," urged Alix, with the large reckless gestures of despair. Peter shook his head. "They fought all the way out and they landed on the beach fighting. We're better off without them."

"Maybe they'll make up, now that they're alone," said Alix.

"It's not that kind of a fight," said Myra. "He's trying to, well I don't know what you used to call it but the kids call it 'making out,' and of course she thinks she has to put up an argument for the looks of things, but you know she's just dying to."

"I'm not only going to pull off your fingernails," said Peter, "but I'm going to bend every finger back until it cracks."

Myra giggled. "But Miss Horne must have met these compulsive Don Juans before. Not that he isn't really charming, with that adorable accent, and awfully talented too, not just in bed, but—" She blushed suddenly. "I do babble, don't I? At home they used to call me the Brook, after that poem. 'Men may come and men may go, but I go on forever.'"

Alix laughed. "Come out in the kitchen. I've been out all day and I'm famished."

As she led the way through the living room she knew they

were as eager as Karen to see everything at once, and she couldn't treat them as ten-year-olds. She walked rapidly ahead, hoping they'd take the hint.

"Oh, what a fabulous face!" Myra cried. "Oh, I love that man!"

Without looking around, Alix knew where Myra had come to a stop. She went on into the kitchen and Peter said, "Come on, Myra."

"But come see this marvelous portrait—" She stopped short as if Peter had clamped a hand across her mouth. The silence made the back of Alix's neck prickle. What was he mouthing ferociously at her? *That's the man, you nut, you imbecile.* Alix rummaged blindly in the cupboards for something to eat, and after what seemed like a long time Myra's voice said, meek and propitiating, "There's a wonderful display of perfect arrowheads here, Peter, and you know how crazy you are about Indian stuff. Did you ever see one with this purply-red color?"

He said as if between his teeth, "Come *on.*"

Alix put the teakettle on, and found a round tin of Scottish oat-and-cheese biscuits. She spread these on an earthenware plate to warm in the oven, opened a jar of Madge's currant jelly, and set out mugs. Myra gave her a bashful smile whenever she caught her eye, and then sighed deeply as if she couldn't contain herself. Peter picked up the sketchbook from the table and began looking through it. "Very nice," he murmured. "Very nice indeed. You can draw."

Alix resisted an impulse to snatch it from him. Still holding the sketchbook, he sat down where Jonas had sat that night. Myra had to look out all the windows first, talking about the view. She didn't need any responses from the others.

"Have you decided yet what you'll enter in the show?" Peter asked Alix.

"No. I haven't much here to choose from, that's the trouble."

"That self-portrait of you is great." Tactfully ignoring the other portrait.

"But it doesn't do you justice!" cried Myra, plumping herself down in a chair and staring intensely at Alix. "You're just too modest, Miss Horne."

Alix smiled as she measured instant coffee into the mugs. Madame President of Coven Number Five of the International Witches' Union, Shane called that one. "I'm rather fond of one I did of Ozzie down in his fishhouse," she said. "I may ask him to lend that. Tell me about your work, Peter. What's your thing?"

He became stern with unexpected self-consciousness. "Well, I don't dig holes and fill them with white paint and call them sculptures, or wrap up buildings, but you'd probably think what I do is just as far out."

"It really isn't," said Myra loyally. "I mean it *is*, but in such a marvelous meaningful way. All those other things are just stunts, you know. Now Peter uses color like Gauguin—"

"He uses color like Peter Ruskin." Peter glared at her. "I don't even *like* Gauguin's color."

"Maybe I shouldn't have brought it up," said Alix. "You're likely to go home with no fingernails at all, Myra."

"Oh, he talks up a storm but he's really sweet," said Myra comfortably. There was a loud knock on the front door, and Peter growled, "Oh, hell."

"Well, I told you not to ask them along, dear."

"I didn't ask them. There they were, hanging on like barnacles. I'd have had to scrape them off with a shovel to get rid of them."

"They sound delightful," said Alix. "Let them in, Peter." He gave her a defeated look and left the room. She whisked the sketchbook to the top of the refrigerator where it was almost invisible.

"Poor Peter," Myra mourned confidentially. "He hates to have anyone else in on this." She leaned across the table, hunching her shoulders up, and talked fast. "Miss Horne, I wish you'd come to dinner with us some night, and then Peter could show you his stuff, and we could have lots of nice arty talk, and we could put you up for the night." She sat back, bright red, and blew upward hard enough to flutter her bangs. "There, I said it. Peter will kill me."

"I won't tell him," said Alix, "but I can't promise anything. Not now. I've only been here a little while, so I'm not really here yet, if you know what I mean."

"Oh, I do know," Myra assured her. "But if you'll just not say *no* right off fast."

"I won't."

Myra in her pleasure looked younger than Karen. She hugged herself, then sat back in her chair as the others came in. "And young Peter's nearly two," she said loudly.

Alix played up. "You mean you're old enough to be a *mother?*" she asked, then turned a bright hostessy gaze on the others.

The girl's name was Judy Grant. With her dark hair falling like portieres from a center part and reaching to her elbows, her eyes peering out from heavy black fringes, her mouth done in large reckless strokes of brownish red, her loops of lightly rattling chains and amulets over an electric blue velveteen blouse, her broad hips in a tight casing of striped bell-bottom pants, she was a stereotype. They all looked alike, dressed alike, wore the same make-up—and she probably had long dangles hanging from her hidden ears like prisms from a chandelier; they all stood alike, and expressed presumably the same thoughts in the same accent with the same stresses, as if they had all been turned out by some Aldous Huxley factory in *Brave New World.*

The drawled "Hi" and remote nod were exactly in character —if one could use the word character at all, Alexia thought unkindly. Myra's cheeks turned almost winesap red, and she started to speak but instead stared angrily at Judy.

"And this is Soren Michaels," Peter said in a neutral tone. She thought for a moment he was going to kiss her hand. He didn't, but as he bent over there was the slightest suggestion— not the sound—of clicked heels; the little bow was slight, formal, and charmingly executed; blue eyes smiled into hers from a sunburned Nordic face, and in an accent exactly like Victor

Borge's he said, "Miss Horne. This pleasure has been entirely too long in coming."

"Thank you," said Alix. All we need now is for the orchestra to strike up "The Blue Danube" and we'll whirl off before the cameras, she thought. She extricated her hand from his and said, "I think something's burning."

There was a muffled snort from Myra, which she hastily muffled even more in a tissue. Beyond her Judy stared with tragic remoteness out across the field, the effect somewhat spoiled by all the hair. Of her profile only her nose showed; it had a peculiar bulge at the tip.

Alix took out the plate of oat-and-cheese cakes and put it on a trivet, and got out two more mugs. "What a wonderful day this is, eh?" said Soren. "A good sail, and that's one of the greatest delights of life to me, and at the end of it to meet this lady." He playfully rumpled Peter's head. "Did you have this planned all the time? You're a deep one. Very deep. Isn't he deep, Myra?"

Peter stared at his mug. Myra smiled up at Soren. "Deep as the ocean, to coin a phrase. That's why I married him. I knew there was a mystery behind those whiskers."

Judy sighed. "Come and sit down, Judy," Alix invited.

"I don't like instant coffee," said Judy remotely, "and neither does Soren, but he won't admit it. Haven't you any beer?"

"I can speak for myself, my girl," Soren said. "Sit down." He pulled out a chair. His gaze was pleasant, even twinkling, but as she met it there was a quiver of juvenile uncertainty in her face, and she sat down quickly in the chair, then reassumed her aloofness like a garment. "I'll have water, please," she said without looking at anyone.

"We need fresh water," Alix said. "Peter, would you take that empty pail and go to the well? It's right down there." She pointed, and he jumped up and went out. "I'm sorry I don't have beer," she said to Soren.

He lifted one hand. "Whatever I drink in Alexia Horne's kitchen will be the perfect thing."

"That's what I think too, Soren," Myra said. She beamed at

Alix. "See what I mean about the accent? Isn't it adorable?"

Soren said dryly, "It would never do for you to go to Denmark, Myra."

"Oh, I'm crazy about all kinds of accents," said Myra. "I almost married a boy just because he had the most beautiful Scotch one." She rolled her eyes to the ceiling. "Ooh, it sent me! That was the only thing about him that did," she added practically. "What are these?"

"They have a Scotch accent too. Oat-and-cheese biscuits. Judy?"

Judy sighed again. Was it because she'd finally refused Soren and was sorry, or because she had promised to give in and was sorry? Soren began talking to Alix; he was glib and amusing, and the accent was enjoyable even if the content of the conversation was negligible. Peter returned in a better humor, as if going to the well for her had re-established his claim on knowing her first. Determined to hold his ground, he seized the first break in the conversation to say, "Miss Horne, you get textures like nobody else since the Flemish painters. I feel that if I touched a child's cheek in one of your paintings, it would be warm. And there's one of yours where there's a ship in a greenish glass bottle—it looks as if anyone could pick the bottle off the canvas."

"Come on now, Peter, none of that fulsome flattery," said Alix. "Isn't that the sort of realism you really despise?"

"Who despises it?" said Soren, setting down his mug. "*I* don't. It gives me a good deal of artistic pleasure—*sensuous* pleasure, I should say."

"I never said I despised it," Peter was bristling. "It's not my thing, maybe because I can't do it, maybe because I wouldn't want to, I'm completely committed to what I'm doing. But that doesn't keep me from seeing that she's brought a high degree of creativity to her portraits. And what's more, she makes them tactile experiences."

"That's a perfect description, Peter," Myra said proudly. "Isn't it, Miss Horne?"

"Don't ask me," said Alix. "Thanks, Peter, but this is enough about my stuff. It's unfair, you know, you people discussing me when I've never seen your work."

"When can I give you a drink in my studio?" demanded Soren, leaning toward her, seeking with his eyes as if they were fingers. *I'm the sheik of Ar-a-by,* a nasal voice crooned annoyingly in her head. "Tomorrow? The next day? What about Sunday? I shall borrow a friend's runabout and come and get you myself, and bring you home."

"Oh, whose, Soren?" asked Myra with childish interest, and without looking at her he said, offhanded, "Nell Whitman's. . . . Well, what about it, Miss Horne? Please come."

Judy reached suddenly for a biscuit and began slathering it with jelly.

"She's promised to come to our house first, Soren, so don't try to weasel in ahead of us," Myra warned.

"My darling Myra," he said, smiling at her and touching her cheek. "I wouldn't dream of it. Next, then?" he said to Alix.

She said, "But I haven't even anything definite with the Ruskins." She was tired of them all suddenly, she felt badgered from all sides, and was aware of a sharp sympathy with Judy, who so obviously wanted to be elsewhere. When a knock came at the back door she was relieved, though she couldn't think who it would be. "Come in!" she called, and the door opened and Sidney bounced in, delighted to find all the people, and Jonas came in behind him carrying a clam roller.

He was grinning. Then he stopped short on the threshold, the expression wiped away. "I didn't know you had company," he said.

"Come in and meet them," said Alix. "Sidney's already in." Sidney was whirling between Peter and Myra in paroxysms of happiness as they talked to him. Soren was on his feet. Judy, like one who has finally returned to the bottle, was compulsively eating oat-and-cheese biscuits.

"I brought you some clams," Jonas said grumpily, putting the roller outside.

"Thank you! I haven't had any yet this year." It was like listening to a tape. "This is Jonas Hallowell, everybody, and that's Judy Grant over there, and Soren Michaels." Soren reached out for a hard manly handshake. "How do you do?"

Jonas murmured something.

"And the two with Sidney are the Ruskins, Peter and Myra." Peter got up to shake hands. "I've seen you around the Harbor a few times," he said.

"Likely," said Jonas. Myra said like an earnest child, "Hello, Mr. Hallowell."

"Hello." He turned to go, saying, "Come on, Sidney," and Alix said, "Don't hurry. Have some coffee with us."

"I can't stop," he said. "I work for a living." There was the slightest, but still perceptible, emphasis on the *I*.

He went out. When the door had shut behind him there was a short silence broken only by the sound of the spoon scraping the last of the currant jelly out of the jar; Judy was still eating. Then Soren said, "Well, we know what lazy wastrels we are, don't we?"

"He a friend of yours?" Peter asked Alix.

"A neighbor."

"Who does he think he is, anyway?" said Peter. "And what does he think *we* are? Playboys? Kids fingerpainting in nursery school? You're a painter—how's it happen he can speak to *you?* Christ, he's not paying our bills, he's—"

"Peter, watch your language," Myra said. Soren sat back, his arms folded, smiling broadly. "A square from Squaresville, eh? A true Philistine. A member of the Establishment, or what passes for the Establishment around here."

Myra said, "So what if he thinks painting is kid stuff? So does my father. So do a lot of decent kind people. That doesn't put them beyond the pale."

"He didn't have to be rude," Alix said. Now she was more tired than she'd been before he came.

Myra said, "He couldn't be any different. He was upset. He probably expected to find you alone . . . I liked him. He looked exactly like a Welsh terrier we used to have when I was a kid."

The men began to laugh and she protested, defending herself. "Well, he was a wonderful dog! He was brave and smart, and faithful to the end!"

"Tell me, Myra," said Soren, "do I make you think of a Great Dane?" He and Peter were off again, laughing immoderately; she was half-laughing herself while she sputtered, enjoying the attention. Judy looked bored to the point of anguish.

That's it! thought Alix. That was the association she couldn't understand. Jonas had the same bright tawny eye and cocky self-assurance as the small sandy mongrel terrier brought home from the Animal Rescue League for her birthday present when she was eight. She thought she had never loved her father so much as when he put Sandy into her arms. Sandy was her fearful joy; she went from peak to peak of the emotional range with him. Agony when he was lost, ecstasy when he returned, horror when he started fights with bigger dogs, rage when he chased cats. Looking at him in his basket at night, weary with his day and innocent in sleep, she swore to him that if anything ever happened to him she would die also; she couldn't imagine life without Sandy, she didn't want it.

My, you've been remarkably consistent through the years, Alexia, she mocked herself now. Still prepared to die for the loved one, even if right now you can't seem to find the time for it.

The sacrifice hadn't been called for in Sandy's case. To everyone's surprise he lived into a very active old age, and died peacefully in his sleep when she was away at college. He had outlived Alix's father. "If only everyone could have as good and as long a life as Sandy had," her mother had said wistfully.

"Miss Horne . . ." Someone was speaking to her. "Alexia Horne," said the accented voice, drawing the syllables out teasingly. Soren Michaels' face was close to hers. She could see the creases at the corner of his eyes and the lines raying out from the pupil through the blue iris. "Are you dreaming, Alexia Horne?" he asked her.

"Dreaming of peace and quiet," said Peter grumpily. "Why don't you get into her lap, Soren, and be really close?" He scraped back his chair and got up. Myra, pensive after her star turn, got up too, and began carrying dishes to the sink. Judy arose, scattering crumbs, and drifted rather than walked through the door into the living room.

Soren, ignoring Peter and smiling as if at some secret and humorous communication between him and Alix, sat back and took out his cigarettes. She said, "I'd forgotten I'm going to supper at the Goodwins' tonight. I must clean up first."

"You've been great to put up with us," said Peter. "I promise we won't make a habit of dropping in and interrupting your work."

"It's been a pleasure to have you," she said. "Sometimes it's necessary to be interrupted—though not too often," she added with a grin to show she was really a good sport. A brick, as her mother used to say.

Soren said, "Something tells me we're being dismissed." He got up, taller than any of them. "I look forward to that hour in my studio."

From the other room there came a tinkle of guitar chords. Myra said snippily, "I hope she doesn't start to sing. Joan Baez she isn't."

Without seeming to push, Alix got into the living room first. Judy sat on the arm of a chair with her hair streaming forward over the guitar. She looked up through elf-locks and said, "It's out of tune."

"Yes," said Alix. Her lips felt parched and tight. "But don't tune it, please. I'll do it myself." If she doesn't hang it up this instant I'll take it out of her hands, she thought. Unhurriedly Judy arose and hung the guitar back on the wall. "You play?" she said indifferently.

"Yes," said Alix, "but nothing you'd recognize."

"Come, Judy," said Soren, holding out his hand. For the first time life came into her face. She smiled slowly, cautiously, and looked faintly intelligent. She put her hand into his and they went out.

"You wouldn't believe it," Myra said, "but she's over twenty-one. Otherwise I'd be having a fit. She's a born victim for somebody like him."

"There's one brought down every hour," said Alix. She could hardly wait for them to be gone, and was afraid of showing it. Though why shouldn't she show it, so they'd never come again? But she could not do it, and besides, they had gotten her through an afternoon. She owed them something for that, if only courtesy.

She walked across the lawn with them to get them out of the house; William came to meet them and was a good topic of conversation for the Ruskins. It seemed that Judy, in addition to fancying herself a lyrical singer of protest songs, got interestingly hysterical if a cat approached her, and needed brandy and male consolation. This got them to the edge of the bank, and triumphantly Alix saw them push off the dinghy without Myra's reminding her again of dinner. She did call something when they were halfway out to the yawl, but Alix pretended she didn't hear what it was, waved vigorously, and went back to the house before they'd gotten out of the cove.

When she went back in with William, the place still seemed in an upheaval, like the beach after a flood tide had tossed everything around. Nothing was physically out of place, but the influences were there, foreign and jarring; she herself had a scattered feeling, as if she too had been tossed around and had lost her hold on something. "Oh my God, Shane!" The words broke from her in a groan. "No longer—no longer—"

William jumped up on a chair arm, then onto its back, and began craning his neck toward the mantel, his head weaving in the familiar preparation for leaping onto the forbidden shelf. Dully she watched him, waiting for the agony to recede and thinking, This time it won't, this time it will drown me.

William jumped, miscalculated, hung on with forepaws and

[1 2 9]

claws while his hindquarters scrabbled in space. She moved automatically to catch him and stood holding him under one arm, gazing at the line of points on the mantel under the portrait. Myra's voice repeated, tiny but very clear like a recording: *Did you ever see one with this purply-red color?*

What one in purply red? There was no point of that color. Shane had found chips of glassy, almost translucent, wine-red jasper, and had always been looking for a point or a knife of the same stone. But he had never found one.

The one on the mantel now, which she had never seen before, was not of jasper but of a rich plum-colored felsite. It was a graceful tapering point, side-notched, perfect, delicately fluted, the edges still as sharp as when it was new, several hundred years ago; it must have been buried all this time.

She put the cat down and touched the point with a finger. It felt warm, as if it had been in someone's pocket or hand. It lay off by itself, over near the pewter tankard from which Shane had ceremoniously drunk ale at least once a summer. Holding to the edge of the mantel with both hands she felt the room slowly tipping over. She shut her eyes against the motion and saw Shane crossing the room barefoot, wearing faded chinos and that sweatshirt; he carried his pipe in one hand and the point in the other. He put the point on the mantel, standing it up against the tankard, looked at it with a tender smile of satisfaction, then went away. Literally. She did not see him leave the room. He was simply not there any longer.

She opened her eyes. The room had stopped its sidewise tilt. William was digging his claws into upholstery somewhere. Two gulls flew past the windows, one in screaming pursuit of the other.

☙ CHAPTER 13 ☙

JONAS DIDN'T APPEAR at the Goodwins for broiled halibut, and Madge fretted. "He came by earlier and said he was off his feed," she said. "I hope he isn't coming down with something. If he is, he'll have to move right in here so we can look after him."

"He's not sick," Ozzie said. "He took off for the main a while back."

"Well, something's ailing him."

Sulking, Alix thought with neither malice nor complacency. He'd come with the clams, expecting acclaim, and found her already taken possession of. When she left for the Goodwins' she found the hod in the shady grass by the back doorstep, the clams white-shelled and clean on a bed of fresh rockweed. She would have to thank him; another of these entanglements, the spiderweb nuisances of human relations.

But she would not have to thank him tonight, and Ozzie and Madge made no demands on her. Madge had had company from the mainland that day too, a woman left at Beauty Cove while her husband went on out to set traps around the Pumpkin Shoal. She'd brought Madge enough news of the Harbor

Road to take her well through supper, and even Karen was sufficiently fascinated by Madge's dramatic delivery not to stare at Alix the whole time.

When she got home Alix went directly to the mantel. The point was still there. She took it upstairs with her and went to bed in her own room. She slept with the point in her hand, tucked under her pillow. When she woke up the eastern sky was the color of Malaga grapes, and Venus was shining into her eyes. She had lost the point and there was a moment of frantic groping until she found it again where it had slid from her relaxed hand. She put extra pillows behind her and lay watching the sky lighten, holding the point the whole time. William, who had remained independently downstairs all night, came up and sat on the foot of the bed, washing and purring.

Do I actually believe Shane brought this point? she asked. If he didn't, who did? He always wanted a red point. He never stopped looking.

But there was no real comfort in it. She wanted Shane himself; she was like the child who, when told that God was with him in the dark, wept that he wanted someone with a skin face.

Blast your eyes, Shane, for feeding on all that nauseating Daddy-dribble and being a sentimental idiot who couldn't resist the picture of himself walking down the aisle with his virgin (maybe) daughter on his arm, Cathleen watching with tears in her eyes. She was so far from being human that her eyes probably never got red and her nose never stuffed up. . . . *The blessed damozel leaned out from the gold bar of heaven.*

"You don't understand Cathleen," he'd said once. "It's not that she hates sex but that she doesn't need it. It's my soul she's worried about. She's in actual terror that I'll burn for adultery."

That's not what you said before, my boy. Love me, you said. Love me, I'm starved for it; she always looked at me as if I were a rapist, the licentious soldiery sweeping through and taking the women, and she was so damned submissive about it it

[132]

would turn your stomach. I swear she was play-acting some ravished saint.

This helpless, nonventable anger got Alix up, to William's pleasure, and he cut a few juvenile capers on the way downstairs. Letting him out, she again bleakly faced a perfect day. She shut the door on it and huddled over a cold stove. The point in her pocket meant nothing at all. She did not believe or disbelieve. She wanted Shane alive. Without him she wanted nothing of life, only to be out of it.

Voices out of her childhood, from her earliest time of remembering: *Don't waste food when so many people are starving. Don't mock a deformity. Don't envy. Don't wish ill.* It was never added, *Don't wish death when so many are dying and don't want to die,* but who would ever think it necessary to tell Alexia that? Green eyes, greedy gut, Eat all the world up, that was Alexia.

Karen was right, the black sink was in a shocking condition. She wouldn't want them casting long glances at her sink when they came in to find her, and saying, Poor thing, she really did go to pieces, didn't she?

Moving with the energy of a hurricane she brought in rain water and washed her face in its icy softness, then put more on to heat. She dressed, brushed her hair and fastened it back, made coffee and drank it. Then she washed yesterday's dishes, remembering unwillingly who had had each cup; she was unwilling because she didn't want them cluttering her up again even in reminiscence. Good God, what was in that lipstick of Judy's? Pure burnt sienna? She scrubbed with a scouring pad and scalded the mug twice.

When the dishes were washed, she scrubbed the counter and drainboard, then went to work on the sink. The scouring pad took off the thick rings of rust, then she scrubbed with crumpled newspapers till she had the iron smooth and dry.

She was rubbing in a thin coating of mineral oil when someone knocked at the back door. It was undoubtedly a masculine knock. "Come on in, Ozzie," she called. One thing about it now, a knock at six in the morning couldn't mean bad news about Shane.

Jonas came in. He looked repellently cheerful. He shoved his cap to the back of his head and stood against her door with his arms folded. "Come on," he said.

Yes, that was Sandy's eye, all right.

"Where?" she said blankly, oily bunches of newspaper in her hands.

"Never mind. Just get dressed for the water. You won't need anything except your sketchbook."

"I don't want to go anywhere," she said. His arrogance was almost laughable. "I don't like being taken by storm. Who do—"

"Who do you think I am? I'm a man who's running away from Karen. And if you've got an ounce of sense left you'll run away with me. She's up bright and early these mornings, making her rounds. If I'm not out to haul by daybreak, I have her at breakfast, and believe me, my girl, that's no way to start the day."

"The child obviously adores you. Don't be cruel."

"She's no child. She was born grown up. I get this feeling sometimes that she's a reincarnation of my mother, and some day she's going to say in my mother's identical voice, 'Now, Sonny, this isn't the way Mother brought you up.' "

"Did your mother *actually* call you Sonny?"

"She did, and it's probably the cause of all my troubles. Well, are you interested in my escape route or not?"

"Yes, I am," said Alix, dropping her cleaning papers into the wastebasket. "Because I can't stand the thought of Karen this morning either. And it makes me feel like a rat."

"Rat fink, they were saying when I left the continent."

"That'll do." She washed her hands and went up the back stairs. Now she could hardly wait to get away from the house and off the land, and as she put on warmer slacks and a jersey she kept looking nervously up the hill toward the woods for the first glimpse of Karen. I suppose we fascinate her because we're different, she thought uncomfortably. She's really just an ordinary kid. She went downstairs again, shoving her tin box into one hip pocket on the way and a small sketchbook into the other.

Jonas was sitting on her tall stool, smoking and looking out over the sea. "Fastest change I ever saw," he said.

"Panic can do it every time."

When she locked the door he said, "Do you always do that, way out here?"

"I never did before Karen. I may be slandering the child, but I think she prowls and pokes. Not that I blame her, I was a nosy one myself." She was talking too much, too fast. "But there are things that I don't want her to touch, that's all. I don't want anyone to touch them."

He didn't answer, and when she looked around he was already going past the corner of the house. She shrugged. If he didn't want answers he shouldn't ask questions. She lost the impetus that had hurried her back in the house, but at the thought of the day ahead she moved faster again to catch up with him.

The dory was nosed up onto the sand below the beach. "Safe," he commented as he pushed off. "That is, if the engine starts." Alix, up in the bow, looked apprehensively back at the land, positive the small figure would appear past the rose-bushes. Only genuine rat finks could go off leaving a child standing there to watch, and she wasn't sure how genuine she could be. She was surprised by the volume of her relief when the engine started and the dory swung in a wide circle and headed out of the cove.

They went northeastward past the yellow-gleaming eminence of the Head and up the bay. She couldn't help looking back, perfectly understanding Lot's wife. Tiree's woods breathed opalescent mists as the sun touched them; its rocks flashed like burnished metal above a sparkling riffle of surf. Land of Heart's Desire, Shane used to call the island when he had one of his Celtic moods; Tir-nan-og, Land of the Forever Young.

Her face seemed to be glazing into a mask, and she turned her head quickly away before Jonas could notice. But he was seemingly preoccupied with steering the dory through a rainbow spatter of buoys that meant a rich kelpy bottom for lobsters.

"Where are we going?" she called to him.

"You'll see."

"I'm too old for surprises."

"You're never too old."

He was right, she thought dryly, turning her face forward again. Still, she was glad she had come; motion was something. The boat seemed to rush gladly forward as if her bow were outstretched like the long neck of a Canada goose. The distant mainland was a band of melting pastels across shimmering water. The islands looked as insubstantial as clouds, reminding her of watercolors of the Romantic school, of dream cities rising from dream seas.

Occasionally water rolled toward them in satiny undulations, the dying wake of a lobster boat crossing their course. Sometimes the cries of medricks pierced the sound of the engine; one stood bravely on a nearby pot buoy as they passed.

After about a half-hour the course shifted more easterly, and then she knew where they were going. Griffin's Island. She had been there before. The weight of the knowledge dragged physically at her, and she kept her head down, pretending to watch over the side. The new island emerged from the dissolving lilac wreaths of morning fog and became corporeal rocks and spruce. A great blue heron took off from a tree as the dory moved along the shadowy west side. The water was dark olive-green with the reflection of the woods that grew thick and untouched down to the very edge of the rock. A cold, damp, resinous emanation came from them.

This approach was unfamiliar to her, and for a moment she hoped that she was wrong, that it was a different island. Then they came around a point, and she saw the long sand beach,

lavender-blue in the shade of the woods, and in the cove the remains of an old weir. She knew it was the same place. Though
she and Shane had landed on the southern side, they had come
to this cove in their explorations.

Just inside the point Jonas edged the dory in alongside a ter-
race of rock that made a natural wharf. Long ago someone had
driven a bolt into it to hold a painter, and he made the dory
fast there. "She'll be afloat at low water," he said.

"I can see you've been here before," she said, trying her
voice out.

"I head for here whenever I've got a spare day." He lifted a
half-bushel basket out of the stern, then looked at her again
with that sharp terrier glance; the faintest movement in the
leaves never got by Sandy. "Have *you* ever been here before?"

"No," she said.

"Good. I'd hate to think my grand gesture of apology was
wasted."

"Apology?" She was honestly taken aback.

"For sniping at your friends yesterday. Tact's not my strong
point, and as somebody once told me, there's no call to be so
damn proud of it."

Abruptly he started walking away with the basket. She followed him, saying, "I'd forgotten all about it. Anyway, they're
not my friends. I'd met Peter Ruskin before, but not the others. They just dropped in, uninvited. . . . However, the men are
working artists. You probably think that's a contradiction in
terms."

"Not necessarily," he said over his shoulder. "You're a working artist, aren't you?"

"Well, if I'm acceptable, why should your hackles rise"—a
good metaphor, that—"at the sight of a couple of males who
have the same profession?"

They reached the sand and he set down the basket and
turned around, pushing his hands into his pockets. He looked
tough and compact, and almost dapper in the fit of his slacks
and windbreaker. "It's that hair. Does it to me every time. He

must spend more time combing out his lovelocks and his goatee than he does painting. Draft card burners. Hippies. Protesters. Radicals. That's what I think of."

"Peter's been in the Navy, not that you deserve to know that," said Alix. "Condemning anybody just because his hair's long. I'm a kind of hippy, and I've always been a radical too, in one way or another. Haven't *you?*" She jabbed a finger at him, and he blinked and then grinned. "If you aren't forever objecting to something, if there isn't something either inside your life or outside it that you want to turn upside down, you're just a vegetable, and not a crisp fresh one but a rotten one. Right?"

"Right," he said. "If you put it that way. I'll go that far with you, I've been a thorn in a lot of hides during my lifetime. But I still don't like long hair except on my women. The Dane there—is he a painter too? He looked like a seafaring character."

"He's the Sheik of Araby," said Alix.

"Huh?"

"Didn't you ever hear that song?" She began to half-sing it. "He's looking for a tent to creep into. Anybody's, mine included."

Jonas burst into a yelp of surprised laughter. "Well, what about young Vampira, with the make-up an inch thick? She was gaffling down all the grub. She just run out of fresh blood?"

"I don't think she's as bad as she's painted," said Alix. "She was pretty nervous yesterday, speaking of tents and sheiks. What's a Scandinavian version of the 'Desert Song'? If he was a Finn he could sing, 'Come with me to my sauna,' but I don't know much about Denmark except that they have lots of butter and eggs. Oh, and those marvelous open-faced sandwiches with raw beef and herring, stuff like that. How's that for sexy?"

"That doesn't make me feel like a lecherous old bastard, just a hungry one."

They both laughed and began walking again below the woods. She felt almost jaunty with accomplishment. If she could keep on this way she'd do all right. He said, "My girl's the one with the bangs and the pink cheeks."

"She liked you too," she said so nicely it sounded even suspicious to herself, but Jonas was squinting up at the dense hedge of rosebushes and bay between the sand and the spruces. Blackberry vines wound through the thicket, binding it even more tightly together.

"You should have brought your sword," said Alix, "and slashed your way through, and for your reward you'd find the Sleeping Beauty."

"No, thanks!" he said emphatically. "That's the last prize I want to find. There's a break along here. I made it last time with a machete. Here."

They climbed up into the spruce wood. Only slivers and wisps of sun could penetrate the thick ceiling of dead branches and green tops, and very few plants pushed up through the muffling carpet of old spills. In midsummer there had been spatterings of toadstools and mushrooms, vermilion, rose madder, chrome yellow, violet-colored, ivory. Now thrushes called secretively, *Whit! Whit!* through the russet duskiness, but in midsummer many of the birds had been silent because it was the time of raising the young. There had been crickets, though. She was glad there was no such drowsy trilling today.

Jonas led the way up through the woods from ledge to ledge. More sun began to get through and there was finally light ahead, a breath of dry warmth, the sound of more birds. Suddenly Jonas, without speaking, moved aside and she stood in the mouth of the branchy tunnel and looked up at the house.

She knew he expected her to be surprised. It was not hard to act speechless at first. She and Shane had planned to come back here this year and bring sleeping bags. It was all wrong for her to be here with Jonas. It was incredible, a nightmare, she would wake up at home or go mad. The protest almost burst past her lips. Instead she heard an almost-unrecognizable voice saying, "What a place! A *mansion!* And way out here!"

Its roofline against the sky presented at first a medieval cluster of turrets and chimneys; after the first shock to the delighted eye it became the sumptuous "cottage" of seventy-five
years ago or more, with tower rooms, dormers, and glassed-in
bays. A broad veranda ran halfway around it, and smaller
porches and balconied nooks were tucked in wherever it was
possible to tuck one.

The chimneys wore gold lichens, and some slates were gone
from the roof. A few windows were boarded up, but most had
remained miraculously unbroken. Where there had once been
a formal garden, a kitchen garden, a tennis court, a lawn, the
woods had begun to move in. The smaller outbuildings were
overgrown with bittersweet and blackberry vines; the barn sat
in a tropical luxuriance of greenery.

"Who does it belong to?" she asked. "And why don't they
live here?" She sounded like the least talented member of the
Eighth Grade Dramatic Society, but Jonas, still staring at the
house, answered out of some preoccupation of his own.

"Family named Marston. The old man made a fortune in
shipping, but he hated high society and wouldn't go near Bar
Harbor when everybody else was discovering it. He bought this
island for about two hundred dollars, and built his castle on it.
It was quite an accomplishment in its day."

"It is now, when it's just a ghost," she said. "What happened? No heirs, or did they all rush to Bar Harbor the minute
he died?"

"The son died in World War I. The daughters married out
of the state. Some of them might have come back now and then
when they were still young, but that was a long time ago. Right
after World War II a couple came here and tried to make a go
of it, but they didn't stay a year. I don't know anything more
than that. The family used Port Edwards as their mainland
harbor, got their help and their caretakers from around there
and so forth."

"But if they still own the place, maybe somebody has hopes

of coming back here. There may be youngsters growing up who dream of this island in Maine."

"They'd better come quick, while the house is still in good shape. It's time and neglect that have done what damage there is. It hasn't been vandalized yet, but any day now the plague can strike." He said very softly, "God, I wish it was mine. There's enough here to keep a man busy for the rest of his days. I'd fix up the house and keep a few sheep, some hens, fish some lobster traps around the island, maybe even put the old weir back into shape." He became silent, then roused himself to add, "Have a garden," and subsided again.

" 'Nine bean rows,' " said Alix, " 'and a hive for the honey bee.' "

"I'm not that crazy about beans, but I kept bees once for my blueberries . . . was that a quote?"

"From 'The Lake Isle of Innisfree,' do you know it?"

"No, but it sounds fitting to the occasion, as the feller says. How's it go?"

She shook her head. "I'll have to look it up," she lied. The words had sprung out only because Shane had said, on his first sight of the house, almost the same thing that Jonas had said. Then later, as they half-drowsed in the warm silence listening to the crickets, he had sleepily tried to remember the poem.

She reached for her sketchbook, saying, "I must get this exactly as it looks from here." It seemed to her that she was gabbling; she always felt self-conscious and a show-off talking about her work except to other painters. But as she sat down on a ledge and flipped open the sketchbook Jonas looked down at her with a kindly expression. "Well, I'll leave you to it."

When she looked up again he was almost to the house along the winding trail among juniper and bay. The next time he had disappeared. The very sunshine took on a different quality. She let her breath go and put the back of her hand to her wet forehead. Then, willing the hand to steadiness, she began to sketch again.

When she had finished with the house, she made notes of
colors; there was a particular iridescence of the slate roof when
the sun first struck the wet places, and there was a deep violet
shadow on the western side in which the windows glinted like
pools among ledges at night.

She got up, stretched, and went up the trail Jonas had taken.
Now, as if the sketch were an alcoholic's first drink of the day,
she began to see things everywhere. The sad tilt of the weathercock on the barn. A swallow lighting on it. One apple tree
standing out in full sunshine against the chiaroscuro jungle behind it, arthritically twisted, scaly, woodpecker-drilled, scanty-
leaved; yet bearing along every dark limb, even to the smallest
twiggy ends, nosegays of pink and white. It was so quiet, except
for birds, that the bees were audible. *The bee-loud glade.*
Jonas once kept bees. It gave him another dimension; it trans-
ported her to a summer at Nahant when she was twelve and
had read rapturously through her grandmother's collection of
Gene Stratton Porter. *The Keeper of the Bees.*

Was it true that you had to tell the bees if someone in the
family died? Whittier's poem "Telling the Bees" had always
inexplicably moved her mother; she would often start to recite
it at Alexia's request but never finished.

I wish I knew now. I wish I had remembered to ask her.

She had a lost feeling, thinking of all she didn't know about
her parents, and now would never know. Angrily she rammed
her sketchbook back in her pocket. Why the notes about the
purple shadow and the iridescent shingles? She'd never paint
the picture she had in her mind. She was only holding a pose
because Jonas expected her to act like an artist, and if she kept
busy sketching he wouldn't try to talk to her.

Then in the next instant she had come into that deep dark
shadow and was looking at something else, and groping for her
sketchbook again without taking her eyes from the scene.

The way to the shore south of the house was a long slope of
lichened gray ledge half covered by the flat spreading rosettes

of juniper; they had kept anything else from getting a foothold in the rare pockets of earth, and so had kept the view open. She and Shane had landed at the old stone wharf at the foot of the field and had come up to the house that way.

Now she went among bay and wild roses to the front steps of the veranda. Some child on a picnic here last year had left a line of mussel and sea urchin shells on one step. Winter had spared it. She made a drawing, called it "Last Summer," but when she printed the words their poignance ran her through, and she got up quickly, wondering where Jonas had got to. It seemed as if he had been gone for a long time. What about the old wells? Her heart began to beat very fast, and she was suffocatingly warm. She threw down her parka and sweater and ran down the steps on the east side and followed a path to the back of the house.

When she heard him whistling and hammering from behind a screen of vines growing up over a back porch, her relief annoyed her. At home on Tiree she was angered when he appeared on the scene, and on this alien island she was worried when he failed to appear. It was almost as if he knew it and was amused.

He was nailing boards over a broken window. He looked around at her with a cheerful, mischievous expression and finished his job, whistling all the time.

She sat on the railing watching him. When he turned around with a self-satisfied smile, she said, "You didn't just happen to have that hammer with you, did you?"

"No, there are still a few tools here and in pretty good shape too, except for rust. I was up here a few weeks ago and cleaned them up and put them away in a chest out there." He started toward the nearest shed. "You don't very often find a broken window. The island's too far out for kids to run all over it." He said with a quick twinkling grin over his shoulder, "It's a great place for lovers."

She stayed where she was, watching him go. His whistle was like a bright thread trailing in air behind him. She was experiencing again that double-exposure sensation she'd known on the wharf at Tiree. Jonas walking away along the overgrown track, he and the whistle growing smaller, and Shane and herself coming here as lovers. It became a triple exposure as the red point entered it. She had been trying all morning to keep the point out of her thinking, as if when she came to it fresh again some revelation must be automatically forthcoming. But it came now as if by the spear for which it had been intended, and with it her—hallucination, was it?—of Shane crossing the room and putting it on the mantel.

❦ CHAPTER 14 ❦

SUDDENLY JONAS crashed through to her.

"You're milk-white! Hey, you aren't going to pass out, are you?"

"This fish-belly color goes with red hair," she snapped back at him. "I never passed out in my life."

"Is that so?" It was Sandy again, spoiling for a fight. "Well, this morning you weren't that color. Damn funny you lost your tan all at once."

"I'm hungry," she said loudly. "I never had any breakfast. I'm dying by inches."

"And you look it. Okay, let's go around and see how well I did in Emery's gourmet food department. That's the section over behind the rubber boots and outboard oil."

They sat on the front steps in the sun and drank strong black coffee, ate old-fashioned Vermont Cheddar sliced off a huge wedge, homemade bread, Norwegian sardines, little dill pickles. "When did you whip all this up?" she asked.

"Yesterday afternoon, after my star performance in your kitchen. You want this heel?"

"That one or the other one. I can't possibly let you have

both. . . . You mean you had this trip planned then? So that's why you skipped supper with the Goodwins."

"Well, hell, I had to do something to redeem myself."

"I have to admit you've done it magnificently. Is there another can of sardines?"

"I like to see a woman eat," he said, chivalrously opening the can for her.

"I really was starved, you know, and when I get hungry I feel terrible. It's probably something to do with my metabolism."

"Ayuh," he said. He filled his pipe and settled his back against a post, his legs stretched out before him, ankles crossed. "Can I see what you did this morning, or is that like asking a lobsterman how he did today? *Verboten?*"

She fished the sketchbook out with two fingers so as not to get sardine oil on it and shoved it across to him. "They're just working sketches, you understand."

"Mm." He looked seriously at the pages. "A year or so ago I'd like to have had you for a draughtsman. They seem pretty perfect to me, each in itself. But why not a camera, if you want something to go by later?"

"Because the photographs would be bound to have their own atmosphere, and that would wipe out or at least confuse what I wanted to remember. See, I want to get more into a painting than just lines, shapes, and so forth. There's the feeling, the whole thing you want to convey—" She was waving her hands around as if trying to catch the impossible in them. "I mean, I have an emotional reaction and I want the viewer to have one too, though it may not be the same as mine."

He nodded. "It hits you. Sometimes worse than *hits*. Stabs. Makes you think of something, maybe something absolutely different. That what you mean?"

"That's it," she said. "Well, in the working sketches, if I'm lucky, I can almost imprint that atmosphere, that special quality, on my brain. You keep looking at it, soaking it in, while you're drawing. You find out how this line goes, that curve, this shadow. It's the next best thing to feeling everything with your hands. Well, you ought to know. You're a creator."

"Makes me sound like God."

"I didn't capitalize it . . . more coffee?" He nodded and she poured some into his cup and slid it toward him. "Anyway, what it all boils down to is that if I snapped photographs, afterwards I'd just be copying them. This way I make the house, that weathercock, those shells, my own."

He nodded again, and went back to the first sketch of the house. "When you're through with these, will you sell me this one?"

"You can have it," she said. "And the others too. It'll be small enough pay for bringing me here. I wanted to be away from the house today, even away from Tiree."

He looked hard at her for a moment, his eyes narrow and bright in their creases. Then he said diffidently, "I'm sorry about your trouble. From what Madge and Ozzie say, he was one hell of a guy . . . but the way I've been acting you wouldn't think I had much feeling, I guess."

"I don't expect people to act as if they're at a wake when they come where I am." It helped to be disdainful of the sympathy that could destroy. "Anyway, you've got it said, so that's over with. Forget it." *Alexia, your manners,* a soundless voice breathed horror. She said after a moment, "But thank you. And I'm sorry that you've got troubles, whatever they are."

"Didn't Madge tell you? Come on, sure she did."

"I guess so, but I wasn't listening."

He laughed. "That's the best way to hear about other people's troubles. Think of something else. Anyway, it stinks." He looked away from her out at the water. "Marriage breaking up after twenty years. No kids—I used to be sorry about that, but I'm glad now. Nobody else to be hurt but somebody old enough to take it."

"They might have made a difference," she said, thinking, It would have to me, now.

"Maybe. I used to think so. Here, have some dessert." He

tore open the remaining package in the basket and laid it between them: dark red cherries, lacquer-bright.

"They're too beautiful to eat," she said, and ate one. Expertly she spat the pit a long distance out into the tall grass.

"Hey!" he said. "You're pretty good."

"I can whistle on two fingers too," she said modestly. "I've
got all kinds of gifts."

"God, you're too talented to be true." He got up. "I'm going
around back again. There's something I want to steal."

"Now I'm glad we ran out on Karen. That's a terrible example to set a child."

"Not Karen. When I don't think she's my mother I think
she's a born criminal."

"We're carrying this too far," she protested. "It's cruel. She's
nothing more than an unlucky little kid."

"You're just salving your conscience because you ran out on
her, as you call it." He stood looking down at her.

"No, I'm being objective, the way I can't be when she's
around where I am. She's unlucky because she's a kid adults
can't fall for, and probably other kids. At least I can't see her
having giggly secrets with other little girls. She's a loner, and
not from choice." He sighed, and she said, "All right, I'm
through preaching. What are you going to steal?"

"There's an old block plane in the workshop that I covet
every time I come here. Today when I saw nobody'd stolen it
yet I decided it was for me. It wouldn't mean much to you," he
said, turning away, "but for me, every time I see it left there
it's like seeing an abandoned animal."

"Then you should take it," she said emphatically, "and I
wouldn't call it stealing."

"Thanks for the blessing. But after all this discussion I've got
so oversensitive I'll probably send five dollars to the heirs."

"They don't deserve it. Give it to your favorite charity."

"But that's myself," he said. He laughed and went away
around the house. She tidied up the remains of the lunch, leaving the cherries out, putting the sardine cans and used paper

napkins into a bag by themselves. Then she went into the house by the front door. Its massive oak dignity was sadly weathered now, but it swung easily open and she wondered if Jonas had oiled the latch and hinges when he oiled the tools. There was something touching about his tenderness for these things, and when he said an abandoned tool made him think of an abandoned animal she had felt a pain as if she had been forced to feel something else besides her own woe.

The big dusty rooms echoed in their emptiness. Most of them were dominated by imposing fireplaces, in which many a picnic fire had been built when rain took the picnickers by surprise. Some had been untidy, and last year the place had been cluttered with refuse. This year the place looked considerably cleaner. Jonas again? She imagined him moving contentedly around the house, all alone on the island, whistling, patching, cleaning up.

He was bitter about his spoiled marriage and for the first time she wondered how deeply he had been in love—how capable he was of complete commitment, or if that were a purely female phenomenon. And was it worse to try to make over your life knowing the lover was still alive than knowing he was dead? Perhaps death wasn't the ultimate catastrophe in a love affair, married or not. Rejection was, departure, the turned back; the beginning of a new life for one and for the other the tortures of loneliness and jealousy.

I don't believe I could have endured that any better than I can endure this, she thought, going slowly up the stairs toward the open door of a room she remembered. So it all comes to the same in the end, for me, anyway.

She walked into the tower room where she and Shane had made love with the rain beating on the roof, blowing past the windows propped open with sticks, splashing and gurgling in the gutters. The air had been tropically warm, scented with soaked grass, juniper, the woods, and an ivory and gold wild honeysuckle that wreathed exotically everywhere. They had laughed a lot that day, making idiotic jokes and bad puns. Now through the loud singing of the spring birds it seemed to her she could hear the midsummer rain falling and see the blanket on the floor, not the scatter of mildewed old books that someone had pawed out of the bookshelf and left lying around. Automatically she knelt to pick them up and put them back. She had one of those flashes of incredulity that still ambushed her now and then. Shane couldn't be dead. Then she heard Jonas whistling on his way up the back stairs and she knew that Shane could be dead, that he *was* dead.

She realized she'd been hoping for some sign of Shane's presence here with her, only she'd kept it secret even from herself. Blindly she was turning damp-stiffened pages when Jonas came to the door.

"Found something *you* can steal?"

She shook her head without looking at him and put a mouldy *Penrod* back on the shelf. Shane had been delighted to find all of Booth Tarkington here.

"Good," Jonas said. "I thought maybe I'd corrupted you."

"That was done long ago."

"Don't disillusion me. I'd like to think there's some innocence left in the world."

"Madge," she said, and he nodded.

"I guess you're right. When she comes up against something bad she just can't understand how people can be that way, and then she forgets it with the next bird or flower she sees, or the next perfect cake she bakes."

"Or the next pleasant person she meets. All Madge's realities are the good things." She knelt on the window seat, looking out over the slope of pale ledge and silvery-green juniper toward the sea.

He came and sat down near her and looked out too. "Of course the life she lives pretty well guarantees her peace of mind, as long as she and Ozzie are all right, and her kids. She doesn't have to be in contact with the real grinding, squalid, killing kind of human misery. Not that I want her to be," he said, looking earnestly into Alix's face. "You understand that. I think it would kill her. She could never get hardened to it, she'd go crazy trying to mother everything and everybody at once."

Alix nodded. "The only trouble is, when something *does* get in—" She couldn't finish for thinking of Shane and Ozzie, but Jonas said at once, "Yes. She's worrying about Thelma now. Makes me mad as hell. Somebody ought to shake the teeth out of that girl. How well do you know her?"

"Not well at all. She's very pretty and lively, I know. I've seen her a few times when she came for a visit when Karen was a baby, but now she comes in the fall, when her husband goes hunting. I know Kenneth better, because he comes with his family for a couple of weeks every summer."

"Ken's all right," he said. "Solid." A pair of barn swallows banked by the windows and he smiled. "I like swallows," he said.

"What about Thelma?" He'd brought it up; she had no intention of letting him slide away. "And what did Karen have that caused her to lose the rest of her school year?" And when is she going home? she would have added, but Jonas couldn't tell her that.

"I don't think Karen's been very sick," he said. "Oh, pneumonia, some virus, something like that, but she wasn't acting very frail when her mother brought her and dumped her. No, she's inconvenient, that's the trouble. I think she's been appearing around corners when she's supposed to be in bed. Einar works at night."

"Oh, good God," said Alix in disgust, standing up. "I hope you're wrong."

"So do I. But it's not just my troubles and yours that bug Madge. Ozzie's not too happy either. . . . Thelma's not a bad kid but she likes excitement. She's romantic too, and that can raise hell with a marriage."

She wanted to ask him if it had raised hell with his. But she was tired of everything all at once, the last few hours seemed infinitely wearying. She stood aimlessly in the room, lacking the impetus to get out, to do anything, wishing that something would strike her dead where she stood if she could not manage to do it for herself.

Jonas looked around at her and got up too. She saw a change in his face but the alarm-reflex was too deep and too sluggish for her to escape before he could speak.

"You've been here before," he said bluntly. "You came here with him, didn't you?"

It was like being accused of a crime. She could hardly meet his eyes. "How do you know that? What makes you so sure?"

He let out a harsh single bark of laughter. "Not by reading your mind, don't worry. In the back part of your sketchbook. You brought the same one with you last time, and dated the sketches."

"Then you knew at lunch," she said, "but you didn't say so. You're quite an actor."

"No, I didn't know till a few minutes ago. You left the book on the porch with the basket. I wanted to look at that drawing again, the one I want. I started at the wrong end." His grin was quite savage. "Well, it's like eavesdropping. Listeners never hear good of themselves."

"It's *nothing* like!" she objected, astonished at his temper. "Why are you so mad?"

"Because you thought you had to lie to me. I was a kid whose feelings had to be saved." His eyes were fiery.

"I didn't think I *had* to *lie* to you," she said, spacing the words with contemptuous emphasis. "I simply—"

A door slammed shut somewhere. "We'd better pick up and go," he said curtly. "It's airing up." He walked out of the room. By the time she reached the balustraded stairwell he was almost at the foot. She followed. At least his illogical outburst had a therapeutic value; she was no longer too enervated to move, and her mind raced from one start to another. *Now listen here ... Now just a minute ... What gives you the right ... Look, neither of us is a child ...*

He was going out the front door, very stiff and square in the shoulders. She sat on the next to the bottom step and watched him pick up the basket without a glance back at the hall. She wanted to laugh mockingly aloud and cry at him, "But this is *incredible!* A grown man taking off in a tantrum about *nothing!*"

Suddenly he straightened up and half-turned his head as if he were listening. For her? She could not bring herself to hurry along or even to call accommodatingly that she was on the way. He looked springily poised there on the steps, like an animal sniffing the wind; the dark blue mass of the spruces beyond made him stand out as if outlined with light, and his profile looked clean, sharp, and young against the dark background.

"Listening" would be a good title. Or "The Listener." For what? She caught herself in disgust for having gone instinctively to painting.

She had got up to go when she heard a shout from out of sight, and realized he had not been listening for her at all. A girl appeared running past the spruces from the field, twisting to look back, her long light hair flying out around her head. She let out an unmusical screech which was answered by a male guffaw; she cried unconvincing threats and a youth broke out past the spruces and made a flying tackle in her direction but got only a fleeting handhold on her as she sprinted laughing for the house. In the thin May sunshine and against the wild setting they were nymph and young satyr. His tight trousers and her flowered bell-bottoms rather detracted from the scene, which would have been really charming, Alix reflected, if they had been nude.

Oh well, give them a little time and some solitude, and they will be, she thought.

At the sight of Jonas on the steps the girl stopped with a squawk like a gull's, and the boy crashed into her. His triumphant male outcry was choked off. They huddled together, staring with widened eyes at Jonas and at Alix as she came out behind him. The girl picked apprehensively at her lips. The boy gave the sidewise jerk and toss of the head that had become the common tic of long-haired boys. He said loudly, "What are *they* doing here, for Chrissake?"

"We're not playing hookey, for Chrissake," Jonas said ferociously. The girl flung herself at the boy, clawing at his shirt.

"You *told* me," she whimpered. "You said one more time would be all right, they'd never know, but honest to God, if they find out about the notes I'll be *expelled*—my mother will *kill* me—"

"Relax," said Alix coldly. "We don't know who you are, where you came from, or where your school is. And we couldn't care less." She went past Jonas down the steps. The boy's face was hard and sour in the page-boy frame of dark hair, innocence gone rotten; a girl was to screw or to lay, not to fall in love with. Alix said to the girl, "Not to spoil your fun, but I'd remember that 'one more time' bit. You can't go on forging notes forever."

She went around the corner of the house where now sunshine had driven away the deep sharp violet shadow of morning. Jonas came behind her. "So long, Dad!" the boy called, and then with the same volume, "Jesus, wouldn't you think at that age they'd be past it?"

The girl hissed something at him and he hooted. Alix looked around at Jonas' set face.

"Devout chap, isn't he?" she said. "Prays constantly."

"Little bastard," said Jonas. Then the severity broke up. "I suppose we should be flattered. He sounded surprised."

"He did, didn't he? Over thirty is over the hill, you know. When they restructure society, we'll be shot."

"From them I'll go without a struggle," said Jonas.

She laughed. "I asked someone once if he had the courage of his convictions and would honorably shoot himself on his thirtieth birthday. He assured me that the new bunch was going to be far different at thirty from us leftovers. What tires my patience is the complete lack of humor."

"Do you think those two have anything on their minds about the future of the human race besides how not to add to it?"

"Well, I think she's a little worried about those forged notes."

"They both need their bottoms warmed." He made a gesture for her to go ahead into the woods.

"Wait a minute," she said. "Jonas, I did lie to you because I didn't want to spoil your surprise—" He flushed and started to speak, but she shook her head. "And because I wanted to make believe, if I could, that I'd never been here before." She talked fast so that no weakness could have time to get into her voice. "I was grateful to be gotten away from the house today and from the island. Everything there is just saturated with—" This time she shook her head at herself in frustration, and then turned around and walked on down into the woods.

He didn't say anything until they came out to the beach.

"All I do is apologize," he said in a bemused voice, "and it's always my fault too. I know that . . . I ought to. It's my biography."

"You don't have to apologize. You had a right to get mad at what looked like a kid trick. A silly little unnecessary fib that made you feel foolish. I've felt the same way. Got into a fury about it, in fact."

"Don't be so cussed sweet and womanly, you make me feel even more foolish. Look, I'm sorry. Okay?"

"*Okay!*" she said, mimicking the jerk of his chin.

❧ CHAPTER 15 ❧

As soon as she got into her house she ran up the back stairs, ignoring the hungry cat, and looked at the point. When she saw it lying just as she had left it, she had an indefinable reaction, as if she had been hoping or fearing that the point had been moved, and was now suffering from anticlimax. *Shane, you had a chance*, she thought irritably, and then with remorse, *It's because I don't believe enough.*

She didn't go to the mainland with the Goodwins on the weekly trip for mail, groceries, and to sell Ozzie's lobsters. Madge could collect the parcel of books for her. She gave Madge also two neatly lettered notices advertising the catboat *Golden-Eye* for sale. One was to go on the bulletin board at Emery's, and the other in Bert's office on the wharf. Her name wasn't mentioned. Interested parties could view the boat at Ozzie Goodwin's, and talk business with him.

The weekly trip had been fun once, in what now seemed a previous incarnation with a half-dozen other existences layered cloudily between then and now. Now it simply meant that when the others had gone she would have a chance to be entirely alone on the island for a few hours. There would be the blessed certainty that Karen wasn't about to appear under her elbow. Jonas would be absent too. He was going in with the Goodwins and then driving down to Rockland on business.

"It's to see his lawyer, I think," Madge said in a hushed, tragic voice. "He didn't say so. Probably couldn't make himself talk about it. He's lost his business too, you know, and he started it from scratch. It's a shame."

"Bankruptcy?" Alix asked.

"Oh, no!" Madge said in horror. "He'd never lose it *that* way! *She* gets it. She gets everything."

"Good Lord," said Alix, more because Madge expected a shocked reaction than because she was really shocked. Losing a wife and a business through divorce wasn't the ultimate tragedy.

She'd found Jonas likable on the Griffin's Island trip, but when she was away from him her original irritation always returned. She realized her own prejudices, that no man could ever possibly compare with Shane. But even considered objectively Jonas seemed to have an extra capacity to annoy, an ebullient and overriding presumption that she didn't know what was good for her.

She made a clam chowder from the clams Jonas had brought, and invited the Goodwins to supper that night. They'd bought Karen a notebook and a package of ballpoint pens at Emery's, and she sat crosslegged on the rug before the fireplace, shoulders hunched protectively over the notebook, and wrote in it all the time she was there. What is she writing? Alix wondered. Isn't anyone curious but me? Maybe she's secretly a genius and is writing a novel. Maybe she's writing about *us*. A chilling proposition.

William, who always lay before the fireplace when there was a blaze in it, was there now, warily facing Karen. He gave the impression that if anyone were to be driven out in a contest, it wouldn't be William. Sidney, worn out by a rapturous afternoon of socializing with the Harbor dogs and having at least one fight, lay under the kitchen stove. Ozzie read his newspaper, and Madge gave the news; there always seemed such an incredible amount of it for a small place.

Meanwhile the parcel of books sat unopened on the study floor. Whenever Alix glanced in at it, which she couldn't help doing quite often, she had a tightening and prickling along her nape and up onto her scalp. Relax, she advised herself cynically. You'll find nothing but a puddle of sentimental slush that'll turn your stomach, or a lot of wishful thinking that you can't possibly buy. There's no magic bottle in that package out of which Shane will emerge like a genie.

The Goodwins left at dusk. She walked down to the wharf with them and after they left she sat there on a lobster crate, with William purring and padding invisibly all around, until she could hear the engine no longer. Far off there was the exciting and excited clamor of gulls over herring, and a lighted sardine carrier was heading north with a muted throbbing of diesel engines.

The house when she returned to it seemed to have been freshly emptied by some new devastation. She had almost gotten used to the emptiness, or at least numbed to it; now, after anyone else had just been here, the return of solitude had the impact of sudden deafness.

She put more wood in the fireplace and sat down on the hearthrug to read a letter from Dodie, who had taken her own advice and was about to go on a Scandinavian tour. "Are you sure you won't come too?" she asked. "Jack doesn't care, in fact he thinks it would be great for me to have you along to go poking around in all the castles and museums with and so forth, so he can sit all day in a sidewalk café and drink beer, and watch the blond beauties go by. We'd have fun, Alix, I promise you."

Why did people think you stayed the same underneath, that these things were simply storms whipping up the surface and never touching the depths? Maybe some human beings did have a core of stability and integrity that nothing could touch; they grew up in foul or vicious surroundings, they survived gigantic natural catastrophes or concentration camps, and yet they remained sweet and whole. They were the chosen ones.

But I'm not one of them, she thought. I just haven't got it, either as an artist or a person. Nothing comes from *me;* I have lived from *others.* I give the impression of knowing exactly what I want, where I am, and who I am. But it's completely false. Facts is facts, old girl.

She got up and went into the study, took a knife from the desk drawer and cut the string of the parcel, chose the bishop's book from the collection, and carried it up to bed with her.

Now there was a hiatus in her affairs. The books possessed all her attention. She fell asleep with one in her hands at night, and read while she ate her breakfast. She read lying on the lawn in the sun, down on the shore, up in the Tangle where the young ferns were knee-high and shimmered delicately like water. She read deep in the spruce woods. If the weather kept her in, she read with her feet on the stove hearth, or she lay on the sofa by the fireplace.

Occasionally, lifting her eyes to rest them by gazing off, she found Karen watching her. It could happen either indoors or out. Sometimes she felt the flick on a raw nerve, but often she was too bemused.

"Do you want something, Karen?" she would ask indifferently from this new distance. If Karen silently shook her head, Alix would say, "Then you'd better go." And she would return to her reading.

When she looked around again the child would be gone. Finding herself alone again after one such visitation, she lay on her back and watched crows pursuing a raven. Far above this traffic and that of the swallows there were the great slow-swinging circles of a bald eagle from the eyrie on Drummond's Island up the bay. She thought of what she had been reading. For the man there had been the stunning release and the assurance of the boy's presence. For the woman, the sudden waves of euphoria as if her daughter were in the room with her and they were laughing together.

For me, she thought, there was the feeling that night that someone was in the house. But it came to nothing. Then the Viking. Then the books and the tiki moved. Then the point. But no joyous conviction with any of it. These people were happy about it. They accepted. Yet they are intelligent and well-educated; they are intellectuals. So was Shane, and he had not rejected the proposition that contact was possible, even though he'd had no personal experiences. Therefore, she tried to reason in a bloodless way, as if the whole matter had no intimacy for her, Shane would logically attempt to communicate with her.

And if that was so—and how else could she explain Thorvald moved out into the open, the shifting of objects on the chest of drawers, the red point?—she could not go yet, not until she found out what he was trying to say to her. Ache with loneliness, be pierced with every sound and scent, but *wait*. Was that the message?

If there was a message, the skeptic answered every time. It came like a cold drench, and she would leave the Tangle, the lawn, the warm rocks, or get up groaning and stretching from the couch, and find something strenuous to do.

But in a few hours she would be back at her reading. Sometimes there would be a flash of revelation when she was surprised by joy like Wordsworth in the sonnet, but the inevitable reaction would then seem all the deeper and blacker.

Shane, convince me! she would implore, waking in the night to the cold wash of moonlight or the thin wintery keening around the windows that meant a bleak day ahead. Prove yourself to me! she would cry silently, waiting for that rush of rapture the others wrote of. But it never came, and she thought the dreariness of these nights was enough to make anyone want to kill herself.

Or to go mad. She was never so thankful for William's solid, egotistical presence. A dog would have sensed her condition and been nervous and anxious. William's serene belief that she existed solely to wait on him was unshattered, and there was no ignoring him.

Shane, be like William, she pleaded. Confront me at every turn. These people rejoice; he hasn't lost his son, she hasn't lost her daughter.

But it was only words. She had lost Shane. She didn't want oblique signs. She wanted Shane in the loving flesh.

What passed for her life went on at various levels. She sketched and painted because she had to fill up the time somehow. She mowed the lawn, she trimmed the paths with the machete. She walked, making work for herself by climbing the rocks, or forcing her way through overgrown parts of the woods where there were no paths but many blowdowns. She talked with Madge like a normal person in convalescence, or at least like one who is holding her own against a possible malignancy.

She didn't see Jonas except at a distance when he was tending his gear. One windy day she sat on the rocks with spray exploding just below her feet and did a series of sketches of his dory in rough water, with a small anonymous figure hauling or steering.

He had stayed in Rockland almost a week, and when he came back he was unsocial enough even for Ozzie to comment on it. "Hard business," he said, mournfully, shaking his head. "Marriage busting up after all those years."

"Which one wants out, or do they both want it?" Alix asked.

"Oh, it's *her*," Madge said, unusually acid. "The way I see it, he's made so much money she's been able to travel, and mix in with society. Or what passes for society in Williston," she added dryly. "So now of course she thinks he's too common for her and she's too good for him."

"You don't know any such thing," said Ozzie.

"I don't have to be told it. I can feel it. I could see vhich way the wind was blowing when we went down there to launch your boat."

Ozzie said, "Well, Jonas has never said a word against her, and I guess we won't either."

"Goodness, I can talk to Alix just like to myself!" Madge

cried. "Alix never would pass it on to a soul, would you, Alix?"

Alix laid her hand on her heart and said, "I solemnly swear." Alix couldn't care less, she thought. As long as he refrained from dropping in on her and shattering whatever mood she was in, she was grateful. The only trouble was that it was like waiting for the other shoe to drop. But he had his own reasons, she supposed, and perhaps after his brief flurry of attention he had become as indifferent to her as she was to him.

For hours she forgot him as if he had never been; she forgot everyone but Shane, and sometimes, trying to find her way into an understandable approach, she half-forgot Shane. It was like a battle of wills when a principle becomes the prize.

One morning as she crossed the living room in the dawn, she looked at the guitar for the first time since the girl Judy had handled it. Today it seemed to thrust itself into her attention as if it had made some desperate move, and suddenly she thought of Jonas again. She saw his serious and gentled expression as he said, "You don't understand . . . every time I see it it's like seeing an abandoned animal."

So the guitar hung there, dusty and untuned. She took it down then, wiped it carefully, and tuned it. William gave up agitating for breakfast and listened, intrigued, as she sang "Flow Gently, Sweet Afton" in her hoarse morning voice, using the only four chords she'd learned.

Halfway through the old song her throat thickened; the wild whistling blackbirds in yon thorny den always meant the Tangle to her. But she persisted to the end of one verse, and then hung the guitar up again, saying in a perfectly steady voice, "There, Shane."

As she walked away from it she wondered all at once what had made her look at the guitar in the first place, what had urged her toward it. A sign to convince her? But it could have been the way the light fell on it this morning that attracted her. Shrugging very emphatically, as if to flatten the invisible adversary, she went to the kitchen.

Yet the action had created a persistent atmosphere of its

own. She felt an actual interest in food this morning, and the untidy kitchen appeared to her with unusual clarity, as if she hadn't seen it for days. The sink needed attention again, you couldn't let a black iron sink go. The floor could stand sweeping. The counters called for a good scrubbing, and the back stairs were dusty. She made French toast for herself and ate it with crisp bacon and puddles of syrup, drank three cups of coffee, and then went to work.

It's not that I've decided to live, she said to the unseen listener. It's just that I'm waiting. You see, I find it hard to swallow everything as those people did, but yet I can't say no, I can't shut a door ... because it just might be true. I mean there are things one can't explain. Anyway, when people come into this house at the end I don't want them saying, Poor thing, how she let things go; you can see how her mind was failing.

Who'd ever think Alexia would ever develop a good-house-wife syndrome? Maybe my mind is failing, she reflected. Am I being compulsive about this goddam scrubbing? Could I take it or leave it? Then she decided that her long sojourn with the books had reacted on her like a long involvement with a painting, after which she always took a few days to attend to her surroundings, her clothes, and herself.

"Cheer up, old girl, you aren't scraping your knuckles and breaking your fingernails for any deep, dirty Freudian reason," she said aloud.

The cupboard doors were fastened with small hand-whittled buttons, and one of those under the long counter was loose; the door didn't shut tightly and William found the crack a handy place in which to hook a big double forepaw and pull. This was a noisy and sure attention-getter when Alix was slow about waiting on him. This morning she took the workshop key from the hook in the windowframe over the sink, and went out to get a screwdriver. The air was noisy with tree swallows. It was always a wonder to her that they could ever settle down and raise their families, they squabbled so. The pair in the house

fastened to the shop roof swooped down on Alix as she unlocked the door.

"Oh, go on with you," she said. "I'm not hurting anything,
and besides, this place belongs to me." Their eyes were gems in
the dark blue masks, their chests made one long to stroke the
fine silky white feathers with a tender forefinger; tiny, fearless,
indomitable, they flew thousands of miles each spring and late
summer in obedience to a built-in command.

It occurred to her that human beings also were driven in the
same way; free will was an illusion that made their instinctive
acts, when they were finally driven to commit them, only the
more difficult and graceless. The rhythm was set, and it was humanity's quarrels with it and attempts to subvert it that made
most human beings infinitely unhappy, and sometimes extremely unattractive.

And she thought, as she looked blindly around the workshop
wondering what she'd come for, of all her efforts and precau-
tions not to have a child, much as she had wanted one. "It
would be wrong," she told Shane. "When they got to the age to
wonder why we didn't live together all the time, what then?
And when there should be a father around all the time, and
not just a mother? Boy or girl, there comes a time when Father's pretty important."

It was one of the few times when she had seen Shane actually
humbled and ashamed, and she hadn't been able to bear it.
"But I'm not really a mother type," she had passionately assured him. "I never looked forward to growing up to be a
mother. I didn't even like dolls," she lied. "It was just a waste
of money to buy me nice ones. I threw them around any old
way. I've got *you,* Shane, or at least as much of you as I can
have—"

"All of me," he had said. "All of me. The rest is nothing."

"And you're enough, you're everything to me. You fulfill me,
Shane. I don't need anything else."

And it had been true, for the most part. Wanting Shane's
child had been a little private crisis she went through and got

over. Still, maybe that young jackass Tony had been right about her sublimating her maternal instincts in painting children.

What in hell had she come out here for? She'd have to go back to the kitchen and start again. . . . She looked down at the broad workbench, lighted by a long window looking southeast, and saw her name.

Cardboard letters spelled A L I, and the x was made by a pencil laid diagonally across a thin sliver of pine.

She clenched one hand around the vise fastened to the edge of the bench, while the other hovered trembling over the letters. Think, Alexia, she admonished herself. Logically. Rationally. She recognized the stiff cardboard letters. She had drawn and cut out part of an alphabet from which they had traced the boats' names on the hulls, *Golden-Eye* and *Sea Pigeon,* with *Tiree* lettered proudly underneath as home port.

The letters were kept in a manila envelope in a drawer at one end of the workbench. That was where she had left them last fall.

All she could think of was her wordless or sometimes spoken plea over the last week. *Convince me, Shane.*

He had. Oh, he had. She stood with her eyes shut, her face lifted blindly toward the sunlight, waiting for the affirmation of Shane's presence. Flies buzzed in the corners of the panes, and through the open door came the shrill war cries of embattled swallows, these sounds enlarged because she stood in the red darkness behind her lids.

I believe, I believe, she cried silently, and waited for joy.

❦ CHAPTER 16 ❦

IT WAS PEACEFUL there in the sun, with the workshop's personal aroma of warm wood and a rather pleasant ghostly whiff of barn, which dated back to a Goodwin wife who had stabled a pet milch goat in one end of the workshop. The flies made a summer sound, the swallows had ceased briefly their internecine rows. A larger bird ran down the roof, sounding like some tiny person rushing about overhead.

Waiting and listening, she began to feel a drifting sensation, as if she could quite easily go to sleep standing up. Already it seemed as if she *had* slept, and for an hour. Nothing had happened that she could pinpoint as a palpable experience, nothing out of the ordinary, unless it was this suspended sunny interval of calm. *So is this winged hour dropped to us from above, When twofold silence is the song of love.*

The words swam capriciously to the surface of her mind, bright goldfish flashing, then gone again. Was *this* it? No inner voice, no unmistakable impression of a presence; maybe that wasn't for her, maybe it was different for everyone. For her, the twofold silence.

She lifted her heavy lids, her eyes blurred with having been shut so long. She looked down at her name again. It was there, it had not been an illusion. And she knew that she had not come out here and arranged the thing herself.

Feeling neither exalted nor deflated, she locked the door and went back to the house. At a certain point in their experiences the other people began looking for advice, either to reassure themselves or to try for a more conclusive line of communication. This meant mediums, and the very word repelled her. Perhaps she was on the edge of discovery, perhaps the discovery had already been made, but whatever it was, it was intensely personal. At least, if she doubted, it would be her own senses and perceptions that she doubted; she could not even imagine herself approaching the most reputable medium without queasiness and a built-in rejection.

She was very hungry, as if she'd been exercising violently, but she didn't want to stay in the house. She made a thick sandwich of sliced onions and canned corned beef and a thermos of coffee, took her watercolors and associated gear, and went down to the beach beyond the wharf. A cold northeast wind had eddied around the house, but down here there was a still pool of June heat. Sanderlings and yellowlegs ran along the wet sand among the half-buried glistening stones. The redwinged blackbirds called in the marshy area that drained onto the beach. Alix ate her lunch sitting on a timber at the farther reach of the curve. William watched the shore birds and drove his claws menacingly into the timber; once he sank them into Alix's thigh when she was a little slow about handing him some corned beef.

It grew so warm she stripped off sweater and shirt down to her bra, but kept on Shane's Anzac hat to shade her eyes. She worked on a watercolor of blue flag blooming in the marsh, just beyond the debris of driftwood and old rockweed. A green bottle half-revealed in the rich rotting mess caught the sun and picked up the exact radiant green of the marsh. The painting was for Madge, if it came to anything, and Madge would exclaim over and over about the bottle, how it looked exactly like glass, you could almost touch it, and how did anyone *do* anything like that? For a long time she would see nothing else but the bottle.

Midday was no time to paint, the sun leached color out of things, but the blue flag was holding its own against the light; sparse, wild elegance in purple-blue, piercing the tangle of snow bedstraw and bindweed; willows and alders were almost diaphanous in the background with the sun coming down through the young leaves, and in front there was the red-brown rockweed, the watery luminous green of the bottle's side, and just a suggestion of the white glare of the beach.

Noon. That was its title, already. She said to William, "Somebody ought to paint me painting the blue flag. It could be a kind of natural history thing. Genus of New England spinster, not yet extinct, painting flowers in water color; some species express themselves in writing poetry, or doing good works, which on the whole is a hell of a lot more useful than water colors or bad imitations of Emily Dickinson."

William sprawled voluptuously flat in the shade of the timber and blinked eyes that matched the bottle.

A boat came around the easterly point of Gib's Cove as suddenly as jet planes seemed to appear overhead. It was a runabout which flashed a great deal of glass and chrome. She thought it was going by, but it slowed down and came into the cove, and she growled inarticulately and reached for her blouse. Alerted by the growl, William flowed over the timber and disappeared under bay bushes. There was no place for her to disappear to as the boat came idling softly straight across to her. The man at the wheel stood up, leaning on the top of the windshield. He was, so far, only a pair of shoulders and a white smile. He waved and called something. She felt herself withdrawing. *You curl up on yourself like a caterpillar,* Shane said.

He shut off the engine and the boat began at once to drift noiselessly sidewise across the turquoise water. He called, "Good afternoon, Alexia Horne!"

It was Soren Michaels. *Oh, bull,* she thought nastily. She gave him a backward flip of the hand, so negative as to be insulting, and turned to her easel. But her involvement had been shattered. If she touched a brush to it now it would be wrong; she couldn't think how she'd done this much. From the boat he called cheerfully, "I shall tie up at the wharf and walk around to you."

As the engine began again and the boat headed for the wharf, she slid her board down to the other side of the timber, facing the undergrowth, and hastily gathered together her gear. She wished she had the guts to disappear as William had, but she could not imagine Soren discouraged. He would set off looking for her and she had a picture of him, amused and determined, turning up at Jonas's camp or over at Beauty Cove, winning them all and being invited to have coffee.

Walking around the beach she rehearsed ways to get rid of him quickly, trying and discarding several. She was quietly enraged. On the edge of eternity—if you wanted to be poetic about it—why did you have to bother with ceremony?

Look, I don't want company. So get lost.

That also took guts. He was on his way; think fast now. *The sun has given me a headache. I have an upset stomach. I am on my way to lie down and rest.* It sounded like a language phrase book. *Please direct me to the American counsul.*

He came toward her, smiling; handsome, with nautical crow's-feet at the corners of his eyes. He reached for her kit bag and easel. "Where is your painting?" he asked.

"I left it there to dry," she said.

"And to collect bugs, flies, and even worse," he said.

"That's my new technique. It's called entomography. I expect to make *Time* any day now."

He laughed. "I get the impression you don't want me to see it, and I would like to, so much."

"Why?"

"To see what Alexia Horne does when she isn't painting those marvelous children."

"Dainty flowers," said Alix. "And birdies, and sometimes dear little pussycats."

He laughed even louder at that, looking at her with his face wreathed in happiness as if she delighted him beyond words. "I'm going to see it," he said. "I have to, after that." He put down her gear and started around the beach. She didn't look after him, but gathered up her things again and walked quickly toward the path. She could say she was due at the Goodwins' to tack a quilt or something, but he was quite capable of saying he'd run her around in that saltwater jukebox, and he'd still end up having coffee with Madge.

He caught up with her when she was halfway to the house. He was carrying the board. "Dainty flowers, did you say?" he asked her. "These wild iris shout! They express the primal urge, spring in its old, dark, and bloody guise. The human sacrifices in the new-plowed furrows, ceremonial sacred orgies. These flowers standing bolt upright in the bog have a sexual significance, Alexia. Who could miss it?"

"Madge could," said Alix. "Me too. A blue flag blooming by the sea a simple blue flag is to we. But you do talk pretty, Mr. Michaels, with all those long words and that accent and all. You sound so much like Victor Borge I keep wondering where your piano is."

"Please! I respect my countryman's success, but I have my own talent, modest as it may be. However, I didn't come to talk about that. I came on business."

"Oh?"

"I would like to buy your catboat." He said it as if suggesting an assignation. They reached the house; she had planned to perch indefinitely on the front doorstep until he realized that he wouldn't be invited in, and would presumably depart. Instead, talking fluently about the *Golden-Eye*, he reached past her and opened the door and she found herself entering with him close behind her.

She put her things on the stairs and turned to face him. "Your technique's admirable," she said. "Very smooth. I might almost say slick. But it's wasted here, I'm afraid."

"Technique?" His eyebrows went up; he was the very picture of a bluff, sincere, and bewildered seadog. "What are you saying? What do you think of me? I wish to buy your catboat. I am a great admirer of catboats, especially this one."

"But the notice definitely said Ozzie Goodwin was in charge."

"I know. I read it. So I borrowed a boat and came out here at the first opportunity. Ozzie Goodwin's boat is not on her mooring, he is out to haul. So I came to you, the owner." He was still hurt, a strong salty man unfairly humiliated. "Can't you say yes or no, I will or will not sell you my boat? And if yes, what is the price?"

"I don't know what price Ozzie has put on it," she said. "I don't care. I wanted nothing to do with the sale, but I don't suppose you can understand that."

"But I do understand," he said gently. "I have seen you and your friend sailing. Do you remember the ketch *Tahiti* in the Morgan Bay regatta last year? She was from Port Edwards, a friend's boat, and I was aboard her. We were very close to you going around the bell." He gestured toward the east. "Remember? We all waved and shouted at each other."

She remembered the brainless laughter of exhilaration, snapping sails, a good wind but not a frightening one as *Golden-Eye* leaned her side down into the bubbling water and ran for home, leaving *Tahiti* behind.

As she remembered, her face began to feel like that of a bare skull. She turned with military abruptness and walked away from him. His behavior was inexcusable, but she couldn't speak to tell him to go.

Behind her he said in a voice like velvet, "I am so sorry, Alexia."

She said, looking at the floor, "You'll have to talk to Ozzie about the boat. I don't care if you buy her, as long as you don't sail her out here under my nose."

"Then I don't want her," he said. "I want nothing to interfere between you and me."

She swung around then in astonishment too strong for indignation, and he smiled.

"My phrasing was unfortunate. I didn't mean that quite as it sounded. I meant simply that I wanted no shadows cast on our acquaintance."

"But what makes you think I want an acquaintance?" She tried to give the word an insulting emphasis.

"You will want friends again. You can't go too long without needing those who speak your own language."

"I don't think you and I speak the same language, and I don't mean Danish," she said.

He laughed at that, heartily, and there was something unpleasantly familiar about being laughed at in this room by a big blue-eyed man; unpleasant because it was a brutal parody. The laughter finally died away into little chuckles and amused sighs. "Oh, Alexia," he said, shaking his head. "No, I shan't buy the boat. I'll continue to borrow the so-called boat which looks like a Chevrolet pickup truck. . . . Who is this?"

He nodded past her, and she turned around and saw Karen standing in the kitchen doorway.

"Why, Karen!" she said, inspired. "I'd forgotten you!" She was positively happy to see the child. "Well, we must get to work." She said briskly to Soren, "I am going to make some preliminary sketches this afternoon. You'll have to excuse me."

"Of course. I'm glad you're working. It's a good sign." He smiled at Karen. "You are a very fortunate little girl." Karen showed no visible reaction to this. "Good-bye, then," he said to Alix with the slight formal tilt of his head. "Until the next time." He went out. As he passed the window on the way back to the wharf, he began to sing softly in a pleasant deep voice. She felt a bout of exhaustion approaching. They did not come so often now, and this one was all out of proportion to the scene just enacted. She knew why. He was nothing like Shane except in build, but there was again this nightmarish sensation of seeing things in negative.

"What is this?" Karen broke in. She was standing before the drawing board, which Soren had set on the old pine commode near the foot of the stairs.

"Look at it from a distance," Alix said indifferently. "Come

[1 7 2]

over this way." She dropped into a chair and began rubbing the back of her neck, digging so hard with her fingers that they hurt. Karen backed off from the watercolor. "Oh," she said. "It's those purply lilies." No rapture of discovery, merely another puzzling item ticked off.

"Very good," said Alix, yawning out the window. "Did you want something special? Got a message?"

"Nope," said Karen, turning around and placing herself squarely in front of Alix, her hands behind her back. Through the open front door they heard the roar of the big engine accelerating past the beach.

"Do you want something to eat?" Alix asked.

"No. Jonas gave me cake. He made it himself."

"Oh? How is Jonas these days?"

Karen considered. "Cranky," she said finally. "He told me to buzz off."

Alix couldn't stop yawning. She said, "You must be lonely for your friends at home, Karen. Aren't you?"

Karen shrugged, and Alix belatedly remembered Jonas's remarks about Thelma. Supposing he was right, did Karen know? And if Jonas wasn't right, but Thelma had no patience with her own child, Karen must know that too. She was unfortunate all around; she hadn't even been able to make a friend of Sidney, who until now had always liked everybody.

Oh well, her grandparents love her, Alix thought, yawning again. "I'm going to take a nap now," she said.

"You said you were going to draw me. You told *him* that."

Alix looked at her in exasperation and despair, and Karen said relentlessly, "Did you just make it up so he'd go away? Like making believe I was s'posed to come?"

"Of course I didn't just make it up," Alix said irritably. She got up, looking distractedly around her; she never knew where she put anything down these days. "Sit down. I'll be back."

She grabbed up paper and charcoal. Three or four quick sketches and she could be rid of the child. *My conscience*, Jonas had called her once. Thelma's conscience too, maybe, but she'd been able to ship her out of sight. Maybe it's good for us, she thought grimly, like a hair shirt, but I don't know what I've done to deserve it.

As expressionless and plastic as a doll, Karen sat or stood motionless however Alix placed her. It wasn't until Alix told her to take off her glasses that she showed any emotion. "I'm not supposed to take them off," she said, and there was a childish softening in her voice, as of fear.

"But it's just so I can get this line of nose and forehead and cheekbone," said Alix, tracing the line on her own face. "Besides, I've never seen your eyes clear."

Red flushed the child's throat and up into her face. She took her glasses off but instantly squeezed her eyes shut. She made Alix think of a newborn white puppy.

"Oh, put them on again," she said curtly. "I didn't realize your eyes hurt without them."

"They don't *hurt*," said Karen.

"I remember," said Alix. "You have a lazy eye. Well, it will strengthen as you grow older. Just be thankful you have nice even teeth and don't have to have all those bars and braces and bits and bridles in your mouth."

"Did you?" Karen asked.

"Yes," Alix lied. In for a penny, in for a pound. And it might cheer the kid up a bit. She had enough to brood on without being ashamed of her eye.

She showed Karen the sketches, and Karen gave them her close attention but without discernible pleasure or disappointment. "I guess I'll go home now," she announced, and went.

Sometime in the past hour Alix's exhaustion had disappeared. She went upstairs and looked at the spear point. It was exactly as she had last seen it. So were the books and the tiki. Then she went out to the workshop, unlocked the door, and found her name still spelled out on the bench. Again she experienced the reaction she'd had the other day when she'd come back from the trip with Jonas and found the point unmoved—as if she'd expected something more, to certify the occurrence. Well, she'd gotten her name spelled out, hadn't she, to certify the point? What more? *Green eyes greedy gut eat all the world up ... I want someone with a skin face.*

She looked down at her name again, and suddenly it was infinitely pathetic. At best it was a cry from a broken, ruined Shane who, if he survived somewhere, was loathing it, who was helpless, bewildered, and afraid.

Tell me how to find you, Shane. If I do it, will I be able to come to you? Tell me how, Shane, and I'll be there.

❧ CHAPTER 17 ❧

THE MOON WAS big enough now to give some light, and she was up and down all night, outside walking till her shoes were soaked and her feet cold with dew, inside drinking first one hot drink and then another, back to bed trying to hypnotize herself into sleep by watching the moon. She would drop off, then snap awake with the familiar sensation of having been awakened. But she was fairly sophisticated about this now, and blamed it on her unconscious mind and her nerves, on William, on the moonlight, or on William's reaction to the moonlight. He went out with her every time, and she thought with mordant humor that if Karen could see her now, wrapped in an old long coat as she paced in the cold faint moonlight with the cat, it might make up for the disappointing lack of bloody ghosts on the island. She must look like a genuine witch. She wondered how many so-called witches had been women like herself, not knowing whether to go or to stay, but existing meanwhile from hour to hour in an agony of solitude.

She finished out the night in the study, reading one of her books as daylight came on. Finally she blew out the lamp and went to sleep to the dawn chorus, with William stretched out along her back like an outsize, fur-covered heating pad with a sleep-inducing sound attachment.

Waking, she knew that everything was unchanged, but she made the rounds just the same and confirmed the certainty. It may be hard to get in touch, she found herself explaining seriously and sympathetically. One doesn't get used to things all at once. One has to learn to send as well as to receive.

Then she was angrily ashamed, as if someone had caught her indulging in furtive magic rites. She hurried outdoors, took the lawn mower from its corner in the roomy toilet, and went to work on the grass. The light wind was northeast, the sky cloudy-bright. Almost overnight, it seemed the field had filled with daisies and buttercups, sparkling in constant motion in the breeze.

When she mowed close to the roses at the edge of the lawn their sweetness blew about her. She held her breath so she wouldn't breathe it. She decided that when she finished mowing she would go away from the house, either in *Sea Pigeon* or on foot, and not come back until dusk. It was the only way to be safe from anyone who came looking for her; who came trapping her, really. She saw in her mind a tiny but bright-colored movie of a fox running and hiding, hearing the hounds in the distance. A red, red fox. A vixen whose heart she could feel pounding in her own breast.

She turned to mow away from the roses toward the house, and there stood Madge and Karen at the edge of the lawn. Sidney's tail was wagging urgently among the daisies behind them as he assisted William in his mousing.

Madge was almost coruscating with delight. "Karen told me last night!" she cried, "and I could hardly sleep a drop, I was that tickled!" Then she became religiously stern, and looked Alix hard in the eye. "Now look, Ozzie's going to *buy that portrait,* and you're not to put a special price on it because we're old friends. Because that wouldn't be right. We'd be taking advantage." Exhilaration burst through again. "Oh, chickabiddy, wait till your mother hears that Alexia Horne's going to paint you! I guess that'll—" She stopped as if her mouth had been slapped shut, bit down on her lower lip, and glanced away from Alix, blinking watery eyes.

Alix, rubbing her palms on the sides of her jeans, was more concerned with her own discomfort. Oh God, this is what happens when I'm driven into a lie. Other people make a career of lying and ride merrily on, but me, *I've* got to answer for the merest fib. *I* get caught. It's the same with everything. I'm a born victim, just like Young Vampira—

"Now, how will you want her dressed, Alix?" Madge was running on. "I've brought over a few things. She's got some real pretty little dresses. One's blue, and that's nice with her eyes, but pink gives her more color. And I've washed her hair. It shines like silver in the sun, doesn't it?" Fondly she stroked Karen's head. "She's real platinum blond, just like her daddy. My, he'll be some proud, won't he, love?"

Alix felt as if she'd never learned to move her facial muscles. It was an effort to talk. "Well, we'll look at the dresses, but what she wears doesn't much matter as long as she's comfortable. . . . I'm not ready to start yet. I have to get a canvas ready."

"I know that, dear, but I just had to come over and talk to you about it, and find out things, you know." She was so happy one kept expecting her to break into song like a bird, or to begin spontaneously to dance. "Alix, I was thinking, there's no way you could get Sidney into it, is there? They'd look some cunning together."

"I just couldn't do Sidney justice," Alix said. "I've never yet been satisfied with any sketches I've made of him. Let's see the dresses." She sat down on the doorstep.

"I'm thirsty," said Karen.

"Run in and get a drink then, honeybunch," said Madge, unzipping the small bag.

"I'll get it for her," said Alix.

"Oh, let her wait on herself, dear," Madge said comfortably. "She's real handy that way." Being very handy indeed Karen slid in under Alix's elbow, sped past the front stairs and on toward the kitchen.

Oh, what the hell, Alix thought gloomily, and sat down again. She barely saw what Madge was showing her, and Madge's voice slid past her like the gurgling and bubbling water along the side of a boat. *A boat.* She should have let the damn grass go and taken *Sea Pigeon* out an hour ago. But it wouldn't have changed anything; she'd already committed herself to the painting just because she hadn't been able to speak up to Soren.

Next time I'll speak to him, she promised herself. *Pow.* Right between the eyes with a crowbar, preferably.

"—could have bitten my tongue off," Madge was whispering rapidly. "Poor little thing, she must know Thelma doesn't think much of her having that eye trouble, and being plain besides. Acts ashamed of her own young one. Now she respects *you,* Alix, and if you think Karen's worth painting, Thelma'll maybe look at her a little different."

"Why don't we have her wear this?" Alix absently smoothed out the smocked blue voile. What was the kid doing in there all this time? Not that it mattered any more. She sagged back against the door frame trying not to listen for sounds from the kitchen. Madge kept on talking. The day dulled as low untidy cloud masses covered the sun. The chalk-white of the daisies seemed to vibrate, the lawn looked dyed. Beyond the starry thicket of the rugosas the sea was choppy and dark, with a dull silver gleam out near the horizon.

"There now, look at that!" Madge cried. "See a sea glin, catch a wet skin. It's going to storm for sure."

"It'll be a change," said Alix languidly, and as Madge gave her a troubled look she grinned and said, "My rain barrels are getting low, and I want to do a washing."

"Oh, there's nothing like rain water for washing," said Madge, abundant with relief. "Even with the artesian well I still save all the rain water I can." Something clattered inside the house and she turned her head quickly.

"Karen! Are you *meddling?*"

Karen arrived, wiping her mouth. "Karen's been inspecting my sink," said Alix. "How's it look, Karen?"

But the child, as if she suspected her of malice, ignored her. "Coffee, Madge?"

"No, thanks, dear, I've been having too much lately, and I must get back. We're going to iron. Karen does the handkerchiefs and pillowcases."

"Isn't that nice?" said Alix. "Send her over tomorrow morning around ten, Madge."

When they had gone, Madge prattling happily and Karen looking inscrutable, the back of Alix's blouse was wet with sweat, and so was the hair on her nape. She went into the house. One cupboard door still hung open, and a drawer below the counter had been hurriedly and not quite shut. She shut it before William could get his paw into it and hook out anything, then sponged her face and neck with cold water.

There was nothing to do but prepare the canvas, if she had any. She couldn't disappoint Madge unless she was prepared to dispose of herself at once, and she couldn't do that until she knew what she had to know. Damn it, life was so simple three weeks ago, she thought. I should have done it then, before everything else had time to happen.

She found a piece of canvas rolled up in a drawer of her work table. "Why did you have to be here?" she asked it. She stretched it and sat down to study the sketches.

They looked awkward and amateurish to her, and nothing germinated from them; she simply could not think how to handle the child. This was a totally new and devastating experience. It was as if she had never painted before. When the time came, she wouldn't know how to mix her colors or handle a brush.

If I forget thee, O Jerusalem, let my right hand forget her cunning. Whom have I forgotten?

She found herself feeling her right hand with her left as if for broken bones or sore spots, then wringing and rubbing the two in a neurotic gesture that repelled her. She went back outside and mowed again.

Light showers came and went on the wind. She kept on

mowing through them, drying out when the sun returned between showers. By the time she was tired the showers were coming faster and harder. She put on dry clothes, built a fire in the fireplace, and lay before it drinking cocoa and eating buttered pilot crackers, re-reading sections in her books.

These people had been forced to believe. They had no other choice but to believe. Thus compelled, they had eventually gone to reputable mediums recommended by reputable people. How reputable? It could be all self-delusion on the part of decent but too hopeful souls. And as far as mediums went, there were more kinds of skullduggery than anyone but a gifted con man could imagine.

But still, if it *could* happen, she thought with a piercing clarity of longing that called her back from the foggy moors of sleep; if there *did* exist a human being above the corruption of self-interest, a pure channel between here and there . . . only what and where is *there?*

She slept finally, and received no messages except from the inherent artist on the best way to pose Karen. This had happened before with other subjects, and was reassuring. Perhaps she would be able to do it after all. She was anxious not to let Madge down. And perhaps by the time she had finished the painting she would know about Shane for sure. She had no illusions of being with him in a sort of Maxfield Parrish heaven; she wanted chiefly for him to understand, and agree to, the necessity for her act.

✤ CHAPTER 18 ✤

WHEN KAREN ARRIVED for her first sitting, Alix still felt inept or worse. She had to produce something from this hour, if it was no more than a study or two. She wondered if her own antagonism toward the child was producing a kind of negative current between them. And why was she antagonistic? Because, like Thelma, she found Karen unattractive? Because she couldn't figure out how Karen reacted to her? She questioned herself without pity all the while she was trying Karen here and there. The child stood or sat where she was placed, but she still resembled a doll whose limbs and head could be turned in any position; except that she breathed, she watched, and there was no doubt that she was thinking. But *what?* Alix pondered grimly. If this is what she does to her mother, no wonder Thelma shipped her out.

Holding the conch shell to her ear or looking at a book, as in the sketches, was too artificial. At last she sat her down in a small armless rocker in the studio, with her hands folded in her lap in the pose of the dream, and began a pastel study.

Almost at once she was involved, and at first her relief was almost euphoric, like the ebb of pain away from a sore tooth or a sprain, and then she forgot that it was happening and simply worked.

Usually she didn't expect children to sit very long at a time, and broke the hour up frequently. Today it was an almost imperceptible twitch of Karen's fingers that snapped her out of absorption, and she realized that the child had been sitting motionless for over half an hour.

"For heaven's sake, Karen," she exclaimed, "you must be stiff as a board. Hop up, now. Stretch, jump, do something. Run, hop, skip!" Karen didn't move, and Alix laughed. "Have you turned into stone? Come on, get up and we'll have some coffee. I'll fix you café au lait." She started for the stairs.

Karen got up slowly, rubbing her bottom. She tucked her lower lip under her upper front teeth in a manner reminiscent of her grandmother, and behind the glasses her eyes were cast down. For the first time she looked shy.

"Can I see?" she asked gruffly.

"Oh, sure. Go and look." Alix went on downstairs to put the teakettle on. She heard Karen cross the floor, then there was silence. After a few moments Karen came down the stairs with her deliberate step. Karen running, hopping, skipping, as Alix had exhorted her to do, could not be imagined. She came into the kitchen, made a full stop, and said, "I thought you were going to use real paints, not them crayon things."

"I am going to use real paints. Today I just made the studies, to find out what way I want to paint you."

Karen continued to stare at her and Alix said, "Do you see what I mean? Next time we'll start with the paints."

After a moment she got a grudging nod. Then Karen said, "I have to go to the bathroom." She went out. Alix grinned and shook her head. But she was eager to get to the actual painting now. The moment she began to know the way a child's hair grew, the convolutions of an ear, the modeling of a mouth, the subject became a different one from the one fetched willingly or reluctantly to the studio. It was happening now with Karen. She doubted that she'd ever know what went on in Karen's

head, but in one afternoon she had become well acquainted
with the exquisite contrast of silver hair and sun-gilded skin.
She knew well the straight, perfect little nose, and as the child
had unconsciously relaxed during the sitting, her mouth had
curved into tender unwariness. The sharp elbows, the stubby
fingers laced together, the scratched knees, all gave off an aura
of vulnerability that made the other Karen a sort of Doppelgän-
ger.

In the kitchen she pinned a clean towel on Karen to protect
her dress.

"I never spill," said Karen sternly.

"So humor me," said Alix.

Karen looked into space as she drank her café-au-lait and ate
saltines and peanut butter. Alix was tired from concentration
and was glad that Karen didn't expect conversation. She was
concerned with the glasses; the time would come when she
must have them off, to see how the eye lay between cheekbone
and brow, and how the lids curved, but Karen seemed to feel
naked or ashamed without them. Thelma would be to blame
for that.

Spoiled brat, Thelma. How could people like Ozzie and
Madge have such stinking kids? Though Kenneth was decent
enough, probably because he was a second Ozzie and all the
relatives hadn't been burbling about his beauty ever since his
bassinet days.

William crying at the door broke up the silent session at the
kitchen table. She got up to let him in and feed him. "Well,
Karen, I guess we've done enough for today," she said.

"It wasn't much," said Karen. "I can stay longer."

"Tomorrow we start. I've something else to do now." Slyly
she suggested, "Walk around by the Home Cove and tell Jonas
you're having your picture painted."

"Unh-unh." Karen shook her head.

"What's 'unh-unh' mean?" Alix challenged her. "That you're
a chimp begging for a banana?"

"It means *no*," said Karen with chilling dignity.

"Then let's use 'no' around here, shall we? Why don't you want to tell him? I thought you and Jonas were pals."

"Nobody's Jonas's pal," said Karen. "When he goes out with Gramp to haul the trawl he won't come up to the house for a mug-up afterwards. Gramp says there's something eating him." Her upper lip curled back, and she put down her mug.

"That means something on his mind," Alix told her, remembering her own early horror of leeches, of poisonous snakes hiding in boots, and of the Spartan boy gnawed away on by the fox under his tunic.

"Oh," said Karen. She began to drink again. "I could drink some more," she said when she'd finished.

"You can have some more tomorrow. Try not to get your dress messed up with any rotten rockweed or pitch on your way home."

"It's wash and wear," Karen told her with a hint of patronage. She was almost airy as she left.

A few afternoons later Ozzie and Madge left Karen off at the wharf on their way to the mainland and a trip to town. It was rather a surprise to Alix.

"We thought you wouldn't want her to miss a sitting," Madge explained.

"Oh, a day wouldn't have made much difference," said Alix.

"No, we don't want to interfere with your work," Madge told her earnestly. "Now you come over to supper tonight. You don't eat enough, and we've got to keep you well and strong. I'm going to muckle on to that Jonas, too. He's still a young man, his life isn't over just because that—"

"Woman," said Ozzie, "stop your noise and get aboard."

"Oh, my!" With Madge it actually was a peal of laughter. "He sounds exactly like his father!" She went down the ladder with a youthful scamper.

When the boat headed out of the cove Alix said, "Well, Karen, let's get to work." They walked slowly to the house, Karen well behind. It was early afternoon, and cloudy with a diffused luminosity that bathed everything in a mirror trans-

parency. Gulls, trees, and rocks seemed to have been dipped in
liquid glass, the field flowers had the gemmy quality of flowers
carved inside a crystal paperweight. There was no wind, no
rote on the shores. Delicate essences arose in warm breaths
from earth and the woods.

It was too beautiful an afternoon to stay indoors, but it was
also an afternoon when it was better to be busy. The light was
good in the studio, and Karen took her position as if she'd
been born to model. Her hair shone on the canvas with its own
light, and the curve of cheekbone around to jaw and chin had a
peachy bloom. But her lack of expression combined with the
glasses gave her the stiff, lifeless air of a ventriloquist's dummy.
The eyes would change everything. Sometime soon those
glasses must come off.

A light breeze began blowing around the chimney, and the
mirror-hush outside was broken. Silver gave way to blue, and
sails appeared on the horizon as the air freshened to a good
sailing breeze.

Alix had begun talking through the sittings even though she
never got much of an answer. Conversations during the coffee
break had never again reached the level of the first day, when
Karen had delivered her long sentence about Jonas. Poetry had
the advantage of occupying Alix's mind and requiring no comment from Karen. Out of desperation or perhaps a yearning
back to the safeties of her own childhood, Alix remembered
whole chunks of verse, and lately *A Child's Garden of Verses*
was coming to her in entire poems which she recited aloud,
with no obvious reaction on Karen's part.

The tall grass in the Head field, seen through the window
behind Karen, rippled light and dark in the wind. " 'Grasses
run like a green sea,' " Alix said. " 'O'er the lawn up to my
knee'. Do you know that one?" She went on and gave the rest
of "The Dumb Soldier."

It wasn't the most fortunate choice for herself; her mind was
attacked by unavoidable images. But she went on stubbornly to
the end. " 'Not a word will he disclose, Not a word of all he

knows. I must lay him on the shelf, And make up the tale myself.' "

They had their mug-up out on the doorstep, with William providing chirpy responses to most of Alix's remarks, and then went back to the studio. Time slid on toward late afternoon. Alix went from Stevenson to Lewis Carroll and was in the midst of "Jabberwocky" when there was a loud knocking at the front door.

William, who had been lying optimistically before the cold Franklin stove, rose and streaked into Alix's room. Even Karen jumped, and showed a normal curiosity.

"Oh, for heaven's sake," Alix said in disgust, putting down her brush. "Now what? All right, Karen, we'll call it a day. Come on downstairs."

The knocking continued, more frantic than imperious. Swearing to herself, Alix went downstairs. More unwanted callers, determined to smoke Alexia Horne out if they had to beat all the skin off their knuckles to do it. "Come on down, Karen!" she called back crossly, hearing no sound from upstairs and remembering that the door into her room was open. "This minute!" she added, then went around to the front door. "All right, all *right!*"

She opened the door. Myra Ruskin stood there looking like a guilty child. "Don't be mad," she begged, so that Alix wondered how she did look. "It's a real emergency, honest. Please believe me. We wouldn't have come ashore, we were on our way to Haddock Island to camp out overnight out there, and this character we had with us—honestly, we know all the weirdest ones, but of course he's Judy's friend—well, he—" she twisted around and said miserably, "Here they come."

Peter and Soren got over the top of the bank with difficulty, half-carrying another man between them who seemed to have legs made of yarn. "What's happened to him?" Alix asked. Her unpleasant anticipation was divided in two parts as she wondered what Karen was doing in the bedrooms.

"He fell overboard just below the Head, and he's a wretched

swimmer *anyway,* and it's so darned cold, and we had to come about to pick him up, and we thought he'd drown in the meantime. Soren jumped in—he was simply marvelous—and got to him and held him up, but Duff fought so hard he nearly drowned them both, so Soren knocked him out, and between being so cold and so scared and the *punch*—well, Duff looked so awful we thought he'd die before we got back to the Harbor. So if we could just get him *warm*—" She looked plaintively at Alix and then back at the approaching group. They were trying to keep a blanket around him and hold him up at the same time, but even Soren's grip around his skinny middle couldn't keep him from slithering downward. Judy paced slowly behind with her usual air of dissociation, her face hidden by a wide-brimmed straw hat tied on with a scarf.

"Well, of course you can bring him in," said Alix, wishing it had happened off Beauty Cove instead; Madge would be simply delighted with all this. Only Madge wasn't home. "I'll get blankets and hot water bottles." And see what that child is doing, she added silently. But when she turned away from the door Karen was sitting on the front stairs as firmly settled as a box-holder at the opera, her glasses fixed on the fascinating action.

Alix went out to the kitchen and put on several saucepans of rain water to heat for the bottles. She collected three bottles from the drawer, and matched up the stoppers, then went into the downstairs bedroom that led off the kitchen beyond the back stairs. Here extra blankets were piled away in an outsize cedar chest Shane had made.

Another door opened into the living room by the foot of the front stairs, and through it she could hear the progress of the three men. The limp Duff seemed to have diver's boots on. Peter was nervously encouraging, biting off profanity which kept getting by him. Myra's voice fluttered around the perimeter. "Now, Peter, he can't help it. . . . Goodness, he could have *drowned.* . . . We'll get you warm in a minute, Duff. . . . My goodness, listen to his *teeth!* Talk about *castanets!*" She giggled. Soren, presumably, was being the strong silent pillar of strength.

She went back to the kitchen with her arms full of blankets, and called to Myra who came speedily, all aglow with undeniable exhilaration. Alix filled the hot water bottles and handed them to Myra to wrap in towels. "Put him on the living room couch," she said. "I'll go up and get dry clothes for him and Soren."

Myra said blissfully, "When I think how we'd be feeling if he'd drowned!" She hurried off.

Alix went up the back stairs. William was lying flat at the top, tail twitching, his head craned forward as he tried to see around the bend. He followed Alix into Shane's room. She hadn't burned all Shane's clothes, just those which had the most personal significance; Madge could do what she wanted to with the rest.

The uproar came to her by way of both flights of stairs. She gathered that the men were trying to strip Duff of his wet clothes and he was fighting them.

"For Chrissake, nobody's trying to rape you!" Peter snarled.

"What about m-my m-m-modesty, you b-bastards?" Duff demanded hysterically between chattering teeth. "Get that kid out of here!"

"Come on, honey," Myra said. "Come out in the kitchen with me."

"And k-keep her out there!" Duff shrieked.

Alix braced herself for handling Shane's clothes. She took out slacks, shirts, underwear, and socks, and went back downstairs before she could think about them. In the kitchen Myra was trying to make conversation with Karen, who was plainly more interested in what was going on in the other room.

"Where did you say he escaped from?" Alix asked her. Myra giggled. "I think he's been kept in a barrel most of his life. He's a real kook. He's a friend of Judy's, and he blew in a couple of days ago on a cloud of pot. Pete, here's the clothes!" she called.

"Gosh, I'm sorry about this, Alix," Peter said sternly, and hurried back.

Myra pursed her mouth, raised her eyebrows, and canted her head slightly toward Karen. "Soren's got what Pete calls the Everest syndrome. You know. Because it's there ... He dropped her in about one week. Very sweetly. Just as I told her he would. So I guess she sent for Duff for sympathy."

"What does she do? Is she a student, a hippy, a model, or what?"

"A *what,* I guess. I don't know. Her aunt's a nice innocent lady who's letting Judy use her cottage while she's off in Iceland looking at birds or something. Heaven knows what it'll look like after she and Duff keep house in it for a week. An old-fashioned opium den, probably."

Soren appeared in the doorway; there was an epileptoid moment for Alix at the sight of Shane's jeans and shirt. He gave Alix his little bow. "How do you do, Alexia? You take all this in your stride; it's very kind of you."

"I'm just glad that no one was drowned," she said. "I'll have some hot tea for him in a minute." She got up and began measuring tea into the teapot. "Are you chilled, too?"

"Oh no, I'm used to this water. Hello, Karen. How does the painting go, eh? That must be the dress you wear in it. It's very pretty."

"She doesn't talk, Soren," Myra said. "Not even to you."

Soren laughed. "Already she has the makings of an exceptional woman. A little unnerving, perhaps, but fascinating. What's happened to Judy? Has she thrown herself off the nearest cliff?"

"—he asked hopefully," said Myra. "She's outside somewhere. I think this is all too much for her. When she feels inadequate she simply freezes and looks off into space."

"He wants her to be with him," said Soren. "He's still terrified. 'All that water,' he, keeps saying. I don't think he even dares to get into a bathtub. Your towels are now quite grimy," he said apologetically to Alix.

"I'll take everything home and put it through my washer,"

said Myra. "Well, I'll go find Judy." She went out the back door. Karen slipped into the living room, apparently to view a nonbather.

"Well," said Soren, pleasantly cuddling his pipe in his hand. "We meet again. A totally unexpected pleasure. We were headed for Haddock Island for overnight. Myra had parked young Peter with a friend, and all was serene until Judy came to the wharf with her young man and begged to come. The alternative was that her aunt's house would be wrecked by a group from Limerock who had threatened to come for a party. Well, we like her aunt very much, and she doesn't deserve to have her house wrecked, so—" He shrugged.

Alix poured boiling water into the teapot. "What prevents them from having their party and wrecking the place anyway?"

"The Harbor Vigilantes, hastily mustered this afternoon. A few neighbors will go down Miss Hester's road at intervals all evening and check the premises."

"Good," said Alix. When Soren was not exhibiting his Everest syndrome, he was all right; she was willing to forget the other day.

Voices came from the other room; Myra had come in the front door with Judy. "And take off that hat, Judy, you look like the Wife of Bath or one of those Canterbury pilgrims or something. All you have to do is hold his hand. For goodness' sake, he's not *dead!*"

Soren and Alix looked at each other and smiled. "My adoration of Myra," said Soren, "is the purest thing about me."

"Tea?"

"Yes, please."

Peter came out and sagged against the counter, blowing hard. "The longest afternoon of my life since young Peter was born. My God, what a madman. He swears something tried to grab him and pull him down out there. I told him it was kelp but he says it was a sea monster."

"A kraken," said Soren. "I addressed it in its native tongue, and it let go."

"How about some hot tea for him?" Alix asked.

"You wouldn't have a little brandy, would you? He's really blue. Maybe he's got a heart condition, and they give liquor for that, don't they?"

If they have time, Alix thought. If it doesn't strike like a pole-ax. She said, "Yes, I have some brandy." She went up and got it out of the studio cupboard. This time William followed her down and slunk into the living room with his whiskers pointing forward and his belly close to the floor. Peter took the bottle and a small glass.

Myra appeared and said, "Can I have some tea, please? Now that it's over, my stomach feels funny."

"Have some brandy."

"That would really do me in. No, tea."

Alix poured for her and for herself. They heard Duff coughing on the brandy and Myra said, solemnly, "He seems awfully frail."

❧ CHAPTER 19 ❧

THE CLOCK struck five. The Goodwins should be returning any minute now. "Excuse me, please," Alix said, and went out the back door. The sudden silence and the cool air flowing against her face were refreshing. She walked around the house to where she could see the way *Marjorie C.* would come. The wind had gone easterly and had the wet, acrid tang of deep ocean. The sun was now veiled by fine gauze, and a mauve bank of fog lay along the outer horizon. It would probably move in by dark. She wondered how long it would be before they could load Duff aboard and continue on their way to Haddock, or go back to the Harbor. They had better tie Duff to a bunk; he could drown himself yet.

Suddenly Ozzie's boat appeared around the Head, and she saw Madge's excited gestures to call Ozzie's attention to the yawl anchored off the beach. She went down to the wharf. Madge was smiling and waving as the boat crossed the cove, and the instant the engine stopped she called, "You've got company! Isn't that nice!"

It was the same tone of loving encouragement that she used to Karen.

"Well, I don't know how nice it is," said Alix. "It's going to keep me from supper at your house, and that's far from nice."

"Can't you get rid of 'em?" Ozzie set her carton of groceries up on the wharf.

She explained briefly, without going into all the entertaining details; they could be saved for Madge's later enjoyment, when there was more time. "I don't know when he's going to get over being blue, terrified, cold, and so forth, but it could be just late enough to mess things up for all of us. So we'd better forget it for tonight . . . Come on up and meet them," she said, reading the desire in Madge's transparent face. "You'll have to pick up Karen, anyway. She's so enthralled by all the goings-on you'll have to pry her loose."

The rest, all but Duff, were drinking tea at the kitchen table. The men and Myra got up to meet Madge, who looked into each face with a shy bright smile to which all three responded with pleasure, the usual reaction to Madge's ingenuous interest. Judy, brooding over a mug held in both hands, nodded somberly.

"How is the poor boy who fell overboard?" Madge asked.

"Judy says he stopped shivering finally, and went to sleep," Myra said. "My goodness, he shook that whole sofa for a while."

"We ought to rouse him up and get going," Peter said.

"Oh, you should give him a *little* while to rest," Madge said maternally. "He'll be all the better for it. Now where's my grandchild?"

"That's right, where is she?" Alix looked instinctively toward the back stairs. Soren saw the glance and shook his head.

"She's fascinated by Duff. I think she's sitting there watching him breathe."

"Oh, Mr. Michaels," Madge exclaimed, "you sound exactly like the nice Danish man my Aunt Frances married."

"That wasn't Victor Borge, was it?" Soren asked.

"No, his name was Fred Larson," said Madge seriously.

"I should like to shake his hand," said Soren in a sepulchral

voice. They all laughed, even Madge, though she wasn't quite
sure why; Alix explained, and Madge said, "But that's why I
like Victor Borge, because he sounds like Uncle Fred." She tiptoed to the living room door and looked in. "I don't see her,"
she whispered back over her shoulder.

Alix went in with her. Duff slept deep in blankets and an
aroma of brandy. He had rumpled, longish, fair hair, and he
looked blue-white, fragile, and almost childish.

"Poor young one," Madge whispered tenderly. "They'd
ought to let him stay put a little while longer. He doesn't look
very strong to me."

"Where do you suppose Karen's gone?" Alix murmured. She
considered going up the front stairs, but a movement from the
study caught her eye, and she turned and saw the child standing in the doorway. Madge beckoned affectionately; Karen
didn't move, but Madge went to her and took her hand and led
her out to the kitchen. She asked everyone to come and see her,
including the noncommittal Judy, and gave them a little solicitous advice about Duff.

"He looks like a pneumonia type to me. You'd better watch
him carefully for the next few days."

"Like a hawk," Peter assured her. "Like a whole covey of
hawks, or bevy or however hawks come."

Madge showed her dimples. "I do like your long hair," she
told him. When she had gone Myra said, "Isn't she *darling!*"

"Delightful woman," said Soren. "Hot tea, Alix?"

"Mr. Michaels poured," said Myra. "Social notes from all
over. Don't you think he'd look adorable behind a silver urn at
the Limerock Women's Club?"

Alix made a frame of her hands and squinted at Soren
through it. "Not bad, with the proper hat," she said. "Wide-
brimmed, with flowers. Big peonies, I think. And a bit of veiling."

"And with a blond wig I would look like Brünnhilde," said
Soren imperturbably. "I can be as gracious as anyone. . . . Tea,
Peter?"

"The human system can hold just so much liquid," said Peter, heading for the door. "I'll be back."

"Oh, darling, I *hope* so!" said Myra.

With Myra around there were no awkward gaps in the conversation. She went on talking, and Alix sipped the tea she didn't want and wondered about feeding them.

Peter came in and said energetically, "Hey, fog's starting to come in! We've got to get out of here. I'm going in and throw Duff out of the sack." He went on into the living room. "Come on, chum, hit the deck! Hey, Duff, get up, we've got to move out of here before dark—" There was a pause. Then Peter exclaimed very softly, and Myra's eyes widened and she stood up.

"He's not *dead*, is he?" she whispered.

Even Soren's head came around at that and he too stared into the living room. They heard Peter coming. His face had turned a red that clashed unpleasantly with its ginger furnishings.

"The little bastard's drunk," he said. "He drank every goddamn drop of that brandy and he's passed out. Excuse my language, Alix. I wish," he added bitterly, "that we'd let him drown."

"You don't, really," Myra said. "But is he actually—"

"Go in and look."

Soren left, and they heard him trying to rouse Duff. Alix thought wearily, Oh, great. If he kills himself on my brandy it'll sound just fine, won't it? Not that I give a damn, but it'll be hard on Madge and Ozzie. Everybody will swear we had a wild artistic drunken orgy out here.

Peter sank heavily into a chair. Judy rested her forehead on her hands and stared at the table. Alix went into the living room where Soren was bending over the sofa. "Is he all right?" she asked. "I mean, he's not in a coma or anything, is he? Does he need artificial respiration? A doctor?"

"As far as I can see," said Soren, feeling for a pulse in a limp wrist, "it's an ordinary drunken sleep and I've seen a good many of them."

"I've seen a few," said Alix, "but Myra and Madge seem to think he's delicate, and they've infected me. He does look white."

"From never going outdoors unless he's dragged out, as Judy dragged him today," said Soren. He dropped the wrist, picked up the empty bottle, and raised his eyebrows at it. "A good brand, anyway."

Peter, Myra, and Judy now came into the room, Judy notice-ably hanging to the rear. "What do you think, Soren?" Peter asked. "Can we get him up and walk him around, give him black coffee, slap his face?"

Soren shrugged. "I don't think the results would be worth the effort. Liquor on top of the dunking and the fright—he's far out on a space walk."

"Oh, Peter," Myra said sadly, "why did you ever suggest brandy for him?"

"Well, how could I know he was an alcoholic? Did *you* know, Judy?"

"Oh, yes," Judy said faintly, looking out a window.

"Then why the hell did you let us give him a drink?"

Judy gazed around the room as if after an invisible bird.

"Judy is stupid," said Soren. "Otherwise she would never have collected such an imbecile in the first place."

"And I'd never have looked at you either!" cried Judy, and burst into noisy weeping. Myra at once hurried to put her arms around her, the good-hearted little girl on the school play-ground who was always first to console the ones who fell down, even the unpopular ones. Judy sobbed into her scarf, saying something through the sobs. Myra looked around at the others and said compassionately, "She says he took up pot to get him off the booze."

"Fine, fine," said Peter. "So she stands there contemplating her navel while we prime him with Alix's brandy."

Judy bawled even louder, making her mouth square. "I hate you all!"

"Come on, honey," said Myra, tenderly guiding her out to

the kitchen. The other three looked at each other over Duff, who was now snoring.

"This is very unpleasant for you, Alix," Soren said. She shrugged slightly.

"I'm not blaming anybody. We'll have to make the best of it, that's all. I think we can stand something to eat."

"Oh, hey," said Peter eagerly. "We've got all this food and beer out aboard the boat. We can go get it. Come on, Soren."

Judy and Myra had gone out. When they came back, Judy's make-up was repaired, and she silently wiped the mugs that Myra washed. Now and then she sniffled, with the effect of bravely holding back tears.

When the men came back with the food their hair was wet with the fog.

"It's what the men at the Harbor call thick as dungeon," said Peter. "Whatever that means. It's got a nice grim jail-cell sound to it. Look, Alix," he said uncomfortably, "This is an awful imposition on you, but there doesn't seem to be much we can do about it. Soren and I can sleep aboard the boat, if you could put the girls up here."

Judy said unexpectedly, "Sometimes Duff wakes up like a wild man. I mean, he has like hallucinations and thinks people are coming after him with knives—"

"Oh, that's dandy," said Alix. "He sounds like a lot more fun than anything. You two men are going to sleep right in this house tonight."

"Oh, boy!" said Myra, then clapped a hand across her mouth, her eyes round. "I don't mean to sound as if I'm *glad* Duff fell overboard, but— You sit down, Alix, and be our guest. We've got everything, even paper plates and plastic cutlery and stuff, so we won't need a thing except your frying pan and your gas stove."

"Feel free," said Alix with a wave of her hand. "While you're getting ready I'll make the beds."

"Do you need any help?" Soren asked.

"No, you stay right there with your beer." She escaped up the back stairs, shutting the door to underline her refusal.

Up in the studio she found that she was shaking. It was not putting them up that was disturbing her, but the fact that someone would have to be in Shane's bed. That would be herself, of course, and to lie there without him, the house full of strangers, was going to be nearly impossible. But she could not let anyone else sleep there.

She made her bed for Judy, then went down the front stairs and made up the downstairs bed for Peter and Myra, the study couch for Soren. She'd have preferred the study for herself, but the men had to be close to Duff in case of his hallucinations. Shane, if you're here, she thought, you must be laughing your head off at this mess. And at me, because I never wanted company, and look what I've got.

Duff snored on.

When supper was over the fog was thick and gray against the windows. Alix lighted the kitchen lamps. "Oh, it's so cozy," Myra rattled on. "We can sit around the fireplace and talk and sing, and—"

"And listen to Duff moan and snore and twitch five feet away?" asked Peter coldly.

"If only Judy had told us he shouldn't have that brandy," Myra sighed, giving Judy a sweet, sad gaze.

"That's right, blame everything on me!" Judy began to cry again. "I'm going to bed!" She left the kitchen, remembering even in her anguish to glide as if carrying a glass of water on her head, proudly letting the tears splash down over her makeup. Though she'd never regarded herself as nasty-neat, Alix recoiled from the thought of all that wet paint going onto her sheets. She murmured, "I'll take up some warm water for her to wash in. It'll make her feel better."

"Cleaner too," said Myra. "I wonder what she really looks like under all that stuff."

"Then you take it up," said Alix, waving generously at the towels and the basin. "I've got to clean my brushes."

She escaped again to the studio. Through the closed door
into her room she could hear Judy sobbing and talking to herself, then Myra's entrance like a resolutely hearty nurse. "Hi,
honey! Don't you want to wash up before you go to bed? Rain
water's marvelous for the complexion."

"Why don't they have electric lights in this stupid place?"
Judy hiccuped. "She makes enough, doesn't she?"

"*Sh!*" said Myra. "It's not dark yet, anyway. Look, she put
out pajamas for you. Isn't that nice? Did you ever sleep on an
island before? There's a poem about it we learned in school
once—"

Judy said with asperity, "Stop talking to me as if I was your
two-year-old infant!"

Alix smiled to herself. Down in the kitchen there was a masculine murmur of voices. Fog filled the north window, and
when she laid her ear against it she could hear the buoy off
Tiree Ledge called the Groaner, heard only on an east wind,
and below, above, and beyond it the immense sound that filled
the night up to the brim: the seas building up on the windward shores, the rote heard through the glass, the chimney, all
through the house whenever you were quiet enough to listen,
as if you were captive deep in the conch shell held to your own
ear.

❧ CHAPTER 20 ❧

She stood there a while. The gray light went fast, the studio became cavernous with shadow. There had been silence for quite some time in her room, and now she recognized Myra's voice downstairs, and the sounds of tidying up in the kitchen. She hated having them there, not so much because they disturbed her isolation, but because they might disturb Shane. This idea, when she had shaped it in words, jolted her; she saw herself turned gaunt and fey, hearing voices and seeing signs in everything. Well, kid, maybe this is how they get that way, because they have seen things they can't deny. And supposing this was the night something else was meant to happen, and he came, and the place was so full he couldn't find his way to her in their own house.

Seal Bay. Table-tipping. Hymns sung in the dark, ectoplasm made of luminous gauze. *Apports*. Wasn't that the word? Miss Spirit World of 1968.

This isn't the same, she whispered at her own raucous mockery. This isn't the same.

Then what is it?

I don't *know!*

She slatted herself away from the window as if from an unpleasant discussion, and lit the Aladdin lamp on her table,
leaving the shade off so that the brilliant yellow-white light
could reach up into the peak of the roof.

From the canvas Karen in a blue dress stared at her even
though there were no eyes yet, just a suggestion of the glasses,
sketched in to do away with the macabre emptiness. It would
not be a living child until the eyes were there. She intended to
paint the weak eye straight, as everyone hoped it would eventually be; but to tell Karen that, to get the whole proposition out
in one complete package before Karen could have time to reject it, was the insuperable problem.

Maybe Madge and Ozzie could do it, but she doubted it.

Karen studied the painting after every sitting. She never
commented but she always came to look. Was she so fervently
attached to her glasses that she wanted them in the painting,
instead of her own blue eyes? But then, how did the rest of
them know whether she even cared about the portrait? It must
be just something she thought she had to endure, because the
rest wanted it and a child had no rights.

Alix sighed, turned the canvas to the wall, and began to
clean her brushes. For a while the studio had seemed like a refuge; now she was glad to leave it for the kitchen.

Myra was reading and yawning. Someone had let William in
and he was going back and forth between Peter and Soren. He
arched his back hard against a firmly stroking hand that went
down his spine to his thick tail, gripped it and lifted him
gently by it. Released, William would bend himself in a circle
to come back with hard-bunting head under that knowledgeable hand.

William liked men; he always made a fuss over Ozzie, he
called on Jonas at Home Cove. But tonight, seeing him behave
as he had done endlessly with Shane, she realized that he might
miss Shane. If not actually *miss,* he still acted as if something
had been lacking, and he was never one to let go a good thing.

She moved quickly to the refrigerator and instantly he left

the game and came over to look inside. She took out his food
and he hurried ahead of her to the counter. "What a character," said Peter. "As big as he is, he looks as if he ought to belong to the Green Bay Packers."

"He's a superior animal," said Soren.

"Oh, he's not all that superior," said Alix. She put down
milk and meat, and William hunched over his dishes with full
and noisy attention. "He's not too bright, and he's terribly
stuck on himself." William looked around and up at her, eyes
opalescent in the refracted light. "But he's a very nice cat,
though," she added.

" 'But he is a very fine cat,' " said Soren. " 'A very fine cat
indeed.' "

"William was almost named Hodge for that cat," said Alix.
"Samuel Johnson's wasted on high school kids. I didn't appreciate him till I was older."

"Oh, you intellectual people," said Myra on a large yawn.
"Suddenly I'm dead. Can I go to bed now?"

"You can, and I'm going myself before long," said Alix.
"Anyone who wants to sit up can, as long as they're careful
about lamps. Do you want one for reading?"

"Read? Me? I can't even see print." Myra shut her book.
"And I know it's fascinating. I'm terribly interested in ESP and
things like that.... Come on out back with me, Peter, I'm
scared to go alone." She giggled. "Not really, but how often do
I get my husband alone on an island?"

Peter arose, stretching and groaning. "Well, don't have any
lecherous thoughts, because you're perfectly safe from me," he
said. "I'm half-dead myself. God, it's been a long time since I
woke up this morning."

Their voices went on beyond the closed door, then faded
out. Alix picked up the book. She knew Soren was watching
her, and she tried not to hold the book so tightly. This was ridiculous; Shane wasn't in this book, nothing was threatening
him.

"And you're tired, too," Soren said. "You look it. Well, if

you'll trust me with a lamp, I'll be glad to retire with a book. Is there any you'd rather I didn't handle?"

"Of course not," she said hastily. "But there are some things I want from the study. I'll go now and get them." She took a flashlight and went into the living room. She could hear Duff's noisy sleep. In the study she gathered up her other books.

Soren had brought a lamp into the living room and set it on a chest near the wall of bookshelves and was looking over the titles. Peter and Myra came back in, their hair glistening with wet; they were laughing secretively, fingers locked. "It's as thick as I've ever seen it in all my years at sea, man and boy," said Peter in a quavery voice, stroking his beard.

"Some camp-out we'd have had," said Myra. "You know that crazy Duff might have walked right off Haddock Island in the fog?"

"Cheer up," said Peter, "he could walk off this one too. Not that he'd be any great loss, but there'd have to be an investigation and they'd probably think we were having a pot party out here."

Myra hugged his arm. "Oh lovey, you better fasten a string from his ankles to yours so you'll know if he stirs."

"Like hell I will. Soren's going to be closer to him. Besides, he's bigger."

"Now that you've got that settled," said Alix, "here's a flashlight. Sleep well, but not too well, Peter. In case you have to help Soren."

"You know you're just tremendous?" Myra said huskily, her eyes swimming. "Who else would take this the way you have?"

"Just about anybody along the coast," said Alix. "Besides, what else could I do? Shut the door in your faces and let him die on the front lawn? Good night." She waved them off. She heard them talking in whispers to Soren in the next room, and they all inspected Duff. Then, as she was getting a lamp for herself, Soren returned to the kitchen.

"I'll take a turn around the house before I go to bed." He was amiable and impersonal, not the Sheik of Araby or the

Scandinavian Sexpot. "Do you want this outer door locked for the night?"

"No need of that, but thanks." He nodded and went out. She lighted her lamp and turned it low, took her books under her free arm, and went through the living room. First her portrait and then Shane's sprang out like living faces in the flickering, moving light, then seemed to withdraw themselves into the shadows as she passed by. William was curled in the big chair near the guitar. He looked up at her and yawned.

She went up the steep front stairs, stepping carefully with her lighted lamp and her armful of books. Her heart was beating unevenly; it seemed to make occasional little jumps. Her anticipation was not completely unpleasant. She didn't expect to sleep, but when the rest of them slept she would feel free again in her own house.

Oh, you're getting there, she said to her reflection in the mirror over the chest as she approached it with the lamp. Round the bend, round the bend, round the bend we go. And isn't it jolly here, forever expecting little messages like a teenager haunting the telephone? *Haunting* isn't the best word under the circumstances.

She took the pins out of her hair and let it fall. With the light burnishing her cheekbones, reflecting in her eyes and gilding the loose outer edges of her hair, she looked younger and less tired than she had felt downstairs when she had to concentrate on not letting the knife-edges of her nerves show through.

She opened one of the seaward windows an inch, and put her lamp on the bedside stand, piled up the pillows, and lay on the outside of the quilt with a blanket over her, still dressed except for her sneakers.

The raw saline wind flowed in carrying the roar of the rote, the thump and suck of seas on the beach below the house and the slower thunder on the points of Gib's Cove and under the Head. Not quite rhythmically the Groaner was heard.

So Shane had lain and read, and listened. He always wanted

the sound of the sea in his ears when he fell asleep and when he woke up. He kept the windows opened on nights when she wouldn't open hers.

Lying in his arms with everything snapping and slapping, the very matting lifted from the floor by drafts running underneath like small animals, doors swinging back and forth, latches rattling as if in ghostly fingers, a roaring past the chimneys, a creaking of ancient timbers around their wooden trunnels.

"For heaven's sake, Shane, the roof's going to lift right off!"

"As long as she creaks, she holds." He pulled her tighter into his arms. " 'Wild nights! Wild nights! Were I with thee, Wild nights should be our luxury!' I'd have liked Emily."

"Forget Emily. You've got me."

"You're jealous of a ghost."

"Of any female you mention, transparent or not."

" 'Futile the winds,' " said Shane, " 'to a heart in port—Done with the compass, Done with the chart.' Poor Emily, all that passion burned out on paper."

"If it had burned out her flesh we'd have never known she existed, so you couldn't be quoting her right now."

They said a dying person's life passed in review before him; in her case it seemed to be all the poetry she'd ever known, the way she was remembering it these days. Maybe it was occupational therapy for the mind, busywork for the emotions.

> *Rowing in Eden!*
> *Ah! the sea!*
> *Might I but moor*
> *Tonight in thee!*

As busywork it had its drawbacks. She got up and took one of the adventure stories from the chest. It had a North African setting, sandy, hot, blazing-bright. She plunged eagerly into its improbabilities, and dozed off finally, sliding down on the pillows as she slid deeper into sleep.

She thought it was her own cry that jerked her upright with

her mouth open and her heart pounding. Then the cry came again, a hoarse and terrible shriek from below.

Something fell over, another crash followed. She remembered everything at once and bounded off the bed and out into the hall. The sounds of a violent struggle came up to her. She ran downstairs, where a dim glow meant that the only light was in the study. The Ruskins' door at the foot of the stairs was closed. She ran across the living room toward the gasping, grappling shadows; the shriek broke free again. "Tigers! Tigers! They're after me! They almost got me! Save me, *save me!*"

Soren grunted out something unintelligible, probably Danish profanity. Duff was an eel with frantic arms and legs; in spite of Soren's size and strength, he couldn't get a positive grasp on a creature turned fluid and ungrippable by terror.

"They're in this house!" he croaked. "They keep coming out at me! Oh dear Jesus, I've got to get away!"

He wrenched himself out of Soren's arms, made a blind leap, tripped over a chair lying on its side, and dived forward on his stomach almost to Alix's feet. Sobbing, he groveled there, trying to pull himself up by her legs. She reached down to him, saying, "You're safe here. Nothing can hurt you."

On his knees he let out another scream, and pointed. In the light from the study William walked the back of the sofa like a Hallowe'en cat on a fence.

Soren moved up quietly behind Duff and felled him with a rabbit punch. He caught him before he collapsed, and carried him back to the sofa. William, exhilarated by all the action, excitedly dug claws into the sofa back. Efficiently Soren shook out the disordered tangle of blankets and tucked them around Duff, while Alix put a pillow under the sagging head.

"You didn't break his neck, did you?" she whispered, thinking that nothing would surprise her now.

"No." Soren, for once, didn't seem amused by everything. She lifted William off the sofa back, and carried him out into the kitchen. Soren came after her with his lamp. He too was still dressed. They looked at each other frowning, still breath-

ing hard. Both glanced back into the dark living room like conspirators, and then a hushed, incredulous laugh burst from
Soren.

"What a mess, eh? But I assure you we hadn't the slightest
idea of what we'd taken aboard."

"Do you think the Ruskins actually slept through that?"

"Perhaps Myra wouldn't let Peter come out, for fear Duff
was running amok with a carving knife. Well, we managed better without them."

"Thanks for the *we,* especially when I didn't do anything."
She put William on the back stairs and shut the door on him.
"Did William actually start all that?"

"If he walked up Duff the way he'd been in walking on me,
and Duff began to wake up without knowing where he was or
what had happened to him—" He grinned. "Horrible, eh?"

"All I can say is that Duff leads a pretty colorful life, if sea
monsters and giant cats are any sample of it. What are you
going to do with him tomorrow? Of course it's none of my
business." She turned on the gas under the teakettle. "Want
some coffee?"

"Yes, I would like some." He was looking at her with a
slight, curious smile and she said brusquely, "Have I got lamp-
black on me, or something?"

"No, it's your hair. Loose, like that, it changes all your features. You look different. Soft, youthful, disarmed."

"I'm just groggy with lack of sleep, that's all," she said, wishing she hadn't suggested coffee. But she was both hungry and
thirsty; she had hardly eaten at suppertime, and it was after
midnight. She began looking through the cupboards.

Behind her Soren said, "What is none of your business?"

"Should Judy be left with him? Or him with her? Running
amok with a knife might be more truth than poetry."

"That is something to be considered, certainly," he said judi-
ciously. "They're both over twenty-one, but Judy might take
some guidance from Peter and Myra. Not from me, naturally."

She didn't pick that up. She had found in her grocery order

a package of the homemade molasses doughnuts they sold at Emery's, and she put some to warm in the gas oven, and cut cheese. Soren lit his pipe and slumped comfortably in the captain's chair.

"How is the work with the little girl coming?" he asked. "Exquisite coloring, and quite a beautiful profile, I thought."

"Yes, as a matter of textures and tones, she's a joy, but then most children are. Even the plainest have something special, you find when you begin to work, and then they're no longer plain."

"You love children."

"I don't know if I do," she said good-naturedly. "I love painting children. I love painting, period."

"I do too," he said, leaning forward. "Do you know what is the thing I dread the most? The day when it's not there any more—or when it's still there in all its fire and passion but I can't do anything about it." He almost smiled. "I am speaking of painting, nothing else. My idea of a good friend is the one who will assist me to make my own quietus after I am paralyzed or blinded or palsied."

She poured coffee with a marvelously steady hand. She was almost tempted to tell him that she wanted to make her quietus; wouldn't it be the thorny irony of her life if he were the one who gave it the blessing of understanding, and not Shane? Unless he said, *Why? You can still paint, can't you?*

He said, "Your mouth is set against something. Against the thought of suicide? Do you consider it a sin?"

She shook her head. "No, there are times when it's justified. When your *raison d'être* disappears, why can't you? That is, if you're reasonably mature and you *know* your life is over, you don't just suspect it. When there's nothing to be gained by waiting." She set the warm doughnuts on the table and sat down opposite him.

"Yes," he said. "Beethoven composed after he became deaf, but he could hear the music in his head, and he had the hands to set the notes down. It's a little different from a painter who loses his hands in one way or another." He grinned. "Well, this is a cheerful conversation for a foggy midnight, isn't it? When will the raven come tapping at the door?"

"Have a doughnut," said Alix.

He laughed and took one. She asked him what he thought of a young painter whose first big show had been a sensation in the early spring. On painting Soren was knowledgeable and committed. The conversation took them through two mugs of coffee each, a half-dozen doughnuts, and a large quantity of cheese. The mantel clock harshly clanging half-past one startled them both. They both looked up at it and, seeing the time, Alix suddenly felt sleepy enough to fall in a stupor over the kitchen table.

"What a pity," said Soren. "Here I've had Alexia Horne with her hair down all to myself in the middle of the night, and we've done nothing but talk shop."

"But it's been nice, don't you think?" Alix said, getting up. She resisted saying, *And probably a change for you.* "Excuse me," she said. She stepped into her short deck boots, took the old tweed coat from the hook in the entry, and went out. Outdoor toilets had a convenience that had nothing to do with plumbing; *in the country,* her grandmother had once said in stately cadences, *a gentleman never asks a lady where she is going.*

The moon was shining through the fog. She took the path down to the wharf, moving through scarves and veils of luminous mist that brushed delicately against her cheeks and hands. She was quickly hidden from the house by a dense screen which took on moving forms as she tried to see through it.

Gib's Cove was hidden except for a glimmer of water seen through thinning fog. The seas had flattened so that the rote was diminished, and from along the beach and around the wharf spilings she could hear the faint sounds and stirrings of the invisible incoming tide. She could pick out the little noises around the hull of *Sea Pigeon* rocking slightly at her mooring. Poor neglected *Pigeon,* she thought, tomorrow we'll go out.

❧ CHAPTER 21 ❧

THE FOG LIFTED, parted, melted together again. Once when she looked back up at the house the wet rooftop and chimneys shone in the moonlight above fogdrifts like a mysterious dwelling glimpsed in a fold in the hills. Toward the west the tips of the tallest spruces seemed to rise along snowy mountain ridges.

It was the way one as a child had imagined the moon to be, a land of perpetual white and silver, snow and fog, clouds that smelled cool and flowery. Alone out here, having it all to herself while the others knew nothing about it, she felt a fierce little surge of something like exhilaration, strange and foreign for someone who was done with the world. But she couldn't help it.

She crossed the wharf and went down onto the ledges on the eastern side of it. She followed the rocks around the eastern arm of Gib's Cove and toward the sand beach. Now there was the musical swash of high tide on a windward shore after the wind has gone down and has left a run on the rocks and gravel. She was below her house shortly, but invisible from it even if the fog should suddenly lift. She walked just above the edge of the water that broke in arabesques of foam on the wet-darkened sand. The dinghy from the yawl had been hauled up above high-water mark at the foot of the path up the bank. The yawl itself was not to be seen.

She sat down beyond the dinghy in the curve of the bank. The little waves came surging and sparkling at her out of the fog, but never near enough to touch before they fell back. Watching them, listening, she felt her lids drooping, and she wished she could sleep here, huddled in the old tweed coat like an Indian in his blanket.

The man was just beyond the dinghy before she saw him. Oh, no! she thought in disgust, Soren has come looking for me. *That* I will not have. Then as he paused, looking up at the illumined sky above the mist, she saw that it was Jonas. His face showed clearly in the moonlight. He wore no cap. The contrast of light and dark gave him a masklike look, rigid, the eyes hidden in shadow beneath the brows, the corners of the mouth turned down. He stood staring up at the moon as if something extraordinary about it had commanded his attention; then he turned his head with that quick terrier motion and looked up in the direction of the house, and stood there for what seemed a long time to Alix, holding her breath.

Then he turned around and went back. The whole thing was unsettling. She felt like a spy, huddling there; it was unfair to watch someone without his knowing it, to witness gestures or expressions you had no right to see. As a child this had been treasure to add to her knowledge of other people; as an adult she was too sensitive of her own rights to deny other people theirs.

A fresh wave of fog blew thick and wet between them. The whole scene in retrospect took on the disjointed quality of a dream fragment. In fact she couldn't be sure she hadn't dreamed it.

The pleasant drowsiness was gone now, and she got up and went up over the bank.

The kitchen was still lighted. She stood a little way off from the first window she came to, and looked in. The lamp was on the counter near the sink, and Soren sat by the table but half-turned from it. He was playing Shane's guitar.

She felt nothing about it at all, she had gone by all that and it seemed ridiculous that it had ever bothered her. He had his head bent over it in the familiar pose of someone picking out chords, and he was singing softly; she could hear the deep tones faintly through the window. His hands moving along the narrow neck and over the strings had also a familiarity, like the shoulders in the worn Viyella shirt.

She went along to the back door, opening it quietly and hanging the coat on its hook before she went into the kitchen. He went on singing; it was a simple, charming little tune sung in Danish, or at least a Scandinavian language; she could tell that much. She stepped out of her boots and went over to warm her hands on the sides of the teakettle. He finished and said, "That was a long trip you took."

"I went for a walk. What was that song about?"

"It begins, 'I can see in your eyes that you love another,'" he said.

"There was something about roses."

"'How can one pick roses where no roses grow?' Do you know what *Jag elsker dig* means?" She looked around and shook her head.

"It means 'I love you,'" he said, and smiled. "You see, you walked straight into it. Would you like some coffee to warm you up?"

"I'm not cold," she said. "Do you generally stay up all night?"

"Do you? ... No, I thought I should stay up in case you didn't come back. I wouldn't know where to look, and I don't imagine William can double as a bloodhound, but I waited, useless as it was."

"Thank you," she said coldly. "But I'm quite used to going my own way here in all kinds of weather."

"And I'm being officious, or presumptuous—is that it?" He saddened. "You're angry because of the guitar."

"No. And if I sounded pompous, I didn't mean to. I'm awfully tired. Good night." She put her hand on the latch of the back stairs door.

"No, wait," he said, putting the guitar on the table and getting up. "You're on guard against me. My fault, because of the other day. Will you forgive me?" He lifted both hands and touched her loose hair. "Your hair's wet. Are you going to bed with it like that? What a wonderful color it is in this light. Could I paint it, do you think? "Alix by Lamplight." Or simply "A Woman in Lamplight," with hair you could warm your hands at, and sad, cynical eyes set in shadows."

" 'Cynical,' is right, the other word is 'bleary.' You should have been a poet, Soren." She moved her head backward from between his brushing fingertips. "Good night." He wasn't so flagrant a hunter as to try to hold her.

She had no flashlight, but the studio was faintly illuminated by the drifting sea of moonlit fog outside. William's purr came from her work table. She picked him up, as flaccid and slithery as Duff had been in the afternoon, and slung him over her shoulder. As she crept through her room, Judy stirred and mumbled.

"It's all right," Alix said. "Go back to sleep." Judy sighed and was quiet. In Shane's room Alix dropped William on the foot of the bed, peeled off her fog-damp jeans, and crawled in. She went at once to sleep and when she woke up it was full morning. The fog hadn't cleared away but had come in thicker. The first horrifying picture that burned into her consciousness in its entirety was that of a day of imprisonment with the rest.

She was completely and frantically awake. She pulled on her jeans, which felt so clammy her flesh cringed away from them. William lounged in the crumpled bedclothes, purring loudly and working his claws, meeting her eyes with slumberous blinks. "Come on, get up," she whispered to him fiercely. He rolled over, kneading the air, and she hauled him out of the blankets. To go down the front stairs risked arousing the Ruskins, and she had the feeling that Soren slept more lightly than

William and was just waiting for her to pass the study door.

When she moved stealthily through her room, Judy said distinctly, "What time is it?"

"Not five yet," Alix lied. It was nearer six.

Judy groaned and dug deeper. Alix slid into the studio and latched the door behind her, put William down, and they went downstairs side by side. She stood in the gray light of the kitchen, listening. No sound except for the hoarse ticking of the clock. Duff had stopped snoring. She hoped objectively that he was still alive. William hooked the corner of the cupboard door not tightly buttoned and jerked it toward him with an earsplitting vibration. She seized him, put him out, got into her boots and a jacket, and went out. William stood with ears flattened and tail lashing; his stock imitation of an enraged cougar.

"You won't die if you don't eat right off," she said. "You're too fat now." She set off at a run along the path up the hill toward the woods.

When she came into the house at Beauty Cove, Ozzie and Madge were eating breakfast. Sidney sat under Ozzie's elbow, too fervent for bacon to give her more than a perfunctory nod. Karen wasn't up yet.

"My lands, look at you!" Madge said. "Hair down like a young one, pink cheeks and all. That company must agree with you."

"Oh God," said Alix, rolling her eyes starkly at the ceiling.

Ozzie asked, "You in full retreat?"

"*Am* I! I ran most of the way here. Like a deer."

Madge set coffee before her and seductively held up a brown egg. "It's fresh since last night."

"No thanks to the egg, but yes to the coffee. . . . Ozzie, if you want me to write my name in my own blood, I will," she told him. "I'll do anything, if you come around this morning and pick them up and take them to the Harbor."

"Well, I don't figger on asking for your honor or your fortune or anything like that. I'll lug 'em off for nothing."

"You've just proved that knighthood is still in flower." She reached for a slice of Madge's bread. "Poor William, I threw him out without his breakfast this morning, and for him that's like depriving a man of his citizenship. But everybody was dead to the world and I wasn't taking any chances on stirring them up."

"But that Peter and Myra seemed like real decent down-to-earth youngsters even if he has got long hair," said Madge plaintively, "and Mr. Michaels has such a nice smile."

"Oh, they're all right," said Alix. "It's just that after being up half the night I can't stand being shut up with them today, or with anyone. And this combination of thick fog and no wind is going to keep that yawl anchored right off my beach unless some expert takes her away." She ducked her head and began scratching Sidney's ears. "People like these, and that includes Duff, aren't strange to me. I'm not all upset or horrified or anything like that. But I don't have the patience I used to have, or the resilience."

Madge's face puckered, and she said thickly, "And no wonder."

"This bacon's real good," said Ozzie. "Seems like you could swallow down a couple of strips in the way of soul-and-body lashin's."

"That is a wizard idea," Alix announced very loudly. Madge at once smiled through her tears and put more bacon in the frying pan. "And you'll have that new-laid egg now too," she said.

Before she went home Alix went into the bathroom and did up her hair, all the while giving herself an unrelenting scrutiny in the mirror. You'll do, she thought. This morning you look like a woman in her right mind, in lousy shape though it is. You also look like a woman who's showing signs of wear and tear. Everything combined ought to be pretty discouraging to Soren, unless he really prefers veterans to virgins.

When she got back to the house everybody was up, making

breakfast of what was left of their camping supplies. William had been let in and fed raw hamburg, and he was now being incredibly jovial. Judy, looking naked without her eye make-up and with her hair tied tightly back at the nape of her neck, was working her way morosely through a fried-egg sandwich with mustard oozing out around the edges. Soren was making toast on top of the wood range with the air of a continental waiter making crêpes suzettes. Each slice was an artistic production, and Peter and Myra received it as such.

"I never tasted anything so gorgeous," Myra told Alix with her mouth full. "From now on, toast made in a toaster will be just absolutely *blah*."

"This one is the perfect color for you, Alix," Soren said. "I'm an alchemist this morning. I'm changing base baker's bread into pure gold."

"How do you know the baker was base?" Alix asked. She shook her head at the toast. "It's simply stunning, it has thrust and perception, its meaningful tensions communicate the dichotomy of *now*, but this morning I'm in a mood to reject. I'm dropping out. Besides, I've had breakfast. Why don't you eat it yourself?"

"Create a new art form, Soren," said Peter. "The predatory clash of teeth crunching through toast into the soft heart; a delicate yet virile sound that lacerates the eardrums, tears at the vitals, and—uh—what—" He snapped his fingers frantically.

"Exacerbates the soul," suggested Soren, buttering the toast.

"That sounds dirty," said Myra, "but I don't suppose it is."

"The title," said Alix, "will be 'Viking, 1968'."

Soren said with a crinkling around the eyes, "I have the feeling that was a low blow."

"Not at all," said Alix. "After all, nobody would let you go very far today burning houses and raping and murdering." She seemed to go away from her voice, hearing it as if from across the room, while she was seeing Thorvald Yellowmane on the desk blotter. How had he got out of the drawer that day? A Dane. This Dane. Coincidence?

The Ruskins had picked up her theme, exaggerating it and laughing madly at her, themselves, and Soren. They were like healthy children after an unexpected adventure and a good night's sleep. Soren went along with them. Judy got up and went out. Duff sat huddled in his chair wearing several sweaters; the large outer one was Soren's. He gripped his mug with both hands, and after an obvious and frightful period of concentration he brought his mouth down to it and sipped very carefully.

He seemed not to hear the rest. All of his world was there in his hands and the mug which he couldn't lift. His face was faunish and small, and the straggling fine hair and overwide eyes with bluish scallops under them made him look like a Gainsborough child.

'How are you this morning, Duff?" Alix asked.

He looked at her from under thick lashes. "Not very well," he answered in a moderate, elderly voice. "Fragile. Gossamer, in fact. A finger pointed at me could destroy me. I'm sorry I drank all your brandy." He gave the mug a depressed glance. "Have you got anything else? I got up early this morning and looked in all the cupboards, but I couldn't find anything." He stopped as if to regain his balance and added, "Just two cans of beer in the fridge, but they weren't much help."

"I'm afraid you'll just have to go on feeling gossamer," Alix told him gently. "If you had just one drink this morning you know what would happen."

"You *have* got something else," he reproached her.

"But not for you. You've got to go ashore this morning."

"I suppose so." He bowed his head lower over the mug. "But I wish I could stay here forever. It's so peaceful. I haven't slept so soundly since I used to go to my grandmother's farm in Vermont."

"Well, I'm glad you slept so well," Alix said graciously. How blissful to have no memory of nightmares.

"Listen, everyone," she said. "Ozzie Goodwin's going to take you in and tow the yawl."

When they had gone, when the Head had shut off sounds of engine and voices calling through the fog, she walked slowly back across the soaking lawn and in through the front door. A warm bouquet of woodsmoke, cooking, and tobacco met her, and almost as strong was the atmosphere that other people left behind them like a patina on all they had touched or even looked at.

Myra had stripped the beds they had used and taken the sheets and towels with her. Judy had stirred herself enough to wash the dishes and had even wiped the sink clean. Duff's blankets had been folded tidily. His performance hadn't included being sick, which was an agreeable surprise, though Soren would probably have taken over. He seemed capable of anything.

Anything. He'd left his mark on the study, all right. Savagely she stripped off the couch cover which he had replaced, and put on a Navajo blanket from the chest. She took the other cover and the blankets outdoors and hung them on the lines in the fog. Turning back to the house she found herself crossing the spot where she had stood last night and looked in at Shane with his head bent over the guitar, picking out chords and singing. No, not *Shane!* She put her knuckles against her mouth and ground them into her lips.

Freudian slip, Alix, Freudian slip! It was *not!* she cried silently back at the guttersnipe jeering. He had Shane's clothes and Shane's guitar, and even with them all here the house was full of Shane, he'd had years to leave his touch on everything.

✌ CHAPTER 22 ✌

THE WIND TURNED northwest, the sun came out, the fog was burned and blown away. The last shreds of the others were also blown away as the wind came down over the spruces and poured through the open windows. The blankets snapped like sails, and blew to the ground; when she gathered and folded them they smelled of warm wool, grass, and sun.

She took one of the blankets and went up to the Tangle. The wind struck only lightly here, casting a perpetual shimmer and dapple of light and shade over the covering of starflowers, anemones, bunchberry blossoms like miniature dogwood, blue and white violets, and all the other nameless, infinitesimal flowerings. The birds were numerous and active. She lay on the blanket under the high rustling ceiling of moosewood leaves, and slept.

It was a loud fussing of robins close by that woke her up, and she found William sprawled on the blanket with her. It was midafternoon. She went home and fed William, took a bath in tepid rain water and put on clean clothes, and went out again.

She was now consciously staying out of the house, as if she

were hoping for a surprise when she returned to it for the night. She hadn't remade her own bed or gone back to Shane's room since she'd left it that morning. When she went upstairs for clean clothes she didn't look around; she hadn't even gone into the studio to take her usual glance at the work in progress. The wind may have cleansed the house but nothing could clear her mind of the fear that the last twenty-four hours had destroyed any filaments she had laboriously spun between her and Shane.

She went over to Beauty Cove early, and found Madge and Karen looking for wild strawberries on the old pasture ground. Myra had asked Madge and Ozzie to a picnic supper on the first day of the show. "You're going, aren't you?" Madge asked anxiously. "We wouldn't go without you."

Alix hadn't planned to attend; when Peter had been going on about the show, how this year they were running it for three days instead of just on Harbor Day itself, she had thought calmly, *Perhaps I won't be around by then. I never intended to be here this long.*

"All those artists," Madge was saying. "I've never been to any such thing before. Myra said to bring Karen, there'll be other young ones there, so it won't be wild or anything like that. Well, Ozzie said he'd go if I wanted to, but I'm not going if you don't. I'd be like a cat in a strange garret."

She gazed hopefully at Alix, who said, "We'll get off in a corner and giggle behind our hands at the sights."

Relief made Madge rise and expand like good yeast dough. There was no need for Alix to make conversation, Madge made it all, breaking off occasionally to tell Sidney to stop rolling in the berries, or to call and ask Karen how she was doing. For a child whom Alix would have suspected of deliberately crushing ripe berries, Karen did very well, and brought a tin mug of fruit to add to the bowl.

"There, we can all have a little dish of berries tonight," Madge said. "I always think the first taste of strawberries is the most special, no matter how many you have afterwards."

Jonas was there for supper. He nodded agreeably at Alix as if they had been introduced once, by accident. The island trip and the almost-intimacy of their sharp words might have never taken place. Remembering his face as he stood by the dinghy in the moonlight she thought, Perhaps he has washed his hands of me because of their all coming in on me like that, and Duff getting drunk, and so forth; probably he thinks, This is the kind of person she is, she draws people like that, crazy, irresponsible. . . . She's an artist too, isn't she? They're a different animal. Like calls to like. Water seeks its own level. Any more old rags, bottles, and clichés today?

Well, I don't really care, she told the omnipresent Ear. I don't want him around any more than I want Soren. One's a virtuous know-it-all, and the other's a lecherous know-it-all.

But when she got up to go, Jonas said, "I'll take you around in the dory."

"I don't mind walking. You were going to watch something, weren't you?"

"I'll take you home," he repeated curtly. She shrugged.

"Will you come about nine tomorrow, Karen?"

Madge answered for her. "Oh, she'll be there! Wouldn't it be nice if you could show that picture, Alix? Just think, Ozzie, *our* granddaughter up there for everybody to see, all these people coming from far and wide."

A picture with no eyes, thought Alix. "Why not, if it's finished?" she said. She thanked them again for her meal, and was loaded down with things to take home in one of Madge's seine-twine carryall bags. Jonas took the bag, and the others walked down to the wharf with them. It was a still evening, with the clear beautiful Wedgwood-blue light that came between sunset and dark on a clear night.

"The moon's rising, but we can't see it," Madge said wistfully. "That's the one thing I miss over there, watching that big moon rising all gold out of the sea, and then turning silver as it climbs, and the path from it coming in to the beach."

"You're in some sentimental mood tonight, old lady," Ozzie said, putting his arm around her. "You must be mellering.

Those were the lights you wanted to swap the moon for." He pointed toward the twinkling sparks on the mainland.

"Well, there's nothing to keep you from coming over and watching the moon rise," said Alix, "and then coming back here to look at your mainland lights."

"If we didn't have our young boarder," said Ozzie, "we'd go up on the Head and neck while we're watching it, the way we did when we were courting."

"You crazy mixed-up kids are what's wrong with this country," said Jonas. "Got sex on the brain."

They all laughed. Karen stood on the end of the wharf looking toward the mainland, a small solitary pale-haired figure in the pure light. She didn't turn around when Alix and Jonas called good night to her. "She's wishing on the evening star," said Madge comfortably.

The dory cut away through the satiny water, shattering into glittering fragments the reflection of the evening star. The woods looked black, but between water and sky the hyacinthine light seemed to hover indefinitely without losing its quality; a positive medium in itself through which they moved like fishes in an aquarium of tinted water.

They passed the Home Cove, where Jonas's cabin was invisible against the ebony mass of woods. When they rounded the next point they saw the moon as Madge had described it, turning from gold to silver in a pale sky.

She thought, I will not think back. I will not think *If only*— She had an old exercise for diversion, that of deciding what colors she would use to get the exact tint of the water just either side of the moon-track. There was also, if you looked at it hard enough, almost a faint flush around the moon, dissolving subtly into the surrounding sky; and was that a grayed violet, a ghost of apple green, a true blue? How deceptive were one's own eyes?

It was like a form of hypnosis, but the trance was shattered when she felt the boat swerve; for an instant she didn't recognize the shape of her own cove. The rocks of the eastern arm against the moonlit sea, with light pouring onto them from above, were like volcanic ledges off a distant and exotic isle; the names Zanzibar and the Seychelles came to mind, smelling of cloves and cinnamon. Not that she'd ever wanted to go there, it had always been Greece, but the words had such lovely hot colors and scents.

The engine stopped, and the dory glided sibilantly toward the wharf. William spoke from the top of it. In the moonlight he was striped in jet and silver.

"Hello, Barnacle Bill," Jonas said to him.

Alix slowly unlocked arms and legs. "That was a lovely ride. Thank you very much."

"Oh, I liked it too," he said. "Been a long time since I've had a moonlight sail."

But you walk in it, she wanted to say to him, except that it would have disturbed her mood; she wanted to hold on to this quietness and take it up the hill with her into the house.

"I'll hand your bag up," Jonas said. She stepped onto the ladder and went up the few rungs to the top, bracing herself for William's heavy and impetuous greeting. She knelt to reach for the bag, but Jonas was still sitting in the stern by the engine, holding onto a spiling and looking up at her.

"I haven't been much good to myself or anybody else lately," he said.

"You've been strangely invisible."

"You must have missed me the way you'd miss a rock in your shoe."

"Don't put words in my mouth." She sat back on her heels and stroked the leaning William. "But speaking of shoes, for a while there waiting for you to show up was like waiting for the other shoe to drop. Then I got news by the bush telegraph that you were some cranky these days."

"Bush telegraph?"

"Karen. The longest sentence I've ever heard her say dealt with you."

He laughed whole-heartedly, looking merry and apparently carefree. "Hey, she talked to me about you too."

"What'd she say, what'd she say?"

"You're painting her picture, and you talk to yourself all the time."

"Well, I can't talk to *her*. I recite poetry. She shows less interest than William. I may just break into a soft-shoe routine and see if that gets her."

"It would get me," said Jonas, "especially if you wore long black net stockings with fancy clocks."

"Why, Jonas Hallowell," she said. "If you'll give me my bag I'm going home."

He stepped up on the middle seat and handed it up to her. But he kept a grip on the handle after she took hold, saying in a much quieter voice, "I'm now what's termed a free man. Supposed to be an occasion for celebration but it hasn't been feeling that way."

"Your divorce has gone through, then," she said.

"Yup. I'm unencumbered by anything except a dory and two hundred and fifty second-hand traps."

"You must have wanted this divorce very much, to give up your business."

"Let's say that one of us wanted it very much," he said dryly. He let go of the bag.

"And it wasn't you, I gather," she said, uncomfortable and a little resentful. She wasn't to be able to keep her mood after all. "I'm sorry. But she's alive, and that means there's always a chance to—"

He shook his head. "No chance. If there ever was one, I blasted it to hell and gone. However, I'm not looking for sympathy. You didn't make your misery but, as the feller says, I am the author of my own misfortunes."

"What feller was that?" she said.

"Oh, one of those Greeks or Romans that always talked in quotations."

"Well, misfortune is misfortune, however it comes. Some other feller said that sweet are the uses of adversity, but right now I can't see it." William knocked over the bag by trying to get headfirst into it, and she was glad of the diversion. The emptiness of the house behind her was as palpable as a crouching beast.

It never got less. It just kept coming back in different forms.

She stood up. "Good night," she said. "Thanks again for the ride."

"You're entirely welcome," he said. She waited a moment longer while he pushed away from the wharf. Then as he started the engine, she turned and walked away up the wharf, William hurrying ahead; their shadows fell dark-blue and scissor-edged on the moon-bleached planks.

The sound of the engine had died away completely as she reached the house. William ran in ahead of her, across a floor patterned with askew panels of moonlight. Without lighting a lamp she gave him more to eat, and put away the food she had brought from the Goodwins'. She brushed her teeth and washed her face, and went up the backstairs to her room. Nothing was wild in her tonight, or outside her. No emptiness had devoured her, it had become simply the emptiness of a house without Shane.

She walked through the studio and into her room, back to moonlit windows again. The door was open into Shane's room. More moonlight lay shattered on the floor. She stood looking down at the uneven shapes until she recognized them as something broken, then she went down on her knees and cautiously picked up the largest piece, holding it up to the windows. She recognized the flowers painted on the sky-blue glaze: edelweiss. There was also a bit of gleaming gold border intact, and a couple of gold letters in German script.

She'd seen the mustache cup trying to shine through its dust in the window of a second-hand shop, crowded with a dreary collection of junk, and she had bought it for Shane as a joke when he was starting to let his mustache grow.

She'd last seen it on a shelf in the studio; she'd brought it up to use in a still life and hadn't taken it downstairs again.

❧ CHAPTER 23 ❧

SHE LISTENED in the house at night, and in the days she sometimes stopped in the woods or on the shore with the impression of an unusual sound, not in her ear but in her head. She often felt as if she were going to explode with this expectancy that never came to full term. One night she sat at the kitchen table and wrote to Shane about it, as if she were in a rage at him that couldn't be contained. After five pages of a large notebook were filled, she felt slack and loose, trembly in her hands and legs, her head heavy on her neck. She looked at the torrents of handwriting with a twisted grin.

"Well, at least I knew what I was doing," she said aloud. "I haven't gone in for automatic writing yet." Clinically she studied the script; it was no more erratic than it ever was when she wrote in haste, a strong and flowing line. Then she tore the pages out of the notebook and used them for kindling.

It seemed a pity to waste this relaxation, so she lay on the sofa in the living room, her spine perfectly straight as one of the books taught, and tried to follow its advice for getting into a receptive state. William spoiled this by jumping unexpectedly onto her stomach.

When the tension built up again she wrote another letter to Shane. "It's better than taking Seconal," she remarked to William. She was still saving the Seconal for the final occasion, but if it weren't for the letters she would have been tempted to swallow the whole lot in one unsplendid, sneering, guttersnipe gesture at whatever was doing all this to her. "It simply can't be Shane," she said. "He'd find a way to make sure. He wouldn't torture me like this."

But this always led to another sort of torture, as agonizing as splinters driven under the nails. What if this was the only way he had, and she was the stupid one?

There must be honest mediums. These people swore to it. But how did you find one? In the telephone book? Even if in one of the nearby towns there was such a person, how could she bring herself to inquire? It made her think of furtive, frightened girls trying to locate abortionists. *This friend of mine, well, she's in trouble, and—*

Seal Bay. Drive up there. Ask. The only trouble was that she could get fouled up with the lunatic fringe and lose her courage before she found what she was looking for. These mediums in the books were quiet, ordinary in appearance and manner. How did you reach *them?* Perhaps if she wrote to one of them she'd get the name of someone she could trust.

She pulled herself up short and said aloud, "I don't know what to do." She was walking through the woods and she felt so sick and breathless that she had to sit down on a boulder. "Shane, if you love me," she said in a voice unrecognizable to herself, "give me a sign."

There was no sign, at least nothing she could identify as such. But after a while she felt better, and started walking again.

At the same time that she was living like this, she was also living in public: sketching, painting, keeping house after a fashion, apparently making the slow climb up from tragedy. Brave Alix. She wrote to Dodie saying she was too well-occupied on the island to think of going on a cruise, but thanks for thinking of her, and thank Jack too. She and Madge picked wild strawberries for shortcake and jam. She spent one afternoon sketching gulls in action as Ozzie and Jonas dressed codfish. The Ruskins came one day in a borrowed outboard dory, but they were all business, Peter austerely resolved not to take up her time. They brought back the sheets, towels, and borrowed clothing, everything washed, pressed, and in some cases mended.

"You did too beautiful a job on those old things, Myra," Alix said.

"I used to be a 4-H girl, can you imagine it?" said Myra.

"I can imagine it very well."

"So long," said Peter sternly, hauling Myra by the hand toward the door. "Oh, hey, Alix, you want me to take your picture in for the Show?"

"It's not ready yet. I'll bring it in."

"Okay!" He resumed forcibly moving his wife out of the house. Alix laughed and said the rush wasn't necessary.

"Yes, it is. Once she gets her fanny on a chair and a cup of tea in front of her, she puts down roots. And I said after the last time we weren't coming in on you again for a hell of a long time."

"But maybe I miss you," said Alix. "What about Duff and Judy?"

"They've gone!" cried Myra happily. "She drove him back to Boston because it was the only way to get rid of him!"

"Poor kids," said Alix. Myra crooned something compassionate, and Peter growled, "You're too soft for your own good. That's why these nuts get away with such performances. Sympathetic women. Look, Alix, I'll be working at the Grange Hall hanging pictures all day before the opening, so I'll meet you there, okay?"

"Okay!" she said. Myra giggled and Peter took her by the nape of the neck and marched her toward the wharf. Alix watched them go, wondering with a kind of all-over soreness what it must be like to be so young, to be married and in love, to be parents. The wondering increased the difference between them and her to a lifetime instead of the ten or twelve calendar years that existed between her and Peter.

"Is there any medical reason why Karen couldn't take her glasses off for a few minutes at a time?" she asked Madge.

"Not that I know of. Of course as soon as her eye gets tired it begins to turn, but she's gone without them at home. With the good eye patched, though."

"Karen, does it hurt you to take your glasses off?" Alix asked her the next day.

"Unh-unh," said Karen.

"What was that? I heard a funny noise."

"No, it doesn't hurt," Karen said loudly.

"Then why won't you take them off for just a few minutes? The instant your eye begins to feel tired you can put them on again. I can't finish this picture until I can put the eyes in."

"Just put my glasses," said Karen.

"But they don't show you. It could be a doll sitting there."

Karen settled harder into the chair, her mouth primly tightening.

I'd like to wallop you, Alix thought, right on the seat of your little blue bloomers. "All right," she said amiably, "you can go home now."

Karen looked slightly surprised. "I just got here."

"Well, there's nothing more I can do to your picture, so I'm going on to something else." She put the painting face to the wall and began to clean her palette. Karen sat watching her. Finally Alix glanced around and said, "Haven't you gone yet? It's a lovely day to be out. You'd better hurry."

Karen got up slowly, keeping her glasses focused on Alix. She seemed about to speak, and for a moment Alix believed with a quite illogical excitement that the child was going to capitulate.

But after a suspenseful moment Karen started downstairs. "Good-bye," Alix called after her, receiving no answer. She set the painting back on the easel and studied it. She had put in a background of the Head in sunshine, and past a shoulder of grass there was a patch of blue-green sea, wind-whipped to the horizon, with a sail showing. The sail and the indication of field flowers in the grass were for Madge, who always took a profound pleasure in the most minute detail.

It could have been a charming work, a little girl in a blue dress against a bright summery scene like the mythological setting of childhood. But it had no eyes, and that changed the myth to something else, not at all charming.

Madge might have some photographs that showed Karen's eyes. It wasn't the way Alix liked to work, but she wanted to finish the picture; the thought of an uncompleted project nagged at her like a hangnail, and besides it would always be an aggravation if not a torment to Madge, a painting all finished but the eyes.

When she was done cleaning up in the studio she went to wash her hands at the kitchen sink. A tiny sound from the living room startled her far more than such a small sound should. She knew it wasn't William; she could see him through the window over the sink, lying on his back in the grass batting at the tree swallows who buzzed him.

She heard the sound again. Her scalp tightened. *Is this it?* She turned her head slowly, listening for more, and identified it as the sound of pages fluttering.

Heat engulfed her like a blast from an explosion. Even her eyes felt scalded. *"Karen!"* she shouted. "Are you in there?" She reached the door. Karen stood by the sofa, stiffly motionless. In the midst of a disappointment almost too dreadful to be borne, she remembered a squirrel freezing when Sandy discovered it, and how she was always wrung with pity for its silent terror, and would drag Sandy away, scolding him at the top of her voice.

She was not, all these years later, that emotional about Karen, but she spoke in an easier voice. "I thought you'd gone. What were you doing?"

"Reading," said Karen, just audibly. She made a small tight gesture with her right hand, which could have indicated a book on shore birds. Alix's special books were on the floor beside the sofa, but they'd be safe from a child, having no pictures in them.

"Would you like to take it home with you?" Alix asked. "I'm sorry, we don't have more things for people your age."

"I don't want anything," Karen said huskily. She swerved out around the sofa and headed rapidly for the front door. I must look like the Dragon Lady, Alix thought.

Madge had no photographs that would do. In snapshots the figures were too small, and in the few posed photographs and school pictures, Karen wore her glasses, and also that same tight-lipped impassivity, as if no photographer would get anything from her, not even the pretense of a smile. In comparison with her cousins, she was a miniature Stone Face.

"Seems like we could insist on her taking her specs off," said Ozzie.

"I don't know how you're going to insist and make it work," said Alix. "I think it's a matter of principle with her by now, and I don't like to pull rank on a kid, so to speak. Just because we're bigger . . . If she doesn't do it because *she* wants to, she'll be all tightened up and probably squinting, and I still won't get what I want."

"I'll ask her to do it for Gram," said Madge. "I'm sure she'll do it for me if I ask her just right." She clasped her hands against her bosom and looked distraught. "Oh, I'm just *dying* to see that picture in the Harbor Day show!"

"Well, try it if you want," said Alix, "but don't badger her. She's got her reasons." One way to keep us all in our places, she thought. "Perhaps it's self-consciousness, somebody's made fun of the eye. Or maybe she thinks it'll get better that much quicker if she never takes them off except to go to bed. Look, I've got a week before I take my exhibit in. If she doesn't concede, it'll be either you or Ozzie."

"Ozzie," said Madge at once. "A real picturesque fisherman is what all those summer people want to see."

Ozzie preened modestly. "You want to watch out, somebody'll be wanting to know who that handsome romantic critter is, and they'll be lugging me off to Hollywood, rubber boots and all."

✋ CHAPTER 24 ✋

KAREN DID NOT give in for Gram, Grampa, or either of her parents, though Madge in her extremity invoked their names. Alix wrapped and tied Ozzie's portrait and took it to the Harbor in *Sea Pigeon* on a flat-calm sea under nacreous skies. Both men were out hauling, and she promised Madge that if the wind blew she wouldn't start out for Tiree alone but would wait at Roger Goodwin's until someone came for her.

The lobster buyer was alone in his office in the slack time before the boats began coming home, and she talked with him for a few minutes about the catboat. He'd had several inquiries and wondered if any of them had been followed up.

"Not that I know of," she said, excluding Soren, whose quest had not been for a boat. "Do you suppose the price is too high?"

"Not for a Saul Goodwin cat," Bert said. " 'Course, that don't mean much to anybody that's ignorant, and there's an awful pile of that kind around. Some days in summer I don't know whether I'm in a kindygarden or a home for the retarded."

"I know what you mean. A few of the inmates have turned up on Tiree. Well, I guess we'll hold on and wait for somebody who knows the difference between a Goodwin cat and just any old boat."

"Sensible," said Bert.

She passed the time of day with two women who'd walked down to the wharf with their children to watch for their men to come in, then she had a cup of coffee and a piece of fresh chocolate cake with Daisy Goodwin. After that she drove to the Grange Hall through the silent afternoon. The air was heavy and enervating, and she kept yawning so that she had to stop once and wipe her streaming eyes.

The Grange Hall was located on a rise above the cluster of houses and wharves at Putnam's Cove, to the east of the Harbor. This had been the original village once, where the fort had stood with the cabins huddled around it in fear of Indians. Then one Christopher Baker quarreled with his family because he married an Indian girl; he loaded her aboard his boat and sailed a mile west and settled in a cove of his own, and called it Baker's Harbor. One of his daughters married Ozzie's great-grandfather, thus providing the Goodwins with their Indian ancestor.

The Grange Hall had once been the residence of a local cod-fish-and-clam king. It was an agreeably Victorian house with a mansard roof, and gingerbread painted a gleaming, buttery yellow against maroon clapboards. Two great bride-and-groom maples guarded the driveway. The carriage house had been re-finished inside for dances, and this was where the show would be.

There was no one in sight, but a station wagon was backed up to the open main doors of the carriage house. She parked beside the wagon and carried her painting inside. The walls had been painted white, and there were already a good number of paintings hung. She could hear hammering beyond the open door to what had once been the tack room.

"I'm here, Peter," she called. She leaned her painting against the wall inside the doors and walked around to look at the others. Her curiosity was a reflex action. Though she saw herself as a woman done with life, she had been a painter too long not to react now to the presence of other painters' work.

She was drawn at once to a silver or steel or aluminum ribbon hanging in loose coils in azure space, reflecting the blue with a gemlike lustre on its polished curves. It looked three-dimensional and gently moving, as if in another moment it would float out lazily free. Freedom, liberty, weightless ease, a light wind blowing in space without limits. She felt a conscious relaxation in her chest. The pleasure increased when she saw that the painting was signed by Peter Ruskin.

"You *are* good," she said softly. "You're damned good."

After that the other nonobjective art made no impression, except of slight claustrophobia in the case of someone's boxes within boxes to infinity.

There were some unaffected and pleasing amateur works, mostly scenery and still lifes. The two big professional names were represented by one of Eva Landry's exquisite *bijou* canvasses—they were getting smaller every year so that her people and buildings looked as if they could be found under a toadstool by a very astute small child—and a vast seascape by Todd Polanski. A shaft of broken sunlight struck down through roiling clouds onto surf piled over red rocks in slathers of whipped cream. The name of the picture should be Strawberry Shortcake, Alix thought, but it turned out to be "Gale Warning," which was predictable like all Todd's titles.

Something was dropped in the tack room and there were footsteps approaching the open door. She called, "You're right about yourself, you know!"

"I'm so glad you've decided that." Soren appeared benignly in the doorway. "It will make everything so much nicer."

"I thought I was speaking to Peter," she said coldly. "Where is he?"

"Don't be so belligerent, dear Alix."

"I'm not—" Seeing the satisfied amusement in his eyes she stopped walking into one of the oldest traps known to men.

"Oh well, I can leave the painting with you," she said, walking toward the doorway. "There it is."

"Please don't go yet," he said, coming behind her. "Peter will be here any minute. He had to go and pick up a canvas. The lady sprained her ankle and can't drive. He'll be so disappointed if you don't wait."

She paused, looking out between the maples and over the roofs below toward the pearly stillness of the cove and the sea beyond. *A ceiling of amber,* she recollected, *a pavement of pearl.* "I don't imagine Peter's disappointment will maim him for life."

"He'll accuse me of driving you away. Is that the truth? Am I driving you away?"

He joined her in the doorway, not touching but close enough so that the effect was there, setting up a layer of heat between them. She prevented herself from moving skittishly away. A gracefully dignified departure in an aura of indifference was called for. She used to manage it quite well back in the world.

"I must get home before the wind springs up," she said.

"The wind isn't going to spring up. Come and see my entry. At least pretend a decent interest in it, it's only professional courtesy." She turned her head toward him and his smile deepened. "You're quite safe. I've never raped a woman in my life. Come along. It's not quite like a visit to my studio, but we have that to look forward to, haven't we?"

"No," she said succinctly, but walked with him to see his work. It was an interior which jarred her with its immediacy; it was like hearing a voice one knows well but can't identify, like being nagged by the memory of a face that once meant something out of the ordinary. It was accompanied by a flood of associations experienced in all the senses but taste.

He said behind her, "Have you ever been there?"

"It's the living room of the mansion on Griffin's Island," she said slowly. "But you've turned it into a haunted house."

"Only for the few. Others will see merely crumpled papers in the fireplace, a Coke bottle on the mantel against magnificent paneling, sunlight falling through dusty windows onto bare dusty floors. Sunlight and emptiness are what people will see."

"But the emptiness is"—her hand felt in air for a word—"heartbreaking or frightening, I don't know which. And the sunlight is grayed. The spruces outside are menacing, as if they're crowding and shoving at the windows to peer in, and at what?"

"Yes, at what?" he murmured. "What do *you* think?"

"You're the one who's supposed to know," she said with a shrug. "You know what you had in mind, nobody else does. My reaction is simply that of an over-romantic imagination. As far as the work is concerned, it's not what I expected of you."

"And what did you expect?" He was leisurely in his enjoyment of this.

"Either boats under sail, or nudes."

He laughed. "Come and visit my studio and see. There are enough marines in this show, and you have to admit it's not the place for nudes."

"But *this*," she said, with a wave toward it, "surprises me."

"Because you didn't expect me to be a good painter, eh?"

"I didn't say that," she protested, but she felt a little embarrassed.

"Let's see what you've brought," he said.

When he had unwrapped the painting he looked pleased. "It's very fine. You have got the essential man there. All who know him will take a closer look at him from now on, trying to find out what they've missed."

"Oh, I think they all know Ozzie for what he is."

"No, he has unguessed dimensions, as everyone has," he lectured her seriously. "You haven't painted merely hands and a face in a picturesque setting. Why do you call yourself solely a painter of children? The man over your fireplace is superb."

She walked away, saying offhandedly, "I don't need to wait to see the picture hung. I'll leave it to you and Peter."

"No, wait, Alexia." His voice deepened and roughened. "Is he a forbidden subject? He shouldn't be. I only wish I'd known him. The man who could follow him would be very proud, he would be honored—"

"Nobody can follow," she said. "Nobody will. And you're right, it's a forbidden subject. Good-bye." But he took her by the shoulders before she could escape and she stood rigid, staring past him with glazed eyes, waiting for him to let go.

"What do you imagine about me, Alexia?" he asked. "That I'm simply a Don Juan, a lecher? You are surprised that I can paint; are you so surprised that I want to be a friend? That I know how to be a friend?"

"I have friends," she said, her gaze fixed on a point past his ear.

"But not like me. Sooner or later you must turn to someone. You're a young woman full of life, no matter how much you deny it."

"Is this the line you gave Judy?"

He squeezed her shoulders quickly and hard enough to hurt. "Judy gave me the line. She's a greedy child. I never did take her to bed, if that's what you're thinking. After I met you that day she ceased to be. Listen, Alexia, you can't deny it—you feel intensely, you exist passionately. Now it's a passion of grief, but it can't last forever. You're too young, too talented—"

"I'm also brave, trustworthy, loyal, and clean in thought, word, and deed," said Alix. A jeep swerved into the drive, spraying gravel. Soren sighed, and released her.

"You aren't half so cynical as you sound," he said. As Peter bounded over the side of the jeep with a painting under his arm, Soren was saying in a professional tone, "I'd expected to see the child's portrait."

"It's not finished and I don't know when it will be. She's not a coöperative subject."

[239]

Peter was delighted to see her, and praised the painting inordinately. "Did you see the other portrait there? It's so darn slick it looks done with an airbrush. He sells them, I don't know how."

"Because they're pretty," said Soren. "Like the shampoo advertisements."

"People have a right to buy what they want," Alix said. "If they don't want to pay for 'warts and all,' why should they?"

"Our charitable Alix," said Soren. "Still, I can see why she sticks to children. The question of 'warts and all' doesn't arise. All her subjects have the charm of youth, if nothing else."

"I want to talk about Peter's work," said Alix. "Only I don't have any words for it, except that I love it, and you don't have to be wistful about anybody else's textures because you have them."

Peter blushed deeply and became inarticulate for once. Soren said, "I don't know why the three of us don't have our own cozy little show and just go round and round admiring each other."

"Well, damn it!" said Peter crossly, "we *are* better than anybody else around here."

Alix laughed. "I've got to move along. The last time I stood around talking to you, Peter, the wind breezed up and I was scared foolish on the way home and had to be rescued."

"Honest?" He gave an alarmed glance out at the water.

"But it's not going to blow today," Soren assured them. "I give you my word."

"God isn't dead, He's alive and well, and living in Baker's Harbor," said Peter.

"I wish it were so," said Alix. "I've a few questions I'd like to ask. Good-bye," she said to Soren, turning away from him.

"Not good-bye." She knew by his voice that he was smiling. He was as bad as the doctor for being endlessly, secretly, and infuriatingly amused by her; unless it was really a defense? *When you're smiling, when you're smiling, the whole world smiles with you.* "It's only until tomorrow," Soren was saying.

"I've enjoyed our talk. I found it profitable and I hope you did."

"Perhaps I should have been an art critic," said Alix. "I seem to do so well at it. But then, I said only nice things, didn't I?"

"Touché," said Soren, bowing her out.

Peter walked to the car with her, talking agitatedly. "Hey, did he try anything with you? God, I'm sorry I let you in for that. Bess is a good soul, but hard as hell to get away from. I tried to get Soren to go collect her picture, but he wouldn't."

"I've met people like Soren before. Believe it or not, we did talk about painting—mostly," she qualified it with a little grin. "He's very good and so are you."

"Thanks." He reddened again. "You're coming to our party, aren't you?"

"Of course!" She achieved a brilliant fire-burst of enthusiasm, and considered adding that wild horses couldn't keep her away, but that might be too much even for Peter to swallow.

❧ CHAPTER 25 ❧

As if Soren were at least the god of the winds, no breeze sprang up until she was back in Gib's Cove and putting *Sea Pigeon* out on the mooring. A light southwest wind began to stir the weighted air. The cloud cover became as luminous as a thin shell held against the sun, and the ruffling water began a slow subtle shift toward blue.

The next dawn was mercilessly superb. There was no chance of the supper picnic being postponed, and the prospect of the evening became the Minotaur, the guillotine, the Black Death. (She could not even discern in herself the slightest tendency toward a genuine malaise, beyond what she felt most of the time these days.)

Karen came in midmorning, bringing what at first looked like a reprieve. Madge wrote in a shaky hand that she had been hit in the night with summer complaint. Now she was in bed between trips to the bathroom, and there was no chance of her going ashore this afternoon.

"I'd swap places with you, Madge," Alix muttered as she read. "Back-door trot, the heaves, and all."

"I'm so mad," Madge wrote, "that I could spit, or bawl like a baby. Of course Ozzie won't go without me, he wasn't fussy about the whole thing in the first place. So will you take Karen along with you? She's been looking forward to it so much. Ozzie will take you in and come back for you."

"Have you really and truly been looking forward to it?" Alix asked Karen.

"To what?"

"This picnic tonight."

Karen shrugged. "I don't know." There were times when Alix thought it was not possible for a human being of normal intelligence to be so phlegmatic.

"If you don't know, who does?" she said. "Look, either you want to go or you don't. Which is it?"

She got the mechanical shrug again. "I don't care."

"Oh, for heaven's sake!" Alix breathed hard through her nose in exasperation. "Your poor grandmother thinks you're simply dying to go, because she is. Well, we'll go for her sake. But I'll be darned if I'll go any earlier than I have to."

Karen, with her hands behind her back, observed her as she wrote a note back to Madge. She sent Karen on her way without the usual tidbit.

The evening ahead now assumed the menace of an expected jaw-splitting toothache. One could think of nothing else, the dreadful anticipation dominated all.

She knew that she could endure several hours of listening to and making conversation that rattled like dry corn husks in her ears; at least she could stand it better than she could have a few weeks ago, when the prospect would have made her physically sick, instead of simply depressed. But Soren was the focal point of her discomfort now. The problem that nagged at her like the preliminary tenderness before the toothache was how to avoid him. She had the feeling that he'd use the presence of other people to his own advantage, thinking she wouldn't hurt the Ruskins by walking out on their party, so that he could be even more outrageous than he'd been yesterday.

She was lying on the sand beach shortly past noon when she

[2 4 3]

saw Jonas coming home from hauling. It occurred to her that
he could be the solution; that was, he could be if he and Ozzie
didn't have something planned, and if he felt accommodating
enough. His interest in other people's affairs might not extend
to making an effort, and this would call for one. Her pride
jibbed at asking it of him; but she had only to recall Soren laying hands on her and speaking in her ear, and pride was a lost
cause.

She gave him time to clean up his dory and himself and get
his noon meal. Then she took a short cut through the woods to
the Home Cove. It brought her into the alders a little distance
from the cabin. The bay was Italian blue, of such a depth of
color that it seemed far more than a reflection of the sky. Everything shimmered in waves of heat; the beach rocks seemed to
be in slight but constant motion as if seen under water. The air
was aromatic with earth and sea smells, the sun heavy on Alix's
eyelids. She walked toward the cabin with her eyes half-shut
against the vibrating glare.

"*Hey!*" someone shouted. She jumped, and nearly lost her
balance. Very close to her Jonas said, "Talk about the swan
drifting along like a maid in a heavenly dream. You were bearing down on my lettuce as if you'd lost your rudder."

"I'm sorry," she said.

"You all right?" he asked, his face close to hers. His hair was
damp and falling over his forehead. Under it his eyes sparkled
like wind-struck water, missing nothing.

"I'm fine for a sleepwalker that's just been yelled at," she
said. She sat down on a boulder in the shade. "Happy Fourth
of July. Have you got your ladyfingers and torpedoes and giant
salutes and everything?"

"The Fourth's got no guts now since they made it illegal to
blow off your fingers." He went back to hoeing a row of onions
whose shoots were celadon-green against the dark loam. He was
stripped to the waist, tightly muscled, tanned and sweating. He
looked tough, springily fit, and combative even while so peacefully engaged.

Like him, his tomato plants were aggressively healthy. There were also four hills of cucumbers, a row of radishes, a row of lettuce, and then the onions. "It's a lovely garden," Alix said. "And I see you have assistants, or maybe they're dependents." An adult robin and a speckled juvenile hopped alertly around the edges, never far from the hoe.

"Oh, that's Marthy and The Boy," said Jonas. "He's a little backward. The others have left home, but he hasn't got much ambition."

Marthy seized a worm turned up by the hoe, and The Boy rushed to her. "Why should he leave a doting mother?" Alix asked. "He's no fool." She sighed and began fitting her finger-tips together.

"What was that gust for?" Jonas didn't look around. "You can't have all my worms, Marthy." He covered one before she could get it.

"What are you doing this afternoon?"

"Why?"

"I asked you first."

He dropped down onto his heels to work the soil around a lettuce plant. "What do you want me to do? Nail a shingle, re-hang a door, put a pane of glass in? I'll do it."

"It's not that easy. This is a really difficult favor I'm asking of you. You might even consider it a sacrifice." She looked at him under the arch of her fingers as he straightened up. "I need an escort at this supper thing at the Ruskins' tonight."

"You mean you need me to protect you at a wild party? By gorry, I hope they don't need the police to break it up. Our constable could never handle one of those riots. He's a dite slow, and a real innocent kind of feller, too."

"Gee, I'm sorry," she said. "It's not even going to be a pot party or a drunken orgy."

"That settles it. If it's not an orgy I wouldn't go anyway. Pot I can do without, but I haven't been to a good orgy since I was in high school."

"That must have been some high school," said Alix.

"It was. And these kids think they've discovered—what do they call it now?"

" 'Group grope' is one name for it. But I'm pretty positive this won't be one. They even asked Madge and Ozzie. So—" She lifted her hands in a gesture of despair. "What can I say after I've said I'm sorry?"

They both laughed. He put down the hoe and came over and sat beside her, wiping his forehead with his arm.

"With those two chaperones, why do you need me?"

"Madge has got some bug and can't go, but she thinks Karen will be heartbroken if she doesn't go. So I'm taking her."

"I still don't know why you need me."

"To fend off the Danish Dessert. He says I need a man to console me, and he wants to be the man."

"You mean he wants to climb your rigging?"

"That's one way of putting it. I can manage him, usually, but I don't want to create an incident at Peter's and Myra's party. . . . I wouldn't go at all if Madge weren't so set on Karen's going." She looked despondently out to sea, ashamed of having come, sounding in her own ears like a fool.

Jonas sat with his elbows on his knees gazing at his tomato plants with the preoccupation of a parent checking the children's ears. After a moment he said, "You could keep Karen between you and him. She'd scare him off. She unnerves me, specially first thing in the morning."

"Apart from a male escort sticking by me no matter what, nothing short of a shotgun blast would unnerve Soren Michaels. Besides, I can't be sure Karen will stay with me. She may disappear and start walking home to Connecticut." She got up, in a hurry to go now. "Well, I'll let you get back to your gardening."

"Oh, sit down again and stop being so damned clipped and Bostonian," he said irritably. "I'll go. What time?"

"Around four, if you want to go to the Fair and the show first."

"I don't need any potholders and ruffled aprons, and I went to enough shows when my wife discovered Art to do me for the rest of my life." He grinned suddenly, his eyes dancing under his forelock. "Now tell me all you needed was a plain yes or no."

"Oh, it was plain enough all right. Five, at Beauty Cove, then?"

"I'll bring the boat around to you," said Jonas. "All right if I turn up in rubber boots?"

"Do. They'd adore it." She stood up. "I'm very much obliged," she said formally. "I appreciate the sacrifice, even if I'm not going to pieces about it. I guess I'm so relieved I'm flattened."

He had that too-merry-for-a-grown-man look again, as if he had no worries and never expected to have any. "Why is it a sacrifice? If there's a lot of girls in mini-skirts I'll consider myself privileged."

"Oh, there'll be mini-skirts, and bikinis too," she promised him. "But you're supposed to stick closer to me than a brother, so you can't go scampering off after them like Harpo Marx. That's where the sacrifice comes in."

"So I'll probably go up in smoke like one of those burnt offerings. Oh well." He shrugged.

She walked slowly home, spinning out the time so there wouldn't be so long to wait. She was glad now to be going off for the evening, away from the exhausting expectancy that permeated all her hours in the house. I'm not really running out on you, Shane, she explained. It's just to rest a little. I'm trying so hard I think I'm defeating our purpose. Maybe if I'm away and then come in fresh, I'll get the sign I'm supposed to get.

It seemed so entirely possible and reasonable that she felt her spirits go spinning euphorically free in a spiral, a reaction she had known since she could first remember. Perhaps that was why Peter's silvery spring or ribbon had affected her. She ought to buy it from him. She would, and the gay decision was a part of the spiral. Anything was possible that was good, creative, positive.

And this could be the night. At the words her heart began a heavy, tolling beat, and she remembered how it had been in the days when she had first been certain of loving Shane and of being loved by him. With Cathleen in the background, neither of them had yet said the words to the other. Whenever she knew she was going to see him her heart would beat in the same ominous way, and she would think the same words. *This could be the night.*

The night when they walked through the looking glass. Or through a door which, once they had used it, they would never be able to find again. The step over its threshold was an irreversible one. She had known it before she ever made it. What she had not known or even suspected was that another such step was waiting for her, ten years on.

✸✸ CHAPTER 26 ✸✸

WHEN JONAS BROUGHT *Marjorie C.* into Gib's Cove that after-noon, he wasn't wearing work clothes and rubber boots. Fresh from the Goodwins' shower, discreetly scented, he wore houndstooth-check slacks and a maroon blazer over a yellow sport shirt.

Alix wolf-whistled. "Oh, you *doll*, you. Karen, isn't he gor-geous?" Karen, lovingly got up by her grandmother in pink-checked playsuit and new white sneakers, contemplated Jonas with a delicate frown between her pale gilt eyebrows.

"She thinks it's a dirty word," said Jonas. He pivoted in the cockpit, holding out an imaginary skirt. "My mother told me always wear yellow for my brown eyes."

"And she was so right, dear," said Alix. "All I can say is, a thing of beauty is a joy forever."

"I know I'm a thing of beauty, but just don't start calling me Joy where people can hear you."

Alix began to laugh, unexpectedly lighthearted. It wasn't going to be so bad after all.

It wasn't. The guest mixture included young fishermen, farmers, and clam-diggers and their families, the Ruskins' clos-

est friends in the art and summer colony, and some local business and professional friends. Jonas as an escort was never far
from her, yet not noticeably militant about it, and he managed
to get involved in conversation with all sorts of people, some of
whom were extremely exotic. Myra made a fuss over Karen and
introduced her to the other children. Some of these were immediately friendly in a casual, kindly way, but Karen hadn't responded and stayed close to Alix.

There was swimming (with at least two of the promised
bikinis) and baseball in the field above the beach. The food
was abundant and good, a seafood *paella* and pitchers of *san-
gria* for the daring; mussels steamed over a beach fire; frank-
furts, hamburgers, ham and potato salad for the conservatives;
beer and soft drinks, coffee by the gallon. Karen was not at all
reluctant or withdrawn when it came to eating.

Alix was drawn into shop talk by other painters who con-
gratulated her on Ozzie's portrait, and she couldn't resist it any
more than she'd been able to resist it with Soren that foggy
midnight on the island. It was good, like the food; it was en-
grossing, and it made the time fly.

Soren came over to greet her when she first arrived, and
shook hands with Jonas. He was amiable and twinkling, as if
he saw through the whole thing. After that he devoted himself
to an elegant blond woman with a *belle époque* hairdo and a
transparent silk pantsuit.

At dusk there were fireworks brought in by someone's out-
of-state guests. When the last shower of gold and silver had
died out in the dark Alix and Jonas said good night to the
Ruskins, it was great and thank you very much, and walked
back to the harbor.

The picnic was still going strong, strewn between house and
shore, adults talking, a group singing around a fire on the
beach, and children running wild. Their shouts rang with a
kind of pagan exultation through the silence of a summer
night.

"They get wilder and wilder as the dark comes on," Alix

said. "I remember . . . it was the best time of day in summer."

"Night was always my time," said Jonas. "I could haul traps all day and ram around all night. Speaking of ramming, your friend and *his* friend left early. You ever see anyone make asking for a light sound like an invitation to rape?"

"What's rape?" said Karen.

"Stealing," said Alix. Jonas chuckled.

The road curved out of the spruces toward the water. Someone was rowing across the harbor, the small rhythmic splashes perfectly clear. House lights shone out onto lawns, and Bert's office on his wharf was illuminated, the doors standing open as he waited for the truck to come and load up with the crates tailing in a long string off the lobster car. New masthead lights like very low stars above the outer harbor meant that two sailing yachts had come in at sundown.

Jonas turned off to speak to Bert, and Alix and Karen went on. *Marjorie C.* lay at Roger Goodwin's float. As they reached Roger's wharf, Karen said suddenly, "I have to go to the bathroom."

"I asked you about that before we left the Ruskins'," said Alix, "and you said no."

"I didn't have to go then."

"Well, that's as good a reason as any. We'll go up to your Aunt Daisy's. Did you have a good time at the picnic?" she asked as they went toward the house.

"Yes," said Karen, with a finality that discouraged further foolish questions. But at least it was not negative, and Madge would be happy. On the kitchen doorstep they heard through the screen door the unmistakable uproar of a television cattle stampede. Alix tapped and went into the dim kitchen, calling, "Hello, it's us."

Daisy came from the living room. "I swear I'm going to take an axe to that TV or else have one of my own out in the woodshed. I've had so much of the Old West I'm gun-shy and saddle-sore."

She was a thin, dry-spoken woman who, by some instinctive

talent like a gift for art, music, or mathematics, always looked effortlessly *chic*, even while hanging out the wash or fishing for flounders off the wharf. This probably accounted for her amazing number of cosmetic sales along the road to town and in the town itself, rather than any seductive sales talk.

"Did you get my note I left aboard the boat?" she asked. "On the wheel?"

"I haven't been to the boat yet. Karen wanted to go to the bathroom."

"Run along, Karen, you know the way. You've got company, Alix. She came by taxi from Fremont just a little while ago."

Alix's mind seemed to stop functioning. She said out of the blankness, "I'm not expecting anyone."

Daisy came closer and lowered her voice. "Well, I thought it was queer. I kept asking her if she was sure this was the right place, but she said she wanted Alexia Horne, and that's you."

"I've just become Mary Jones who's worked all her life in the insurance business. I wish."

"Can't you just send her back?" Daisy whispered under cover of tempestuous accusations of blame flung across the drovers' campfire. "I'd be glad to keep her and get her back uptown in the morning, or even tonight."

"Thanks, but I'd better see who it is, and so forth," Alix said. It couldn't be Dodie, she'd just gotten a postcard from Oslo in yesterday's mail.

"She's just not your kind, Alix," Daisy said. "I can't feature her being a friend of yours. Well, come on in. She's staring at that television as brainless as Roger. The two of 'em look hypnotized."

Silently resisting at every step, her *paella* a nauseating mass in her stomach, Alix followed into the living room. Roger beheld her with a slight start, gave her a smile like Ozzie's, and waved her to a chair.

"No thanks, Roger, I can't stop. Don't let me interrupt your program," she said mechanically. I never saw that girl before in my life, she thought, but she had a floating, hallucinatory sensation as if adrift in a fragment of nightmare. Perhaps this was someone she should know but she'd been stricken with amnesia.

The girl on the divan took the cigarette from her mouth and got up with slow ungainly movements, like a puppet being hauled up and straightened out by loosening strings. The impression of a large marionette was sustained because her face was oddly indistinct, wearing violet-tinted sunglasses, and framed by a Polynesian fall of long black hair. She was swathed around the neck in yards of scarf, tie-dyed in explosive colors. The streaming ends fell below the hem of her sleeveless orange dress, which came to halfway between waist and knees. In the Goodwins' small living room her legs looked unnaturally long, sheathed in orange-tinted nylons ending in large, flat, shiny yellow sandals.

If I have amnesia this must be what drove me to it, Alix thought. Karen's sudden appearance in the room snapped her out of her brief catalepsis. She gave Daisy a conventional smile and nod.

"We'll go out in the kitchen. Would you mind?" she said to the girl. "Watch television a few minutes, Karen." The girl followed her to the kitchen. She was no taller, but she was broad-shouldered and seemed to hulk over Alix. In the dimness she looked even stranger, with her face a blur and the two big shadowy circles for eyes.

"Were you looking for me?" Alix asked politely.

"If you're Alexia Horne I am," the girl said. Her voice was a surprise; it was penetratingly clear with precise endings to the words. "I'm Bunny Mannering."

"*No,*" Alix said sharply. "What sort of bad joke is this?"

"It's no joke. Or perhaps it is. I'm Shane Mannering's daughter. You aren't going to refuse to take me in for the night, are you? Your lover's child?" The crisp lucid tone gave the words a lacerating insolence.

What if she'd dreamed the whole thing, even Shane's death? She heard Jonas coming, whistling a song they'd all been sing-

ing at the picnic. *I don't work for a living, I get along all right
without.* "Hey, where'd my women go to?" he called as he came
in, then stopped as if icy spray had hit him in the face.

"It didn't take you long, did it?" the girl said to Alix with a
sarcastic curl of her long pale mouth.

"Do you have a bag?" Alix asked coldly.

"There." She tipped her head. A suitcase stood by the sink, a
black raincoat draped over it. She was carrying a large canvas
and leather tote bag.

"Would you take that bag, Jonas?" Alix asked him without
looking at him. "This is Bunny Mannering. She's going out to
the island for overnight."

"Bunny *who?*" asked Jonas.

"You heard correctly," said Alix. "Come on, Karen," she
called. "Thanks, Daisy, and good night!"

"Good night," Daisy called back. "Put that outside light on
so you won't break your neck."

In a sort of awkward rush, untidily bumping each other,
they were outside and then spreading out on the way to the
wharf. Jonas went ahead, and Karen ran down the wharf after
him. Bunny was behind, pulling on the shiny black trench
coat, which was a trifle longer than her dress.

Down aboard the boat Jonas switched on a light in the cockpit. Alix saw him discover the note fastened to a spoke of the
wheel with an elastic, then Karen crossed the float to the boat
and climbed aboard. Alix stopped Bunny at the head of the
wharf just outside Roger's fishhouse. A refrigerated lobster
truck was backing cautiously down Bert's wharf, and the noise
masked their voices.

"Now just what are you doing here?" she asked. "And how
did you find out about this place?"

"I went through my father's papers after he died, and there
was a letter from you."

Alix burned in the dark, not from shame but rage. She had
never written anything that would shame her, but to know that

someone alien had read something so private was almost unendurable.

"We'd known about you for years," the girl was saying. "But not where you and he hung out. You mentioned getting a letter from Baker's Harbor and going to Tiree. It was easy enough," she said scornfully, as if breaking the cover of a very inept secret agent, "to locate Baker's Harbor on a chart. He even had one on his wall, all nicely marked. So I thought I'd come and take a look at you."

"You weren't in any great hurry, it seems," said Alix in her Louisburg Square manner.

"I waited until my mother had gone to Europe. She's much more of a lady than I am. She'd never have let me come. To lower myself," she added, so that Alix couldn't miss the point.

Alix began walking again toward the ramp and the lighted boat, whose engine was now softly idling and making phosphorescent bubbles astern. Karen's head shone under the cockpit light. Jonas was handing the child her jacket and warm slacks. It looked blessedly dull. Behind her Bunny stumbled, and Alix said, "Be careful. You could fall and there are rocks down there."

"If I broke my neck that would be convenient for you, I imagine."

Alix didn't answer. Chills ran over her from a painfully tight spot on her crown down to her feet. As they reached the ramp the girl said in her clear insulting voice, "Is that child yours?"

"No," said Alix. She crossed the float and stepped aboard. Jonas held out a hand and she ignored it, but he took her hand anyway, and gripped it hard, looking closely into her face. She didn't look at him. Karen, zipped into jacket and hood, leaned back with her elbows resting on the guardrail and her glasses fixed on the stranger, who came aboard with an overdone nonchalance and at once dug into her tote bag for cigarettes.

Jonas turned off the light, and put the engine in gear, taking the boat away from the float. They glided slowly past the floodlit car where the crates were being hoisted up to the wharf and the truck. As they went among the moorings the lobster boats rocked slightly in the wake of luminous bubbles and ripples. Alix pulled on her parka and pushed her damp and doubled-up hands into the pockets.

They passed by the yachts and out of the harbor onto the star-streaked dark glass of the sea.

No one spoke on the trip out. Alix stood where she didn't have to look at anyone, seeing nothing herself, trying to make order out of chaos. She wasn't obliged to be intimidated, shamed, or even angered on her own ground. The girl would be sent back tomorrow, and that would be the end of it. But another chill shook her in spite of her dispassionate reasoning; for she had never in her life been spoken to as this girl had spoken to her.

Well, what do you expect? she argued. She's been left on her own, and she's out to raise a little hell. But she can't take away anything you've had, she can't pollute your memories. Even by walking into your and Shane's house she can't do it. She's come, she'll go. Have the courage of your convictions, for God's sake. No, for Shane's sake and your own.

It worked quite well. At least when the boat turned into Gib's Cove the chills had stopped, her hands and feet were less clammy, and she spoke naturally to Jonas.

"Thanks again. You were a big help. I think he got the message."

"He did some circling around, didn't he? Put me in mind of William when he thinks there might be a mouse in my wood-pile and he's going to take it by surprise." With a candidly hostile glance toward the girl he said, "What about right now? You still need some help?"

Karen yawned loudly. Alix said with a smile, "No, and Karen's ready for her bed."

"Well, you know best." He sounded as if he didn't believe it. He took the suitcase up the ladder and left it on the wharf.

"Thanks again, Jonas," she said when he came aboard the boat again.

"Don't mention it," he said irritably.

"Well, Bunny, do you think you can manage the ladder?" Alix asked. Without speaking Bunny swung a long leg up and stepped onto the washboard, then went clumsily up the ladder, her knees and her tote bag all getting in her way. Alix waited until she'd got onto the wharf, then went up. "Good night, Karen, good night, Jonas," she said.

Karen answered with another yawn. "I'll see you tomorrow," Jonas said in a tone that could best be described as portentous.

"Yes, please," Alix said tranquilly. "Bunny will be going back."

"I'll be around early then."

Alix gave Bunny the flashlight and walked ahead of her up the path, carrying the suitcase out of practical considerations only. Bunny was having enough difficulty getting herself to the house, judging from her mutterings, hissing breaths, and one anguished outcry when she stubbed her toe. The flashlight went soaring from her hand and landed in the midst of a prickly rosette of juniper, still shining valiantly up at the stars. Alix went out into the field and got it. When she handed it back, Bunny snatched it. There was a catch in her hard breathing as if she were near tears, but she didn't speak, and in the starlight there was nothing to see.

William howled off in the field and came galloping. Alix swung him up over her shoulder, glad of his warm grass-scented weight against her.

"Is that a *cat?*" Bunny demanded. "I can't stand cats. Neither can my mother. I inherited it from her. We have ailurophobia."

"Is it usually fatal, or can you get shots?" Alix asked. She picked up the suitcase and went on. William bumped his big head fervently against the side of hers, purring deafeningly into her ear. In the house she put him down and lit a lamp. Wil-

liam ripped at a cupboard door and Bunny said with distaste,
"Does that cat have the run of the house?"

Leaning over the table adjusting the flame, Alix said, "William does, but you can keep him out of your room. You'd better go to bed at once, and there'll be no chance of his coming
near you." She carried the lamp into the small bedroom the
Ruskins had used, then took off her parka and began getting
bedclothes from the chest.

"The toilet's out back," she said. "I'll show you. If you want
to wash up I'll heat some water. You can bring a basin in
here." She snapped sheets out of their folds and the lamp flame
flickered in the draft they made; the shadow-play on the walls
and ceiling was grotesquely dramatic, all of a piece with Bunny
herself, who stood in the doorway with her hands in her pockets. In the short shiny black trench coat, with her long hair and
the big violet lenses, she looked like a caricature of a woman
agent in one of the more incredible James Bond stories; as if
she had nothing on under the tightly cinched coat but a gun
belt and twin holsters, filled, of course, with Colt .45's. Water-
proofed, because she'd just swum a lagoon to get here, carrying
the raincoat in her teeth. . . .

Without knowing it Bunny matched her tone to the picture.
"I didn't come here to be sent at once to bed. I came here to
get a look at you and ask some questions." *We have ways of
dealing with your kind, Miss Horne. Besides, that man is
mine!*

Alix tucked her lower lip under the top one to keep it
steady, at the same time tucked a blanket in at the foot. "Questions such as?" She straightened up, sure now that her face was
perfectly composed. "Look and ask. Here I am."

"I won't be rushed. I'm starved. Will you give me something
to eat, or can't you bear to?"

"Don't be ridiculous," said Alix with her most three-cornered smile.

She built up a wood fire, heated water, and got out sandwich
materials. Bunny sat on the edge of the captain's chair, never

taking her eyes off Alix except to throw wary sidewise glances at William.

"Help yourself, Bunny," Alix said. "Build your own."

She sat down opposite her with a cup for herself. She didn't want it, but she felt that somehow she had got the advantage, and she didn't intend to lose it. The girl was probably half-frantic with what her daring had led her into. Contemplating the food as if it were a dish of poisonous toadstools, she swallowed visibly, picked up a knife, and immediately put it down. She unfastened the top button of her trench coat, then resolutely picked up the knife again and buttered a slice of bread. After that she ate three more slices and gulped down two cups of tea that should have blistered her throat.

Then she sat back and took cigarettes and lighter from her tote bag. She made a beautifully detailed bit of business out of lighting up, blowing smoke out from her nostrils, and giving Alix a long heavy-lidded stare through the smoke.

"So that's what you look like," she said. "I don't know how he could have done it. My mother's a beautiful woman."

"So I've always understood," said Alix.

"The ghost of a beautiful woman, I should say. You killed her long ago. You cut the heart out of her, like one of those Aztec sacrifices."

"Oh, come now," said Alix. "Your father and mother had separated before I ever came into the picture. You may not remember, but I assure you that's the truth."

"The truth is," said Bunny, fastidiously enunciating, "that he'd have come back to us if you hadn't kept him away." There was more than a faint echo of Bette Davis; she must have been watching late movies.

"You see things in black and white, Bunny," Alix said. "I hope you never make a disastrous marriage, but if you do you'll discover a lot of intermediate shades you didn't know existed. As far as your parents' marriage goes, there was nothing for your father to go back to."

"There was a woman who adored him. There were two chil-

dren who thought he was better than God. I suppose that's
nothing!" She rubbed out her cigarette with another studied
gesture. With the part of the mind that observes details when
the rest is in turmoil, Alix saw that the features were less indef-
inite than at first sight. Her nose and chin were finer versions
of Shane's, but the oversize glasses blurred the shape of the eye
sockets and brows.

"Can't you speak?" Bunny asked. "Or are you too ashamed?
But maybe you don't feel shame. That's why you could do what
you've done. If you were a woman of integrity you'd have made
him come back to his family."

"My dear girl," said Alix, "nobody could *make* Shane do anything that he didn't want to do. Now you've had your say,
you'd better go to bed. Would you like a hot water bottle to
warm your feet?"

"Don't patronize me!" Bunny's hand began to shake so that
she couldn't work her lighter. "I'm warning you!"

"Of what?" Alix got up and carried her cup to the sink.

"I'll make you wish you'd never been born. I've been hating
you for a good long time now. If it hadn't been for you, my
mother wouldn't be the way she is, and I wouldn't be—"

The lighter clattered on the table and she stopped talking.

"You wouldn't be here, is that it?" Alix said calmly, facing
her. "Look, Bunny, it's natural for you to resent me. I don't
hold it against you. But coming in like this, threatening and
insulting, won't gain you anything but the realization that
you've put yourself at a disadvantage." She was going to say
that you've behaved like a fool, but it seemed a little harsh.
"Go to bed now, and tomorrow you can go back to Philadelphia or wherever you came from today, and the thing'll be
over."

"It'll never be over for me, can't you see that or are you stupid like all the rest of them! Ten years—*ten years!*" she repeated incredulously. "All that time we could have had him instead of just on holidays, and little visits to the college, and
telephone calls on our birthdays, or big packages coming when
we wanted *him*. And you *had* him. You *kept* him. If you'd

been a decent woman and refused to sleep with him, loneliness would have driven him back."

"Don't you think there'd have been other women?" Alix felt herself beginning to shake, but it was inside; her hand was steady and so was her voice. Damn the kid, you couldn't throw at her that when he lived at home her mother had refused to sleep with him. At the same time her own words knifed her: *other women.* She couldn't imagine even hypothetical women without suffering the wounds of jealousy and deprivation.

"Never mind other women," Bunny said. She had made a quick rally after the long impassioned speech of a cheated child. The immaculate accent was back. "You're the one who should have us on your conscience. And him too. If my mother had been taking care of him he wouldn't have died like that. She said you made his life a hell of guilt and it wore him out. She just thanked God he died in her arms instead of yours."

Alix winced. She wanted to double over from the blow, but she kept her back pressed hard against the edge of the sink, and gripped the cold iron rim with both hands. "Go to bed," she said wearily. "If you don't want to go out back in the dark, there's a chambermug in there you can use. Either go to bed or sit here alone in the dark. Because I'm going."

Bunny said with a brattish smirk, "You won't sleep tonight, will you? My mother hasn't slept well for years, just for knowing you exist."

"There have been times when her existence has been a trial to me too," said Alix. She took a flashlight from the lamp shelf. "Here." Bunny sat there, still with her fixed little grimace, and didn't offer to take the light. Alix stood it on the table. "Keep your door shut and the cat won't bother you."

She blew out the lamp and went up the back stairs, the picture of the girl imprinted on her vision like the memory of an apparition. When she reached the top she stopped and listened. She heard a chair scraping back, the flashlight dropped and a savage whisper, a chair bumped into, and then the slam of a door.

❧ CHAPTER 27 ❧

SHE SAT ON the edge of her bed in the dark for a long time. William slept across the foot of the bed, purring absently whenever she moved. After a while she got out of her clothes and into pajamas, and lay down.

Blankets couldn't warm her, and along with the cold there was the dirt. Even if she didn't deserve it it had been flung, and not what Madge called "clean dirt," but filth. A child jeering, she kept telling herself, but she wasn't so sure it was a child; it was a physically mature female who hated her enough to want to murder her with words if she didn't dare to do it any other way. You could read in her the enormous aching desire to spit out a killing venom at Alix. It was in the very way her mouth worked when she spoke.

But how did you know she didn't dare do it any other way? It was an old house and a dry one. If she should wander around in the night, provided she could do it without knocking over any chairs or toppling books, she would see her father's portrait and other signs of his male possession. She could be unstable enough to want to destroy it all and Alix with it.

"Bunny's a cuddler," Shane used to say, and Alix had imagined his younger daughter as small and chubby. Maybe she had once been a little girl with a round stomach and black pigtails, crawling into her father's lap to talk confidentially, but she was eighteen now, and she was as mysterious to Alix as a strange attaché case with a ticking inside.

What do you care? she asked herself. You want to die anyway . . . but not that way! My own way, in peace, listening to the birds outside and thinking of Shane and then maybe dreaming of him. The damnable part of this girl's being here, one of the damnable parts, was that she had turned him into an object that women had fought over when he was alive, as if he had no right to possess himself but was simply an article of property, and brawled over when he was dead. Yes, brawled. She'd been fool enough to answer the girl, and that made it a brawl. This object, this parcel of property, bore no relation whatever to Shane Mannering, the man of this house.

She couldn't even weep for him. She felt as if the capacity for tears had been dried up long ago. She lay watching the slow procession of the stars and looking forward to tomorrow and getting rid of Bunny. Her life before the girl appeared on the scene represented the essence of rapture as compared to what it was at this moment.

There were no sounds all night except the usual ones, the clock striking, the creaks and ticks of an old house, a plane going over far up; a sardine carrier taking a short cut between the Head and Tiree Ledge; a rhythmic swash and thump on the shore as the tide came in. William snored in a delicate cat fashion.

Ailurophobia, Alix sneered, knowing the sneer was as childish as Bunny's had been.

She fell asleep when it began to grow light. William woke her up by standing on her and smelling her face, and the room was ablaze with sunshine. She remembered at once all that had happened and sprang up, pulled on a robe, and ran downstairs.

The door was still closed into Bunny's room. She couldn't hear anything through it, and tiptoed around through the living room to listen at the door by the front stairs. No sounds. She returned to the kitchen and washed her face and hands, fed William, and let him out. When she was dressed she made coffee and took it out to the front doorstep and the sun. The sea was all a dazzle of aquamarines, and a light wind blew from it and across the rugosas toward her. She shut her eyes, breathing the scent, hoping to quiet the crawl in her stomach. She wondered if Jonas would go to haul before he came to get Bunny, and how best to avoid another confrontation with the girl in the meantime.

"Good morning," Jonas said.

She opened her eyes and saw him black against the sun-struck sky. She put a finger to her lips and gestured toward the bedroom window, and stood up. They walked in the wet, muffling grass around the far corner of the house.

"Still in bed, huh?" he asked.

"Yes." With repulsion she poured her cold coffee out onto the grass. "*Yuck!* as the kids say. Want some hot?"

"Not right off. I don't have to ask you what happened last night. You look like hell this morning."

"Thank you, you've just made my day. My beauty was all I had left and now that's gone."

"Good God, you don't have to keep up that stiff-upper-lip business with me. I got her name last night. And I saw the way you looked. The Walking Dead."

"So now I'm a zombie." She kept the smile on her face, and warned him, "Don't be sympathetic. It'll kill me, but only because when I'm short of sleep I fall apart, that's all."

"The way you turn feather-white when you're hungry. I remember. You're full of these cute little quirks. What'd she do, call you a scarlet woman, to put a pretty pair of words on it?"

"It's really none of your business," she told him gently.

"She didn't try to slap you around, did she?" he demanded.

"No, no, she talked and then she went to bed. Let's have some hot coffee."

"We'll get her up first, by God. There's an eleven o'clock flight for New York and she's going to be on it."

"I think if you drop her in Fremont that'll be all right."

"I think if I dropped her overboard that would be better, but with her build she's probably a long-distance swimmer," he said gloomily, following her to the back door. "Hi, Bill. It's a pleasure to meet somebody who seems to be enjoying life." This morning Alix was glad of Jonas's proprietary interest in her troubles; his presence should prevent a scene before it was time to take Bunny away.

In the kitchen she put the teakettle on the gas stove. Jonas took a pail and went to the well, and she knocked on the bedroom door. "Get up and have breakfast, Bunny," she called. "It's almost time to leave."

There was no answer, not even a sound of creaking bed and stirring bedclothes. She took dishes down from the cupboard and measured coffee into the pot. When Jonas came back they talked in normal voices about the level of water in this well compared with the one at the Home Cove. Then she knocked and called again.

"Not a sound," she said to Jonas.

"You sure she's in there? She may be up and prowling around the island somewhere."

She tried to open the door. It was buttoned on the inside. She found the other door also fastened. "Do you suppose she's all right?" she whispered to Jonas, who had followed her.

"She's either sleeping hard or sulking." He rapped loudly on the door. "Time to get up. If you don't start moving pretty soon I'm coming in through the window and roust you out."

"Leave me alone," Bunny moaned. "I'm sick."

"A likely story," Jonas said. "You need fresh air, that's all. You're hermetically sealed up in there."

"I *am* sick!" It was followed by authentic sounds of vomiting.

"You got an heirloom quilt on the bed?" Jonas asked Alix. "If you have, it's a goner."

"Maybe she got the mug in time," said Alix morosely. "I wonder what ails her."

"Typhoid?" suggested Jonas. "Smallpox? Bubonic plague?"

"I can hear you out there." Bunny sounded thick and tearful.

"Bunny, can you get up and open a door?" Alix asked. "I can't do anything for you if I can't get in."

"I'd *die* before I'd let you do anything for me!" Bunny wailed.

"Well, die then," said Jonas, "and we'll give you a burial at sea."

"*Jonas!*" Alix whispered. "Stop that! I don't think she's acting. She sounds really sick."

"Well, she brought it on herself," he said loudly. She pulled him away from the door.

"That's beside the point. If she's sick, she's sick, and she can't stay locked up in that room."

He said in male exasperation, "Let her suffer it out. If it's summer complaint she won't die of it. She's not your responsibility."

"She's in my house, and she's not much more than a child. I know you expend all *your* sympathy on old block planes, but—"

"You mean you've got sympathy for her, after the way she ripped into you?"

"If you want to know, I'm trying to contain my rage," said Alix. "I thought I'd get rid of her this morning, but I can't chuck her out in this condition."

"She'll probably be all right tomorrow, but that sounds as far away as next year, doesn't it?"

"How'd you guess?"

"Oh, I've been there once or twice." They exchanged unamused grins. "Well, what more can I do?" he asked.

"Not a thing, I guess, until you take her ashore." She felt lifeless; not wounded, not degraded, but worn out. She forced herself to walk decisively back to the kitchen as if she had things to do and wanted to get to them.

"Look," Jonas said, "leave her to sleep it off and come on out with me to haul. I can put you back ashore whenever you say."

The temptation almost undid her. Then as they heard more retching she said grimly, "She shouldn't be alone. I may be able to get her to open the door, and if she's too weak I can go in through the window the way you threatened to do."

"Well—" For once he seemed uncertain of his next move, neither aggressive nor over-confident but oddly mild, and she thought, It's not just abandoned tools that get his sympathy. Not that she wanted it, even if she could stoop to clutch at crumbs, and she was sorry for the sparse admissions she had made to him. But she did want his practical assistance, without dragging Ozzie and Madge into this, and that meant a *quid pro quo*.

The teakettle was at a jumping boil, sending out clouds of steam. "Would you like that coffee now?" she asked him.

"No, I'll get along and leave you to it."

"Thanks for coming in this morning. I'm sorry you held up your work for nothing."

"Oh, that's all right," he said absently, lingering in the doorway. "Madge'll be over to see the sights as soon as she gets her legs under her. If Karen didn't get the name she got everything else. She didn't miss a detail, down to that bracelet on her ankle."

"It sounds as if you didn't miss anything either. I didn't even see that."

"Well, hell, I didn't die when I was divorced," said Jonas with dignity. "So long, and be sure to have a kitchen chair handy when the tigress comes out of her den."

"Good-bye, Jonas," she called loudly after him so Bunny would know he had gone. Then she tapped on the door again. "Are you all right?"

"Is that man gone?"

"Yes."

Bare feet heavy on the floor, the button turned, and the thumb latch clattering. Bunny opened the door. She looked like a gigantic child in her short nightgown and long hair. Her eyes were red, her mouth trembling and pathetically loose. She was shivering, but the room behind her was hot with the sun pouring in, and reeking with vomit.

"Good Lord," said Alix. "Come out here. Have you got a robe?" Bunny shook her head. Alix got out her old tweed coat from the entry and handed it to her. "Put this on. Right now," she snapped when the girl's jaw started to push out. Holding her breath she entered the room and opened the window to the sea wind, and swung wide the far door. She found the girl's shoes and brought them out. "Put these on, too," she ordered. "And sit down before you fall down."

She made another foray into the room and brought out the chamber without looking at it and set it out on the back door-step. She replaced it with a new white enamel combinet. Then she returned to the girl huddled shuddering inside the old coat. "I'll make you some hot tea and a piece of toast to settle your stomach," she said.

With a wailing moan Bunny lurched to her feet and toward the back door, where she was sick again. Alix took her by the arm to guide her back in, and was not driven off. The girl was frighteningly white and sweating heavily. "You'd better get back into bed," Alix said.

She had managed not to throw up on any of the bedding. Alix covered her up and put the washbasin on a chair beside the bed, and went out to get a hot water bottle ready. When she came back with it Bunny said, feebly, "Did that man stay here last night?"

"Good Lord, no," said Alix. "He has a home of his own."

"Would he have stayed if I hadn't been here?"

"Just get that bee out of your bonnet," said Alix. "He's a neighbor, a relative of the other people on the island. I am not having an affair with him. Not that it's any of your business."

"You're my business." She raised up on her elbows. "Don't think I'll be meek because I'm sick. Don't think I'll be grateful because you clean up after me. I've hated you for too long. We all have. It should have curled you up like burnt paper. You're a—" She began to retch again, leaning over the basin. Alix pushed a box of tissues within reach and left the room.

She left the door ajar, fully expecting that Bunny would get out of bed if she had to crawl to shut and button the door. But there was no noise from the room except some deep, groaning sighs and the sounds of turning over. To keep herself occupied Alix washed out some underwear and blouses. When she came back from hanging them out there was a different character to the stillness. Moving stealthily she looked around the door and saw that Bunny was asleep. Her face was turned toward Alix, the long black hair pushed back from it. She was so pale that the black brows and lashes looked drawn by a pen and India ink. Her expression in sleep was of innocence and peace. Undistorted by hatred, her features showed a classical generosity and distinction. The bare throat was long and strong. When she learned how to manage herself she would be a handsome woman rather than a beautiful one, and she would still be handsome when she was ninety.

Shane's daughter. It was incredible, but she was here. There was no chance of a hoax. She had his forehead and peaked black eyebrows; the very shape of the lids veiling the eye in sleep was the same, and the thin strong sweep of nose, the tranquil folding of the lips, even the deeply dented chin.

Alix could not take herself away. Shane, Shane! she called him without sound. Did you really suffer such guilt that you can't now come into this house while she's here? Look at her now, the cuddler; she sleeps as you did, in total surrender. But she'll wake up fighting, and Shane, what's my defense against the poison Cathleen's dripped into her brain all these years?

There was a fresh horror to confront as she wondered for the first time what Shane had been like away from her, especially when he was with his daughters or had to meet Cathleen. She'd never visualized him as different from her Shane, a warm and confident man who moved in a serene yet vital atmosphere all his own. But supposing he'd been disturbed enough by Cathleen's air of pious martyrdom and the children's questions to act ashamed and uncertain, letting them think he was a man possessed against his will.

Oh no! She nearly shouted her rejection of it. But it might turn out that the fatal act Bunny had committed here wasn't to make her feel defiled, but to destroy Shane.

❧ CHAPTER 28 ❧

SUDDENLY BUNNY opened her eyes, Shane's eyes in their shape and blueness but with no other resemblance.

"Are you spying on me?" asked the lucid, brittle voice. "I hate people who watch me while I sleep. I couldn't even forgive my mother that." She pulled the bedclothes defensively around her neck.

"How do you feel?"

"Better now. It's gone by, I think. I ate some fried clams at the airport last night. It's a wonder I didn't die of ptomaine poisoning."

"I'll bring you something. Tea, or bouillon?"

"I don't know," said Bunny, gazing at the ceiling. "I'll get up and then make up my mind."

"All right." Alix left her. Bunny came out shortly, barefoot in western jeans and a man's plaid shirt with long tails hanging free. Her hair was fastened back from her face with a wide band. She washed at the sink, went out back, and when she came in she announced loftily that she would have coffee and toast. She wasn't wearing the glasses.

Silently Alix prepared the meal. William came in and she

[271]

talked to him; she had decided not to attempt even insignificant conversation with Bunny. Manners were no currency in this case. If Bunny began an attack, she would walk away from it.

She left Bunny eating and went upstairs. William followed her and wandered around polishing the furniture and making plaintive comments. "I know it," Alix told him. "Just wait until tomorrow and we can breathe again."

She made her bed, and invented a few chores for herself in the studio. When she returned to the kitchen Bunny was absent, leaving everything on the table amid a sprinkling of crumbs, jam smears, and spattered coffee. It was a little too much to be natural sloppiness.

She cleared away and wiped the table, then glanced into the living room. Bunny was standing before the fireplace, looking up at Shane's portrait. Her back was toward Alix, so she couldn't see the expression. But she too looked at Shane, and felt a thrill of pride and possession. This was no man hag-ridden by guilt. This was the man of the house, robustly at home in it.

She stepped back out of sight before Bunny turned away from the portrait. She could follow her movements by ear, and William stopped in midbath to listen with turned head and pricked ears, one hind foot pointing balletlike to the North Star.

In a few moments she heard Bunny on the front stairs, and she ran quickly up the back way. Ignoring Bunny didn't extend to giving her the freedom of the bedrooms and studio. She had left the doors open all through, and when she crossed the studio she saw Bunny standing in the middle of Shane's room, hands in her hip pockets, looking all around her. There was color in her face now, like that of fever or an emotional flush, which it probably was, either from anger or something else.

Watching, Alix was capable of a detached pity for her. If the girl's arrival here had disoriented her, it must have disoriented the girl even more so.

Then Bunny passed out of her line of vision, and she heard a drawer being opened. She went swiftly across her room to the door. Bunny was rummaging through the contents of the drawer, some of Shane's clothing.

"I'd rather you didn't do that, Bunny," Alix said. The girl turned her head slowly and contemptuously. Her jaw was set as if she had her teeth clamped together.

"He lived here with you."

"Yes," said Alix, "this is our home."

Bunny began picking up things on the chest, looking them over, putting them down again, reading the titles of the books. She opened the leather box, handling the objects inside. It was a rather obvious performance. Flicking the wheel of the defunct lighter she said as if absently, "How can any decent woman just start living with a married man? But then, you wouldn't know about that, would you?"

Alix folded her arms and leaned her head against the door-frame. She looked over Bunny's head at the ceiling and said, also absently, "The rain must have come in around the chimney in the last big storm. There's a new spot."

Bunny put down the lighter and picked up the tiki. "What made you decide on my father anyway? Why would you pick out a professor of government in a small college? Where was the excitement, for an artistic type like yourself? Was it just because he belonged to somebody else?"

"Your father was a grown man," Alix said patiently. "He made his own decisions. I didn't draw him by witchcraft out of the bosom of his family. He'd already left. I don't know why I tell you this," she continued, "unless it's to defend your father because he's not here to do it for himself. We didn't begin to live together until he'd given up hope of a divorce."

"We don't believe in divorce," said Bunny proudly. "We have a religion. My father did too, till you seduced him away from it. My mother never believed he could stay away from *it* —and her—for good. She'd try to be brave, but she'd cry at night. She never stopped loving him."

There was a slight tremor in her voice, and as if she heard it she dropped the tiki and stood staring out of the windows at the water.

"He'd have come back too," she went on. "I know he would have if you'd been different. But he was weak and he was too kind. You probably made him think he owed you everything because you gave him your honor." She looked around with that derisive one-sided sneer. "It's a wonder you didn't have a child or two, just to hold him. He was the kind who'd think the little bastards needed more protection than his legitimate children."

"That's enough, Bunny," Alix said. "Go on downstairs." Bunny turned around to face her and Alix kept walking slowly toward her, thinking, I can't force her physically. What if she doesn't move? But suddenly Bunny wheeled and strode toward the door. She kept her hands in her pockets presumably to show her nonchalance, which was shattered when she cracked one elbow against the doorframe. With a gasp that was almost a sob, she ran thunderously down the front stairs. Alix buttoned the bedroom door behind her, then went back through the rooms, scooping up William on the way.

The door at the foot of the back stairs wasn't one of the originals; some later Goodwin had replaced that with a conventional inside door, and it had a conventional old-fashioned lock, though it was never locked. As Bunny ranged noisily around her room, Alix rummaged in a wooden salt-cod box among cup hooks, odd nails, and old bottle openers for the key. She locked the door and put the key in her hip pocket and buttoned down the flap over it.

"*Now,*" she said softly to herself. It didn't mean anything in itself, but it was like a signal for the end of something, or the beginning.

She and William went out. The day was fresh and fragrant, still earlier than noon though it felt as if it had already been fifteen hours since daylight. She stood on the back doorstep looking up the slope toward the spruces in full sunshine against

blue sky and a few puffball clouds. This aspect always had an
Alpine air for her, as if the field were really a mountain
meadow in Switzerland. Beyond the barrier of deep-sweeping
green boughs the Tangle lay like a secret garden and aviary.

Watching William stroll up the path, leisurely and lustrous
in the sun, she was powerfully tempted to take a flying leap off
the doorstep and keep on running.

Which would doubtless give Bunny a sour satisfaction. *She
couldn't face me. She ran out on me. I told her a thing or two.*

Suddenly a strong draft swept through the house and
slammed the back door behind her. She went in and found the
front door wide open to the strengthening wind. Bunny was almost out to the edge of the lawn where the roses were, carrying
her tote bag and a blanket from her bed. "Small favors grate-
fully received," said Alix, shutting the door. She left the house
rapidly by the front door, taking an orange with her, and some
soft pencils and a note pad from the study rather than unlock
the door and go to the studio for materials.

The Tangle in July was almost tropical with ferns and birds.
William wandered through a bracken jungle like a tiger by
Rousseau. Today the place represented to Alix not unbearable
memory but sanctuary. However, she was fully prepared for
Karen to come tramping through.

But Karen never appeared. Alix made some sketches of William in the bracken and up in the crotch of an apple tree, and
she slept in a hollow cushiony with bracken. She was tired
enough to sleep soundly, but she knew in her sleep what
waited for her back at the house, and she woke reluctantly. Yet
there was nothing else to do but go back. This wasn't something she could take to the Goodwins, as she'd taken the others
on that foggy morning.

For my sins, she thought as she walked slowly home through
the cooling, darkening woods. *If I hadn't taken up with Shane,
his daughter wouldn't be here now. That's simple enough for
anyone to understand. She'll victimize me because I've victim-*

ized her—she thinks. Given ten years more, she might see it differently, or at least more charitably. But I doubt it. Not after growing up to the sound of her mother's prayers and tears. No, this is something to put up with until tomorrow, and I've had so little of it in my life with Shane I should be thankful, and endure her presence here as gracefully as possible. Though the only way I can be graceful is to stay out of the line of fire.

William had left her while she slept, and he met her at the back door with loud cries. A fragrance of fried bacon floated out through the screen door, tantalizing him. He rushed in ahead of Alix and straight to the gas stove, where a still-warm frying pan remained. There were fresh eggshells in the sink, and the table was littered again so obviously that it had to be a token of contempt.

Alix fed William and inspected the living room. The guitar had been taken down and left in a chair. A few books had been removed from the shelves and not replaced; this wasn't the sort of thing that would ever annoy Alix, but she was irked to find one book dropped and left face down on the floor with some pages bent over. There'd been a shifting of articles on the mantel, the pewter tankard moved, the arrowheads stirred around. The red-purple point was missing, which gave her a bad jolt until she found it shoved carelessly behind Shane's masterpiece at the other end of the mantel, a ship in a rum bottle.

The sofa pillows were on the floor, and an ash tray had been upset on the hearth rug and left in a spill of ashes and butts. No poltergeist was at work here. Bunny left a visible spoor wherever she'd been.

Alix hung up the guitar, put back the books, shook the rug. In the study, some of the desk drawers had been left open. She was glad she had burned all of Shane's notebooks. Thorvald's drawer seemed undisturbed. She took out the Viking and stood him on the palm of her hand. "Friend, I could use you now," she said dourly, and returned him to the drawer.

After she tidied the kitchen, she fixed a light supper for herself and ate it. As sunset approached with its long golden George Inness interval she began wondering if Bunny was lost and she would have to organize a search party. Sidney always picked up a foreign scent at once, and perhaps if they brought him to the house he could follow Bunny's trail. "You're certainly making your presence felt, my girl," Alix said. "Getting sick, getting lost, all in addition to being generally objectionable."

She went across the lawn and looked down at the sand beach, empty except for a flock of gently peeping phalaropes, and then along the top of the bank toward the northeast, around the bay and juniper clumps. Bunny wasn't on the rocks below. She went all the way up the steepening rise toward the Head, but the only moving things she saw in the roseate light were birds of both land and water, and some bees working late in the wild roses. Coming to the thrust of the Head itself, she climbed up to the top by familiar holds and lay flat with her head at the outer edge. The tawny rock was comfortably warm against her belly and thighs. She felt restfully isolated up here.

Live like that stoic bird, the eagle on the rock. Yes. She sighed, and resting her chin on her folded arms she studied the slow-motion balletic interplay of the currents below as they met, formed, and separated in long lines of foam. There was a constant complex shifting of patterns and designs, with a lovely deliberation in the blossoming, the swirling erasure, the blossoming again.

For a few moments she forgot why she was here, and it was like other times when she'd lain here for minutes or hours, mesmerized by the scene below. Finally she extricated herself from the spell and looked down along the shore to the north. Nothing moved among the irregular masses of stone.

Up on the Head the last of the sunset still ignited everything it touched, but when she left it and came down into the shadow it was like walking into quiet water. Listening to the long flute-notes of the whitethroats and the evening calls of robins, she was bemused enough to pass the house, and when she saw the figure climbing the path from the wharf, she was startled. Then she remembered who it was. The irony was that this was the first evening since she had come when she had been completely immersed in the mood of the evening, an entity free for a time of memory or even thought, simply reacting through her senses.

Bunny came trudging toward her, head down and hands in her pockets. When she reached Alix she stopped, as if Alix were an obstacle she was too tired to walk around. She looked exhausted; the shadows under her eyes were almost the color of the tinted glasses she had left off.

"I thought you were lost," Alix said.

"Too bad I'm back." The insolence was faint.

"You must be hungry."

"No, I fixed myself something before I went. I've been halfway around this place, I guess."

They walked on toward the house. "I'm going to have a cup of coffee," Alix said, "and you're welcome to join me. Or you could have something else."

"Gee, thanks." The sarcasm was as weak as the insolence had been. "I'm going to bed and read."

✺ CHAPTER 29 ✺

THERE WAS A brief thundershower early the next morning, consisting of a few long cannonades and a hard rain that roared on the roof and gurgled in the gutters and down the spouts like a spring freshet. Then everything stopped abruptly and the sun came out. There was a spectacular rainbow.

Alix made coffee for her thermos bottle and buttered some bread and wrapped it up, and went down to the wharf to bail out *Sea Pigeon*. It would be a wet job, so she wore shorts and was barefoot. All around her the fields sparkled with tremulous prisms. Tiree glittered through its own fragrant steam.

She went down on the beach to pull the boat in. When *Sea Pigeon*, heavy with her load, beached out in shallow water, Alix waded in and bailed from outside, then got into the boat to finish up. William sat on the wharf, watching the bright flying arcs of water. The wet wharf planks and fishhouse roof gently smoked in the sun. When she had finished Alix regretfully returned the boat to the mooring, thinking of all such dazzling mornings when she could have taken *Sea Pigeon* out but hadn't; now, just because she couldn't feel free, it was the only thing in the world she wanted to do.

She got some dry old magazines out of the fishhouse to sit on,

and perched on the edge of the wharf with her legs dangling
over, and had her breakfast. It was the best-tasting meal she'd
had since the picnic, when the *paella* had been so very good
and then had felt so very awful afterwards.

She took her time about eating. If it didn't breeze up southwest after Bunny was gone, she'd take *Sea Pigeon* out.

On her slow homeward course, she was met halfway by a wet
and enthusiastic Sidney, who whirled around her and leaped
into the air like a lamb, then rushed off down the path in
search of William. Madge and Karen were coming along the
path from the woods. Alix waited for them at the edge of the
back lawn.

"It's some wet in the woods, but doesn't it *smell* good!" said
Madge. "I told Karen to breathe real hard. We get all this for
free, and some folks never draw a clean, sweet breath in their
lives, poor souls." She was overcome with sadness, but rapidly
cheered up. "I hear you've got company, dear! Isn't that *nice!*
A big girl, Karen said. You weren't expecting anyone, were
you?"

"Never in a million years, and guess who? You can't, so I'll
tell you. Shane's daughter."

Madge went completely out of character. She said simply,
"Why?"

"To read me out," said Alix unemotionally. "She's done so,
now she's leaving, and that's that."

Madge gave Karen's uplifted and transfixed face a harassed
glance. "I don't know how much they take in," she murmured.
"But didn't you have any *idea*? I mean, was she just there at
Roger's, out of a clear sky?"

"Yes, she was just there."

"But how did she know where to find you?"

"She found the address in Shane's desk at the college. Hark
to the sweet music—Jonas is coming." The big gray dory came
fast around the farther point of Gib's Cove, Jonas standing in
the stern. He cut down his speed to cross the cove to the wharf.
When he saw them up by the house, he waved.

"I'm really beginning to appreciate him," said Alix as she waved back. She turned to meet Madge's expression of compassionate anxiety. "Oh, don't worry, Madge," she said tartly. "It's all right. *I'm* all right."

"But to have this happen when you were just beginning to feel better. I think it's a wicked shame."

"She thinks things were a wicked shame too, Madge. I have to see her viewpoint."

Jonas had tied up at the wharf and was coming up the path, whistling exuberantly. He walked as if his rubber boots weighed nothing at all. Such springy gaiety could be bruising, but not this morning when he was about to take Bunny away.

"Good morning, ladies," he said, sweeping off his cap and holding it over his heart. "How are the flowers of womanhood today?" He made a lightning snatch at Karen's nose. "I want that, it's a lot prettier than mine." She ducked away from him, disapproving of such juvenile foolishness. He laughed at her. "You want to ride in with me, Flora McFlimsey? I'll treat you to a bottle of pop at Bert's."

Karen's shoulders went up to her ears.

"Is my passenger ready?" he asked Alix.

"If she isn't she soon will be, if I have to get her out of bed and dressed myself."

"In the meantime I'll drink some of your incomparable coffee." With a Gallic flourish he kissed the tips of his fingers. "Ah! Pure nectar!"

"The secret must be in the way I spoon it out of the jar," said Alix.

Madge was still visibly upset; she looked from one to the other as if bewildered by their joking at a time like this. Alix laughed and said, "Come on in. Bunny!" she called, "time to get up and have breakfast! Jonas is here."

She was rather pleased with her manner, which hovered between that of a kind aunt and an efficient Nanny.

"Can't he go away and come back?" Bunny answered faintly. "I can't hurry. I'm dizzy."

"You don't have to hurry," said Alix. "There's plenty of time. But you may be just hungry."

Bunny made a gagging sound, and Madge looked apprehensive. Karen stared at the door as if the intensity of her curiosity could dissolve the panels. There was a tinkle of breaking glass in the bedroom, then a long moan and a heavy crash, as if a bed had collapsed.

"Oh, my stars!" Madge breathed with her hand to her heart. Alix sensed disaster like a split in her head, though it felt more like a pumpkin hurled against a stone wall. She and Jonas reached the door at the same time and their glances met like signals. "Fake," he said.

"I don't think so."

She got into the room first. Bunny lay on the floor by the bed, half-naked in her short nightdress. The small stand had tipped over with her, and the glass had gone first. It lay about her head in glinting fragments.

There was no faking the marble whiteness and the graceless out-of-joint sprawl. She looked dead, and for an instant Alix froze where she stood. Jonas pulled a blanket off the bed and dropped it over the girl, then he knelt amid the broken glass and lifted Bunny's wrist, feeling for a pulse. Alix's own heart beat in a wilder rhythm of suspense. Finally he nodded at her and laid down the hand. With a peculiar delicacy in his fingers he turned back one eyelid. "The real thing," he murmured.

"You stay out here, Karen," Madge said with unusual sharpness. She came around the door and stood looking down at Bunny. "Looks like her father, doesn't she?" she marveled in a whisper.

Jonas began picking up the larger bits of glass, and putting them in an ash tray. "She must be one of those fainters," he said. "Roll up their eyes and turn up their toes at the drop of a hat. Comes in handy when they don't want to do something. Stay to hell out of this glass in your bare feet," he growled as Alix moved. "Get me a dustpan and brush."

Madge, nearest the door, went to get it and collided with

Karen. "Karen, you go and sit in that chair and *stay* there!" she exclaimed.

"Well, at least put a pillow under her head," Alix told Jonas. He hauled one off the bed and lifted the heavy black head and put the pillow under it. Madge returned with the dustpan and Jonas cleaned up all the glass in sight.

"Thank you, Jonas," Madge said. "Now why don't you go out in the other room and see what Karen's doing?"

He cocked his head at her with a wry speculation. "Just *see*, and let her go ahead and do it?"

"You know what I mean," she said crossly. "She's dying to get in here and it's no place for *either* child or man. Alix and I can manage now."

"Thanks for getting to her first, Jonas," Alix said. "I was sure she was dead, and it paralyzed me for a minute."

He nodded. "Yep. If you need me again, holler." He took the dustpan out and shut the door. Madge laid a hand on Alix's arm and nodded her head toward the far side of the room, well away from the unconscious girl. They went to the window that looked across the lawn toward the roses and the sea. "Before we bring her around," Madge murmured, "I wonder . . . she was real sick yesterday morning and then got right over it?"

Alix nodded, mystified.

"No runs with it, just throwing up?"

Alix nodded again.

"And this morning she gags and then faints," said Madge. She looked out at the lawn, her palms pressing into her plump cheeks and dragging down hard over her jaws. "Now Alix, you know I don't have a dirty mind, don't you?"

"But you've got a hunch, and I wish you didn't."

Madge said, "I wish I didn't have it, too. I may be awful wrong and I hope I am."

"But you don't think so." Alix leaned her forehead against the glass, which didn't cool it. "Great," she said. "Simply great."

"But it's not for you to worry," Madge whispered agitatedly. "When she's gone you can forget all about it. I only mentioned it so you wouldn't think she was really sick and not able to travel."

"She looks really sick to me," Alix objected.

"But she'll probably be fine when she comes to. Some do faint awful easy, the way Jonas said. And it's so early yet, she may not even know it herself. *If* it's so," she corrected herself.

"But damn it, after this collapse I can't just rush her out of here!" Alix whispered. "Supposing she faints over at the Harbor, or in Fremont. She could fall through a store window or in front of a car. She's only eighteen, and her mother's in Europe. I can see her onto the plane, but I should call someone to take care of her at the other end."

They both looked at the silent form under the blanket. "I can see how you feel," Madge whispered back. "I'd feel the same way. But you look just awful, Alix. It's extra-bad for you, the whole thing. . . . Look, there has to be a boy, and they'll likely get married as soon as he knows about this. Seems like there's more of those weddings than the other kind these days."

"I never even thought of a boy. I hadn't got that far."

"Well, she certainly didn't pick it up out of thin air like you catch a cold."

"Why, Madge Goodwin!" whispered Alix, testing herself cautiously for signs of rising spirits. Yes, they were lifting; she wanted to giggle insanely at Madge's expression.

Bunny returned to consciousness meek with fright. Dazed and quiescent, she responded obediently to being put back in bed with a hot water bottle at her feet.

Jonas had taken Karen outdoors. She made a tight sullen bundle at the edge of the field, knees hugged to her chest, staring at the toes of her wet red sneakers. Jonas sat on the workshop doorstep in the sun, smoking his pipe. Sidney raced back and forth yelping at the swallows while William tolerantly watched.

"I'm sorry you've lost another early start out to haul," Alix said to Jonas. "Next time it'll be at your convenience, not hers."

"Isn't she going today?"

"Not after that faint. She's pretty shaky. I want to find out who can take charge of her when she gets home."

He raised an eyebrow at Madge, who gazed up at the weathervane with ostentatious interest and never a blink.

"I take it the conference has reached a decision to believe the worst," he said.

"There's nothing I hate more than a male gossip, Jonas Hallowell!" Madge told the weathervane.

"Who's gossiping? When I get sent out of the room with the kids, I know why. By the prickling of my thumbs or the twiddles in my ears, or something."

"Well, there are all kinds of *worsts*," said Alix. "This doesn't have to be one of them. If it's so," she added meticulously.

He got up and stretched. "Well, I'm going to work. Want a ride around, Madge?"

"Come on, Chickabiddy," Madge called winningly to the gloomy one. "We're going for a sail. Boat, Sidney, boat!" Sidney threw himself at her, and Karen slowly arose. "Let me know, Alix," Madge said meaningfully.

"She can send the message by me," said Jonas. "In code, to protect my innocence."

"I never knew he could be so provoking," Madge complained. "And at a time like this, too."

"At a time like *what?*" he teased her as they headed for the wharf. Madge's expostulations floated in her wake, and Karen followed like a small, balky skiff being towed against its will.

❧ CHAPTER 30 ❧

BUNNY WAS LYING in bed gazing at the ceiling with her hands folded on her breast. She didn't turn her eyes toward Alix but went on watching the flickering waves of light that endlessly crossed the ceiling from one side to the other.

"Hypnotic, isn't it?" Alix asked. Bunny didn't answer. Alix sat down on the foot of the bed.

"Do you feel sick now, lying down?" she asked. Still gazing upward, Bunny slowly moved her head from side to side—cautiously, Alix guessed.

"You'd better stay in bed for a while, at least," she said. "I'll bring you something to eat when you want it, and something to read if you want that."

"Trying to keep me out of the way, I see," said Bunny huskily.

"Don't be ridiculous," said Alix. "If getting you out of the way was the prime factor, I could have got you aboard Jonas's boat this morning if we'd had to carry you down in the wheelbarrow. I hope by tomorrow I can put you on a plane, but I want you moving under your own power. I'd also like the name of someone I can call to meet you when you get home."

Bunny's gaze flashed toward her, and her folded hands jumped. Then she laced them tighter and said languidly, "Now you're being ridiculous. I don't need to be *put* on the plane, and I don't need to be *met*."

"I think you do," said Alix. "Where does your sister live?"

"In Hawaii." Bunny displayed a sort of smug triumph. "Her husband's stationed out there. And we don't have any relatives around. No faithful maiden aunts."

"No close family friends?" asked Alix skeptically. "You mean your mother's gone to Europe and you've been left absolutely on your own?"

Bunny twisted her shoulders restlessly. "Why not?" She turned her head away and appeared absorbed by a sketch across the room. "Times have changed since you were young. At my age we're grown up now."

"So I keep hearing," said Alix dryly. "Over and over. Well, what about a boy friend, then? There must be one."

She received an eloquently scornful look. "Why *must* there be one?"

"Well, Bunny, grown-up or not, boy friend or not, you aren't well, and someone has to be responsible for you." Bunny sucked in an angry breath, but Alix allowed no interruption. "If there's no one to meet you, I'll have to put you in the care of the stewardess, and have the Traveler's Aid people take charge of you at the airport."

It sounded ludicrous as she said it, and the echo was worse. She waited for Bunny to laugh in her face and call her bluff. She'd counted on shock tactics to knock reason out, but Bunny might be more intelligent than she knew.

Suddenly Bunny said thickly, "All *right!* I'm staying with some people in Paoli. But I came down to Boston to visit a girl whose people have a summer place at Gloucester. They know who she is, and my mother does, and everything. So I'll just go back there, to Gloucester, I mean. I can call Sal from the airport in Fremont to meet me."

The rush came to an end and she sat up and reached for her

cigarettes. The start of the motion was bold enough, but her trembling hand fumbled the package, and the lighter slid onto the floor. Alix picked it up and held it, and after a futile reach for it Bunny turned her head away.

Alix sat silent, watching the line of brow and cheekbone that must have been like Shane's as a young boy, and the familiar way the black hair grew back from the temple. The silence began to brim, and finally the girl's voice spilled over it, thickened and shaking.

"Why the third degree? You work for the FBI or something? It's none of your business what I do!"

"You told me that you'd made me your business. And when you came into my house you became *my* business. You don't like it and I certainly don't, but here you are and in rotten shape."

"I'm all right!" she shouted. She snapped her head around. Her eyes were streaming. "Just because I picked up some stupid virus or ate those rotten clams, why can't you get off my back? I'll go this afternoon if I can get across." She began to thrash around in the bed. "Will you get out of here so I can get dressed? I'll go ask that man to take me. I'll pay him plenty."

"That man is out hauling," said Alix without moving. "I could take you across if it stays calm. But I'll want to know you've called your friend so she'll be sure to meet you, and I intend to see you onto the plane. If you fainted again it could be in front of a truck or on a pavement that would split your head open. It could kill you."

"I don't care!" she shrieked. "Just leave me alone!" She clapped her hands over her ears and kicked her feet convulsively under the covers, trying to dislodge Alix. She had the insane concentration of a child in the grip of a tantrum.

Alix got up and went to the sea window. The view set in this frame was beginning to take on a hideous familiarity. She had never looked out at it so much under such grim circumstances.

It was taking all her courage now to remain there apparently unmoved by the turmoil behind her. She felt the gut-wrenching futility of watching an animal gone wild in pain and terror, unreachable no matter how great the watcher's desire to help it.

Finally there was no sound behind her except some small, stifled hiccups. She turned around. Bunny lay on her stomach with her face buried in the pillow. Alix went to the bed. "Who's your friend in Gloucester, Bunny?" she asked quietly.

No answer. She said, "I can keep you here on this island indefinitely. Nobody will take you across."

"You have to let me go," Bunny said into the pillow. "I have to be in Boston tomorrow afternoon."

"Why? Your friend won't be wondering what's become of you because there isn't any friend, is there? At least not the way you mean. Why do you have to be in Boston tomorrow afternoon?"

No answer. Alix was not enjoying herself. She felt like a Gestapo interrogator, except that he'd have been enjoying his work. She wet her lips and said, "Bunny, are you pregnant?"

She saw the shoulders go rigid, and then the whole long body sagged and flattened in the bed.

"And nobody in your family knows?"

"Are you kidding?" said the muffled voice. "It would kill my mother, on top of all she's suffered from you and my father."

"What about your sister? She'd understand, wouldn't she?"

"What could she do?"

"All right then, there's the boy, or the man, whoever—"

Bunny surged over onto her back and sat up, hair in a maenad tangle, eyes swollen, her face creased as if with red scars from wrinkles in the pillow case. "Listen, you've done your duty as a busybody. I don't think you really give a damn, but just to round out the story and make you feel good, I'll tell you I can take care of myself. I don't intend to go on being pregnant. I've made all the arrangements and that's why I have to be in Boston tomorrow afternoon. Is that clear? Now if you'll get out of here I'll get dressed, or don't you intend to allow me that much privacy?"

"What you're saying," said Alix carefully, "is that you're going to an abortionist in Boston."

"You read me right," she said with a sardonic grimace. "You do indeed. And if he'd kept the original appointment it would be all over by now, and maybe I wouldn't even have bothered to come down here. I'll bet you could cry about what you almost missed."

"When was the original appointment?"

Bunny sent a rapid, furtive glance toward the tote bag across the room on the chest. Then she counted on her fingers with a savage gaiety. "Last Tuesday. The day before the Fourth. I thought it was a wonderful way to celebrate independence! But when I called the number from my hotel, she told me to call again Saturday for a new appointment. So I thought I'd give you a whirl." Suddenly her bravado teetered too close to the edge. "When I think it would have been over by now—oh *God!*" She put her hands over her face and rocked back and forth. "I've been so scared, and it doesn't get any better, it gets worse, having to wait like this. I thought if I came down here and raised the devil with you I'd stop being scared, but it didn't work. I got so sick yesterday; that was the worst it's ever been." She took her hands away but kept fingering her lower lip as if to hold it steady. "Yesterday afternoon I kept jumping off high rocks, and I climbed trees too and dropped down hard, trying to start a miscarriage, but all I got was so tired I could hardly walk back here."

She stared incredulously up at Alix. "And I never fainted in my life before today! That was what gave it away, wasn't it?"

"Not to me," said Alix. "But never mind now, you're freezing." She moved to wrap a blanket around Bunny's shoulders, but Bunny recoiled and took the blanket from her. "It's just nerves," she said. "Have you got a couple of aspirin? Then I'll get up and eat, and you can take me over. It's calm enough, isn't it?" She stretched her neck, trying to see the water.

"I'm not taking you ashore just to send you to an abortion mill."

"You've *got* to! It's my life, and you've got no right to meddle with it!"

"Maybe not, but if I let you go without a fight and you died or were maimed for life from this operation I'd be responsible."

"Huh!" she hooted. "Easy to talk about responsibility now, isn't it? Who do you think is responsible for my being here in this mess in the first place? *You* are! If I'd had a full-time father I could talk to and who was around when I needed him, I wouldn't have got in with that bunch. I wouldn't have got so drunk at a party that I didn't know who or how many made out with me the night I got knocked up." She laughed raucously. "How does that grab you? You never were that immoral, were you? You never went around in such a nasty, revolting, sexy gang; you got yourself a married man and a nice cozy little playhouse, and to hell with what happened to his kids without him."

Bette Davis was conspicuously absent.

"I should have thought," said Alix, "that your loyalty to your mother would have kept you out of trouble. You've been conscious of her suffering all these years; didn't you feel any guilt about adding to her suffering?"

Bunny opened her mouth but was unable to think of an answer right away. After a moment she burst out, "She's coming back the first of August! I've got to get this over with! Can't you see, I don't care about the risk, I don't care about anything except her not finding out!"

"She'll find out if something goes wrong."

"Why do you keep harping on that?" Bunny cried in despair. "People do it all the time! The girl that fixed it up for me has been three times, and *she's* all right. Can't you leave me alone? Haven't you done enough to us already?"

The thrashings of a terror-stricken child weren't to be classed as accusations. "Well, Bunny, after that fainting spell you can't go today anyway," she said. "But I'll leave you alone. I'm no more infatuated with the subject than you are. Now do you think you can eat?"

Obviously Bunny hated to admit it, as if taking food from Alix would be a form of surrender. "I guess so," she muttered. "But I'm going to get up."

"Good, if you feel strong enough." Alix departed at a brisk pace. Out in the kitchen she resisted an impulse to sag into a chair. William's howls outside the screen door were a welcome link with a world where Bunny didn't exist. She let him in and kept talking to him to keep his purr going.

Bunny came out in her jeans and shirt. "Oh, that's who you're talking to," she said. She and William regarded each other dispassionately, William's purr ceasing for a moment. It began again at new volume when Alix opened the refrigerator.

"How about some hot oatmeal?" Alix asked.

"Oh, sure," Bunny said indifferently on her way out. Alix was cynically amused by her own instinctive reaction to pregnancy, even one that was to be terminated shortly, if Bunny could manage it. She wanted to stuff the girl with large quantities of milk and nourishing food.

Bunny came back in and washed up at the sink. "Makes me think of camp," she remarked grudgingly. "No comforts. It's supposed to build character that way.... I was a counsellor there this summer but I resigned."

"Formally, or did you just leave?"

"Oh, I left them a note. Otherwise they'd have the state police out dragging the lake and beating the bushes, and wiring my mother." She added gruffly, "I forgot I told you something different. But I really was at camp."

Alix said nothing, just went on stirring oatmeal. Bunny ate two soup dishes full, then got up and went to the door. "I'm going for a walk," she said curtly. She didn't wait for a response.

Alix did sag then. "Shane," she murmured. "If you love me, if you hear me—if I ever needed you, it's now, and where are you?"

She went through the house, stopping wherever there had been a so-called sign. Thorvald first; then the broken fragments of the mustache cup where she had left them in a small box in a corner of the studio cupboard. The things on Shane's chest had been moved around by Bunny, of course, and the tiki dropped inside the leather box. But her name was still on the workshop bench, and she studied that for a long time.

At last she went to the spear point, remembering how she had visualized Shane on that day with an anguished super-reality. But today the memory was dulled like a steamy glass, and it seemed very far away. She felt deserted. She stood looking at the portrait until the face began to move, and then she got away from it as quickly as possible and went outdoors.

❦ CHAPTER 31 ❦

SHE HAD A desire as strong as the extremity of thirst to be away from all human contact for a while. She knew Madge was dying for a good talk over coffee cups and had probably baked a cake on purpose, expecting her to show up at Beauty Cove. But she couldn't make herself go. She walked to a cove halfway between Gib's and the Home Cove, a steep little niche dug out of a stretch of rusty-blackish rock that looked like the petrified aftermath of a volcano. The spruces grew thickly to the edge of the turf, some with roots exposed by the wash of the high tides, and there was no path among them. She felt well-hidden here. Once she saw Ozzie hauling traps just offshore, but he didn't see her where she sat among the trees. Later Jonas came into the mouth of the cove, watching the shore for old traps or pot buoys; but, stippled by light and shadow, she felt camouflaged enough for him to miss her.

There was nothing to think out; at least nothing that thinking could solve. She wanted not to think, she was as tired of the inside of her brain as a prisoner of his solitary-confinement cell. She sketched rocks, fragments of sea-urchin and mussel shells washed up into the salt-burned turf, infinitesimal plants, but without the usual concentration. She worked on the details of the roots of old trees, but these turned into scaled and predatory Arthur Rackham claws. The changing colors of the sea and the floating weed couldn't absorb her. The moving play of shadows cast by the trees as the wind freshened meant only that another day was inching toward night.

The edible plant called lamb's quarters grew in fresh green profusion here out of a rich fertilizer of old rockweed. She spread her cardigan out on the beach and heaped tender silver-green tips on it, then tied up the bundle and went home with the idea of getting a hot and substantial supper ready for Bunny. She was still amused at the way she'd seized on this as something she *could* do.

In May she had been living from day to day, and then later from week to week, so she had not laid in supplies as she had done in other years. Today, looking over her scanty store, she remembered those early days and nights, and how they had blended into one another so that she couldn't separate them, and the sickening swings between incredulity and realization. When she had come, she had expected to be dead within a week. The letter for Madge and Ozzie was still locked away in the studio with her will, the Scotch, and the Seconal.

I won't see September here, she thought matter-of-factly, studying the contents of the kitchen cupboards. If Shane had ever been here, he had withdrawn. The merciless realities of the last few days had turned the whole thing into a memory of delusions that had gone on for a time and then had suddenly ceased.

There is nothing to wait for, she thought. Dead is dead, and they don't walk. All I've got is the word of people who couldn't accept the facts, who'd have gone mad if they couldn't take the escape route. . . . What happened here, I *could* have done all myself if I was turning a little schizophrenic . . . except for the point; I swear I never saw that before in my life.

But maybe I did . . . Nothing to wait for, once Bunny's gone.

She decided on a baked cheese, egg, and rice dish, with the

lamb's quarters for a vegetable. All the time she was putting it together she kept thinking, *Once Bunny's gone* . . . The simplest solution, which she ached to follow, was to say no more and let her go. If the abortionist hadn't put her off, by now she would have been through the mill, either recovering or found in her hotel room dead or dying from hemorrhages. Alix wouldn't have known anything about it. Let her go tomorrow morning, and forget, except that now that she had it to forget, she could not.

She put the baking dish in the gas oven and went outside. There was no sign of Bunny in any direction. She wondered if she were still climbing trees and dropping out of them. Too bad it wouldn't work; it would be an easy way out. "Oh, why did that miserable girl ever have to come here?" she groaned.

William, who was just arriving from concerns of his own, chose to interpret this as an affectionate greeting, and fell heavily against her legs. She looked abstractedly at him and went off and left him kneading air. Suddenly she had a totally unexpected desire for a drink.

"Driving me to drink, that's what that brat's doing," she grumbled. "Between her and Karen I shudder to think what I might have given birth to."

She took her glass up to the studio and unlocked the little corner cupboard where the liquor and Seconal were. After she poured her drink she didn't really want it. "Think of it as medicine, dear," she said in a smarmy voice. "For your poor tortured nerves."

She sat on her tall stool by the work table watching the osprey family hunt in wide swinging circles high over the Head. Let her go, she thought. Maybe she's right when she says she's no concern of mine. If I had no conscience once about Shane's family—according to Bunny—why this sudden explosion of virtue now, when it can only be a nuisance?

She lifted her glass in a toast to the absent girl. *"Git,"* she said. "And maybe you'll be lucky and have three abortions like your friend . . . and live through it."

She drank, but the whiskey turned rotten in her stomach, and came boiling up in fumes of nausea. *It's Shane's daughter you're talking about.* She ran downstairs with her hand over her mouth and threw up in the sink. Then she washed the sink with a half-bucket of rainwater, and washed her face. Still sick but with nothing to bring up, she hung to the edge of the sink as if defying a cyclone to bear her away.

Shane's daughter. Drunk and in bed or on the floor with she didn't know whom or how many. On her way to an abortionist represented by a telephone number sneaked to her by another girl in the network of frightened kids who thought they knew so much.

"Shane, I can't do it to you," she said. "You're in your grave and your spirit doesn't walk. You're gone. But I still can't do it to you. At least I can't do it without a fight."

Bunny wasn't in sight from the sink window, or from any of the others. She bolted both front and back doors and went into the bedroom. The tote bag stood open on the chest. Her reluctance to delve into the bag was instinctive, and she had no certainty that she'd find what she was looking for, just a hope based on Bunny's fast sly glance toward the bag.

She took it up to the studio, and turned the contents out on the work table. Bunny had crammed a fantastic amount into it. The oversized glasses, crumpled tissues, a clutch of odd combs, scattered items of make-up, pocket books, chocolate bars, half-used rolls of Life Savers and Tums, cigarettes, at least a dozen paper match packets, some empty; a package of letters fastened with an elastic band.

As a compromise with her honor Alix ignored everything that couldn't possibly contain a telephone number. She was hoping for an address book so she wouldn't have to look through the letters. There was a little memorandum book finally, but nothing was in it but a big black scrawl across one page—*Dentist,* and his number. She read meticulously both sides of sales slips, receipts, used envelopes with lists written on them, business cards. She examined the bag for secret pockets.

A zippered slit in the lining gave up a letter, and she thought triumphantly, This must be from the friend, making the arrangements.

She turned the envelope over and saw Bunny's name and the address of the Mannering home in Paoli, written in Shane's hand.

It was one of those surprises again. You believe you can think objectively about something, that at last you've taken control of it, and then comes the ambush. It never goes away; it just comes back in different forms.

To see his handwriting now was like hearing his voice say the written words. She shut her eyes, seeking after the voice, waiting for it to say something else, but it didn't.

She looked at the other side of the envelope for a scribbled notation, but found none. She put the envelope back and fastened the zipper. As she replaced the other items she studied each one for something she could have missed. Presumably one of the three business cards could have been a blind, but they were for a music teacher in Philadelphia, a dressmaker in the same city, and the third belonged to a salesman in a custom-floorings firm based in Hartford. The abortionist was in Boston.

Boston, Boston . . . what *was* it about Boston? . . . She opened the little red imitation leather memorandum book, and knew what it was. The dentist's telephone number had a Boston exchange.

It must have registered on Alix at the first glimpse, because the numbers of the exchange were now immediately familiar. Up until a year or so ago she used to call an elderly cousin at that exchange several times a year. The old lady was dead now.

Why would a Pennsylvania girl have a Boston dentist?

She copied the number off on a slip of paper, then finished putting things away in the bag. As she looked up from this she saw Bunny standing on the brow of the Head, facing the wind. Her hair streamed back from her head and shoulders like dark seaweed in flowing water. She was outlined in light from the sun that shone across the island over the top of the woods; a romantic and mysterious figure, or she would have been if one didn't know the truth about her. The truth was that there was something pitiful and sordid about her pregnancy because there was no love, not even imagined love, involved.

Alix buttoned the telephone number into the pocket of a tartan wool shirt hanging up in the studio, and went downstairs. She carried the tote bag into Bunny's room, followed by William, and put it back on the chest. How observant was Bunny, if everything hadn't been replaced in order? As if the jumble including crumpled tissues and empty match folders could be called order.

"What would the CIA do?" she asked William. "What would they do on *Mission Impossible?* Well, this is what any redblooded, intelligent, sneaky secret agent would do if he had a cat around to blame things on." She tipped the bag off the chest and left it where it lay, its contents spilling out. Then she unlocked the doors, and put the greens on to cook. When Bunny came in she was setting the table.

"Hello," Alix said. She was short, knowing that anything else would make Bunny suspicious of attempts to undermine her. "What will you drink, tea, coffee, or milk?"

"Water." Bunny was already in her room. The next sound was a furious exclamation.

"What's the matter?" Alix called.

"My bag's been knocked onto the floor!"

"Oh, that cat!" Alix looked at William, who was sitting in the captain's chair. He gazed blandly back at her. "I should have warned you about his getting into things. I hope there wasn't anything breakable in it."

"No, but there could have been," Bunny answered sternly. In a few minutes she came out, ostentatiously shutting the door behind her. "I never liked cats," she said. William blinked genially at her as if she'd complimented him.

The food was good and they both ate well, with no conversation. Bunny didn't seem as exhausted as she'd been yesterday,
but relaxed enough to be almost limp. She was yawning before
she was through the meal. "I don't know why I'm so tired," she
said heavily. "I don't feel sick or dizzy, but just so—" She lifted
one hand and let it fall.

Alix didn't tell her it was probably a result of her confession
this morning. Bunny would have rejected that in outrage. She
said, "It's this air."

"I'm going to bed and read," Bunny said. She started to
leave the table, then she said offhandedly, and looking elsewhere, "Excuse me."

"Certainly," Alix said. Bunny shut herself into her room.
Alix sat there drinking her coffee. She could hear Bunny moving about, and then getting into bed. It was after sunset and
soon it would be too dark for reading. She didn't light a lamp
for herself but sat on into the twilight, until there had been no
sounds from the bedroom for quite some time. William had
gone upstairs. She opened Bunny's door carefully, and said,
"Do you want a lamp?"

There was no answer, and she could hear the even breathing
of deep sleep. She backed out and closed the door with infinite
care; a thumb latch released too quickly could make a diaboli-
cal clatter. She listened again with her ear against the door, but
Bunny didn't even turn in her sleep.

Alix went up to the studio, by habit avoiding the places that
always creaked, and put on the wool shirt. When she came
down she listened again. She didn't doubt that Bunny was
probably sleeping better now than she had for weeks.

She took a flashlight with her, though she didn't need it out
in the open in the long hushed twilight that always made
Shane quote Thomas Gray. *Now fades the glimmering landscape on the sight, And all the air a solemn stillness holds.*

Don't you know anything else about twilight? she teased
him.

I am a walking dictionary of quotations about twilight, he

said. I happen to like that one best. It fits perfectly. It's the only one that does.

How about your friend Emily?

Her twilights are too portentous.

This is a portentous twilight, old boy, Alix said. Disaster is plunging toward us through it like a meteor.

⚜ CHAPTER 32 ⚜

THE DARK ARRIVED precipitately when she took the short cut through the woods. The dancing beam from her flashlight made the night seem all the blacker. It was warm in the woods with heat stored from the day, and almost perfectly silent until she heard the rhythmic hooting of a barred owl, like the far-off barking of a dog. Another one answered from nearby, and she sensed the noiseless flight of a night hunter.

She came out to the flickering sparks of fireflies and the smell of the sea. The precise rows of the garden were bright green in the ray of light, the dew standing on the leaves. The cabin was dark, and she hoped he hadn't gone to bed. She knocked softly on the door, saying his name. There was no answer, and she opened the door and went in, flashing the light around. The place was as tidy as Jonas was, the bed as tightly made up as an Army bunk.

He'd be over at Ozzie's now, playing chess or watching television. Unless there was something special on, he shouldn't be late. The men got up at dawn to go hauling, and in summer dawn came much too soon after midnight to allow for late nights.

There was a roomy old-fashioned rocking chair pulled up to one of the front windows, and she sat down in it and put her feet up on a homemade stool that seemed to have been put in exactly the right spot. He'd widened the windowsill into a shelf for ash tray and coffee cup, and beneath it there were more shelves holding books and magazines. All the comforts, she thought with grim humor, and freedom too. He may not know it yet, but some morning he's going to wake up and realize that's the pure medium he's breathing.

She turned out her flashlight and lay back. At once the ticking of a clock became loud but not intrusive; it accentuated the silence as the fireflies glowing and fading outside the window emphasized the dark.

Toward the south a distant lighthouse was an intermittent gleam on a horizon only guessed at. Other lights twinkled low in the west. The stars were becoming brighter and more plentiful. Lying back and looking up at them was hypnotic. A sense of dissociation crept over her, a velvety stupor from which she was aroused once by remembering she hadn't locked the door to the back stairs. But Bunny wasn't likely to wake up and go prowling, as exhausted as she was. If she did get up she'd probably stub her toe on something, and be immobilized at once. Alix sank into a euphoric deep-blue mist charmingly pricked with spangles of light.

The sound of the door opening was magnified by sleep into a metallic crash that brought her upright with a cry, not knowing where she was and what she was hearing. Her head cleared almost at once, and she groped for her flashlight, but before she could find it a stronger beam blinded her like a locomotive headlight.

"*Jesus!*" said Jonas.

"Thank you, but no," said Alix, shutting her eyes against the glare. "Look again. What time is it?"

"You sound drunk." He stood the flashlight on the table with the light directed at the rafters. "It's twenty after ten."

"I must have been asleep." It hadn't helped, she felt terrible.

[3 0 3]

"I'm sorry I woke you up, then. You must have needed the rest." He scratched a match and lit the lamp on the table.

"Not so much as I need help. I hate asking for it, but there's no other way. I'd do it myself if I possibly could," Alix said.

He put the flashlight on a shelf and sat down across the table from Alix, leaning on his folded arms, annoyingly chipper when she felt so sodden.

"All right," said Jonas, "you've made it clear that you've got your pride. We'll take that as stipulated, as they say in court. What's got to be taken care of before I remove your boarder tomorrow?"

"A telephone call," she said. "I don't know if it'll work, but it's the only thing I can think of." She felt in her shirt pocket to be sure the slip was there. "Look, I'll gladly reimburse you for your time if you'll go over tomorrow morning and call the number I have here. I'd go myself, but I can't leave without making her suspicious."

"And when they answer, what do I say?"

"I hadn't got that far. The truth is, I've been hoping you'll get a recording that says the number's been discontinued."

"What does this number represent?"

"An abortionist, I hope," she said. "I mean, I hope I found the right number." She explained how she found it. "She said that when she called they told her to call tomorrow for another appointment. Now I'm hoping they've put her off because they're on the run and there'll be nobody to answer."

She got up and took the other straight chair across the table from Jonas. He hadn't even raised an eyebrow yet, and she blessed his matter-of-factness. "I want to find out before I let her leave, because if she gets to Boston and finds they've given her the runaround, I don't know what she'll do."

"If she hadn't come here to raise the devil with you, you'd never have known."

"But she did come and I do know. The moving finger writes, you know, and all your tears can't wash out a word of it," she said derisively. "That's her trouble as well as mine . . . and in my typical over-thirty way I'm interfering, and she hates me even more for that."

"Quite a shock to find yourself in the Establishment, huh?" said Jonas. He began filling his pipe. "All right, I'll make the call. But what if somebody answers? What do I say then?"

"Oh, *hell*." She stared bitterly at him. "I guess I was hoping so hard for one thing I refused to consider alternatives."

"Listen," said Jonas, "who says we have to tell her the truth?"

"I'll admit it's straining at a gnat after I've been through her bag."

"Then we'll lie," he said decisively. "She'll suspect us, but she can't do anything about it. Oh, I'll go and call, all right. Might just be that they've cleared out, so we can have a clear conscience about it. Hey, then what? If they're still in business she'll soon find out, no matter what we tell her. You can't hang on to her forever."

"I don't *want* to! I'd like to see the last of her tomorrow!" She ran her hands through her hair. "But if I could just find somebody else to take the responsibility. There *has* to be somebody, damn it!" She slapped her palm down so hard on the table that the lamp flame jumped.

Jonas moved the lamp to the counter by the sink. "I wouldn't want that to hamper you next time you feel violent. Look, there's a man involved, unless this is one of those immaculate conceptions. I had a great-aunt who swore nobody'd ever touched *her*, so the other ladies used to remark she must have got little Millicent from the tea she drank, but I never set much store by those stories."

"And how did little Millicent turn out?"

"Great. Taught school, played the piano, and married a senator and once had dinner at the White House. Cleveland was President then. She named her first one Grover. Some folks thought it was a funny name for a girl, but Millicent was a loyal Republican. . . . Well, did you find any letters or pictures in her stuff?"

"I didn't look in her billfold or at the letters. Just at the handwriting on one."

"Talk about straining at a gnat and swallowing a camel," he said in disgust.

"I asked her about him, but she won't say anything, she won't even admit that he exists," she lied. ·

"Well, she's got a mother, hasn't she?"

"She's got a martyr, a saint, Joan of Arc at the stake. She can't tell her the truth, because it would kill her on top of everything I've done to her." She hadn't meant that to slip out. She turned her face away from Jonas's eyes, straining toward the cool dark outside. She saw his reflection in the glass, but he was looking down at the pipe in his hand as he listened. "Oh, I'm unfair to the woman. She may be in a very bad state of health, nerves, and so forth. The sister's in Hawaii, newly married. But there has to be *someone* who can take over. ... If I could just keep at her, but I've no stomach for that sort of thing."

"Especially when she spews venom with every breath," he commented. "She stopped here the first day for a drink of water. Asked me if I was sleeping with you, and added a few more choice bits. I threatened to wash her mouth out with soap and water, and she left."

"She'd spent that afternoon throwing herself around trying to bring on a miscarriage," Alix said. "It's a wonder she didn't merely break both legs, instead. She's a lot quieter today ... she thinks she's leaving tomorrow, and she's scared half out of her mind, but more scared of having her mother find out."

She rested her head on her hand, shading her face from the lamp. She felt an immense ennui about the whole thing.

"Time for coffee," said Jonas decisively.

"No, thanks, I've had so much coffee the very word makes me burp."

"Cocoa then, and don't refuse because it won't do you any good. Your blood sugar's probably low and you need a lift."

"Thank you, doctor," said Alix. "When did you graduate from Harvard Medical?"

"None of your sarcasm now." He put a dented but well-scoured teakettle on the bottled-gas plate, and took mugs from his cupboard, cocoa, and canned milk. "Tell me something. Would you do this for any kid?"

"Wouldn't anyone try to keep any young girl from walking into this mess? Oh, I know it's possible to have an abortion done under safe circumstances, but this is a telephone number handed around among the kids. This hasn't been arranged by a knowledgeable adult. Now if somebody else takes Bunny over, somebody with authority to act for her, and *they* manage the affair, all right. Good!" She spread her hands in finality.

He nodded without speaking as he mixed the cocoa paste in the mugs.

"But it would be easier with a stranger," she admitted, "because she wouldn't be blaming me for her trouble."

He said sharply, "How does she get around to blaming you? You didn't put her into bed with the guy."

"Because if she'd had her father close to her all these years she wouldn't have become wild and reckless. This sounds like a soap opera, haven't you noticed?" He poured boiling water into the mugs, stirring, and set one before her. She looked dreamily at the steaming surface. "What nags me is the fact that she may be right. It nags me enough so that if Bunny kills herself, or dies after an abortion, I'll feel guilty."

"Christ, *why?*" He stood with his hands braced on the table, leaning toward her; his face was strained and his eyes sparkling oddly. "Why you? You've lost him, isn't that enough punishment or do you have to go on flogging yourself forever?"

"No," she said thoughtfully. "I don't have to." To gain time she sipped cocoa. The hot sweetness was strengthening, as he'd predicted. "But call it a Puritan conscience if you want . . . working a little late, according to Bunny. When I went into this—oh, I hate the word *relationship*."

Jonas sat down, and she had the impression that he was deliberately relaxing from whatever tension had gripped him a few moments ago. "Nobody ever just plain fights or loves nowa-

days. They have relationships. If bed's involved, it's a meaningful relationship. Even if it's just a one-night stand. Or lay, he
said like the vulgar clod he was."

She laughed. "Well, at that time I was positive nobody could
be hurt. I had no family left, and Shane had left his. As long as
we weren't married, we wouldn't have children. We had it all
worked out, you see. Nothing could go wrong." She forced herself to look squarely at him, and to keep any trace of self-pity
out of her manner. "I never expected this. It's like one of those
viruses they've discovered that take years to mature and then
hit you when you least expect it. In this case it's not a disease.
What hits you is the far-reaching consequence of your acts."

"You're pretty conceited, you know it? Taking so much
credit. Many a girl has picked up a little by-blow when she's
had two parents working together to raise her right."

"I know that, but in this case I'm forced to consider all the
possibilities. Shane might have gone back, he and Cathleen
might have worked out something. If Bunny really has the peculiar temperament she seems to have, maybe his constant presence would have kept her in balance. He said she was a cuddler, very affectionate and seeking affection. So if she couldn't
get it from her mother—"

His set face, almost as if he were taking this as a personal af-
front, irritated her. "All right, what am I to think?" she demanded. "I don't know why I told you all this anyway. Just to
hear myself think out loud, I guess. I don't seem to get anywhere thinking in silence and I'm not doing any better—"

"Oh, shut up," said Jonas. "I should have known you'd end
up like this, the minute you started analyzing. Whenever anybody starts using the word *guilt* so loosely I know what I'm in
for. Talk about four-letter words, that five-letter one turns my
stomach."

She stood up. "Thanks. Forget about the telephone number,
I'll figure something out."

He braced his hands on the edge of the table as if to rise, his face suddenly gaunt. "Sit down. I've listened, now you can listen."

"I suppose I owe you that much," she said politely, sitting down. "What's your advice? Turn her out and forget her, I suppose."

"Hell, no. Do what you can for the girl, but stop flagellating yourself for what might have happened. You were just one part of this mess, not the whole cheese. And you don't know the first thing about guilt."

"What do *you* know about it?"

"Everything!" he snapped.

She felt laughter beginning in her belly like a convulsion of her intestines, then shaking irrepressibly under her ribs, aching in her chest, turning her mouth broad and silly. "What I can't stand," she gasped, "is your guiltier-than-thou attitude."

He had been staring at her, his mouth open, then he began to laugh too.

≋ CHAPTER 33 ≋

THEY KEPT ON laughing until the thing wore itself out. Wiping her eyes Alix said, "I feel even drunker than before, if possible."

"Naturally. I serve only 100-proof cocoa. Listen, you're blaming yourself, or trying to, for something you did a long time ago. You didn't just come slam-bang up against yourself as a stranger and a pretty deadly one at that."

"No. Did you?"

"I did. That's why I'm here. That's why I won't take a drink. That's why—oh, the hell with *that*. Well, my wife wanted a divorce so she could marry another man. They'd had one of those meaningful relationships," he said with a mordant grin, "for about a year before I found out. He was a good friend of mine. I don't know whether I felt worse about losing my wife to my friend, or the other way around. And her having his kid, not mine."

"But taking everything together it was rotten," said Alix.

"Stinking rotten," he agreed. "But simple. I was to let her get the divorce on mental cruelty, because the law won't let you be honest about it. She asked for nothing—just the chance

to marry my old friend. She thought she was pregnant by him."
He shrugged. "All right. Because you've got to be a good loser,
that's civilization. As soon as your head stops spinning and you
straighten up from that belly blow—if you can focus your eyes,
you poor slob, you say, 'Of course I'm going to be a gentleman
about this, dear.'"

He fell abruptly silent, drumming his fingers on the table.
"But where does the guilt come in?" Alix asked. "For you? Unless you did something once that drove her away from you, neglected her for your work, had other women—"

He shook his head hard. "No! She was interested in the yard,
she liked the atmosphere, the people we met because of my
boats, the launchings, all that. And I never looked at another
woman after I met her. I thought we had something pretty
near perfection. With a kid or two it would have been perfection. But if she didn't want them—was scared to try it for some
reason—well, I had *her*, and she was all that mattered." He
couldn't sit still any longer, he got up and ranged around the
small space, looking everywhere but at Alix. She didn't want
him to go on if it was too intolerably private to tell, yet she
knew that for him to have even begun meant that the pressure
had become too great.

"Anyway, when she told me she had to have the divorce so
she and Jock and their child could be together, I promised to
be the little gent while I was still numb. Then I went off to
the yard. It was around midnight . . . we'd been to a party."
His eyes looked into time past, squinting as if against a blinding glare and yet unable to close entirely or to turn away. "I
couldn't stand the house. In the morning she'd been mine, and
by night I'd lost her. It couldn't have been any more final than
if she'd suddenly died." His eyes shifted from that night and focused on her. "You know about that."

She nodded.

"I went into my office and started work on a design for a cut-
ter. I tried to keep at it, but the feeling started to come back
and I was one big toothache. Well, I always kept a bottle in the

office, to have a drink with a customer now and then—for ceremonial purposes, you might say. That night I went through the
bottle. . . . At daylight I went home. It was snowing. A thick,
wet, March snowstorm. I had the sense to know I couldn't
drive, so I walked."

He was back in the past again, watching a dark solitary
figure going home through the slushy, soaking snow in the gray
light. "I kept skidding and falling down. I felt like staying
down, if I could freeze to death fast, but I kept thinking I had
to get back, because I was going to make her stay with me. I'd
talk her around all right. This whirl with Jock didn't mean a
thing."

Suspense was driving cramps like knives under Alix's ribs.
She wanted to move, to stretch, but she was afraid of breaking
some spell and never hearing the end of the story. If I didn't
know she's still alive, she thought, I'd think he was telling me
how he committed a murder.

"The more I thought about it the wilder it was. I was almost
convinced I'd dreamed the whole thing. . . . I went into the
house all covered with wet snow from taking a header in the
driveway, and tramped through the house over those carpets of
hers and up into our room. She woke up when I put the light
on, looked up at me, yawned, and said, 'Been out building a
snowman?' Then she laughed. That's when I knew it wasn't a
dream."

He turned his back to Alix and walked to the door. He
opened it and stood on the threshold looking out. Past him she
saw the fireflies' dreamy erratic flight.

"I don't remember the first move I made, but I found myself
kneeling on the bed strangling her. And it felt so damned
good." His hands made a gesture she couldn't see. "I was killing her, and glad of it, me that couldn't drown kittens, that
never went hunting!"

"There's a difference," Alix said. "The animals are innocent.
Not your enemies." So a murder *had* been contemplated. "But
you didn't kill her," she finished aloud.

"Something got through to me, and I let her go before she

blacked out. She wasn't too much damaged—a little hoarse, and scared half-foolish. I cleared out then, and if I thought I'd been in shock the night before, now I knew what it was really like. When I went back to the office I didn't know myself any more. I just wanted to get rid of myself quick, because I was a killer. I didn't own a shotgun, but I could go off one of the wharves and start swimming out among the ice cakes, and I'd last just about five minutes. It was early Sunday morning and there'd be nobody around to interfere."

He was quiet for so long that Alix thought he didn't intend to go any further. After a few moments she said, "Obviously you didn't do it."

"No," he said vaguely. "I remember getting up to go and do it. I must have tripped and hit my head, or passed out, because I came to on the office floor, and Jock was there. Good friend Jock. He was making coffee and being so damn' solicitous and helpful I was fooled again, into thinking it had been one long nightmare. Or that I *hadn't* been back to the house and attacked her in the meantime, and she'd been worried about me all night and had decided she loved me and couldn't leave me after all."

"And there was no baby," said Alix.

He shut the door and came back with a battered and cynical grin. "Hell, I was going to take him over too. I saw it all in a flash. *Jonas Hallowell and Son!* You can see how punch-drunk I was. . . . Well, Jock, all flustered and apologetic, told me that if I'd turn over the yard to her, as well as everything in our joint accounts, the house, the boat, all the securities, she wouldn't have me arrested for assault with intent to murder. What did you say about life being like a soap opera?"

"It's very like." She felt a cold rage with the nameless woman who could betray, humiliate, and finally blackmail a man. The thing was appalling, and yet the curious thing was that she didn't doubt Jonas in the least. She was accepting his story as the truth, knowing all the time that he could be a very convincing liar. She said, "So there was a murder after all."

He knew what she meant, and nodded. "Can you stop loving

somebody just like that"—he made a chopping sweep with the side of his hand—"when they've been your blood and bones and heartbeat for twenty years?"

"You can, I suppose," she said thoughtfully, "if you find out you were loving an idea, or maybe your own creation, and not the real thing. And then you find out what the real thing *is.*"

He walked back and forth, hands in his pockets, scowling around him as if everything in the cabin were strange and puzzling. "The way I see it," Alix said, "they did this thing to you and then when you were driven to strike back, they didn't even stop to examine their own consciences, they just moved in with their blackmail so fast it wasn't even—I was going to say *decent,* but I guess that's not the word."

"Hardly," he said dryly. "But—strike back? Some strike. I tried to murder my wife. I almost did. Never mind how fast she and Jock slapped down their ultimatum—I laid myself open to that when I grabbed her by the throat. Until then I'd been the injured party. I still had some dignity in my own eyes, not that I saw it until I'd lost it."

"Being preoccupied with that one giant toothache."

"The toothache was preferable to what I felt when I got out of the house that morning. I didn't know myself any more. I thought I'd gone insane. Christ! And you talk about guilt." He went back to the open doorway again. "Me—a murderer! Something stopped me, but I'd had the intent. I couldn't believe it, couldn't even face it. It wasn't the thought of prison that made me give up without a struggle. That was no more than a fly buzzing around my head compared to what I'd discovered about myself, on top of what I'd discovered about *her.*" He gave that short harsh bark of laughter she'd heard once before. "Horror, shame, guilt—with them on my neck I was ready to give up everything."

"Which she knew," Alix pointed out. "And it's no use saying they'll pay for what they've done; some people never have to pay up. . . . It's July now. Hasn't the edge worn off just a little?"

"Not enough. I don't take even one drink for thinking what it could start. I never was one of those hog-wild drinkers, but now I don't know about myself, you see. I could take off for Williston and break loose again, and this time finish the job."

"You'd have to be very drunk, and that means you couldn't drive that distance."

"Aren't you the practical one. I could get drunk after I got there, couldn't I? . . . Listen, I'm still sore about what she did to me. I don't have to resent her having another man's child when she wouldn't have mine, because she lied about that, either on purpose or because she believed it herself then. But I still resent the fact that I can't look back on any part of my married life without wondering if this was a lie or that was an act, and did she really mean it when she said so-and-so?" He wheeled around and strode back into the light. "At least you still have what you had. But twenty years have been stolen from me, only not enough so I can forget them as if I have amnesia. And along with all that I have to contend with being a potential murderer."

"But I don't think you are," she protested. "She shattered your life that night, you got drunk, she laughed at you when you were in agony. You were like the poor bull when they keep driving the darts into him."

"She's a human being. If I'd killed her, I would have killed myself." He said it so serenely that she was stopped. Yes, he would have done it as unspectacularly as she planned to do it, and would have gone to his grave just a little before Shane. She would never have known him except as a figure in a sad story told by Madge, to which Alix, preoccupied with her own concerns, would have paid no attention.

"What's the matter?" he asked, coming closer. "I didn't do it. I'm not a ghost standing here."

"You are, in a way. Because you were so close to it."

"Are you horrified?" he asked defiantly. "Disgusted?"

She shook her head. "It's odd, but Soren asked me almost the same thing—if the idea of suicide shocked me."

He said with an incredulous, angry laugh, "Don't tell me that one's been confessing private nightmares, too. I didn't know I was standing in line."

"Oh, stop it," said Alix. "We were talking about painting, and he said that when he couldn't paint he'd have no reason for living and he'd kill himself."

Jonas looked slightly abashed. "Well, now, you see that gives him a different dimension. I thought it was all women with him. Shows how you can't ever tell."

The interlude had slackened the tension in the small room. Alix relaxed in her chair, gently wriggling her shoulders and stretching her hands. "Anyway," she said, "I'm awfully glad you didn't do it. One, because it would have made things so damn' easy for those two, and two, because what would I be doing now? I couldn't take this mess to Madge and Ozzie."

"Thanks. What's left of my self-esteem appreciates any small crumb."

"Listen, you must have got drunk a few times in your life and didn't want to kill anybody."

"They always told me it improved my disposition. I got very peaceful and benevolent. Seraphic was her word for it."

"You must have given her quite a turn then, for a few minutes anyway. Look, you'll admit that she's the only object of your so-called killer instinct, won't you? You don't really believe that after a few drinks you'll wipe out anybody who comes within range."

"How do I know what'll happen?" he demanded belligerently. "It could be a personality change."

"Do you want my opinion or not?"

"I don't recall asking for it. I only told you all this so you could see you were sticking pins into yourself for nothing. But go ahead, analyze away! Be my guest." He waved an arm at her.

"Oh, honestly, Jonas!" she snapped. "You bring out the worst in me. Here I've been enraged for your sake, suffering every step of the way with you, and now I feel like either slapping or kicking you."

"Why don't you just tell me your opinion? I don't want to deprive you of the pleasure." He sat down and began to fill his pipe again.

"Well, you did stop in time. So you lost control only so far. And when you stop caring anything about her, you'll stop worrying about killing her."

"*Caring* about her? Haven't you been listening, for Pete's sake? I told you all that stopped with a karate chop."

"*Loving* stopped," said Alix, "or what you thought of as love. Now you think it's hate, but that's caring, can't you see? She's still the most important thing in the world to you."

"I wouldn't have her back on a bet."

"No, but she's right there all the time, isn't she? And so is what she did to you and what she took away—and I don't mean the yard."

He sat looking at the unlit pipe in his hand, then a dry raspy sound faintly resembling a chuckle came from him, and he nodded his head at the pipe. "Yes, she's there, damn her eyes. You'd think it would be Jock, but it hardly ever is except when I remember how jumpy he was that morning. Took quite an effort for him to get the terms out. Dawned on me afterward he was all ready to dodge in case I made a flying leap for his jugular."

"Will they ruin the yard, or lose it altogether?" Alix asked.

"They're not stupid. They know enough to keep on the men, those who'll stay. Two who were with me from the start of the yard quit when I did. They'll be missed. It's hard nowadays to find boatbuilders like them." He slapped his palms down on the table and said briskly, "Well, that's it. Ozzie and Madge don't know about Jock or any of the rest of the story. They think I'm letting the yard go in place of alimony, because I don't want any more ties down that way. Now how about carousing around with a second cup of cocoa? We'll drink to each other and then hurl the mugs at the stove."

"Gee, I *hate* not doing that," said Alix. "But it's after midnight and tomorrow, or rather today, is going to be a hard one." She got up, stretching for the rafters. "Thank you for everything."

"Including the True Confessions hour?"

"As long as you don't hate yourself in the morning."

He said seriously, "You're the first person I've told it to. My lawyer thinks I'm a maniac for giving up the yard—I built a ketch for him, by the way. A little beauty. I wish you could see her." He grinned. "Nope, I guess it didn't do me any harm to lay the whole thing out, even if I don't think much more of your comments than you did of mine. So thanks for listening."

"Oh, you're welcome!" Their laughter was tired and their voices hoarse. He came out with her and she said, "You don't have to walk home with me."

"I want to get out of here long enough to let the dust settle. Seems like that bedroom and the office at the yard are right here in this camp, and the voices—this makes me sound a little nutty—"

"No, unless we're all a little nutty." She looked up at the stars thick as pollen over the dark water. "They put us in our places," she said.

"Restful, isn't it? To know what useless, insignificant little insects we are. All this prattle about meaningful relationships doesn't amount to a hill of beans."

"Except that we have to go on dealing with the consequences," said Alix, yawning. "If we could convert everybody to the doctrine of unimportance—" Another yawn caught her, jaw-stretching and eye-watering.

"Go on home and go to bed," said Jonas. "I'll be around in the morning."

❧ CHAPTER 34 ❧

SHE HAD EXPECTED to lie awake, swinging like a pendulum between Jonas's story and the day to come. But she was wrung out, and fell asleep almost as soon as she lay down.

She woke up hungry in spite of the dread that awoke with her, as if her very tissues had been depleted by the emotional excesses of the day before. She cooked oatmeal again for Bunny and ate a bowl of it herself before the girl was up. Bunny arose and wandered through like a sleepwalker in her bare feet, yawning and heavy-eyed, uttering vague syllables when Alix spoke to her.

This relieved Alix of any residual compulsion to make hostess-like gestures. She left a place set for Bunny and took her coffee and toast out to the sunny front doorstep, where she began at once to think about Jonas. She realized he had not once called his wife by name, and Madge had never used the name either; it was always *she*. Shades of Rider Haggard. She had not been described, either, which was a small matter, since for Jonas she'd been Helen, and over the smoking ruins of his own Troy he loved her still.

For Alix he had ceased to be the inquisitive and ubiquitous

terrier. He was a complex man whose whistling was literally a charm to keep off the dark, and the dark was in himself; nothing would convince him otherwise. Ah well, she thought, he's entitled to it. It's his, and I've got mine. *The bright day is done, and we are for the dark.*

"Can I sit here?" asked Bunny, with a mug and a doughnut in her hands.

"Oh—yes." Languidly Alix moved over, drugged by the strong morning sun and her own introspection. Bunny sat down and squinted out across the water, wriggling her bare toes in the wet grass. Well-fed and slept out, she had a fresh natural color of her own, enhanced by new tan, and her lashes and hair had the live sheen of healthy youth.

"It's nice here," she said grudgingly. "I can't say I'm glad I came, but still ..." She contemplated her large feet in the grass. "It fills me in on him. I mean, up till now part of each year was a big gap when I couldn't even imagine him." She looked around at Alix. "Did you know," she asked in solemn amazement, "that when an old star dies it leaves a black hole in space? Can you imagine anything so *tremendous* that it can make a hole in *space?*"

"It's difficult to conceive," said Alix. "But yes, I can imagine it." She hoped it was the right answer to what the girl seemed to be asking. It was too much to believe they had any area of agreement whatever, but if there should be one, it would be Shane.

William came around the corner of the house and set a hypnotized course for Bunny, eyes fixed on her with an unwinking, burning, green-gold stare.

"What's he want?" she exclaimed in alarm. "He's gone mad!"

"It's not you, it's your doughnut," said Alix.

Bunny wilted. Cats," she grumbled. "Wild animals." She broke off a piece of doughnut and threw it at William as if to placate a vampire. William pounched, crouched, and ate it with tigerish pleasure. "I guess I'll go down on the beach," said Bunny hastily. "Will he follow me?"

"I'll divert him," said Alix. She picked him up and carried him around to the back of the house. The swallows were driving off a merlin and returned to use up their excess spleen in strafing William. He took off for the fishhouse.

Alix's dishes had never had so much immediate attention. Washing them after each meal made her feel as if she were on a treadmill, but there was nothing else to do in this new schedule, or nonschedule, of waiting around for someone to make a move. After she put the breakfast dishes away, she swept the kitchen and the back entry.

The clock struck ten. It took a very long time and with relief, not to mention eagerness, she recognized a new chore. She was standing on a chair winding the clock when she heard the front screen door slam and then Bunny called from her room, "He's here! I'm going to change!" She began moving things noisily about, dropping small objects and bumping heavily against large ones. Her coördination suffered when her nerves did.

Alix went out and down the path to meet Jonas halfway from the wharf.

"*Good* morning!" he called blithely. "How are you after a night of riotous living?"

"How are *you?*"

"Oh, so's to be about." He was smiling with what she had once considered offensively high spirits. "Well, we don't have to lie. I dialed direct, and the number didn't answer. Then I got the operator to try it. After an assortment of clicks and buzzes someone said, 'Good morning, this is your friendly Boston Police Department, you have just won two weeks in our luxurious House of Correction!'" He broke out into laughter at her expression. "Sorry, but the calls are being switched through to some police lieutenant's office. Identified himself like a gentleman and told me the parties I wanted are under arrest. Managed to make me feel like a rat trying to arrange something for a poor young girl he's got in trouble."

"Oh, boy," said Alix. She kept lightly smacking one fist into the other palm. "She's going to hate us for this. *Hate* is a feeble word. It won't make any difference to tell her they probably got caught because something went wrong with one of the customers."

"Kids," he said reflectively. "They always think it can't happen to *them*. And kids aren't the only ones who think it."

"No," said Alix. "You know something? I'm almost tempted to let her go without knowing."

"Oh, not feeling quite so guilty this morning, huh?"

"Just as guilty, but tired of it. My moral fiber has jungle rot."

"That's a good healthy sign."

The manner she'd once called smug no longer made her hackles rise. "You should talk," she retorted. "No, I've got to tell her I went through her bag for that number, and do I dread it. Well—" She dragged in a long draught of sea air, which didn't help in the least. There was a sound from the house, and Jonas looked up past her, then shielded his eyes with a histrionic sweep of his arm, and staggered back.

"My God, a nuclear explosion!"

Bunny had just come around the house in her orange dress. She was carrying her luggage and raincoat.

"I can see why she wears tinted glasses with it," said Alix. "Just looking down at herself in sunlight must make her eyeballs vibrate." She folded her arms tightly and dug nervous fingers hard into her ribs. "Have I thanked you yet? I meant to."

"If you're trying to get rid of me, you haven't a prayer. How about my telling her? I'm not so emotionally involved. Didn't I get that one out some slick?"

"Just like a psychiatrist," said Alix. "Thanks, but I'll do my own dirty work. You'd better leave."

"Oh, I'm sticking around out of morbid curiosity, like going to a stock car race to see the crack-ups." For an instant she experienced again the early reaction to him, but it didn't last. Everyone had his own cover-ups, she had a variety of them. Just the same she wished he would go.

Bunny was close now. The violet lenses gave her an odd contradictory appearance of fragility, as if her eyes were deep in shadowy hollows. She was panting a little, and Alix could feel in herself the constriction in throat and chest, the thudding labors of the heart.

Bunny started to speak and had to wet her lips. "Well, let's go," she said huskily to Jonas.

"I don't know why you're in such a hurry to leave this place," he said. "Look at that water out there." He waved his arm at the sparkling sea. "Feel that sun! Smell that unpolluted air!"

"Can we get going? *Please?*" She picked up her bag again and started to go out around him.

"Bunny!" Alix said, the explosiveness startling even herself. Bunny kept on going. "You called it your dentist's number, didn't you?" Alix called after her. "But why would a Philadelphia girl have a Boston dentist?"

Bunny stopped. She faced the cove and the wharf, but she was absolutely still, as if she had suddenly felt a gun at her back. And so she had, Alix thought, but there was no time for analysis. You had to talk while she was struck mute. "I looked for the number, Bunny. I had to try to make sure it was all right for you to go. Jonas went over this morning and called it. The police answered. Something must have gone wrong after an operation and that's how the police found out."

They were all three quiet, the girl facing the water, the man and woman looking at her rigid back. Then with an unintelligible cry Bunny hurled her things away from her, the suitcase tumbling end over end into a hollow. The tote bag strings loosened and the contents began to spill out across the cinquefoil and blue-eyed grass. The raincoat fell in a heap.

As she started to turn, one sandal skidded on the slippery short grass of the path, her action became a twisting lurch. She caught herself by a frenzied windmilling of the arms before she could fall sidewise into the field. Her face was blotched with dark red. "You sneaks," she said in a low trembling voice. "You liars. You sons of bitches." She pointed a finger at Alix. "You. Going through my bag. How dare you, how *dare* you?"

Her voice rose with the words until with a scream she plunged toward Alix, but Jonas's arm dropped between them, and his other arm caught her around the waist. She fought him, sputtering and swearing, tears running down her face. The glasses flew off and disappeared. Alix stood immobile, her throat dry and aching. On the practical side she was glad Jonas was so strong, but she wondered how long he could hold the thrashing girl. She was wiry and agile herself, but Bunny was heavier, with big bones. In all her dread of a scene she'd never dreamed of anything beyond screaming accusations.

"Watch your language, darlin' mine," Jonas was saying. "Remember what I told you the other day. And don't think I can't do it, and turn you over my knee too."

Bunny sagged all at once. The tantrum trailed off into a harsh sobbing, and she sank down on the path on her knees, hiding her face in the tie-dyed scarf. Jonas stood looking down at her with his hands on his hips. "You'll feel better now," he said briskly. She didn't answer. Alix eased her own cramped hands out of her pockets and flexed her fingers.

"Full house for this performance," Jonas said with a signal of his head. Karen stood on the path just above them, her hands behind her back, her glasses shining.

"Nemesis," said Alix. "Or conscience again, but whose?"

She looked down at Bunny's head and saw with an unexpected pain—as if she could have any more of them—that Bunny had a cowlick like Shane's. "Get up and come to the house, Bunny," she said, "and we'll talk this over."

Bunny gave no sign of hearing. She moaned softly, huddled over and rocking back and forth.

"She'll be all right when she runs down," said Jonas heartlessly. "Well, I'd better go haul."

"Thank you for staying," Alix said in a low voice. "I didn't expect she'd try to tackle me."

"The thing is, will she try it again? Maybe I'd better take

her off anyway, just to save your neck." They contemplated Bunny. Set against the magnificently illuminated blues and greens of high summer, the crouching figure in brilliant orange with the long black hair streaming over its face was a Gauguin creation. But I could make it my own, Alix thought. I must remember the way the tawny hawkweed in the grass picks up that orange—

She was ashamed of herself. Always the little painter, she sneered. You'd make a composition out of your own funeral if you could manage it.

"I don't think so," she said to Jonas. "She builds up to these storms and collapses afterward. I may be able to get through to her at low-water slack."

"Ayuh," he said skeptically. "Just don't let her get near any hammers or carving knives. If she starts on a rampage, lock yourself in somewhere."

Karen had come closer to Bunny and stood gazing down at the moaning huddle. "What's the matter with you?" she asked finally. Getting no answer she stepped nearer and continued to stare. On the path above her William strolled, tail straight up as an indication of sociability.

"Oh, Lord," said Alix. "Everything's collecting. I'll get them away and leave her alone. Thanks again, Jonas."

He gave her a backhanded wave and went on down to the wharf, starting to whistle. Even with all he had on his mind he was luckier than she was, Alix thought wistfully. He was going out on the water for the next few hours, and later he would return to blessed peace and solitude at the Home Cove.

"Come on, Karen," she said crisply. Karen didn't move at once, and Alix took her by the shoulders, and turned her forcibly around. "Now *march*," she commanded. She stuffed items back into the tote bag, pulled the strings tight, and set it by the suitcase. Then she scooped William up and carried him under one arm, keeping the other hand free in case Karen loitered.

Karen kept glancing back, but Alix was always between her and the fascinating figure down the slope. William squirmed, trying to get his hind feet braced against Alix's hip for leverage, and thus back rapidly out of her grip, but she managed to hold him till she got him into the house.

Enraged, he ran up the backstairs. "Now," she said to Karen, "What's on *your* mind? Is this business or pleasure?"

Tight-lipped, Karen handed her a note. Madge invited her to supper, and Bunny too of course, if she was still there. Poor Madge, in suspense since yesterday morning, and she couldn't stand it any longer.

"Tell her we'll come," said Alix recklessly. She certainly couldn't see Bunny tamely accompanying her across the island. But at this point she couldn't even visualize the arrival of tonight. Today seemed to have been frozen indefinitely at one point: *now*.

"Good-bye," she said pointedly to Karen.

"But what's the *matter* with her?" asked Karen, screwing up her face.

"She feels sick. Now run along."

"Is that why she's crying outdoors where everybody can see her? What was Jonas doing to her?"

"Karen," said Alix softly. *"Go."*

She saw Karen out to be sure that she started in the right direction, then went out around the house and peered under the shade of her hand toward Bunny. She lay sprawled on her side among her things like someone struck down in mid-journey by a surrealist accident in a dream landscape. Alix went down the path, tentatively. Bunny didn't move; she had cried herself into sleep. Alix stepped stealthily around her and picked up the raincoat and laid it over her. She found the glasses, and brought them and the suitcase back to the house.

She was surprised to be as hungry as if the emotional stress of the day so far had been physical exercise. She warmed up the rice-cheese mixture from the night before, with the greens cold and vinegary on the side, and ate at the kitchen table, reading something picked at random from the shelves. It was a relief to put her mind on something besides Bunny. When she had finished eating she went upstairs to the studio and began sketching the mourning woman she had imagined this morning.

Lost in it she heard only dimly the opening and closing of the screen door, and it hardly registered on her until she heard the dipper clatter against the edge of the water pail. She was as astonished by her forgetting as by the fact that the girl was here. She ran downstairs. Bunny stood leaning against the sink drinking a glass of water. Her eyelids were swollen and her face had a sodden calm.

"Why did you do it?" she asked in a quiet, faint voice. "You and he together—*why?* What are you trying to do to me?"

"Save you," said Alix. "A typical busybody over-thirty trick."

"*Save* me." Her long mouth twisted in a mournful and cynical smile. "You mean crucify me. If I have to wait any longer it'll be too late."

"Bunny, first the number was not answered. Then when Jonas called the operator, she connected him with a police officer who told him the people had been arrested. If you'd gone today you'd have got the same answer, and you'd be as desperate in that hotel room as you are right here."

"But I'd be desperate on my own!" Bunny exclaimed. It could have been Alix's own cry as she fled from sympathy. "And if it *is* so, and not just something you two cooked up to torture me, then I'd find somebody else to go to."

"From whom?" Alix asked. "A bellhop? A cab driver? Sit down and eat. It's all warm in the oven. You probably won't want the cold shore greens, but I've got some frozen asparagus I'll cook for you."

"I don't care about that." Bunny slumped in a chair and began to cry again, silently this time, working to hold it back.

Alix sat down beside her. Instinctively she put her hand on Bunny's, but the girl pulled free and turned away in her chair.

"Bunny, you can go as soon as you tell me someone who can look after you. Your mother should know—she has the right and the duty to know. But what if somebody else did the telling for you? How about your family doctor? Do you have one?

A lawyer? Old friends of your mother's? Your clergyman," she
said with inspiration. "He'd be the one. Tell me who he is and
I'll call him myself for you."

Bunny spoke with immense patience, or exhaustion. "But
don't you understand? No matter who told my mother, or how
they did it, and even if it was Father Tom, it would be the
same to her. Something just—just awful. She's so good. It
would be like driving another knife in her. I couldn't face her.
I'd rather die than have her know."

There was a dreadful sincerity in the quiet words. Alix
wanted to hit in the face the saint whose purity had reduced
her daughter to this desperate pass.

"No mother would be happy at the news, Bunny, but most
mothers are stronger than their kids think."

Bunny shook her head. "Not mine."

"This may sound like a foolish question, since you've been
trying to get an abortion, but do you want this baby? I mean, is
the abortion for your mother's sake or for your own? Really."

"I don't want it," Bunny said rapidly. "It's not a baby to me,
it's just a kind of growth to get rid of as fast as I can so I can
forget about it, and *she'll* never know, and I'll be able to go on
living. That's why I have to hurry with it."

"Your family doctor might know how it could be arranged,"
said Alix. "Especially where this pregnancy could do a lot of
emotional harm to both your mother and you."

"You've got to be kidding," said Bunny with a slight show of
spirit. "To him an abortion's a crime against the Holy Ghost,
or something. If I told him I'd kill myself, he'd lecture me on
that sin. He's worse than Father Tom could ever be. One time
—" She caught herself up short and said coldly, "I'll eat now
and go out somewhere. I'll leave my suitcase locked and take
my tote bag with me, not that it would hold any secrets from
you now."

"I didn't read your letters," said Alix, "if that's what you
think."

"And tomorrow I'm leaving. Do you understand? I'll find a

way to get off this island somehow. You can't keep me a prisoner any longer." Bette Davis was back, beautifully done.

Alix went back up to the studio, not to work. She'd lost that.
In Shane's room William lay stretched at full length on the
coverlet. She sat down beside him, reaching up to knead her
aching neck. Well, I tried, Shane, she thought. But she's right.
I can't keep her here.

In retrospect the time spent alone in the house, reading her
books and trying to receive communication from Shane, and
even the frustrating period of painting Karen, seemed far pleas-
anter than they could have possibly been. She thought kindly
of the Ruskins and charitably of Soren. She almost wished they
would appear unexpectedly now, to help pass the time until
Bunny left. Perhaps they would even take Bunny away with
them; Myra would love seeing Bunny to her plane, and Bunny
would hate it.

She fell over onto the bed and put an arm over William's
solid middle. He began to purr in his sleep, whiskers and ears
twitching as her breath touched them. The minute she shut
her eyes the summer sounds of the island took over; gulls, the
chattering swoop of swallows past the windows, the water
noises that never ceased blended with the somnolent hum of
engines. Crows broke out in a wrangle over the woods, and
William tensed and lifted his head, tickling Alix's nose. Then
he sank back into sleep again. Waiting for Bunny to go out,
having had only a few hours of sleep the night before, Alix almost slept but was never quite submerged.

Bunny's movements downstairs were marked by sudden
knocks and bumps. Finally the front screen door slammed—it
always did behind Bunny—and Alix bounded up off the bed
and over to the seaward windows. Bunny, statuesque in a black
bikini, was crossing the lawn. Alone, presumably free of the
disturbing influences of other people and temporarily purged
of her terrors by the outbreak on the path, she moved well,
with a straight back and a high head.

❧ CHAPTER 35 ❧

ALIX SPENT the afternoon in an aura of peace, picking wild strawberries on the slope toward the woods. She hulled a bowlful, sitting on a scaly ledge near a bay thicket inhabited by a passionately busy pair of song sparrows and their voracious young. When she walked back to the house she was still in the mood evoked by the field, the birds, and the incredible purity of light. She met Bunny with equanimity and invited her to supper at the Goodwins'.

Bunny gazed over her head and aloofly refused. "Besides, if I were tempted—which I'm not—that weird kid would put me off." She shuddered theatrically. "Wild. Straight from outer space."

"She's not bad, as ten-year-olds go," said Alix. "They all take everything and store it away, like computers."

"Well, *I* wasn't a monster when *I* was ten," Bunny said self-righteously. Alix went on getting things out of the cupboard and refrigerator.

"There's plenty of milk, and salad makings. This canned chicken à la king is very good stuff and you can make toast over the gas flame for it, or here's some instant rice. And for dessert, wild strawberries."

Bunny's eyes followed her gestures without expression. Alix didn't expect any, knowing the girl was as obsessed by her own disaster as Alix had been with hers before all the interruptions began. She left.

When Madge sent Karen down to the fishhouse to call the men to supper, Alix told her the hunch had been a valid one. She made the account as brief as possible, glad that the presence of the men and Karen would preclude any discussion of it. "She's still all at sea. I've been trying to convince her that she should tell her mother, and perhaps she will. She leaves tomorrow, and that's that."

(*I hope.* If only anyone could call in amnesia at will, I'd like the last few days wiped completely off my brain.)

"My goodness, what about the *father?*" Madge exclaimed. "Has he just walked out on her?" She was stricken by a new thought. "Is he *married?*"

"She won't talk about him. I wish the sister weren't so far away, Bunny's awfully on her own at the moment. But you can't go on worrying about someone who doesn't want even a kind word from you."

"But why did she come to see you, if she—if she—" Rosily flustered, Madge shifted plates unnecessarily.

"If she hates me? I don't know," said Alix. "Morbid curiosity, maybe." She opened the door to Sidney, and the men were close behind him.

"I know," Madge went on fussing, "but a young one like that, not knowing where to turn—they stick in your mind. You keep thinking there ought to be *something* you can do."

"Madge, love, there's nothing. Don't think I haven't tried."

"But you'll always wonder—" She stopped as Karen came in.

At supper she and Jonas gave an antiphonal account of the Ruskins' party, of which Madge had heard nothing whatever from Karen. Their performance was so successful that Ozzie laughed outright several times, and Madge alternated between shocked delight and disappointment.

"Never mind, Madge," Alix comforted her, "they *are* going to do it again and you *are* going to be there."

She walked home at twilight, having refused Jonas's offer of a ride. The day of splendid light had been a weather-breeder, and there'd be an easterly wind in the morning, with a chance of rain or fog. Ozzie had offered the use of his boat, in that case; he wasn't going to haul anyway, he'd hauled all around today, and baited everything up for two nights' set, and planned to spend a day working on gear.

The tree toads had long grown past their singing, and the Tangle was silent and shadowy as she passed through it, but not empty. The fireflies were there, and the nests hidden among the leafy boughs and in the hollow dead trees. The birds heard her walking below, as quiet as she was. After she was gone, they would sleep again. The thought carried with it a hypnotic suggestion of peace and sleep, perhaps because she longed for it so much. She could not remember when she had had more than a couple of hours' sleep at a time. Before Bunny came, yes, but it felt as if Bunny had been there for years.

Her eyelids were heavy; awake, she dreamed of sleep. The warm still atmosphere of the dark woods was Goethe's *Wanderers Nachtlied,* which she'd learned in her high school German course and which, repeated to herself at night in those days, could always make her sleepy, the last lines like a gentle hand laid over her eyes. *Warte nur; balde ruhest du auch.* Only wait; soon thou shalt rest too.

Sleep tonight, guaranteed with one Seconal. Tomorrow, sweet solitude again ... and maybe Shane. Incredible how the hope came back, frustrating in its very sweetness, like the evanescent hopes and despairs of beginning love.

William met her in the field. He went straight to his dish in the dark kitchen and began loudly to finish his supper. Bunny's door was closed, and the house was silent except for William and the mantel clock. The drinking water in the pail was warmish, and Alix poured it into the teakettle for morning and went down to the well for a fresh pail. When she came back there were still no stirrings on the other side of Bunny's door. She took a glass of water and went up the back stairs. She hadn't locked that door before she went out; Bunny had been there in the kitchen, and it would have been insulting.

Besides . . . *things.* It didn't really matter after all. Especially since she had come to the end with the girl. She would not always wonder, as Madge suggested, because she would not be around to wonder. As for the time between, she intended to create her own amnesia if there were no gods to confer it.

In the studio she went to the corner cupboard where she kept the liquor and the Seconal, and found it unlocked. This startled her until she remembered opening it to get a drink, and then becoming sick. She'd rushed downstairs and hadn't thought of the cupboard again.

Was that only yesterday? Woman, you need a long night's sleep, she thought, or your head will be taking off over the rooftop and out to sea like a lost balloon.

She groped around confidently in the dark corner for the little plastic bottle, and found nothing. She flashed the light in; the two bottles of Scotch were there, and in the opposite corner the long envelopes holding her will and the note and money for the Goodwins. Nothing else. She sat back on the floor and switched off her light. The Seconal was gone.

If this had happened before Bunny came, it would have been the unmistakable, ultimate sign of Shane. She could not believe that now.

I couldn't face my mother. I'd die rather than have her know.

She ran downstairs and knocked lightly on Bunny's door. No answer. She lifted the latch carefully and went in. At first she heard nothing but her own heartbeat, and she was sickeningly sure that there was nothing else to hear but the peculiar silence left when breath has stopped. The black hole in space.

She could see the dark hair spread on the pillow. The room

was cold, or she was. Automatically she went across to shut the eastern window, then came back to the foot of the bed, straining eyes and ears.

The figure stirred suddenly, an arm was flung out as if to strike off an attacker. "Who's that?" Bunny demanded clearly. "Who's there?"

"I just shut your window," said Alix. "The wind will be coming up soon. I'm sorry I woke you. . . . Good night."

Obviously Bunny hadn't taken anything yet. She was relieved but not overjoyed. Her own chances for a night's sleep, either natural or assisted, had been destroyed. And how she longed for unconsciousness now to make her forget that Bunny could refuse to admit she had the Seconal; that she could take it away from the island with her and swallow the lot in her Boston hotel room, or perhaps in some more isolated spot if she could find one, and hope that nobody would discover her for a long time.

She lay in bed hearing every stroke of the clock—wishing she'd let the striker run down—and watching the stars mist over as the weather changed. Queer, she thought. Three of us so different, and all thinking of suicide. Jonas from horror of himself; Bunny from manic fear; herself from the devastation of a burnt-out life.

Jonas had seemingly pulled himself back from the abyss, though he still had his nightmares; she recalled the feverish look of him at times that night, the spasmodic violence of his gestures.

She hadn't canceled her own plans. Each night her future extended only through the next day.

Bunny was the one to worry about. She was too young for the abyss, and she was Shane's daughter, Shane's cuddler; he had been the one to nickname her Bunny.

It was like so many of Alix's nights. She dozed off sometime after the clock struck three, and did not wake at sunrise because a heavy cloudiness had moved in and made the morning dark. When she did wake, a wet wind was blowing in, spitting rain. She was cold, she was depressed, she wanted her coffee. She jumped out of bed and pulled on her robe, drove her feet into fleece-lined moccasins, and ran downstairs without even a passing glance into her mirror.

When she came into the kitchen Bunny was sitting at the table drinking coffee. She looked at Alix as if she were an apparition and not a friendly one, and Alix, giddy with her fast departure from bed, grinned and said, "Well, which is it? Old Lady Witch, the Dragon Lady, or Medusa?"

Bunny said distantly, " 'Witchcraft celebrates pale Hecate's offerings.' "

"Your father's daughter," said Alix. "Always the appropriate quotation. I haven't thought of pale Hecate since we learned Macbeth's soliloquy in high school." Energetically she put kindling into the stove. "We called her 'Heh-Kate' because that sounded a lot more supernatural than 'Heckety,' which sounds like expurgated profanity. By Heckety, I'll have your gizzard for this."

Bunny said nothing but went on sipping. William sat in the captain's chair, his eyes moving from her to Alix. "How come you're not charging around here, William?" Alix asked him.

"I gave him some milk," said Bunny indifferently. "I had to, he made such a pest of himself. Cats are so stupid. A dog could tell if I didn't like him."

"William doesn't care, as long as you know how to open a refrigerator." After she had the wood fire going, she washed her face and went upstairs to dress, and to brush and pin up her hair. She didn't give herself a chance to prepare an opening statement, but returned quickly to the kitchen, and as she stepped off the bottom step she said, "Bunny, where have you put my bottle of Seconal?"

At the words the mug jumped in Bunny's hands and clicked against her teeth. She winced and put her hand up to her mouth. After a moment she said, "I don't know what you're talking about."

Brittle and transparent as glass; no inflections.

"I'm sure you do know," said Alix pleasantly, fixing her coffee. "And I want that bottle back. In fact I must have it. I don't intend to let it go away with you."

"Supposing I did have your bottle, which is absolutely ridiculous because I'm not a thief, why should I want it? Why should I take it away with me?"

"To take all the capsules at once, because you don't know where to turn but to death." She sat down opposite Bunny, who laughed very loudly and artificially.

"Sometimes suicide is justified," Alix said. "But I don't think yours would be, because no matter how bad the next few months might be, you're still almost brand-new, you have a whole lifetime ahead, and too many potentialities to throw away in a gesture."

"You know something?" Bunny put her chin on her hands and stared at her. "*You're* not carrying this thing that you can't get rid of; *you* don't have all these people you can't get away from; you're your own boss. So how can you sit there and tell me I have something great going for me, and if I just manage to hold together through hell it'll be roses, roses all the way?"

"I can tell you because I know that if I could wake up eighteen again—even pregnant—oh, never mind. The fact is you can go to people who will help you; if not your family or your priest, there are *people*. It's in your own hands, if you weren't so obstinate. But there's nothing that I or anybody else can do to change my situation. My life ended the day your father died. There's only one thing left in my hands. Now do you see why I want my Seconal back?"

A slow flush washed into Bunny's face and then receded. She actually gaped. Her mouth worked without a sound. "Do you mean what that sounds like?" she asked finally.

"Yes."

"But you've gone on painting—" She swallowed visibly. "Well, I couldn't help seeing things. All right, I did go into the studio. I'll admit that much," she said aggressively. "And you were at some party with Jonas and that weird kid the night I came. You even had a picture in a show over there. And my father's been dead three months."

Alix showed her Cheshire-cat grin. "You mean I should have done it then? Well, there were things in this place that I didn't want anyone else to handle. Clothes of your father's, his papers and notebooks. Stuff of mine. Things that were too personal to leave." She looked down at her hands, folded before her on the table. "This is something you don't know about, but you may someday, if you ever love a man as I loved your father, and you outlive him."

"But you still haven't done it," Bunny said relentlessly. Her blue eyes had a hard light.

"Because nobody's given me the chance." It was an astonishing conversation, and astonishingly easy, if she concentrated on each word and not on what it or the whole meant, and if she throttled down each picture that arose. "Karen, at first. I knew Madge would be terribly upset, and I thought it would upset the child, do traumatic damage maybe." Her smile returned. "Now I don't think anything could upset her. But there's been one thing after another getting in my way. You're the latest, and I've made up my mind that you'll be the last."

"But—but—even my mother wouldn't think of k-k—" She couldn't get it out. "She'd think it was a sin anyway. But she didn't even collapse, and everybody thought she would. And she's gone to Europe. Everybody says she's been simply wonderful."

Happy as a clam because she's got Shane away from me, Alix thought. She said, "She has children. It makes a difference if you have someone to live for."

"I should think if you thought it was all right to live with him openly you'd have had children too."

"You're right. If I was willing to do one thing I should have done the other. But I didn't think it was fair to involve anyone else in my life." Alix got up and went over to the wood stove, intending to put wood in, but forgot to; she stood over it absently rubbing her hands and looking out the sink window where the rain had begun to beat harder.

She had confessed on impulse, hoping to startle Bunny into common sense. To save her for *what?* What guarantee could she give Bunny that life would indeed be good? She might be doing her a favor to let her take the Seconal away with her, except that she wanted it for herself.

William jumped down and walked over to the door. She heard him but felt far away from him, withdrawn as she was into the full, vigorous reacquaintance with defeat.

He spoke and enthusiastically polished the inner doorframe. The rain came again in a blinding rattle against the glass. Bunny's chair scraped back and she went past Alix, saying, "I said you were stupid and I mean it. Going out in this." She opened the outer door and William left.

"You see?" she said in a falsely breezy tone. "No brains. Or maybe I should say no raincoat." She stood by the table, picking up things and putting them down. The silence drew out. I can't talk any more, Alix thought. It's not humiliating this time, I'm too tired even to feel that. If she's triumphant, I don't care.

"I guess no boats would be out in this, would they?" Bunny asked tentatively. "I mean, Jonas couldn't take me across in that dory. It's a real storm, isn't it?"

"I imagine he could take you over in the big boat," Alix said, still staring at the rain-obscured glass.

"Well, I wouldn't want to put anybody to all that trouble. I mean, in weather like this. I—" She had to clear her throat. "I'd be willing to stay over another day. I mean, it's not as if anybody was expecting me anywhere."

"Then stay," Alix said bleakly. She recalled what she had got up for, and put more wood in the stove.

"Well, do you mind if I fix something to eat? I—would you —I'll fix you something too." The fact penetrated to Alix's brain that Bunny sounded thoroughly subdued. "I do very good scrambled eggs. Everybody says so."

Everybody says she's been simply wonderful.

"All right, Bunny, I'll eat some of your scrambled eggs," she said.

❧ CHAPTER 36 ❧

Now IT WAS Bunny who tried to talk, making embarrassed, juvenile, little rushes of speech to which Alix gave forced or absent-minded answers. She suspected that she had frightened the girl into believing she was shut up with someone who was about to go mad at any moment, if it hadn't happened already. But in that case, why didn't she want to leave, regardless of wind or weather?

It was beyond Alix, and she didn't really care. She ate and drank apathetically, her thoughts wandering far from the kitchen in the wind-whipped house and even beyond Shane, ranging erratically over a variety of terrain but never staying long anywhere.

All at once Bunny said loudly, "I've got the Seconal. I didn't know that's what it was, but it said for sleeping and not to be refilled, so I knew it was strong." As Alix's gaze moved slowly to meet hers, she began to bluster. "All right, I admit I was prying! I know better than that, I was brought up to know better. So I apologize. And I'll give you the bottle back, but not till I'm leaving."

"What's the matter?" Alix said. "Do you think if you give me the Seconal now I'll take it all while you're still here?" She laughed at Bunny's indignant mortification. "Excuse me, Bunny, but this conversation reminds me of another one, when right in the middle of feeling utterly foul I began to hear the conversation from the outside, like a tape recording, and it struck me as ridiculous."

"I don't see how anything so serious can be ridiculous."

"It can be when you can't bear something any longer," said Alix. "It's a different form of bursting into tears."

"Oh." She considered. "And better than pounding your head and your heels on the floor, I suppose." She turned her head away, her ear was red. "I can do these dishes," she said. "And I suppose I'd better sweep up my room. Wherever I hit—*voom!* —instant slum." She gave Alix a bashful sidewise smile, and seemed reassured. "Oh, hadn't I better walk around and tell Jonas I'm not going?"

She was candidly eager to get out, and Alix was just as eager to be rid of her. "Go ahead if you'd like. You'll be in the lee once you get past Gib's Cove. Ask Jonas to show you the short cut back through the woods."

"Ask him nothing," said Bunny, disappearing into her room. She came out with a pair of sneakers and sat down to put them on. "I'll be lucky if I get anything said before he's down my throat. He doesn't like me much."

"He doesn't *dis*like you. His patience is short, that's all, and he has worries of his own."

"I thought he seemed pretty uptight." She was busy with shoe laces as she added, "I was awful yesterday. I don't know where all that language came from, but anyway—"

"But anyway, you'd better get going before the storm's worse. Here." Alix handed her a sou'wester, and Bunny said, "Hey, groovy! I feel like the skipper's little daughter in *The Wreck of the Hesperus.*" She buckled the black raincoat and left.

Alix built a fire in the fireplace with a long-lasting birch backlog, replenished the kitchen fire, and went up to the studio. As usual in an easterly or northeaster, the studio resem-

bled the bridge of a ship at sea. Water poured unceasingly
down the glass and the roar of the wind obscured all other
sounds. She worked for a while on the sketch she'd begun yesterday, making changes in the composition. When she had
done all she could before transferring it to canvas, she put it
aside and studied Karen's portrait for a while. The thing was
good; she couldn't doubt it. She hated to give up on the eyes.

Those two kids have really defeated you, my good woman,
she thought. Nor all your piety nor wit nor your most passion-
ate reasoning got anywhere with either of them. So give up. Beyond a certain point you become a garrulous crank. Not that
you really give a damn what you sound like, but it would be
more artistic to leave a memory of some intelligence behind
you.

She whiled away more time in the studio, looking at other
sketches and studies, surprised by the amount of work she had
done since May. Finally, when she could find nothing else to
do, she went downstairs to put more wood in the kitchen stove
and the fireplace.

It was quiet down here compared to the studio. Bunny's
sneakers were under the wood stove, and William lay beyond
them, snoring faintly. She went quietly to the living room, expecting that Bunny had fallen asleep on the sofa before the fire,
but she was gazing up at Shane's portrait.

Alix started to retreat, but Bunny, without looking around,
said, "Don't go away."

Alix went around to the fireplace and put more wood on.
When she straightened up, brushing her hands on her jeans,
Bunny said hurriedly, "I wouldn't really look at it before. I
kept avoiding it. But now I've done nothing *but* look at it.
You're good," she said tersely. "He said you were."

Taken by surprise, Alix had nothing to say. She looked into
Bunny's set face, the black eyebrows drawn sternly together,
and then up at the painting.

"I've seen him laugh like that," Bunny went on. "But not
very often. So it's Daddy, but it isn't, if you know what I mean.

It's like the first discovery that he was a man *separate* from Daddy. I mean I *knew* it, but it's as if I never believed he had the right to be something separate." The reviving firelight on her uplifted face gave her a devout look. "Seeing him like this. The longer I watch him, the more I know that he *was* separate, whether I wanted it that way or not. So I wonder how many more Shanes there were. . . . I know," she said diffidently, "that my mother's Shane wasn't the same as"—she made an obvious effort—"yours."

"We're none of us one person. Don't you know already that you're several versions of Bunny?"

Bunny's smile was the first natural one Alix had seen. "Oh, brother! Meet Mary-Kate, Mary-Catherine, *Miss* Mannering, and the Scourge of the Hockey Field, Attila Mannering."

Alix laughed. "Meet Alix, Alexia, Miss Horne, then my own idea of me—"

"And Shane's Alix," the girl said. "You see? I'm admitting it." She picked up the guitar from beside her and plucked the strings at random, as if she wanted something to do with her hands. "He was happy here. I wanted to think he was suffering all the time. That he was just plain miserable with you. But I knew the truth the minute I stepped into this house and saw the portrait, and his room, and his guitar." She patted it. "I remembered it from his rooms at the college, because once when I was little I scratched my initial on the back of it. See?" She turned it over and traced the wobbly B which Alix knew was there. "He didn't find it till after I was gone. Even my sister didn't know I'd done it. I wanted something for him to remember me by."

"He wouldn't need that," said Alix. "He talked of you and your sister a great deal. You were his cuddler. And musical. He was so proud of that."

"Well, I'm a pretty good pianist, and I play a few other instruments, but not as well as the piano." She stroked the strings, drawing forth a crisp, expert-sounding arpeggio. "What was terrible about coming here was the feeling that I'd *almost* found him, that he was here if I knew where to look. It was like one of those nightmares. If I went into a room he'd just left it."

"Yes, I know." Alix sat down on the sofa.

"But I didn't *want* to find him here. So that was another terrible thing. He'd lived here all those years, he loved you, and even if I set fire to the place it wouldn't wipe out the truth. It's one of those irreversible facts like my being pregnant."

The word dropped into the comparative peace of the moment like a rock. Simultaneously it seemed to land in Alix's stomach. Bunny said, "Do you want to know why I can't tell Mummy? Because she'd say, 'You're just like your father.' She always said he was lustful, and she prayed we wouldn't be. I shouldn't talk about her like this—"

"I don't want you to, Bunny," Alix interrupted firmly.

"But I think perhaps you'd understand Mummy even if she never in a million years would understand you. She's not really cold, unless that's what frigid women really are, just so repelled and horrified by sex. I know Daddy tried to help her, but going to a psychiatrist is one of the big sins to Mummy. Besides, she couldn't talk about something so private to a *man*. The big battle about that took place when I was having my tonsils out. My sister told me about it, a long time afterward."

"Bunny, if it's any comfort to you, your father never blamed her."

"But he just couldn't live with her, and maybe if she'd done what he asked, he could have. Don't you see?"

"If she couldn't make herself—"

"If she cared all that much about him and us—I mean," Bunny said earnestly, "she never took any of the blame, it was all Daddy's fault for being so lecherous. She brought us up to believe he must have been some kind of sex fiend when they were alone." She stretched her mouth into a trembling grin. "You know how in those old novels they write about 'unspeakable horrors' in the bedchamber, and so forth. Crazy as we were about him, we thought he was Jekyll with us and Hyde with her, until she said exactly the same thing about the first boys who wanted to date us."

She kept looking up at her father's portrait as she talked. "He's so alive," she half-whispered. "You think if you can just look at it long enough and forget everything else, you'll go out of this world into that one, and he'll be there to welcome you, with his arms out—" She had to stop, shaking her head irritably and saying something to herself. She went through her pockets and brought out her cigarettes, jabbed one into her mouth and held her lighter to it with a shaking hand. It took quite a while to light.

"It's not her fault," she said suddenly. "I mean, not all of it. I suppose she couldn't help herself. You realize that when you 'see how she's been ever since. She's—blossomed."

Alix got up and went away from the sofa. "I think it's letting up," she said. "Look." A watery gleam of sunshine struck the floor.

Blossomed. Of course. She got him at last the way she wanted him: a dead bridegroom.

"Let's get out of the house," she said without looking around. "I'll make up a thermos of hot tea, and we'll take some crackers and cheese and sardines, and eat somewhere out of the wind." She felt as if she couldn't face another meal in that kitchen ever.

"Oh, great!" Bunny bounced up from the sofa. "I'll go get my sneakers back on."

They went to the narrow deep cove to the south of Gib's Cove, because Bunny remembered seeing something bright floating in the turbulent water. The tide had brought it ashore, and it lay in the fresh debris of green-brown rockweed like a globe of fire, if there could be such a thing. Bunny pounced on it with greedy triumph. It was a pot buoy painted with fluorescent red paint.

"Hey, wild!" she shouted, swinging it around her head on its remaining bit of nylon warp. Alix walked toward a wing of dark wet driftwood projecting from a rubbery tangle of kelp. Bunny's voice followed her, indistinct as the medricks' cries over the crash and tumbling roar of surf.

"What was that?" Alix shouted back at her.

"I said, Daddy loved beachcombing, didn't he?"

"Yes!" Alix pulled the driftwood free and held it up.

"Wings!" Bunny cried, happily slithering toward her. She skidded and sat down hard, laughing, in the drenched weed. Alix went to her at once, reaching out a hand.

"Are you all right?"

"Oh, sure!" Bunny caught up a festoon of dark green translucent weed like entwined strips of cellophane, and draped it over her head. "Look, I'm Undine—" The laughter was suddenly wiped away as if by an obliterating paintbrush. She looked stricken. "I forgot," she said. "I actually forgot, for the first time in weeks." She ignored Alix's hand and got up slowly, as if she were old. "If I could bump something loose I'd be the happiest creature in the world. Happier than those birds up there, and I've been watching them out the window and hating them." Her eyes stretched wide in defense against tears. "I *mean* it. I'd never ask for anything again *ever*. It would be enough of a favor to last me my whole life long."

"Have you given any thought at all to what you're going to do?"

Bunny's grin was a phantom of Shane's. "Well, I did have a wizard idea, but you've conked that, making me promise to give the stuff back. Oh, I'll probably go to Father Tom after all." A gust of wind whipped her hair across her face and she muttered, "This mess. I'm going to chop it off." She turned back to Alix, facing into the wind, and as her hair blew away from her face she tied her scarf tightly around it at the nape. "There! Oh, look, there's a bunch of net floats coming ashore!"

She plunged off toward the water again. Hoping this time for a successful fall? Alix wondered. She'd been a little too non-

chalant about talking to the priest; no, there was going to be
an abortion if she could possibly manage it.

Bunny picked up the cluster of floats hung on a fragment of
torn seine, and wandered on with the foaming wash surging
about her ankles. Her sneakers had been soaked from the start,
and now her jeans were wet to the knees. Beyond her the tumbling waters of the cove were thick with churning rockweed
and flotsam, outside the cove the seas were silvery blue and
green, and jets of spray flashed in the sun. The warm air was
heavy with a blend of salt and iodine, and the resinous and
herbal scents of the rain-soaked land.

Alix climbed the steep slant of beach toward the woods. William picked his fastidious way along a log, crouching as a myr-
tle warbler shot by his head. Alix spread out the lunch on a flat
rock already dried by the sun. In a few minutes Bunny came
up the beach, walking slowly this time and occasionally picking
up a pebble and studying it. She looked like any young girl
watching for pretty stones. Someone coming upon them both,
not knowing them, could not possibly imagine what plateau of
despair each of them inhabited. Any more than I could have
imagined it about Jonas, Alix thought. What a world can be
contained in a human brain. What a universe, really. Full of
Bunny's black holes in space where our stars have died.

Bunny sat down cross-legged in front of her.

"Can I stay a while longer?" she asked bluntly. "For a week?
I'll stay out of your way, honestly. But I'll never have another
chance to be in a place that meant so much to my father."

Alix, still bemused by her own speculations, looked at her
without answering. Bunny's lashes flickered, but she kept her
eyes on Alix. "You've been better to me than I deserve."

"The answer is that you're Shane's daughter," Alix said finally. "Yes, you can stay a week. We'll have to let Jonas know."

"I told him I'd let him know just when I was going." Bunny
reddened even more. "Well, I mean—"

"And what did he say?" Alix handed her a thermos cup of
tea.

"He didn't say anything. I don't think he was enchanted. He's been around how many mornings, and hasn't had a chance to have a cup of coffee with you yet."

"I think he would rather have an early start on hauling his gear," said Alix dryly.

❧ CHAPTER 37 ❧

NOW BEGAN THE great suspension of belief. Whatever Bunny thought in her hours alone, whenever Alix saw her she seemed to have put her troubles completely out of mind. To have willed them out of existence, in fact. She became enthralled with Shane's arrowheads and spent hours patiently searching the beaches. She swam, and dug clams. She played the guitar, singing to herself, working out chords; she lay in the sun and read. Sometimes she was observed closely in these pursuits by Karen, who no longer hovered at Alix's elbow when there was newer, more fascinating material at hand.

"That weird kid bugs me," Bunny said one day.

"Welcome to the club," said Alix.

Bunny spread out a handful of felsite flints and chips and began examining the edges with Shane's magnifying glass. "I nearly knocked her out with my elbow when I turned around quickly," she said. "I tried to talk with her, but all I got was the stare. Are you sure she's not a Martian?"

Alix laughed. "She might be."

"Well, I prefer William's company to hers," Bunny said grumpily. "At least I get some response if I speak to him."

"Did you say you were an ailurophobe?"

"Oh, I just threw that in. Mummy's one. I wonder if that's got some psychological tie-up with—"

"Did you offer yesterday to bake a cake?" Alix interrupted, "or was that something else you just threw in?"

"No, I meant it. I really can bake, you know. And from scratch."

"Be my guest." Alix waved at the cupboards and went out. Karen was nowhere in sight, and she wondered how Bunny had managed to get in without her. But Bunny was still child enough to be tougher with Karen than the adults could be unless they were driven to it.

Bunny was keeping to her word about staying out of the way, so much so that Alix was goaded by her conscience into activities which the girl could share. They went out in *Sea Pigeon* one hot calm morning at low tide, first to Tiree Ledge where the seals lay untidily around in the sun and playing in the water. While the boat drifted almost imperceptibly Alix made quick sketches. Bunny sat in the bow with her knees almost under her chin, watching; there seemed to be nothing whatever behind the dark blue eyes but a totally sensuous reaction to her physical environment.

The sea was as still as blue porcelain, and the only hazard was running out of gas. They went to Old Bull Ledge where the young gulls were, watching them from the water, and then headed for a sand bar which appeared only at dead low tide. It shone like sugar in the sun. They beached *Sea Pigeon* here and walked the length of the bar to where water began rising over it and turning the sand and shell to a pale green floor. Bunny had to wade in it, to know how it felt. She was like a child, far more of a child than Karen in her relationship to her surroundings; she was Shane's daughter in that she could be utterly, mindlessly happy around or in salt water.

Back at the island they drifted without power above barely submerged rocks and gardens of swaying plants, leaning over

the sides to behold an aqueous world pierced through with refracted light This went on with very little said until the dying
wake from a big cabin cruiser hit *Sea Pigeon* and shattered
both their mood and the scene below.

Alix had to reach for an oar to steady the rolling boat by
turning the bow into the wake. Bunny rose up and stared out
at the impervious craft churning up through the thoroughfare.
"Yankee imperialist pig, go home!" she shouted. She sank back
and said with breathy intensity, "*Actually* though, I'm demo-
cratic and tolerant and all that. I mean I'm all for rich people
having their civil rights and everything as long as they keep in
their place. I mean, how would you like your daughter to
marry one?"

Alix laughed. Bunny's guffaw, allowing for difference in
pitch and volume, was pure Shane.

Alix did not believe that Bunny was going straight to any
clergyman who would then be able to manage Cathleen Mannering. She did believe that Bunny would find another abortionist by way of the grapevine; that she meant it when she said
the risk didn't matter; and that when she asked for this week
here it had been with the fear that she might not survive.

But it didn't pay to dwell on what one couldn't help, or on a
hatred of Cathleen; the acid content of hatred only scalded herself and not Cathleen.

For safety's sake Alix insisted on knowing when Bunny
swam, so she could keep an eye on her. One day when Bunny
came out of the water and lay down on the hot pebbles of Gib's
Cove beach, she said without preparation, "Mummy did something awful."

"What?" Alix asked absently, then heard herself, but it was
too late. She had refused to encourage Bunny to discuss her
mother.

"She had Daddy's beard shaved off. You know." The girl's
voice was subdued. "I was thinking of him while I was swim-

ming here, I always do, and he always has the beard. And then suddenly today I remembered the funeral. Not that I *wanted* to, but—"

"I don't want to know about it, Bunny," Alix said. She got up and walked away. She was shaking again, for the first time in days.

"I'm sorry!" Bunny cried after her. She sounded about to cry. Alix kept on walking, her hands clasped together so hard that the knuckles ached. She saw with a merciless lucidity that the last few days had not really been a kind of peace, but only the exhaustion that comes from being continually beaten down. Now she knew she had not only lost Shane but that any sense of his continued existence in this place had been wiped out by the girl's words. In spite of nine years of his presence, and the portrait like the symbol of the tutelary god, his daughter had just turned him into a well-dressed, clean-shaven corpse in a casket.

Back on the beach Bunny crouched weeping at what her own words had done to herself as well as to Alix. Alix heard her but kept walking away, driving the pain deeper into her hands. What stopped her was the log at the edge of the boggy spot where she had painted the blue flag that day. She turned and walked past the edge of the swamp toward the wharf. She didn't see Karen until she walked into her.

"Is she crying *again?*" Karen moved so she could see past Alix toward Bunny. "I never cry."

"I can well believe it," said Alix. "Go away and don't bother her."

"People act awful funny around here," Karen commented.

"Do you have a message," asked Alix, "or did you just drop by to fill our lives with sunshine?"

"Gram says you and *her* come over to supper tonight. We've got mackerel."

"All right. Please tell her we'll be there, and thank you for bringing the invitation."

"I guess I'll go down there awhile," said Karen, pointing in Bunny's direction.

"I guess you won't."

There was a silent duel between Karen's pink-rimmed glasses and Alix's dark ones, and finally, with the usual expression of either resignation or exasperation around her mouth, Karen walked away. Immediately she became a very small figure in blue shorts and blue and white striped jersey. She went up over the bank by the wharf with the stiff, straight carriage of wounded dignity.

"And don't stop at the house," Alix called after her, thinking that it was a classic example of locking the stable door too late; Karen could have been all through Bunny's belongings before she appeared at the beach with the message.

She walked back to Bunny, who was now forlornly wiping her eyes with her towel. "Come on, brace up," Alix said. "We're invited out to supper."

"I don't want to go," Bunny said thickly.

"You'd better. You'll get a marvelous meal, a lot better than what I've been supplying. And Madge and Ozzie were good friends of your father's. You've got plenty of time to get your face back into shape."

Bunny shrugged, still staring straight ahead at the cove. "All right," she said at last.

"Be ready at five. They eat early." Alix went on up to the house.

The afternoon moved on with a horrible lethargy. Always the moment on the beach was there, a ghastly presence glimpsed from the corner of the eye but not to be confronted face to face. And somewhere near, only waiting for her recognition to make it audible, there was a scream. She would never utter it, but she knew it was there; it had been there in those first days when she had drugged herself so it wouldn't echo through her nights.

She stayed upstairs until five. When she went down Bunny

was in the kitchen feeding William. "I hope you don't mind," she said, "but he was making such a row and I thought you might be asleep." The redness and swelling had gone out of her face and she looked shiny with cleanliness. Her hair hung in two neat braids, and she wore a fresh white blouse and shorts.

"You look very nice," Alix told her.

"So do you. I wish I was slender."

"Skinny is the word for me. If I went to Italy I'd never get pinched."

Bunny grinned. Then she said in a hurry, "I shouldn't have said that on the beach. It just—" She thrust out her hands. "Exploded, somehow. I mean, it haunts me. But now it'll haunt you. I should have kept it to myself."

Yes, you should have, Alix thought. In some respects Bunny's friendship was far more disastrous than her enmity could have been.

"Never mind," she said. "Let's go."

✤ CHAPTER 38 ✤

BUNNY NOW DISPLAYED a new persona, the nicely-brought-up young girl on her best behavior. She showed a good deal of charm, and also a good deal of Shane, and Ozzie and Madge, who had been a little uneasy at first, relaxed. Observing from the outside, Alix saw that the relaxation wasn't one-sided: Bunny was responding to Madge's maternal warmth. It must have been restful to Bunny for a little while to be considered a child, like sinking tired bones and chilled flesh into a warm feather bed.

Jonas had caught the mackerel that afternoon, but he wasn't there. "You know how notional he is," said Madge. "He said he didn't feel like eating mackerel tonight, but I know better."

"All you know is that he don't feel like eating mackerel," said Ozzie. "Nothing more. Been out on the water all day and he feels like putting his feet up under his own vine and fig tree."

Madge rolled her eyes at Alix. "Just the same," she began rebelliously, but gave up. Bunny, playing with Sidney and watched by Karen, apparently didn't even hear the inter-

change. But when they were walking home in the firefly-span-
gled dusk she said, "I was right about Jonas. He is staying
away because of me."

"I told you he had his own troubles, Bunny. What are you
trying to promote?"

"Male companionship for you," said Bunny at once. Her
flashlight bobbed along behind Alix through the Tangle. "I
think you should have it. You don't have to be in love or anything. But he could keep you from being alone too much and
thinking . . . you know." She was running out of nerve, but
kept gamely on. "I mean you shouldn't be thinking the way
you do. Shane would *never* want that! Alix, you've got this
wonderful talent, you're young still, you've got something you
could live for."

"Thank you, Granny," said Alix. They had reached the
stone wall and she stopped and switched off her own light.
Bunny shut off hers. "And who's talking now about something
to live for? Why have I so much more than you? I'm twice your
age. You haven't even begun to live."

"What do you call getting pregnant?" Bunny asked cynically.
"That's living a little, like wow, man."

"Well, it doesn't have to be a permanent state, does it?"

"It might just as well be. The next seven months look like
eternity to me. Look, you wouldn't have a child by Daddy because it wasn't right, you said. So why am I supposed to go
through with it?"

"So as not to take chances with your own life," Alix said patiently. "Give this child up without ever seeing it, and then
begin new. Oh, for heaven's sake, I didn't intend to start
preaching again! But for some reason I get afflicted with this
compulsion to make inspirational noises. So I'll shut up if you
will. Agreed?"

"But I—Oh, agreed," said Bunny sulkily.

By silent consent, they stayed apart for most of the next day.
They were eating supper out on the western side of the house,

using William as a safe topic, when Jonas came into Gib's Cove, with Karen up in the bow of the dory.

"I'll disappear," said Bunny at once.

"You will not," said Alix. "If you do, I'll put Karen on your trail."

"Oh dear God, not that, not that, please, I'll do anything, but not that." Bunny collapsed, moaning. Then she sat up and took her cigarettes out of her pocket. She had smoked very little in the past few days and not at all at the Goodwins'. Now she posed with an elbow on her knee and an enigmatic expression veiled in smoke as Jonas came up the path with Karen behind him.

"Good evening, ladies," he said.

"Coffee, tea, or milk?" asked Alix. "Chicken sandwich? Brownie?"

"Nope, I've et. Wait'll I ask my mother. You want something, Mother Machree?"

"A brownie." Karen held out her hand, not at all tentatively, and Alix put a brownie in it. Karen at once withdrew and sat down with her back to them.

"Your mother's antisocial," drawled Bunny.

"They all get that way after being around where I am," said Jonas. "Anybody want to go mackereling?"

"Yes, we do," said Alix at once, seeing a way to use up the next few hours. "Bunny, you clear up here and I'll get the jigs. Karen, why don't you help Bunny?"

"You don't need to, Karen," Bunny said hastily, which was a mistake. Karen at once advanced stolidly toward the remains of the meal.

"Never mind the jigs," Jonas said to Alix. "I picked up some new rigs at Emery's today. We'll troll."

They went out about a mile east of Tiree and trolled back and forth from northeast to southwest in the pellucid hour before sunset. Jonas tended the engine and let the others fish. They moved under pastel billows of clouds and across the shining reflections of clouds, trolling their lines from small plastic hand-lining reels which they secured with loops around oar handles or the rising, against the heavy pull of two or three mackerel at once on one line.

Bunny was indifferent at first, but at the sudden strike on her line she shrieked, "I've got one! I've got one!"

"Well, don't sit there keening about it, haul 'er in!" said Jonas. Bunny hauled like a madwoman and shrieked again when three blue and silver mackerel came flying aboard. "Everybody dodge," ordered Jonas. He grabbed and unhooked the fish and put them in a clam-roller.

"Oh, brother," Bunny gloated, then turned solemn. "They're so pretty. I don't want to watch them die." She tossed her line overboard again. Karen, perched up in the bow in her bright orange life preserver, was tensely holding her line. She had to struggle to bring it in with two mackerel on it, and Alix decided to wind up her own line and concentrate on dodging Bunny's flying hooks and assisting Karen. Though the child showed none of Bunny's frenzy, she was dedicated to catching mackerel and did so. Her glasses became so splashed that Alix wondered how she could see through them, but Karen sternly refused to let her wipe them.

When they moved out of a school everyone fell into a dreamy silence until there was a new strike.

They headed for home finally so they could get all the fish cleaned while there was still light. The wake bubbled amethyst and gold astern; ahead, the highest spruces on Tiree were almost invisible against the incandescent west.

Karen, up to now as immobile as a figurehead, suddenly pointed. A runabout was speeding past the sand beach in a blurring wave of spray. It turned into Gib's Cove and was hidden by the eastern arm of rock. "You've got company," Jonas called to Alix.

"Out for a sunset ride, I guess," she answered. It looked like the boat Soren had come in. He wouldn't stay long when he saw that she wasn't alone.

When they came into the cove, the boxy, shiny runabout was tied up at the wharf, and someone was going up the ladder. When he reached the top she saw that he was too gangly to be Soren. Something was handed up to him from below. *Luggage.* She felt an exhilarating indignation. Whoever he was, he'd come to the wrong place.

"I see he's got his pajamas and toothbrush with him," Jonas said with a grin.

"Just let's get in there before his friend can go off and leave him."

"Don't you know who it is?" Bunny asked. Alix shook her head, but they were close enough now for her to recognize Soren aboard the boat. He was smiling as he watched them approach. Of course he was smiling, she thought nastily. He was up to something.

Jonas shut off the outboard and they floated alongside the runabout.

"*Good* evening, everyone!" Soren greeted them. "Alix, Mr. Hallowell, young Karen, and—" he paused, with a questioning twinkle. Bunny said as if entranced, "Bunny Mannering."

"How do you do, Miss Mannering?" The accent was like velvet, with an unmusical counterpoint of pure Illinois from the wharf above.

"Hi, there, Alix! I'll bet you never expected to see *me!*"

"That's painfully obvious," Soren remarked, watching Alix.

Tony from Illinois; he who had analyzed her painting, kindly informed her of her repressed maternal instincts, explained his own art to her without end, and had eaten anything she gave him.

"How did you get here, Tony?" she asked.

"Well, I flew to Fremont, and took a taxi to Baker's Harbor." Tony was given to waving his arms when he explained, and his square horn-rimmed glasses made him look intense and scholarly. "There wasn't anybody around when I got out but Mr. Michaels here, and I guess that was just by accident. He was gassing up. And when I asked him how to get to Tiree Island, he said he'd take me." He looked down at Soren with happy wonder. "Gosh, I never expected to run into such luck! And you know what, Alix, I've seen some of his stuff. I know I have."

"Something tells me I should leave," said Soren.

"You want to be careful going back in this light," said Jonas. "If you hit a pot buoy with any speed at all it could drive a hole right through that fiberglass hull. You'd sink in five minutes."

"You describe that with such relish," said Soren, "I can't help feeling there's some deep personal motivation there. Well, good night, everyone. I'm so happy to have met you, Miss Mannering." The caressing inflection and formal tilt of the head did their work.

"It's Bunny," she said. "Mary-Kate, really."

He smiled at her and turned to Alix. "Another time, Alix."

"I'm sure of it," she said resignedly.

He started the engine. Jonas poled the dory ahead until she beached, and Karen climbed over the bow, the others following. Soren backed away from the wharf, waved heartily, and headed out.

Tony eagerly jumped down to the rocks and came to meet Alix. "This is Tony Elliot, everybody," she said uncordially. "Bunny Mannering, Karen Seastrom, Jonas Hallowell."

"Hi," said Bunny, looking as stolid as Karen, who said nothing. Jonas shook hands and began cleaning mackerel at the edge of the tide. William arrived.

"What a sky!" marveled Tony. "It's like being inside an opal. This place is—gosh, I just haven't got the *words!*"

"Well, it's the first time," said Alix. "How did you get my address?"

"Bribed the super."

"You did not. He's not bribable."

"But he's susceptible. No, I didn't bribe him, I just didn't want you to know how I lied. I told him I was your only nephew, and my mother was your only sister, and on her deathbed she made me promise if I ever needed help I'd go to you."

"Is he *kidding?*" Bunny asked Alix.

"I don't know," said Alix, keeping her eyes coldly on Tony. "But he got my address somehow, and Leon never gave it out before."

"It's my coloring," Tony explained. "My hair is sort of reddish, and you can see freckles if you look hard enough. When I pointed it out he saw the resemblance right away. Even commented on it."

"The other question is," said Alix, "*why?*"

"I guess I'll go and get a lesson in cleaning a mackerel," said Bunny with heavily emphasized tact. She went down to where Jonas was working under the combined scrutiny of Karen and William.

Tony watched her go. "What a subject for a life class," he commented. "I'll bet she'd make a magnificent nude."

"I'm waiting," Alix said ominously. "Why are you here?"

"How long since you've spent a summer in New York?" Whatever impetus had carried him thus far deserted him. He became defensive. "Even if you did stay there, you've got that studio. Do you know where *I* live? It stinks. Literally. And I can't go home because they didn't want me to leave in the first place. It would be rank surrender. I've got a job in a supermarket, so I can eat, but all I do on my time off is sleep because I can't get enough sleep at night. Honestly, Alix, I've been so depressed I can't paint, I've turned into this automaton, except a real automaton wouldn't notice the stinks and the ungodly noise, and be so homesick for uncorrupted silence."

"So you just took off from your job. How do you eat when you go back?"

"I've got a week's vacation, but I was getting to the point where I would have taken off anyway. Everybody's gone somewhere, so there's nobody to talk painting with even if I weren't so depressed. My God, Alix, how do they do it? Everybody's poor as hell but they're in Europe, Canada, Woodstock, Montauk. . . . I keep thinking, if I can just get through the summer without freaking out, I'll be all right."

Alix looked with yearning at *Sea Pigeon*. She would like to have been wafted aboard at this moment, and then she would set straight out to sea like Tennyson's Ulysses.

"If you can put me up tonight, I'll find a way to get back tomorrow," Tony said bravely. "I can stay somewhere around the Harbor, maybe. As a matter of fact, you don't have to let me in the house if you don't want to. I've got my sleeping bag."

"Don't be preposterous," Alexia Horne answered. "If I didn't know better I'd think there was a conspiracy. All right, Tony. For a few days anyway, and then we'll see."

He took his glasses off and wiped them; his hazel eyes were very young and glowing. "You're the greatest, Alix. And look, I'll make myself very useful, getting water, doing repairs— *anything,* just ask!" He waved his arms and she expected to see his glasses fly out of his hand and into the cove.

"I'll go up and make a bed," said Bunny without a glance at him. "Where are we putting him?"

We. "In the study. You know where the bedding is."

"Come on, Tony." Bunny jerked her head toward the house. They left, Tony talking and Karen trailing them. Jonas, fending off William, rinsed each gutted fish in salt water and laid it in a bed of fresh rockweed in the clam-roller. He tipped back his head and gave her a twinkling, unreadable glance. "You'll want a good mess since Prince Charming showed up."

"Prince Charming went back," said Alix. "Come and have a cup of coffee. Bunny made a cake today."

"No thanks," said Jonas, washing his hands. "It's between the dark and the daylight, when the night is beginning to lower."

" 'Comes a pause in the day's occupations,' " said Alix, " 'That is known as the Children's Hour.' "

"Yep. Let me know when kindergarten's closed for the summer. What's Peter Rabbit's problem? He's not in an interesting condition, too, is he?"

"Well, it's interesting to him," said Alix. "Lonesome, homesick, and inquisitive."

"I thought for one glorious moment that he was Bunny's boy

friend come to save her honor. You made any headway with her yet?"

"She's half-promised to see her priest, but I don't believe that either. The man in the case may be married," she lied. "She won't even mention him.",

"You shouldn't have this on your neck," he said.

"Well, I've brought it on myself by my meddling, as she tells me," she retorted. "Not that she wants any help. She still intends to manage things her own way. The hell of it is that the more I know her, the worse it is. However," she said, getting up, "I'm not asking for sympathy either."

"Oh, sure, you and I are a pair of porcupines when it comes to that. Sympathy's an obscene word around here. *Karen!*" he shouted. "Come on! And step lively!"

The older ones were just disappearing around the corner of the house. Karen returned slowly. "Do you run an obedience school," Alix asked Jonas, "or do you give her a Yummy every time she comes when called?"

"Neither. It's my personal magnetism."

They both laughed. "I'll invite you to supper by way of a liberation festival when my boarders are gone," said Alix. He stood looking at her without speaking. Perhaps it was the angle of his face, or the light; or the expression was genuinely soft, almost tender. Then Karen arrived, and the illusion was gone.

"Come on, get aboard, Sairey Gamp," he told her, "and if you can't get aboard, get a plank. How's that for a thigh-slapper?" He seized her under the arms and swung her over the side. "And put your life jacket on. No sense of humor," he said to Alix.

"She's discriminating, that's all. Good night, Karen. You're a good fisherman. Goodnight, Jonas, and many thanks." She sounded quite cheerful, and told herself that she really was.

✺ CHAPTER 39 ✺

She heard Tony stealthily leaving the house at sunup, and she saw him from the seaward windows, crossing the lawn toward the roses, walking slowly into the apricot fire of the rising sun. He was carrying his paintbox. She found herself smiling in sympathy. He would come back drunk and dazzled, with nothing set down. He'd been tied to his beige squares for too long.

She found that she did not resent Tony's presence this morning. Except for William, Tony was the most uncomplicated personality of all those around her. He was also a painter, which gave them something in common, a set of reactions, impulses, aspirations, and desires that had to do only with their work and nothing else, and thereby removed barriers of background, sex, and age. It represented a large territory in which explanations were not necessary. Tony would be no trouble, unless at the end of his week he had gone native and decided to join the art colony. In that case she'd make it clear he was on his own.

While she was building the fire Bunny came out bundled up in Alix's toweling robe. She had a bleak, mopish look. "What's the matter?" Alix asked. "Sick again this morning?"

Bunny dropped ungracefully into a chair. "Not that way. I just feel terrible, that's all."

"Terrible enough to be scared? Should you see a doctor?"

Bunny gave her a sad, icy little smile. "I'm not having pains, if that's what you're hoping. I'm afraid it's not a miscarriage. No, it's just like everything's dropped on me, like a brick building collapsing. I'm going back to bed."

When the teakettle started to boil Alix looked in on Bunny. She lay with her arms folded under head, staring up at the light ripples running across the ceiling. She was sniffling, and tears ran from the corners of her eyes down toward her ears. She didn't look at Alix, but the tears came faster and she kept swallowing.

"How about something hot?" Alix asked her. "It's been a long time since supper, and food cheers you up sometimes, I've noticed."

"How long is that kook going to stay?" Bunny hissed.

"You don't have to whisper, he's out," said Alix. "A week, I guess. That's what he asked for, anyway."

"But you aren't going to let him stay, are you?" She sat up, a large and outraged child, her full lower lip quivering. "He'll spoil everything! He's cutting into *my* time, and I've only got a few more days. I could *kill* him!" She shook her fists.

"Listen, Bunny." Alix sat down on the bed. "You can stay longer. You can stay as long as you like."

"I *can't*," Bunny wept in frustration, "because I have to do *something* before the first of August—" She caught herself up with a quick shuddering breath. "I mean, get things lined up with Father Tom and everything before Mummy gets back."

Alix cut in deftly. "How would you like me to talk to Father Tom? I could call him up and tell him, I could do that much for you."

"No, no!" She shook her head violently. "I'll do it myself! I *should!* It's my mess, you didn't make it. But this damn Tony, I could kill him. This is all I'm ever going to have of Daddy, and this creep, this jerk, this—this infantile neurotic is coming between Daddy and me, don't you see?"

Her mouth went square and she let out a long howl of woe and then buried her head in her arms. Alix put her hand on the crown, where Shane's cowlick was, but Bunny began rolling her head from side to side. Alix went out and left her. Pretty soon, she thought, I'm going to sink back into that nice, numb stupor I had last April, and I can't think now why I ever wanted to get free of it.

She wrote a note to Tony, telling him to help himself to food, and propped it conspicuously in the middle of the kitchen table. Then she called to Bunny, asking her again if she wanted a hot drink or cereal, and got no answer. She put coffee in her thermos, buttered some bread, sliced off some cheese, put it all in a basket with her sketch pad, and left the house.

She ate her breakfast up in the Tangle, sitting on the stone wall. William shared her cheese. "We might set up a tent here," she said to him, "and withdraw from the world." William climbed to a crotch of an apple tree and sat there like a large species of owl.

" 'The world forgetting, by the world forgot,' " she said. "I think that was said of a vestal virgin, which hardly applies to me, but it sounds so delightful I'd better not dwell on it."

William went out on a limb in futile pursuit of a redstart, and stretched his length on the sun-warmed bark and drowsed, lionlike. She made a quick charcoal sketch of him thus. Then she went on through the Tangle and into the Beauty Cove spruces, and sat down on the hillside there. It occurred to her that Madge and Ozzie might like a panoramic view of their place at the foot of the broad gentle slope, the fishhouse and wharf, the cove opening out into the western bay and the mainland hazy-blue with deceptive promise across the water. She was working out the composition when Sidney landed on her work with wet and scrabbling paws, licking at her ears and nose.

Alix was holding him off and laughing when Madge came up the slope. "Sidney, behave yourself!" she cried. "Alix, I was just *thinking* about you. Now, isn't that strange? I'm dying to know about this boy who came last night. Karen told me. Is he the *one?*"

"No, he's a young painter I know in New York," Alix said. Madge looked personally bereft.

"And I was hoping so *hard!* That poor, poor girl. Oh, fiddle-sticks," she said sharply, "here comes Karen. They always pop up just when you wish they wouldn't."

"There's no more to tell anyway," said Alix. They walked down toward the house.

"I was coming over to see you today," Madge went on. "Look, blueberries coming there, mind your feet, chickabiddy. Well! Alix, with all you've got on your hands I hate to ask you this, but Ozzie says you can't no more'n say *no,* and it's not as if Karen would be any trouble. She'll be in bed most of the time."

Madge stopped in the path to gaze appealingly at Alix who began to laugh and said, "If you'd just start in again and tell me what, where, and why."

"Roger and Daisy have asked us to go to Lakewood to the summer theatre tonight," said Madge in a rush. "It'll be after midnight when we get back, and we might stay right there at Roger's till morning. So would you keep Karen for supper and the night? There!" She fanned herself with her hand. "I'm all out of puff, but I got it said without running all around crea-tion and half of Brighton, and Ozzie would be proud of me."

"Of course I'll keep Karen," said Alix. "Send her over any time."

"Well, they want to start out as soon as the men get in from hauling and get cleaned up." Madge was flustered with jubila-tion. "We're going to eat on the way! And you know me, I just love that. So it may be about three. Is that too early?"

"No, we've got plenty to entertain her with. Tony will have her spellbound."

"I was thinking, where he's nearer Bunny's age and all, she might talk to *him*," Madge said.

"I never thought of that," said Alix kindly. "She might."

When she got back to her own field it was a shimmering hot noon; the prevailing southwest wind would spring up shortly and cool everything off. Tony was at the well, leaning over and looking down in. She said from behind him, "Lost the pail? We can hook it out with a long-handled gaff."

He straightened up. "No, I've got the water." The full pail stood in the shade of the well-head. "I was just looking in and wondering if it was true that from down there I could see stars at noon."

"Don't try it," said Alix. He gave her a subdued grin and sat down on the well-curb. His forehead and nose were sunburned, and she said, "Haven't you a cap? I'll supply you with something."

"Thanks." He lit a cigarette and looked off down at the wharf and the turquoise lagoon of Gib's Cove cut off from the sea beyond it. Alix sat down beside him.

"Did you paint anything?"

"No. I gave up and just looked and smelled and soaked it in. There's too much of everything unless I surrender to my baser instincts and do calendar art. There must be a hell of a lot of satisfaction in that, huh? All that wallowing around in pure color, laying it on with a trowel."

"Lot of money in it too," said Alix.

"For the sake of my artistic integrity I try not to think about the money," said Tony. They laughed. "But I'm going to paint tomorrow," he added. "If I'm still here."

"Is there any question about that?"

"Look, Alix," he said earnestly, "I don't know if it was such a good idea, coming here like this. I didn't stop to think, and I guess maybe that's my besetting sin. Anyway, you've already got company, and I ought to apologize and take off." He looked hard straight ahead of him.

"Did you see Bunny to talk to?" Alix asked him.

"Sure, why not? We're in the same house." He was too elaborately casual.

"And what did she say to you?"

"*Hi*. That's it. That's what she said."

"If you tell me the truth, I won't get after her, I promise. Come on, Tony, or I'll be mad with the both of you."

He did complicated things with his large hands, studying each move as if he'd never seen such actions before. "Well, actually, she didn't say too much. She was getting something to eat when I came in a little while ago, and I guess she wasn't feeling very good anyway, you know? and some guy coming in high as a kite on fresh air all ready to act like her brother or something—you know?"

"I do not know," said Alix with lethal patience. "She said *what?*"

"That I was a dirty rat for getting your address by false pretenses, that I had one hell of a nerve barging in uninvited and invading your privacy. ... Well, she didn't start right in with that, she sort of worked up to it."

"And then?"

"Well, I asked her—and I was polite, Alix, I was gentlemanly, I never raised my voice—I asked her who the hell she was, and weren't you old enough to speak for yourself, you know? And she said you were too decent and that she had a right to be here because under other circumstances she'd have been your stepdaughter." He turned to her in modest triumph at this dénouement, and when she didn't speak he said, "Well, that really snowed me. You know?"

William began drinking out of the full water pail and Alix pushed him away. "Yes, I can speak for myself, and yes, Bunny hasn't been feeling well. You can stay your week, Tony. But do me a favor and don't send postcards to everybody telling them where you are."

He was laughing foolishly in relief, wagging his head and hands at her. "No, no! I didn't even leave a forwarding address! Thanks, Alix. I'll never be able to pay you back." He jumped up, all energy now. "I'd better get this water into the house. Any chores you want me to do this afternoon? Chop wood, dig clams?"

"The tide's high. Are you safe with an ax? This is no place to slash through an artery."

"My great-grandfather taught me how to use an ax when I was twelve. I worked on his woodpile every summer till last year." He was quite honestly proud of himself. Boys are so nice, she thought. But then, they can't get pregnant.

"Then you can start on that pile behind the workshop and cut it into lengths for the kitchen stove. I'll unlock the shop so you can get the ax."

He set the pail on the counter by the sink and watched her pick out the right key. "Why do you have to keep anything locked on here? This is Eden before the Fall."

"When there's a child on the island I worry about sharp tools," she said. She didn't want him to see her name on the bench and possibly mention it, but she didn't want to destroy it, either, so she upended a half-bushel basket over it while he was looking around him. She gave him a straw hat and watched him start in on the woodpile. He wasn't lying about his skill with an ax.

Reassured, she went into the house and looked in on Bunny, who was lying with her pillows at the foot of the bed and reading. She lowered her book and gazed over the top of it, with large reproachful eyes.

"Come on and get up, Bunny. If you want to read, take your book outdoors. This weather's too good to waste."

"Where is *he?*"

"Chopping wood." She went all the way in and shut the door. "Don't resent him. After all, you were here first, and you do have a position here that Tony can't hurt."

Bunny lowered the book more. "Well," she said stiffly, "as long as he understands that ... But he's such a darned *bubbler!*" she exploded. "Everything's wonderful, everything's magnificent." She waved her arms wildly. "What light, what colors, what fragrances! And you know how it was, I could walk around here in a dream and if I wanted to sit in front of Daddy's portrait for hours I could, and just let myself go. But now we've got this damned happy busy bee!"

Alix smiled. "By way of contrast Karen's coming over this afternoon and she'll stay all night. I have to go make up my bed for her. You'd better get up or she'll come in and stare at you."

❧ CHAPTER 40 ❧

THE ADVANTAGE OF Tony's being a painter was immediately clear at supper. He and Alix talked painting all through the meal of broiled mackerel, while Karen applied herself to her food at one end of the table and Bunny ate moodily at the other end. She was polite to Alix and friendly to Sidney, who had come with Karen, but Karen and Tony were ignored.

Tony offered to do the dishes after supper. "Bunny and Karen are going to do them," Alix told him sunnily. "You can get two pails of fresh water, and then do whatever you please."

He was going around to play cribbage with Jonas, whom he had met again on his day's wanderings. Sidney went with him. After a silent session with the dishes Bunny went out for a walk. Alix, wondering how soon she could decently send Karen to bed, suggested a walk of their own, checkers, or drawing. But Karen said coldly that she had brought her notebook and was going to write.

She did write, until Alix told her it was too dark to see. Without comment she put her notebook away in her bag, took herself out back, brushed her teeth at the kitchen sink, and followed Alix upstairs to her room. "Here you are," Alix said brightly. "Look, you can see the new moon, and I'll be up and tuck you in when you're all ready for bed."

When she went downstairs, Bunny had returned and was making a cup of cocoa. She was uncommunicative, though civil, and took her drink and her lamp into her room.

Karen was in bed when Alix went back upstairs. Her glasses were on the stand, and she was curled up with her face turned away from Alix. "Do you say prayers?" Alix asked her.

"In bed. To myself," Karen added pointedly.

"Here's a flashlight for you, I'll tuck it under this other pillow. I'll be up in a little while, and I'll leave the door open between our rooms. If you feel nervous all you have to do is call me."

No answer. "Good night," she said, leaving. She couldn't imagine Karen's being nervous.

Downstairs the dusky silence beat against her ears, and she felt as if she'd been running a race with two express trains since noon. There was a line of light around Bunny's door, and she spoke softly to her. "I'm going out for a little while. Not far, so don't worry."

"All right," Bunny said.

William emerged from somewhere and went out with her. There was a ghostly light from the new moon, and the crickets were the loudest sound in the mild evening of quiet seas and no wind.

She sat on a crate against the fishhouse wall and let the stillness sink into her. She was not thinking ahead or backward. William got up on the crate beside her and began to wash, bracing his back warmly against her side. She started to yawn and anticipated bed with an actual and almost voluptuous sleepiness. "Come on, Willie," she said. "Let's go home."

She was halfway to the house when she first heard the noise, which at first sounded like the radio-transmitted cries of one of the more far-out rock groups. Then they became a different kind of cry, and she began to run.

Hideous pictures formed and reformed as she ran. Bunny

had tipped over her lamp; Bunny trapped by flames in her room and screaming. Fire spreading through the dry old wood as if through shavings. Karen upstairs, frozen by terror. The men across the island out of reach.

It was like running in nightmares. When she reached the yard she was hardly able to lift a foot, her breath was scalding her throat, and her lungs were hardly able to draw down the burning air. If I open the back door, she thought with fresh horror, it will make everything go up at once.

What fell upon her blurred vision was the cool blessing of darkness inside the kitchen windows. The shouts broke through the noise in her ears, but she saw no Doré version of hell, only a glimmer of spectral light in the living room, about enough to come from one ordinary flashlight.

She opened the kitchen door and went in. "You little monster!" Bunny was screaming. "I could *kill* you!"

Alix did not remember crossing the kitchen, but she had grabbed her big light on the way, and she turned it on Bunny, who gasped and put her arm across her eyes. A small figure in pink pajamas stood by the study doorway, her glasses blind white circles of reflected light.

Alix said with quiet passion, "What is going on here?"

"This little brat—this damned little sneak!" Bunny stormed. "I caught her in the act! Daring to touch Daddy's things! She was in his *desk!*"

"Bunny, get hold of yourself," Alix commanded, knowing as she said it that Bunny didn't intend to hear the command; she wasn't going to surrender the rich satisfactions of this screaming rage. It had been almost a week since she'd had one.

"She's stolen something!" Bunny raved on. "She's got it in her hand and she won't give it up!"

"It's probably an eraser or a paper clip. Bunny, *shut up!* Or I'll throw a pail of cold water on you, so help me!"

"But don't you *care?* She was in Daddy's things! I *caught* her!" She broke loudly into tears. Alix stood her light on a table and went past her to Karen. When Alix put a hand on her shoulder the child was as cold and rigid as stone.

She ran into the study and pulled blankets off Tony's bed and wrapped the immobile child, then carried her to the sofa. "Bunny—"

Bunny slumped in a chair, bawling. Alix took her by the nape of the neck in a merciless grip until Bunny yelped in surprise and pain. "I'm sorry," Alix said grimly, "but you asked for it. Go out and heat some water. Put some on all four burners, don't try to heat one huge kettleful. And you know where the hot water bottles are. Hurry up. If you haven't scared her into convulsions we're lucky. Get a move on or you'll feel that bucket of water, I promise you."

Sobbing, Bunny tramped out to the kitchen. Alix sat down on the couch and put her arms around Karen, holding the blankets in place and hugging her close, trying to will heat from her own body into the stiff, chilled one.

"It's all right," she kept saying against the silky hair. "Everything's all right. Nothing's going to hurt you. . . . Light all the lamps too, Bunny," she called. There was a clash of pans from the kitchen.

What can I ever say to Madge? Alix thought, hugging and rocking. Lamplight brightened in the kitchen, and Bunny brought in two more lamps for the living room. She had stopped sobbing, and was down to sniffling.

"I don't care, she deserves to be scared," she muttered.

"Not out of her wits," said Alix. "Do I hear something boiling?"

Bunny went back to the kitchen and returned with two wrapped hot water bottles. She stood watching as Alix tucked them in around Karen. "Did you see what she has in her hand?" she asked finally.

"No, her hands are all covered up now. Are you getting warm, Karen?" she murmured close to an ear. She put her lips against the temple; the child's skin felt thinner and finer than the rugosa rose petals. "A little warmer," she answered herself. She settled Karen's head more comfortably against her shoulder. The glasses twisted and she took them off and handed them to Bunny. "Here, put these on the mantel."

She felt a slight shudder among the blankets. "They're safe there, Karen," she said. Karen took a deep breath, and when she let it out she seemed to sink more heavily into Alix's arms.

Bunny was now watching with a kind of defensive anxiety rather than resentment. "I didn't think anything could upset *her*," she said.

"She's loosening up a bit now, I think," Alix said. "Bunny, why don't you get yourself something warm to drink and fix a hot water bottle for yourself, and get back to bed? You must be cold too."

Bunny didn't move, her eyes seemed to get bigger as she stared down at Alix, and her lips parted. Finally she said almost inaudibly, "Are you mad with me?"

"No, no," Alix shook her head impatiently. "Go to bed now before you get chilled."

"Shall I bring her something hot to drink? Weak tea?"

"I don't think she wants anything now. She's still pretty tight. You go on to bed and I'll be in later when things quiet down."

"Don't forget."

"I won't."

Bunny went. Alix tried to shift into a more comfortable position, but Karen immediately stiffened again. "It's all right," Alix said. "Bunny's gone to bed. She's sorry she screamed at you. I think she must have had a bad dream. Did you ever have bad dreams and get up out of bed because you're so frightened?"

After a pause Karen's head nodded very slightly.

"Why did you get out of bed tonight?" Alix asked. "Did you have a bad dream too?"

She thought she heard something but wasn't sure. She lowered her head. "Say it again."

"No," whispered Karen. She made a spasmodic attempt to free herself, but the blankets and Alix's arms were too much for her. She went limp in defeat and began to cry. It was different from Bunny's robust howling, and wrenched Alix as Bunny's noisiest outburst had never done, for this was the silent battle of pride against superior forces. The thing was impressive and moving, and it made Alix feel a profound shame in her victory. She hugged the child closer to her. Karen's face pressed into her breast as if she were trying to hide all of herself there. Alix's own eyes were smarting and she heard herself making little sounds. "There, there." Rocking and patting and murmuring. It was all anyone could do.

Finally the tremors died away. She waited until the occasional hiccups had stopped, then tried to get a look at Karen's face. But when she took it gently by the chin to turn it away from her tear-soaked shirt Karen shut her eyes.

"What do you have in your hand, Karen?" Alix asked her. "Whatever it is, I won't be cross about it. I'm just curious, that's all." She unfolded the blankets and with a sigh Karen brought out one hand and opened it. Thorvald lay on her palm.

"The Viking," Alix said. "We found him in the rockweed after a storm."

Karen held him up and opened her eyes to look at him. They were wide-set, with fair curling lashes, and slightly tilted up at the outer corners. They were both straight for the moment and they made her face a unique little one, solemnly but brilliantly alive.

"That's why I got up," she said hoarsely. "To see if he was still there."

"Oh? You mean you'd seen him before? When was that?" Probably the time they'd brought Duff in; Karen had gotten into the study then. Karen gave her a sidewise look.

"Once a long time ago. You were upstairs cleaning all that stuff out of the studio. That's when I found him first." Without the glasses and talking of her own free will she was a changeling in Alix's arms, or else the other one had been the changeling. Something was making Alix's head spin; she knew an intolerable suspense, as if she were looking from a great height and knew she was going to jump.

"And did you," she delicately placed the words, "leave him on the desk and run away?"

Karen nodded solemnly. "I heard you coming, and Gram told me not to bother you."

The jump. Make it.

"You liked him, didn't you?"

Eyes on her face, the head relaxed and heavy against her shoulder. "Yes."

"But there was another little man you didn't like so well. You hid him under the little leather box."

Karen nodded, yawned, and politely put her hand to her mouth. "He was ugly. I didn't want to look at him."

"When did you put the spear point up there?" She nodded up at the mantel, aware that she wanted so much for Karen not to know about the point that she was entreating something or somebody, Please, *please* let it be Shane.

"I think," said Karen, sleepily, "it was the day before you came. When Gram was making your bed. I found it in Jonas's cove but I never showed him. I never showed anybody," she added. "I brought it for *him.*" She looked up at the portrait of Shane and smiled, not broadly, but with pride. "Because he likes those things and he hasn't got one that color."

Alix's nape prickled, and it was not just the weight of the child that impeded her breathing. "And—does he like that point?"

"Yes," said Karen confidently. She looked at the portrait from under her lids. "He does."

"Did you make my name out on the bench in the work-shop?"

Karen was yawning again, rubbing her eyes. "You kept reading and reading. You were right here on the sofa. I just wanted to see what was out there."

"And you knew where the key was."

"Uh-huh." The yawn was wide and uninhibited.

"But why my name?"

"Because it's pretty. I *hate* Karen. I wish I could be Alix. It's almost like my most favorite word of all."

Easy does it. Sometimes people walked around for days without knowing they had concussion. If you acted perfectly normal maybe you could keep your equilibrium and never ever realize what had happened to you. So she said, "And what word is that?"

"*Ibex,*" said Karen with a drowsy smile. The tip of her tongue came out and tasted the word. "*I is for Ibex,*" she said voluptuously. "Ibex . . ."

"It was mine," said Alix. It was true; and like Karen, she had tasted as well as heard its pure beauty. This was apocalypse indeed. "The broken cup," she said. Karen made a jerky little movement, her eyes opening wide, and Alix said, "It's all right. It was just—just an old cup."

"It was *pretty,*" said Karen sternly. "That color blue, and those little white flowers, and the gold letters. I didn't mean to break it."

"I know you didn't, but when was it?"

"I don't remember. Some day when you weren't home but you forgot to lock the door. I came to see *him,*" she said, looking up at Shane. "I always did." She sank into contemplative silence, from which she roused herself to say, "I shouldn've gone upstairs."

"Well, I was curious about it, that's all. I thought maybe William did it. What do you say we go to bed now?"

"All right," said Karen, agreeable if not enthusiastic. She allowed Alix to sit her up and unwrap her. They went up the front stairs, Karen hanging to the railing and yawning loudly, while Alix carried the hot water bottles.

She was amiable about being settled in bed, though she rose up instantly and said, "My glasses!"

"I'll bring them up when I come to bed."

"When will that be?"

"Pretty soon."

"I'll stay awake till you come."

"All right," said Alix. "Here's your flashlight, remember. Are you warm enough?"

"Yes." Suddenly she sharpened to complete wakefulness. "What did Bunny mean about her daddy's things?"

"I don't know," said Alix. "I'll ask her, but I think she's asleep now."

It would not do to tell Karen tonight that the man over the mantel was Bunny's father. Let him be *her* special friend for as long as it could be managed. Shane would have been amused and touched.

Would have been. Dead is dead, and they don't walk. Bunny had begun Shane's death on the beach the other day, and this was how it ended, in a child's drowsy confession.

✖ CHAPTER 41 ✖

BUNNY DIDN'T ANSWER when she spoke to her through the kitchen door. Asleep. That was one blessing, because she felt so vacant. She seemed to be drifting rather than walking through the silent lamplit rooms. She stood for a while before Shane's portrait, but nothing seemed changed here. It was like all the other times this summer when she had come to rest there, pulled irresistibly as the compass needle is pulled to north.

Perplexed, she looked around the room. Nothing leaped instantly to the eye or the senses to underline the fact that it was all over. Instead she saw the tumbled blankets on the sofa and remembered that they came from Tony's bed in the study. She gathered them up, and Thorvald fell from them onto the hearth rug.

She set him on the mantel under the portrait. If I had a fire going now I'd give you a Viking funeral, she thought. Who'd have believed in the devastation you've left behind you?

While she was making Tony's bed she heard surreptitious noises in the kitchen, and Sidney flew joyously at her. Tony appeared behind him. "Hello!" he said softly. "Did I keep you up? I didn't have any idea it was so late, but he skunked me the first time and I've been trying to get even ever since."

"I wasn't waiting for you," she assured him. "I was just about to go up. Do you want something to eat?"

"No, thanks! We went through a whole apple pie over there and about a ton of cheese. We didn't play cribbage all the time, we talked some. Talked a lot, in fact."

"About what?" Alix asked. Sidney settled himself on the foot of the couch.

"Oh, a hell of a lot of things. Boat building and painting, for two of them. I don't know where we went from there." He was sleepy and happy. "He's quite a guy, isn't he? I'm going out to haul with him tomorrow. He's picking me up at the wharf at five-thirty. I can get something to eat without waking up the whole house," he promised. "You don't have to get up."

"I don't intend to." They both laughed soundlessly, like conspirators, and whispered their good nights. She blew out the other lamps in the living room and kitchen, and went up the back stairs in the dark. Karen slept deeply in her bed and William lay at the foot. Alix left the glasses on the stand. William jumped down and followed Alix into Shane's room, where she undressed and got into bed still without a light.

It had been a long time since she had lain in this bed beseeching a sign from Shane. She had wanted to believe, she had finally believed, and now there was nothing. It was, all over again, her first terrifying conception of Space.

I'm glad I don't feel like crying, she thought. There's been enough brine shed around here tonight to pickle a bushel of cucumbers.

Really, there was nothing to cry for. There was nothing. *Nothing.*

William lay stretched along her side and from habit she worked her fingers absently around his ears. One thing about *nothing* as a concept, it behaved like one of those gelatinous, blobby organisms dear to science fiction, that surrounded, swallowed, and digested anything it came in contact with.

It was rather a relief to stop beating your brains trying to figure it all out, because it didn't mean a thing. Everything happened by purest chance, if there were degrees in chance. Pure, purer, purest. One lived and died by it. Somebody's whim created or destroyed, and that went for the alien presence of living tissue in Bunny's womb.

Created by her whim, and the moment life began, it had the power of its own existence. Like a wind blowing through space it had wafted Bunny here. *It.* A growth, Bunny said. The death of her in one way or another. *It.* A growth, certainly, but not malignant except as it threatened Bunny. There was a malignancy, but somewhere else, and full-blown. What was growing in her body even now, adding cells while she slept, was as innocent of its killing power as the sea was, or fire.

Given another month or so it would be *he* or *she*.

Alix sat up in bed, reached for her robe and pulled it around her shoulders. William went down to the foot and began to wash. She could hear the rasp of his tongue on his fur. Something had been awakened and set in motion, and it wasn't the cat; it began as a slow faint light kindling far back in her mind, she could almost see it as a small ruddy glow deep in a dark cave, growing brighter and larger and more vigorous as she approached it.

It. She had called it a baby when talking to Bunny, though she hadn't really seen a baby, or allowed herself to see one when there was so little chance of its ever becoming a baby; and Bunny had never even called it "it" if she could help it, but always spoke as if she had some probably mortal disease.

But it was—even now—Shane's grandchild.

The new concept was a fireburst as compared to the sound-proof dark of *nothing*. She wanted to shrink from its glare but it was everywhere. Bunny was carrying Shane's grandchild. No matter who had fathered it, no matter how squalid the process had been, Shane was its grandfather. The other grandfather existed for Alix no more than the biological father.

One image gave way to another like a series of lightning

flashes. Her heart was beating so fast she felt as if she were running while she was lying still. She got up finally and went down to get some aspirin. She made a cup of bouillon and carried it back upstairs with her, and tried to read while she sipped it. There was a book of Shakespeare's sonnets in Shane's bookcase, one which she had given him but had overlooked in the grand burning. The rhythms soothed her now, along with the aspirin and the hot drink, to the point of sedation, as long as she passed over the sonnets Shane had been fond of quoting. Still, she could hear his voice in a good many of them, and it was not unbearable; she thought how strange it was that his voice should be so clear to her tonight when his ghost had gone for good.

She fell asleep and it was full daylight when she woke up. Sidney was barking outdoors, and she remembered at once what had happened last night, both with Karen and then the later revelation. She felt as vigorous as if she'd had a long sleep. She dressed and gave her hair a harder brushing than it had had for days, until her scalp was stinging. She pinned it up and went down into the kitchen.

Bunny and Karen sat at the table eating corn flakes with bananas. Karen wore her glasses and looked as she had always looked.

"Hello, Karen," Alix said.

"Hello," said Karen laconically, applying all her attention to her food.

"Bunny, you were asleep last night when I stopped to speak to you," Alix said on her way out.

"I was beat," said Bunny. "There are times when I'm my own worst enemy. It's exhausting using yourself for a punching bag, but other people don't like you using them."

"Selfish beasts." Alix laughed and went out. The swallows were sitting now; she stopped to watch the smooth changing of the guard as one parent came off the nest and the other moved on. Sidney and William were out in the field.

When she came back in and was washing her face and hands,

Bunny said, "Did you hear that clown going out this morning? He was trying so hard to be quiet he hit everything. He's got more feet and elbows than I have."

"I didn't hear a thing," said Alix. "Not even Karen getting up."

"Oh, she can be quieter than William when she wants."

"Almost anyone can be quieter than William," said Alix. "The fog may come on little cat feet, but Willie comes on big Clydesdale feet." Karen's glasses looked at her and Alix explained, "A Clydesdale is a huge horse."

"I know it," said Karen. "I've seen one. On a farm, once."

"Do you want toast or not?" Bunny asked her. "While you're making up your mind we'll have time to examine the theory of relativity, plan a space probe, or write Bertrand Russell's biography."

"Somewhere in between there, make me a piece," said Alix.

Bunny balanced bread on the camp toaster set over a burner on the gas stove. "Anyway, I only heard her last night because I got up to get some crackers. And I heard little mouse noises where they shouldn't be. So Lucia di Lammermoor does the mad scene."

"I'll have some," said Karen suddenly. "Then I have to go home."

"So you're running out on the dishes, huh?" said Bunny.

"My gram's bringing me a present."

"First things first is Karen's policy," said Alix. "She knows what's important. You can do dishes any time, but presents are different."

Karen composedly accepted her toast. As Alix set the currant jelly before her Karen gave her a small quirk of the mouth, almost too slight for a smile. Alix responded in kind. The exchange took place when Bunny was putting more water in the teakettle.

When she left, Bunny stood watching her go up the field toward the woods. "She *is* a weird kid, you know? She came down and I asked her if she wanted breakfast, and she didn't act scared, or even a little mad with me. And I *know* how I acted last night. I woke up with the horrors this morning just thinking about it."

"Oh, she loosened up and relaxed after a while," Alix said. "I guess no permanent harm was done. Sit down, Bunny. I want to talk to you."

Bunny pushed her lower lip over her upper and looked at the floor. "I can guess what about."

"No, you can't. Come on. Bring a fresh cup of coffee, or shouldn't you be drinking milk?"

Bunny gagged realistically, and brought a banana instead. Then she jumped up. "Wait till I get my cigarettes."

"You don't need them. You just use them as a prop anyway. You'd better come to earth before I bring you down with the nearest weapon."

Bunny laughed nervously, sank without grace into the captain's chair, and burlesqued rapt attention by staring at Alix and fluttering her lashes.

"Tell me this, Bunny," Alix said. "If you weren't afraid to tell your mother—afraid for her sake or your own—and it could be arranged for you to be looked after through your pregnancy, and the baby put into good hands, would you still be determined to go after an abortion, no matter what the risk?"

Bunny stopped clowning and sat back, registering the sullen withdrawal which Alix now recognized.

"I know I said I wouldn't talk about it," Alix went on. "But this is something different. You see, I'd like to take that baby and bring it up. I mean *him* or *her;* in the middle of the night I refused to call your father's grandchild 'it' any longer."

"Daddy's *grandchild?*" Bunny repeated. She seemed almost dazed. "I never even thought of it as a child, let alone mine, or Daddy's grandchild."

"Would you be physically afraid to go through the pregnancy; as much afraid as you are of the operation?"

"Oh, the pregnancy would be a breeze," Bunny said bitterly.

"I'm as healthy as a horse, and not one of those delicate thoroughbreds. But, there's Mummy, and everything that goes with her knowing, all the things that would be said, or not said—" She looked at Alix appealingly. "There's a whole atmosphere that makes me sick to my stomach just to think of it. And it would go on—and on—and *on* till the time was up, and it wouldn't end there. I'd always be marked, like the lepers in the old days. For her, anyway, and finally for myself."

"I can see why you're willing to take the chance on the operation," said Alix. "But suppose somebody else told your mother, and convinced her it was for the best for you to stay away from her for a while. What then?"

"You don't mean *yourself!*"

Alix grinned. "No, but what about your Father Tom? What if I called him and told him what the situation was?"

"Oh, great!" said Bunny. "Just start in, 'You don't know *me,* but I happen to be Bunny's father's mistress, and—'"

"Shut up, Bunny," said Alix. "I've got some common sense even if I am over thirty, and therefore senile. I'm a friend of yours who's concerned about your physical and mental condition."

"I have to admit there are times when you sound like a social worker who got her degree at Radcliffe," said Bunny. "After making her debut, of course. You should impress him as intelligent, at least. *Alix!*"

Alix jumped. "What?"

"Delayed reaction. You want this baby. Why?"

"I thought you understood that. Because it's Shane's grandchild who'll go into an abortionist's trash can." Bunny winced and went white. "I'm sorry to be so graphic, Bunny, but you must know it's the truth. . . . I want this baby because it will be something of your father. I was a fool not to have had a child by him. But you see, I thought I'd have him a lot longer than I did."

"B-b-but you don't know anything about the father," Bunny stammered. Her eyes were watery.

"I know the mother, and *her* father."

They looked at each other steadily. Then Bunny blew her nose and said in a weak, shaky, little voice, "Could I stay with you till I had it?"

"Yes, except that it would be too much of a deception on your mother, don't you think? Neither of us wants to live a lie to that extent. But if she knew about it, it would be a worse blow than the pregnancy." Bunny was biting her lip in anxiety and frustration. "But if you weren't actually in the same house with me, you could be nearby," Alix said. "I'd stay in Maine all winter, so you wouldn't be left on your own. And this part of Maine is a good, long, inconvenient distance from Paoli, so nobody could drop in too often."

As she talked relief, interest, doubt, hope, and other, indefinable expressions moved constantly over Bunny's face. Fear returned often, and she would look away then, down at her hands or out the window, still biting her lip or the inside of her cheek, her lashes flickering but this time not for fun.

"We'd have to work all this out," said Alix. "In the night I never got beyond asking you to let me have the baby."

"I wish I could give it to you right now!" Bunny said with a groan, and put her head down on her arms.

"I'm not pressuring you, Bunny," Alix said. "I've wanted you to tell your mother, I've wanted you *not* to go to an abortionist, and what I've said now is an alternative. I do want the baby, but it's your baby, and your decision. I don't have any authority, any power at all."

"I wish you did," Bunny muttered from within her arms. "Why can't I just stay away for good, never write or anything, just disappear?" Her head came up. "I burned that letter and the chart so she'd never have a direct lead here, and she doesn't even know your name. Daddy talked to me about you before the—before the wedding—but not to Gerry, my sister. Alix, why can't I just vanish?"

She was radiant. Alix shook her head sadly, not so much at the idea but at the childishness involved. How long before

Bunny would stop dodging the primary fact and look it in the face?

"I can sympathize, because I've wished the same thing for myself plenty of times. But I can't be an accessory to it even if only in my own eyes. You can't do this to your mother, and you really don't want to."

"Yes, I do," Bunny insisted. "I hate her for making me feel like this. I hate her already for the way she'll look when she finds out. *Upset* is all right, and I could stand it if she hit the ceiling. I wouldn't blame her, I guess. But Alix, she's going to be nailed to a cross even if she has to do it herself. I can hear her: 'First my husband and then my daughter.' What I'm carrying would never be a grandchild to *her!* No, it's something filthy, rotten—" She ran out of words and looked wildly around for more. "But I'll have to carry it to the end and she'll pray for me to have a hard delivery so I'll pay for my sins in blood and agony. Do you call that a *mother?*" she cried.

Alix was trembling slightly. "*No,*" she said loudly to reach the girl through the agony she was already suffering. "I don't. But biologically and legally she's your mother, and I, as you put it, am your father's mistress, which makes me feel like Madame Pompadour." Bunny's mouth twitched in a slight grin. "I don't think you two should be together, but I don't have any standing. That's why a third person should do the talking. Is there anyone who'd do better than Father Tom?"

Bunny said distractedly, "No. He's been listening to Mummy all these years, he ought to know what to expect. But Alix, if she knows where I am, nobody on God's earth, not even the Pope, could keep her from coming here." She began to shake. "She'd take over. I wouldn't be able to do what I wanted with the baby, even if I said there was someone going to take it. *No!*" She slammed her fist on the table and the dishes clattered. "That little product of sin would go into a foundling home somewhere, and I'd never be told where—I'd never know what became of him—"

"Bunny, stop this!" Alix said sharply. She moved her chair

close to Bunny's and took her by the arm. "Stop it. You're not doing yourself any good."

"But I want you to have him," Bunny said, more quietly. "He should be in his grandfather's house, and this was Daddy's. The other one has always been Mummy's, even when he was still there."

"All right. We'll find a lawyer to find out just what your rights are concerning yourself and your unborn child."

"Mummy will come with *armies* of lawyers. She'll say I'm emotionally unstable, and have herself made my guardian."

"Well, she isn't coming today," said Alix. "She's still in Europe. That gives us time to see a lawyer and for me to talk with Father Tom, and then we'll make the next move."

Whatever it's going to be, she thought, wondering what she'd started. Yet she had no desire to pull out now; the baby had become too real.

"I've got the operation money with me, and I've got more in the bank, so I can help myself," Bunny was saying. "And when it's over I'll never go home again. I can work and support myself. I'll do anything, except I don't think I'd be a very good waitress. I get so clumsy when I'm self-conscious." She looked worried.

Alix laughed. "Well, at least you're thinking in terms of the future instead of the end of the world."

"So are you," said Bunny, and Alix looked at her without knowing what she meant at first, and then it hit her. If I were so minded, she thought with a rueful yet hopeful humor, I could believe that the real sign from Shane is Bunny.

𝓦 CHAPTER 42 𝓦

Bᴜɴɴʏ ᴀʀᴏsᴇ sᴜᴅᴅᴇɴʟʏ with a large air of decision and said she was starved. She scrambled eggs and they both ate, talking about everything else but what they'd been discussing.

"I ought to wash out some underwear and blouses," Bunny said when they finished eating.

"I ought to mow the lawn."

"Why don't you leave it for Tony the Tiger?" asked Bunny. "He's just dying to justify his existence around here."

"I need the exercise." In truth she needed to keep busy; she couldn't dwell on what might well turn into a deadly tangle before it was finished. Bunny's mother might be the formidable force she described, or she could be something entirely different from what the girl's distorted vision saw. But any woman, let alone the neurotic personality that Bunny painted, would not willingly hand a child over to the Other Woman even if she didn't want it herself. They had to find out what Bunny's rights were, and the rest lay with Bunny herself. No one else could make her strong enough to resist the emotional pressures.

Mowing the lawn didn't keep one's thoughts occupied. She

had to pick a lawyer, and her mind worried at the problem as she went back and forth across the lawn. She didn't want to bring Madge and Ozzie into this yet. But thinking of them reminded her of the lawyer who had handled the sale of Tiree, a Mr. Esmond. She would call him for a starter; if he was no longer in practice, there were several others on Main Street in Fremont. Any one should be able to tell her what Bunny's legal position would be in regard to making her own decisions about her baby.

"Bunny and I are going to town tomorrow, Tony, if it's calm enough to use my boat," Alix told him at suppertime. "We've got a few things to do. You and William will have the place to yourself. How does that grab you?"

"Right in the heart," said Tony. "I'll be monarch of all I survey. Hey, how are you getting back if it breezes up?"

"I think Roger will bring us out. I don't take advantage of his good nature very often."

Everyone was tired and turned in early. Alix was reading in bed when Bunny came up through the studio and tapped at her open door.

"There's something else I have to tell you." She shook her head at Alix's expression. "It isn't anything terrible that I've held back. It's something you ought to know, and you'll be glad to know it, I think."

"Come and sit down," said Alix. Bunny moved the cat over and sat on the foot of the bed. She was oddly bashful, and with her hair in two braids she looked like an oversize thirteen-year-old.

"It's about that so-called orgy," she said. "Where I'm supposed to have got this way. Well, I lied about that. I've never been drunk except slightly on some cheap wine, and then I got sick before I could get smashed. Big disappointment." Her giggle was pure nerves. "And I never went to a love-in, so that's another area where I'm ignorant." She began stroking William with long, painstaking motions, as if this were her chief concern at the moment. "I know who the father is, and I didn't even have the excuse of being in love with him. I guess I wanted some attention, and his girl had just walked out on him because he signed up for the Peace Corps instead of going into his father's business." She shrugged. "Well, we were both feeling sorry for ourselves, and misery loves company, and so it happened."

"And he doesn't know?"

"No. He's in Nepal by now. His plans don't include me, and I don't have any right to shatter them. After all, I was just as responsible as he was, maybe more so. In fact there was a moment when I knew I should stop the whole thing, but I didn't. . . . I just wanted you to know he's a good man and an intelligent one."

"Thank you, Bunny," Alix said.

"When I came, I wanted to say the worst things I could think of, like throwing filth at you."

Alix nodded. "I know the feeling."

Bunny got up. "I guess you still wonder why I don't want to keep the baby even if everything is made easy for me to do it."

"Because you want to put that time in your life completely behind you, is that it?"

"Yes," Bunny said somberly. She no longer looked thirteen. "Of course I realize if you have him—I keep saying *him,* I don't know why—and I want to keep on knowing you, I'll see him. But he'll be yours, Alix. Already I think of him as yours. . . . Remember how you told me I was almost brand-new, I had all my life to live?" Alix nodded, and Bunny went on, "Well, that's what I'm going to do—*live* it. Starting now."

"Good for you, Bunny," Alix said. She could not have said anything more.

"Good night," Bunny said. She went back out through the studio. With a sigh that surrendered to the night all the day's strains and tomorrow's uncertainties, Alix blew out her lamp and lay down to sleep.

Tony asked at breakfast if he could go; he wanted to look in at a gallery Soren Michaels had told him about, and besides, it

was an interesting old seaport worth seeing. "Don't forget, I'm
a Midwestern boy, and this coast is pretty exotic for me."

"Oh, come along," said Alix, "you don't have to wear us both
out with your explanations."

"Tony never uses one word where ten will do," said Bunny,
disappearing into her room.

"Bunny, have you got something else besides that orange
dress?" Alix called after her. "I don't think I can stand it in
full sunlight, even with dark glasses."

"Oh, don't you like my psychedelic get-up? I've been told
that no self-respecting prostitute would appear in public in an
outfit like that, but I thought the remark was inspired by jealousy."

"It's not jealousy on my part, just self-defense."

"Okay, I'll put on my *jeune fille* dress."

"Thank you," said Alix. "Tony, the sink's yours." She went
upstairs, and faced the fact that she hadn't brought any summer dresses with her because she hadn't expected to need any.
And here she was muttering to herself in bad temper about
clothes, not only committed to life but planning to complicate
that life beyond all common sense.

She'd have to get something that was suitable to wear into a
conservative down-East lawyer's office. Let's hope the appointment isn't so early I don't have time, she thought. Dear God,
this is nerve-racking. I feel pregnant too.

She put on her best-looking slacks and shirt and went downstairs. Tony looked freshly scrubbed and changed, if a little
shaggy around the ears and nape. The dark-rimmed glasses
gave him a solid, earnest appearance.

"I don't think you're a painter at all," Bunny said accusingly.
"I think you're an Eagle Scout."

"Good guess," said Tony with a smirk. "I *was* one. Look,
even if I don't go around with a floppy cap like Rembrandt or
minus one ear like Van Gogh, and alizarin crimson on my
knuckles, and—"

"Let's get going." Alix shooed them and William out and

locked the door behind them. There might be a kind of silent *entente cordiale* between her and Karen, but there was no need of putting temptation in the child's way.

In Fremont they left the car in the municipal parking lot near the public landing. Bunny and Tony had been sparring all the way, which was better than Bunny's sulks, and besides, it kept either of them from talking to Alix. They walked out on the dock to look at boats while she called Mr. Esmond's office from the telephone booth next to the restaurant. Mr. Esmond wasn't in yet, but he would be in; no, he wouldn't be in court today. Yes, he could see her today, thanks to a cancellation; would eleven be all right?

"Eleven would be fine," said Alix thankfully. The first step over with before lunch. She waited until they came back up the wharf, Tony talking boats with large gestures and Bunny looking extremely *jeune fille* in pleated blue and white linen with a hat of the same material, her hair still in braids and the huge sun glasses left behind her or hidden in her bag.

"He can squeeze you in at eleven," Alix said to Bunny.

"Dentist?" asked Tony. "Well, I can't buy you anything to eat then, so don't ask me. My teeth just happen to be perfect, by the way."

"How nice. I suppose you go around biting girls instead of kissing them, just to show off."

Tony snapped and snarled at her. "You didn't know I was a werewolf as well as an Eagle Scout, did you?"

"Why don't you two go find the gallery," said Alix, "and meet me here by the car at ten-thirty?"

"Oh, I wanted to help you choose your dress!" cried Bunny.

"This is an ordeal I prefer to face in privacy," said Alix.

Back at the car an hour later, she put away the bundle containing her slacks, shirt, and sneakers. She'd found the dress in a small shop, a silky jersey shirtwaist dress in a paisley design of browns, copper, and gold. It felt comfortable on her, and it seemed the perfect thing for an appointment with a lawyer whose support she might need later in regard to her suitability as a parent. Oh, Shane, if you see me now, she thought with sad humor.

It wasn't time for the others yet, and she sat down on a bench overlooking the harbor. A young woman passed, wheeling a stroller. The baby was excited about the boats, leaning forward and waving his arms and exclaiming. He was a strong-looking little boy with black hair. Alix felt a peculiar jump under her ribs and an attack of breathlessness. Now why are you thinking of *him* all the time instead of *her*, which it could very well be? Woman, you've got to knock it off or you'll never last the next seven months. Good God, I'm committed to winter in Maine. ... Back to New York in the fall and pick up what I'll need ... sublet around till the next fall? ... Don't know ...

"Hi!" Their shadows fell over her as they came around the bench and Bunny sat down beside her. Tony remained standing before them, polishing his glasses. He seemed to be laughing to himself.

"If the show was that good I'll have to see it," said Alix. "He looks a little drunk."

"He is, in a manner of speaking," said Bunny. Her voice was shaky. She kept looking at Alix as if there were something urgent she had to say, but couldn't get up to it.

"All right, tell me," Alix said.

"Well—" Impulsively she seized Alix's hand and held it. "I know you'll think we're really crazy, and irresponsible, but it's really a very sane and responsible thing to do, and the *only* thing ... I mean it will take care of everything, including Mummy, and oh boy, that *is* everything."

"What she's trying to get up steam to say," said Tony in unnaturally measured cadences, "is that we went to the local hospital and asked where to get blood tests. We were directed to the medical arts building across the street, we were tested, and as soon as we find out that neither of us has flunked our Wassermann, we're getting married."

"*Tony.*" It wasn't a shout. She hadn't the breath for it. He stood smiling down at her, as tenderly amused by her consternation as if he were about seventy. Bunny was holding her hand so tightly it was getting numb. Alix pulled her gaze from Tony and saw that Bunny was nodding madly at her.

"When was all this planned?" Alix asked, falling back for support on her Louisburg Square manner.

"Last night after I was upstairs talking to you," said Bunny promptly. "I went down to the study and asked Tony to marry me. He's only committed until I have the baby and turn him over to you. I can pay my own way, so it won't be a burden on Tony, and I'll be *Mrs.*, which will change everything. Mummy can't do a thing."

"Have you thought about this carefully, Tony?"

"How can it hurt me to do a favor?" Tony asked soberly. "It's more than a favor, it means so much to that little baby that I'd feel like a—a murderer if I refused. Of course if I had a girl I wouldn't be able to do it," he assured them, as if eager not to deceive them. "But I'm free, I can do anything I want, and it won't harm me any. And hey"—he started laughing again—"the benefits aren't all on *her* side. I get company, a captive audience, a free model, and a cook."

"What do you think, Alix?" said Bunny. "Don't you think it's great?"

"That's my painting hand you're wringing off at the wrist. I think we'd better call Mr. Esmond and tell him the problem is solved."

"Alix," Bunny pleaded.

Alix said, "I *think* I think it's great, Bunny. Yes. I don't know why it wouldn't be."

"And we'd like you and Jonas to stand up with us," Bunny said.

❦ CHAPTER 43 ❦

"How do you feel?" Jonas asked when they were driving away from the airport outside Fremont.

Alix reflected. "Peculiar," she said at last. "I think I detected slightly maternal qualms of emotion. It wasn't any kind of a wedding except as a legal contract, but I still felt the damndest urge to be sentimental. I hoped everybody would think it was hay fever."

"You didn't fool me any," he said.

"I hate people who say that," said Alix. "They always sound so stuck on themselves. But the way Tony rushed off to get corsages for us because you're supposed to have things like that at a wedding—that got me." She had unpinned hers after the plane took off, and now she lifted it to her nose and sniffed the cool reticent fragrance of the tight Talisman buds. "And Bunny, staring at that man as if he were her first-grade teacher and she was trying hard to get her lessons right . . . Then when they got on the plane, and were standing there in the doorway waving like mad at us—didn't they look *desperately* young to you, Jonas?" she demanded crossly. "Now admit it."

"Indestructibly young," he corrected her. "Far from desperate. As bouncy and tough as bubble gum. Bunny like to broke my ribs when she hugged me."

"You're a stand-in for her father," she said. "You know, when they first sprang this on me, I was flabbergasted. But sometime during the waiting period, I stopped seeing the idea as crazy. It became perfectly sensible and good."

"Well, isn't it? It's based on a lot sounder reasoning than most. Friendship, kids' loyalty to each other in trouble, generosity, kindness, and none of that deadly foolishness about love."

"No Sleeping Beauty psychosis," she teased him.

He took his eyes off the road for a sidewise glance. "You're durn tootin'. And I can do a little needling on my own. For somebody who a few weeks ago was having a fit if anybody touched anything of hers, how come you're letting those two move into your place in New York?"

"That's a practical way of giving them my blessing. . . . Mere things aren't as important as they used to be. Besides, I trust them. There's hardly enough space in Tony's place for him, let alone Bunny. She needs a lot of elbow room, and I don't think she can manage to break the skylight unless she gets a trampoline. Besides," she said offhand, "I won't be going back this year till the cold drives me. There's nothing to go back for."

The words carried their own seeds of fatigue. She slumped into silence. No more telephone calls to and from Shane; no more exquisite and tantalizing expectation of his visits to New York; no more ski weekends on a Vermont farm where they were the only guests.

Nothing to go back for . . . She roused herself to say, "This way they can take their time looking for a place. With Bunny going halves they can get something decent. Of course Bunny thinks that to live in a loft and know artists must be heaven. She's been reading too many books. *Trilby,* for one."

"What does Tony paint after a day at the supermarket? Soup cans?"

"If he doesn't, he's missing a chance to make the big time."

They were well around Fremont now and on the road home.

She thought of Tiree, the quiet, the thick grass in the late afternoon light, cool to the bare feet. The cold sea wind blowing through the roses. Today the crickets had begun; it was early for crickets. Bunny and Tony had divided a handful of blueberries for their cereal. The season was moving irrevocably forward.

They stopped at Emery's and picked up their grocery orders, and stopped again at the post office, where Jonas went in and got the mail. At the Harbor she went up to Roger Goodwin's house to change into slacks for the trip home. Nobody was there, and she was glad of that. It was restful not to talk. When she'd told Jonas she felt peculiar, it had been the truth, and she only vaguely touched on any amplification of the word. She couldn't have explained it even to herself.

She walked slowly down over the lawn toward the wharves, pulling on her hooded rain jacket in expectation of a choppy trip out in the dory. Jonas had carried their boxes to the float and was talking across a narrow stretch of water to a man in a boat tied up beside the lobster wharf.

Alix was at once involuntarily involved in the contrast of the boat's long, shallow, horizontal curve against the dark verticals of the spilings, and the glassy sheen of the white sides against the logs so dark with marine growth and wet that they looked velvety. Staring across at the patterns and textures, she almost walked into the man who stepped out of Roger's fishhouse and stood in her way.

"Good afternoon, Alexia. You're too much of a stranger, all at once."

"Hello, Soren," she said.

"Did I ever tell you that your smile has three corners and your cheekbones are superb?"

"No, but other people have. Coming, Jonas!" she called past him. Jonas's head whipped around. Soren saluted him and said with gentle sadness, "Really, Alix, is it necessary to have a bodyguard where I'm concerned?"

"I don't know, Soren. Is it?" She deepened her smile intentionally, and walked out around him to meet Jonas.

"I never give up," Soren said amiably behind her. "Some day I will sing the Danish national anthem for you, and then you'll understand what motivates me."

"Patriotism? Soren, I have to congratulate you on an absolutely novel and unique approach. And now, good-bye."

"Until the next time," said Soren. He watched her go down the ramp to the float, and then went back up the wharf.

"Was he lying in wait?" asked Jonas.

"Like William." As she stepped around the groceries on the way to the bow seat Jonas said thoughtfully, "I wonder what happened to the one he took home from the picnic."

"Why don't you ask him sometime? Maybe he'll introduce you to her."

"Hah!" said Jonas irascibly.

On the way out of the harbor they met the Ruskins' *Kingfisher* tacking in. Peter and his young son were at the tiller. Myra stood up on the bow deck and wigwagged strenuously, obviously shouting, though they couldn't hear her because of Jonas's outboard. Alix waved back and nodded emphatically until the yawl's port tack took her away across the harbor.

"You don't know what you just agreed to," Jonas called to Alix.

"All I can do is trust Myra," she called back. "And she was a 4-H girl."

"That's no sign of a duck's nest!"

She flapped a hand at him in dismissal and moved around sidewise on the seat, pulling up her knees and bracing her back against one gunnel and her feet against the other. The first spray spattered her shoulder and cheek when the dory's nose poked out past the harbor mouth.

William met her at the wharf. When Jonas was on his way out of the cove she shed her wet oil jacket and picked up the cat, nuzzling gently in his neck. Then she put him down and loaded the wheelbarrow, pushed it across the wharf and onto the path, where she took off her sneakers and put them on the wheelbarrow. The grass was as she had expected it to be, deliciously cool and damp to her hot feet.

She stopped at the halfway place as she always did, looking out at the sea and listening to the crickets. The birdsong was less now while the parents worked hard to feed the young, but a flight of goldfinches came sailing up over the housetop like blowing leaves, and down toward her, passing over her head in a cloud of little excited calls and signals, and then settled on the tall thistles at the edge of the swampy spot above Gib's Cove.

The goldfinches had been seen rather than heard lately; Tony could yodel, and hadn't had so much space to vocalize since he'd last been on his grandfather's farm in Illinois. Her New York studio should offer some entrancing possibilities for echoes, until the neighbors complained. The thought of Shane's daughter eating supper there tonight deserved more reaction than it got. She was too tired to be incredulous any more.

Name me one thing that could jolt you, Alexia. I can't. There's nothing left.

She unlocked the back door and William shot in past her legs, immediately setting up a howl for his supper. She fed him first, put the groceries away, and methodically took her corsage apart, floating the stemless blossoms in a shallow dish. All the time she was aware of the silence of the house behind her, as imposing and dominant as a personage about to receive her.

The silence of a house where Shane no longer was. She walked into the living room. It was just as they had left it this morning, with all the clutter of young occupancy, and the voices were still imprinted upon her hearing. The house was full of impressions left by them like images on film, so that as far as her reactions and reflexes went they were still here, simply out of sight for the moment.

But *Shane?* She looked at him from across the room; he looked back at her with blue sparks in his eyes, the ironical buccaneer laughing at her from where?

Shane, be here! she had cried night after night, and had waited in anguish, punishing herself for having no faith even when she saw the signs. Yet she had kept on hoping because it was better than weeping.

Everyone stopped at the portrait sooner or later. If strangers were drawn to it, if for them he was a presence in the house, why wasn't he much more evident to her, who was a part of him?

Karen had brought him the spear point; how was it that she had been able to find a perfect artifact in the color that Shane wanted, and had at once thought of Shane? What had happened to Bunny in the hours she spent on the sofa staring at the portrait as if willing it to come alive?

And what had sent Bunny here in the first place? Chance. But *why?* And was it chance?

My darling, her lips shaped the words. What am I believing now with no difficulty whatever?

Tomorrow would be time enough to tidy the room. . . . William had come in and was smelling at a sofa cushion on the floor where Tony had been lying in front of the fire last night.

"They'll be back for Labor Day and turn the place upside down again," she told him. "So don't look so forlorn."

The day when they had gone to Fremont to get the results of their blood tests and apply for the marriage license, Tony had brought home a gallon of sauterne, which Bunny thought was a wildly artistic thing to do. But she drank milk instead. Tony drank a lot of wine the next day, carrying the glass around with him, but he really preferred beer.

Now Alix poured a glass of the chilled wine and carried it out to the front doorstep. The osprey family was out, and she

was watching one bird hover in blue space on beating wings
when Jonas appeared noiselessly beside her.

"Have you learned the secret of vanishing in one place and
materializing in another?" she asked him solemnly.

"Ayuh, but don't look too close, I had a hard time getting
back together again this time and I think I left out a few mole-
cules."

"Oh, you'll find them scattered about on the way home."

"I hope so. I can feel a draft." He handed her her mail.
"This was in with mine. I know you want peace and quiet tonight, but I thought you'd want this."

"Oh, thanks, Jonas. Sit down." She moved over on the
doorstep. "Here's a postcard from a friend. She's in Denmark."
Alix chuckled. "She says I'd love it, the Danes are marvelous."

"Talk about materializing," Jonas said. "Where did *she* come
from?"

Karen had just appeared on the bank by the roses. "Oh, you
know Karen," said Alix. "Out of the everywhere into the here.
At least she came by the shore instead of through the house,
and that's a novelty."

"Well, what do you want?" Jonas growled at the approaching
child. Karen ignored him, and recited rapidly to Alix, "Gram
says come tomorrow night for baked beans and brown bread."

"Just her?" asked Jonas. "Not me?"

Karen gave her small inimitable shrug. "Oh, I s'pose you can
come." She sounded bored.

"Thank you, Mother dear," said Jonas.

"Why does he call me 'Mother' all the time?" Karen asked
Alix.

"I don't know, but the next time you say, 'That's all right,
Sonny.' "

"*Sonny?*" Karen repeated doubtfully. She looked at Jonas
and pursed up her mouth. "Is that his name too?"

"Just among friends, and we're his friends."

"I know a kid named Sonny and he's a stinker."

"It goes with the name," said Jonas ferociously. "Now I'd

like to have some adult conversation with this lady, so why don't you go build a sand castle or pick up some mussel shells the way little girls are supposed to do, and I'll whistle to you when it's safe to come back. Okay?"

The tip of Karen's tongue showed as she considered. "Okay, Sonny," she said, and turned and walked deliberately back toward the roses. Alix put her hand to her mouth so she wouldn't laugh out loud, and Jonas grinned.

"If she ever gets to really talking, we may wish we'd left well enough alone," he said.

"Would you like some wine, Jonas?" she asked belatedly. "Or are you afraid one glass will set you off on a murder spree?"

"Needle, needle," he said. "But do you know something? I hardly ever dream of her now. She's still there, and *it's* still there, but with a difference. . . . Did Tony leave any beer?"

"In the bottom of the refrigerator. Go help yourself."

He went into the house, and she looked at her mail again. Not much besides Dodie's postcard, but there was a catalog of art supplies from the shop where she'd gotten the ESP books. She needed materials, having brought so little with her, and she'd go through the catalog in the morning.

In February the baby would be born.

"I know I won't want him, Alix. It's not his fault, poor little guy, but I can't be a mother, I just *know* I can't. I want to finish growing up. And some day I want to fall in love the way Daddy did, and then I'll want a child."

This had been last night, after Tony went to bed.

"Just the same, Bunny, you may do a lot of growing up in the next seven months. You may not have cared about the father, but that baby will be half yours. One look, and you may not want to part with him."

"But Alix, isn't it a known scientific fact that some women don't want their first child, or their second, or their fifth, because of all kinds of complicated psychological hang-ups?"

"All right, Bunny. We'll wait and see."

"But I'm going to take very good care of him, Alix. Or *her*.

You won't mind a little girl, will you? . . . I'm going to a clinic as soon as we get settled, and I'll do just as I'm told. And look, I've stopped smoking. *And"*—with a long stern look—"I've thrown away the Seconal. It's all dissolved in the ocean. You won't need it now that you're expecting."

Oh, you child, Alix thought now. You good, loving, honorable child. You daughter of Shane. She lifted her glass in a silent toast. All she was sure of about next February was that she would still be alive, barring a fatal accident or illness; but for the time being that was enough to go on.

Jonas let William out and came behind him, with a can of beer and a glass. "The way I see it," he was saying, as if their conversation had never broken off, "talking it all out that night was like lancing a boil."

"Oh, Jonas, what a poetic thing to say."

He sat down beside her and poured beer. "It's still damn sore and it will be for quite a while. You know what that's like. But comes the time when you think, oh hell, I'm going to live through it somehow." He took a long pull from his glass. Karen's fair head appeared cautiously over the bank, and he said, "I see the Venusians have their telescopes trained on us."

"Whistle her in, Jonas. She can hardly wait."

He whistled, and Karen came sedately. Her sneakers were wet and her shorts pockets bulged with beach rocks. She stood in front of them with her hands behind her back. "Are Bunny and Tony really married?" she asked Alix.

"They are really married," said Alix, "and by now they're in New York and having something to eat. Tomorrow they're going to Bunny's house and get the rest of her things. Monday morning Tony will go to work, and that night Bunny will have his dinner ready when he comes home."

Karen's nose wrinkled slightly. "Why do people want to get married?"

"I admit it doesn't sound like an absolutely fascinating proposition compared to beachcombing on Tiree," said Alix.

"You know when the time's up that thing could still hold together?" Jonas said. He didn't know about Alix's and Bunny's agreement, only that Tony was supplying refuge until the baby was born. "They could grow on each other."

Alix looked thoughtfully into her glass. The faceless image of a woman passed swiftly through her consciousness. A solitary woman, but not herself this time. Cathleen.

She said briskly, "Karen, would you like milk and cookies?"

"Yes."

"Yes what?" prodded Jonas.

"Please," said Karen without a change of expression.

Alix stood up. "One more thing, Karen." She put her hand on the child's shoulder. "We're going to work on your picture tomorrow and this time we're going to finish it. Agreed?"

After a moment Karen said, "Agreed."

"We'll start at ten." Alix went into the house to get the milk and cookies.